CONSTITUTIONAL CHANGE IN THE EU

Constitutional Change in the EU
From Uniformity to Flexibility?

Edited by
GRÁINNE DE BÚRCA
Professor of European Union Law, European University Institute, Florence
and
JOANNE SCOTT
Reader in Law, Queen Mary & Westfield College, London

• HART •
PUBLISHING
OXFORD – PORTLAND OREGON
2000

Hart Publishing
Oxford and Portland, Oregon

Published in North America (US and Canada) by
Hart Publishing c/o
International Specialized Book Services
5804 NE Hassalo Street
Portland, Oregon
97213-3644
USA

Distributed in the Netherlands, Belgium and Luxembourg by
Intersentia, Churchillaan 108
B2900 Schoten
Antwerpen
Belgium

Hart Publishing Ltd is a specialist legal publisher based in Oxford, England.
To order further copies of this book or to request a list of other
publications please write to:

Hart Publishing Ltd, Salter's Boatyard,
Folly Bridge, Abingdon Rd, Oxford OX1 4LB
Telephone: +44 (0)1865 245533 or Fax: +44 (0)1865 794882
e-mail: mail@hartpub.co.uk
www.hartpub.co.uk

British Library Cataloguing in Publication Data
Data Available
ISBN 1 84113–103–2 (cloth)

Typeset in Sabon 10pt
by Hope Services (Abingdon) Ltd.
Printed in Great Britain on acid-free paper
by Biddles Ltd, Guildford and King's Lynn

Contents

Contributors

Catherine Barnard, University Lecturer in Law, University of Cambridge and Fellow of Trinity College

Marise Cremona, Senior Fellow and Head of European Commercial Law Unit, Centre for Commercial Law Studies, Queen Mary and Westfield College, University of London

Gráinne de Búrca, Professor of European Union law, European University Institute, Florence

Bruno de Witte, Professor of European law, University of Maastricht and European University Institute, Florence

Karl-Heinz Ladeur, Professor of Public Law, European University Institute, Florence, and University of Hamburg.

Carole Lyons, Lecturer, School of Law, University of Aberdeen

Eric Philippart, Senior Researcher (National Fund for Scientific Research), Associate Professor of Université Libre de Bruxelles, and Visiting Professor at the College of Europe, Bruges

Miguel Rodriguez-Piñero Royo Professor of Labour Law and Labour Relations Universidad de Huelva

Joanne Scott, Reader in law, Queen Mary & Westfield College, University of London, (from April 2000 University Lecturer in Law, Cambridge University and Fellow of Clare College)

Jo Shaw, Professor of European Law, University of Leeds

Monika Sie Dhian Ho, Member of the Scientific Staff Scientific Council for Government Policy The Hague

Filip Tuytshaever, Member of the Brussels Bar/Assistant in European Law, Free University of Brussels

Neil Walker, Professor of Legal and Constitutional Theory, University of Aberdeen

Stephen Weatherill, Jacques Delors Professor of EC Law in the University of Oxford, Fellow of Somerville College, Oxford and Associate Director of the Institute for European and Comparative Law in the University of Oxford

Jacques Ziller, Professor of Public Comparative Law, European University Institute, Florence

Acknowledgements

This book originated in a workshop which took place at the European Univrsity Institute, Florence in April 1999, at which the contributors presented earlier versions of the chapters which appear in this collection. We are grateful for the funding for this workshop which was awarded by the Research Council of the EUI. Warm thanks are also due to Susan Garvin and Madeleine de Leeuw for their efficiency and hard work in organising the event, and to all those who attended and participated in the workshop. Thanks also to Jo Murkens, and particularly to Kate Elliot for her characteristically thorough copy-editing work. Finally, we are very grateful to Hannah Young and to Richard Hart for their enthusiasm, professionalism and speed in bringing the book to publication.

Table of Cases

Table of Legislation

Table of Statutory Instruments

Table of EU Secondary Legislation

Table of Treaties

1

Introduction

GRÁINNE DE BÚRCA and JOANNE SCOTT

THE PURPOSE of this collection of essays is to examine the nature, extent and implications of an apparent shift in the paradigm of European governance from one of uniformity and harmonisation to one of flexibility and differentiation.

The story of the European polity, which began with the establishment of the coal and steel community in the early 1950s, has been one of growth from a relatively small, relatively homogenous and defined economic entity to a very wide and powerful entity which is more heterogeneous in political, economic and cultural terms. The changing terminology which has accompanied the various legal and geographic expansions is only one indicator of this: beginning with the ECSC, and subsequently the European Economic Community (these, together with the atomic energy entity, formed the so-called "European Communities"), the EEC was subsequently renamed the "European Community", and most recently the title "European Union" has been used to include the newer institutional mechanisms established to deal with largely non-economic policy areas such as foreign policy, security, policing and immigration.

But the European entity is in many ways a very different entity from that which was formally established in the 1950s, and not only in name. It is not merely that the European grouping of six relatively closely related states has been joined by nine others—with a further ten or more planning to follow suit—but that the geographical limits, political and economic powers and competences, and even the aims and aspirations of the European polity are quite different from those expressed and agreed in the original treaties.

One of the manifestations of these changes, to which the multiplicity of titles attests, is the division and fragmentation of political authority in both functional and institutional terms. Whereas the small, six-member ECSC, Euratom and EEC gradually came to operate as relatively centralised, homogenous decision-making entities, according to what became known as the "classic Community method", this method, represented by the paradigm of integration as uniformity and harmonisation, has gradually changed as the Communities expanded geographically and, in terms of policy competence, to a more diversified and fragmented system of governance. While it is not possible to identify a specific point in time—such as a particular Intergovernmental Conference or

Treaty signature—at which this metamorphosis occurred, it can broadly be said that over the past ten years the paradigm (however notional) of uniformity, homogeneity and one-directional integration is gradually being replaced by one of flexibility, mixity and differentiation.

In one sense, it is quite obvious that a European organisation whose membership has expanded from six to 15 and soon to be 20 or 25 states, whose aims have become more diverse and more ambitious, whose geographic scope and policy competences have widened extensively, cannot sustain the degree of homogeneity, commonality and unity of purpose and method which seemed to characterise the earlier Community. The increased heterogeneity, political, economic and cultural, of its member countries inevitably brings an increase in the degree of heterogeneity within the functioning of its institutions and policies also. It has gradually become not only conceivable but positively accepted that not all members must adhere to every policy, and that different states and regions may adhere at different times and in different ways to various policies, and indeed that European policies may have to be drawn up in such a way as to accommodate a degree of flexibility in their interpretation and implementation by different states. Further, other forms of political ordering, other sites and fora for decision-making involving different groupings of states have evolved alongside and outside the official EC and EU structures, making the idealised "*communautaire*" model of unity and uniformity increasingly unsustainable.

This idealised view of integration has, in the past, been contrasted with the hidden reality of "disintegration".[1] It has been argued that despite the professed aim of achieving "ever closer union" by gradually harmonising the policies and actions of different Member States, the EC's attempts to develop uniform policies at the supranational level have in fact exacerbated and polarised irreducible differences across its territories, resulting in various degrees of social, cultural and economic disintegration. The model of integration can also be considered, however, not only in contrast to the reality of disintegration, but also in the context of the existence of a substantial degree of differentiation: a model of Europe and even of European integration can be imagined in which not all states or areas commit themselves to the same centralised policies, but in which some choose to pursue different policies or similar policies in different ways, while remaining within the overall umbrella of the European polity. In other words, there need not necessarily be one inexorable path of integration implying harmonisation and gradual unification, but rather commitment to a broad commonality within which room exists for varying degrees of difference and diversity.

The gradual shift from an entity in which the notions of unity and harmonization appear not only to have been prized but required as an essential element of membership, to one in which differences in the degree of adherence of various

[1] J. Shaw, "European Union Legal Studies in Crisis? Towards a New Dynamic" (1996) 16 *OJLS* 231.

states to various policies are not just tolerated as a temporary aberration but are positively accepted as a necessary feature has been evident for some time. Although the first discussions of a multi-speed or variegated Europe are much earlier in origin,[2] and many instances of overlapping orders and sub-orders within, without and on the periphery of EC competences such as the European Monetary System (EMS) and Schengen have come into existence without any centrally authorised legal basis, the provisions introduced and formalised in the Maastricht and Amsterdam Treaties have most obviously marked the change taking place in the nature of the EU's framework of governance. Such a development in the *modus operandi* and even the identity of Europe as a political entity has many implications, and the emergence of a complex language of differentiation/multi-speed/variable geometry/flexibility represents one of the stages in attempting to explain and understand the development and its meaning.

This collection of essays is intended to contribute to the attempt to understand these changing patterns of governance in Europe. Some of the contributions reflect on the broader theoretical and constitutional implications of differentiation and flexibility for the European polity. Others examine the continuities with past practice and question the extent to which there has in fact been any major change of paradigm. Other chapters use particular case studies or examine specific policy areas to explore the many different meanings and forms of differentiation and flexibility which exist, and their significance for the EU model of governance. The intention, in presenting this variety of perspectives and methods, is to bring into focus some of the problems and the potential ways forward for Europe which the developments may suggest.

The fears generally associated with the move to a constitutional model which embraces differentiation rather than one which idealises integration include[3] a further weakening of the democratic elements within the polity, legal and institutional complexity and fragmentation which could further alienate an already disinterested and distrustful populace, the absence of unitary authority with which to address potential problems and conflict, loss of unity of purpose, the undermining of past achievements of the EU and possibly the undermining of its future as a credible political and legal actor. On the other hand, some of the potential benefits include, for new and for applicant Member States, a reduction the burden of adaptation which has rested on them in the past,[4] and for current Member States, a possible means of accommodating their commitment to the

[2] See e.g. R. Dahrendorf, "A Third Europe?" Jean Monnet Lecture (Florence: European University Institute, 1979); C.-D. Ehlermann "How Flexible is Community Law? An Unusual Approach to the Concept of 'Two Speeds' " (1984) 82 *Michigan LR* 1274; E. Grabitz (ed.), *Abgestüfte Integration: eine Alternative zum herkömmlichen Integrationskoncept* (Kehl-am-Rhein: Engel Verlag, 1984); H. Wallace and A. Ridley, *Europe: The Challenge of Diversity* (London: RIIA, 1985).

[3] See N. Walker, "Sovereignty and Differentiated Integration in the European Union" (1998) 4 *ELJ* 355.

[4] K. Junge, "Flexibility, Enhanced Co-operation and the Treaty of Amsterdam", European Dossier Series (London: Kogan Page, 1999).

overall EU entity with their desire for greater autonomy in relation to certain political or social policy choices. A more flexible constitutional framework is likely to facilitate enlargement and better accommodate a broader and more diverse European membership. At its most general, there are benefits in the possibility of a new and more pluralist type of framework or *modus operandi* for a continually changing entity whose legal and political nature has long eluded definition.

Several of the chapters reflect in a theoretical way on the general implications of this framework, and of what might be called a flexibility paradigm for the EU. Neil Walker's contribution considers the need for a new set of concepts and a new language—that of "meta-constitutionalism"—both to break away from state-centred constitutionalism and to help us understand and conceptualise the broader changes in international governance and political ordering, including that represented by an increasingly multi-centred and differentiated Europe. Jo Shaw's chapter explores the apparent paradox of the "constitutionalisation" of flexibility which the Amsterdam Treaty amendments seem to represent, and considers, drawing on ideas of relational and procedural constitutionalism, whether the EU as a legitimately flexible polity might better accommodate diversity within uniformity than a more traditional constitutional model. Eric Philippart and Monika Sien Die Ho address the nature of the EU as a system of governance – setting out four different models of EU governance—and consider the implications of a more differentiated Europe for this system. In addition to this broader constitutional level of analysis, they seek more pragmatically to explore the potential capacity of the new Treaty provisions to manage some of the specific problems posed by "diversity" in the EU.

A number of other chapters reflect on the relationship between older forms of differentiation and flexibility and the more recently formalised "closer co-operation" after the Amsterdam Treaty. Bruno de Witte examines the past use of international agreements between Member States on subjects which come within the scope of EC competence, looking particularly at the Schengen model but also at other kinds of agreement. He considers the likelihood of their continued use even after the establishment of EU and EC Treaty mechanisms for closer co-operation, contrasting the strengths and weaknesses of the various options which remain open to groups of states who may wish to pursue different types of policy between themselves. Jacques Ziller similarly puts the newer Treaty provisions in context by examining how geographically differentiated the Europe polity (or polities) has always been, and how its territorial scope has always varied depending on a range of factors. His focus is specifically on the overseas countries and territories and he argues that the differentiated regime applying to these areas needs to be amended. It is worth considering what lessons might be drawn from his study of the complexity of application of EC and EU law to these territories, and whether problems in the future application of the closer co-operation provisions and other newer types of differentiation might be anticipated, including in relation to the interpretative role of the Court of Justice. The role of the Court within a differentiated European legal system is investigated in further detail by Carole Lyons, whose contribution explores the implications of the restructured judicial architecture following the Treaty of Amsterdam. She considers both the extensions and the apparent restrictions of the Court's jurisdictional role, and questions more generally how the internal coherence or intelligibility of EC law as construed by the Court may be affected by the degree of fragmentation which is occurring. Gráinne de Búrca's chapter examines the kind of differentiation between individual Member States which has been accepted for many years within secondary harmonising legislation in the field of the internal market, and uses this case study to consider whether a "core" set of commitments forming the heart of EU membership can be identified, which could be seen as setting the outer limits to the scope of permissible differentiation.

Other contributions address the relevance of various kinds of differentiation and flexibility within particular policy areas and, in so doing, tease out and reveal the nuances and different meanings of the term "flexibility". Marise Cremona's chapter deals with the external relations of the EU, and examines two different but related features of this field: focusing first on the way in which the EU differentiates clearly in its dealings with different groupings of states, on a geographic, economic or "conditionality" basis and, secondly, examining the nature of its negotiations with external partners and the type of "package" which is generally offered to third states. Ultimately she identifies a rigidity and lack of flexibility in the way in which the EU deals with its various partner countries, and concludes that the EU is imposing not only a model of integration on many third countries, but also a set of fixed core commitments, without the possibility of participation in the negotiation of those commitments which its own Member States enjoy. Concentrating on the field of social policy, Catherine Barnard examines the ambiguity of the term "flexibility" in this context, contrasting the implications of the term flexibility in the labour market context with those in the broader institutional and constitutional context. She examines the way in which degrees of difference between states and others may be accommodated through different forms of flexibility: at the "micro" level in the provisions of directives and through soft law, at the more "macro" level in the variable geometry of the Maastricht Social Policy Agreement and Protocol, and finally in the moves towards a kind of proceduralisation of EU labour law and social policy. In a response to this chapter, Miguel Rodriguez-Piñero Royo considers what might be learnt about the constitutional implications of flexibility in Europe from the mixed experience of labour lawyers in dealing with a somewhat different conception of that term over past decades. Based partly on that experience, his assessment of the notion of flexibility in general is both cautious and sceptical, and he points in particular to its vagueness, its formalism and the use which is made of the term to provide a kind of retrospective legitimation of outcomes which have already been decided.

Like Catherine Barnard, Filip Tuytschaever similarly examines the multiplicity of forms of differentiation—primary and secondary, positive and negative, temporary and non-temporary, to be found within one of the policy areas in which its use has most readily been accepted: that of Economic and Monetary Union. He considers also the possible relevance of the closer co-operation provisions of the Amsterdam Treaty in this policy sphere, and he reflects on the inevitable tension existing between the desire (reflected in those cautiously worded Treaty provisions) to "rein in" the different subsystems and forms of political ordering which might otherwise proliferate and the opposing tendency for such arrangements to emerge in response to the desire of Member States to co-operate in less formalised inter-governmental ways. His conclusion, interestingly, is that the practice of integration—the gradual incorporation of *ad hoc* and differentiated arrangements into a more centralised and formalised framework in which all members eventually participate—inevitably seems to prevail over the ideology of differentiation, and that differentiation frequently turns out to be the first decisive step towards "communautairisation". Steve Weatherill's chapter uses the case study of cultural policy to examine the potential of the new closer co-operation provisions of the Treaty and concludes, despite their apparent narrowness, that they may well be open to a more generous interpretation. He is cautious in his overall assessment of differentiation and flexibility as a model to replace the "overstated" paradigm of uniformity, placing side by side both its potential to damage further the legitimacy of the EU as well as its inevitability and usefulness in absorbing and addressing some of the problems caused by enlargement and expansion.

Joanne Scott and Karl-Heinz Ladeur both focus, in their respective contributions, on specific environmental instruments (the IPPC—Integrated Pollution Prevention and Control and the EIA—Environmental Impact Assessment Directives) as a lens through which to examine certain kinds of "micro" flexibility—i.e. the accommodation, in the implementation of these instruments, of different national systems and local choices—in this policy sphere. Ladeur argues, drawing on the example of these environmental directives, for a form of mutual observation and co-operative learning between different national legal and administrative systems, rather than the imposition of uniformity through harmonisation. More generally, he suggests that the study could be merely one exemplification of a broader conceptual shift in the process of European integration from supranationality to transnationality. Scott's case study is the IPPC directive, used as an exemplar of the changing approaches to environmental governance which are clearly influencing the EU. She questions whether the apparent degree of flexibility and discretion accorded to Member States in the substantive provisions of this measure is in fact countered by the extent of procedural prescriptiveness. Some interesting parallels between her analysis of the EU's changing environmental policy and Barnard's analysis of developments in social policy are apparent here, although Scott introduces a note of caution by questioning whether the constitutional implications of an EC role in setting procedural standards for its members have adequately been considered.

The complicated, varied and nuanced language which has emerged to describe the sorts of changing constitutional and governmental patterns which this book seeks to analyse has been criticised both for its complexity and for its opacity. From mathematical and geometric metaphors to speed analogies, they seem to obscure and confuse rather than to clarify. What this collection of essays has sought to do, rather than provide yet another typology of the language or set of definitions, is to reflect both generally through a number of theoretical reflections, and more focusedly through a number of policy studies, on the many ways in which various types of "flexibility" have affected the framework of EU governance. From these different perspectives and studies, a number of themes and conclusions emerge: first, that the project of European integration may no longer be—if in fact it ever really was—one which aims towards ever greater homogeneity of it membership, and that differentiation of many kinds may co-exist with an overall set of broadly defined and shared commitments; secondly, that the explicit acknowledgement and embracing of various forms of differentiation carries with it, as well as pragmatic benefits and the promise of accommodation of greater diversity, both a new set of challenges and a number of dangers and tensions. Apart from the more obvious legitimacy problems including those of democracy, transparency, disunity and effectiveness, there are tensions also between the move towards legalisation of different governance arrangements and the inevitable attraction of less formalised co-operation, tensions between the treatment of non-member countries and Member States, and tensions between an apparent increase in substantive flexibility within EU policy and a simultaneous increase in procedural intervention and constraint.

This book is evidently only a beginning, and there is much scope for further analysis of the changing patterns of governance within and around the European polity, not only through an examination of the future operation of the closer co-operation provisions but also through further case studies and the development of theoretical frameworks to conceptualise and understand what is occurring. It is clear that the emergence of a multi-centred, flexible and differentiated Europe poses considerable challenges, not only for the EU and its policy-makers, but also for its observers and those who attempt to analyse and make sense of this complex and constantly changing polity.

2

Flexibility within a Metaconstitutional Frame: Reflections on the Future of Legal Authority in Europe

NEIL WALKER*

1. INTRODUCTION

AMIDST ALL THE talk—constructive and critical—about the emergence of a more flexible conception of the European order, a key question threatens to disappear from sight. Is flexibility aptly viewed as a discrete and technical legal matter? Or is it a broad descriptor, with only an incidental legal dimension, for the more fragmented, multi-layered order of governance in Europe and beyond which is emerging from the complex mix of economic, cultural, political and technological processes involved in "globalisation"?[1] Or, thirdly, is flexibility best conceived of in plural terms, as possessing both a particular legal dimension and a broader significance? Many writers appear unmoved by this question, their answers, at best, only implicit in their general approach. The danger is that it is simply assumed by some that the legal dimension is axiomatic,[2] and by others that it is a mere reflection of a larger process.[3]

* I would like to convey my appreciation to audiences at Pace University, New York, and King's College, London, as well as to the participants in the Florence seminar, for their verbal and written comments on earlier versions of this Chapter. The usual disclaimer applies.

[1] Cf. D. Held, A. McGrew, D. Goldblatt and J. Perraton, *Global Transformations*, (Cambridge: Polity, 1999).

[2] There is a burgeoning legal literature on flexibility which, however sophisticated in its own terms, pays scant attention to the social and political processes underpinning flexibility. Cf. C.-D. Ehlermann, "Differentiation, Flexibility, Closer Co-operation: The New Provisions of the Amsterdam Treaty" (1998) 4 *European Law Journal* 246–70; H. Koltenberg, "Closer Cooperation in the Treaty of Amsterdam" (1998) 35 *Common Market Law Review* 833–54; G. Gaja, "How Flexible is Flexibility under the Amsterdam Treaty?" (1998) 35 *Common Market Law Review* 855–70.

[3] Some of the most suggestive political science work on flexible polities within and beyond the state tends to ignore or marginalise the institutional specificity of law. See, for instance, Michael Keating's work on asymmetrical government: e.g. M. Keating, "Asymmetrical Government. Multinational States in an Integrating Europe" [1999] *Publius* (forthcoming); David Held's work on cosmopolitan governance: e.g. D. Held, *Democracy and the Global Order; From the Modern State to Cosmopolitan Governance* (Cambridge: Polity, 1995); and Gary Mark's work on multi-level governance: e.g. G. Marks, L. Hooghe and K. Blank, "European Integration since the 1980s: State-centric Versus Multi-level Governance" (1996) 34 *Journal of Common Market Studies* 341–78.

The absence of a more thorough reflection on conceptual foundations is unfortunate, as it is a basic premise of this paper that neither the discrete nor the subsumed approach is a wholly adequate answer to the question of the legal significance of flexibility. Instead, the third, more subtle, answer is favoured. There is, indeed, a distinct legal dimension to flexibility which is not merely epiphenomenal of broader social forces, yet legal flexibility remains intimately and inexorably related to these broader processes.

In grasping law's quality as a "semi-autonomous social field"[4] in this connection, we can appreciate that law both influences and has been influenced by flexibility and gain some measure of the terms of this reciprocal influence. Only in this way, it is submitted, can we understand the enormity of the challenge posed by flexibility to our conventions of European legal order and the great demands and opportunities involved in rethinking these conventions. This in turn provides a platform for the main part of our discussion, which concerns the development of a language adequate to the task of reconceptualisation.

2. LAW AND FLEXIBILITY

As I have argued more fully elsewhere,[5] the present pattern of differentiated integration in the EU is not the outcome of a teleological process. Instead, it is the provisional conclusion of a complex mix of strategic politics,[6] sectoral politics[7] and geopolitics.[8] Strategically, the evolving forms and models of flexibility within the EU may be viewed as a contest between, on the one hand, those states and other political actors who favour flexibility as a way of maintaining the momentum of integration against the caution of nationalist sceptics and, on the other, those same sceptics who favour flexibility as a way of endorsing a less monolithic—and so ultimately less powerful—EU. In other words, flexibility is not an end in itself, but an ubiquitous device which can serve quite different—even diametrically opposed—end-games. Sectoral politics further complicate the picture, in that political actors located at various different political levels, and often with quite different overall strategic visions concerning the balance of power between states and supranational polities, may argue for or against flexible initiatives and arrangements in a discrete policy sector because of their particular ambitions and preferences in that sector. Finally, the geopolitical context is important in that it introduces various external factors to compound the internal pressures towards differentiation. In the realigning international order which has succeeded Cold War bipolarity, other European and global organisa-

[4] S. Falk Moore, *Law as Process: An Anthropological Approach* (London: Routledge & Kegan Paul, 1978) ch. 2.

[5] N. Walker, "Sovereignty and Differentiated Integration in the European Union" (1998) 4 *European Law Journal* 355–88.

[6] *Ibid.*, 369–71.

[7] *Ibid.*, 372.

[8] *Ibid.*, 373–4.

tions and the new wave of EU candidate states make for a more elaborate network of overlapping polities of which the complexly differentiated EU framework is but one seamless component.

Flexibility, therefore, is a "non-project".[9] It is not the product of a single fixed or even evolving vision. Rather it has unfolded in a sequence of strategic negotiations and gambits, of policy-driven initiatives within discrete sectors, and of accommodations of new geopolitical forces. Its composition is marked not by design, certainty and consensus, but by contingency, ambiguity and disagreement.

In turn, the complex and unplanned legal order of flexibility gives rise to at least four sets of governance problems. There is, first, the specifically legal question of delineating the boundaries between legal orders and putative legal orders and of finding appropriate bridging mechanisms between these legal orders.[10] This is difficult enough in a two-dimensional juridical space; regarding the paradigmatic "EC" relationship between two kinds of fixed polities, each making sovereign claims—Member States on the one hand and the supranational order on the other. It is all the more difficult in the multi-dimensional juridical space which is beginning to characterise the highly complex world of differentiated integration, with the fixed polities of the two-dimensional universe of legal sovereigns co-existing with and in actual or potential competition with other "Europes" which are emerging from (e.g. Schengen, the Eurozone) or overlap with (e.g. Council of Europe) the fixed and uniform "second-dimensional" supranational order—each with different jurisdictional scope and depth and claiming a different degree of legal autonomy. The legal boundary disputes and sovereign power struggles associated with a two-dimensional configuration are compounded under a multi-dimensional configuration simply because there is more border territory to fight over and more existing or aspirant centres of power to enter the fight.

There are also broader problems of political efficacy,[11] democratic accountability[12] and social legitimacy[13] associated with the multi-dimensional configuration of authority which flexibility entails. As regards political efficacy, problems of trust, mutual understanding and technical co-ordination between political institutions are exacerbated to the extent that these institutions are domiciled in different political systems. Democratic accountability, too, is posed new challenges in a crowded institutional context, where popular affinity is contested or diluted and lines of responsibility are blurred. These problems of legal authority, political efficacy and democratic accountability also threaten the popular legitimacy of a multi-dimensional order, as does the absence of a discourse of authority and belonging which marks out the non-project of

[9] *Ibid.*, 374.
[10] *Ibid.*, 375–8.
[11] *Ibid.*, 379–80.
[12] *Ibid.*, 380–1.
[13] *Ibid.*, 381–2.

multi-dimensionality as an identifiable and defensible political construct in the same way as nationalism and supranationalism and their associated cultural and constitutional discourses mark out one-dimensional and two-dimensional orders.

If we look at the governance problems of flexibility in the light of its diverse roots, we gain a sense of how law is profoundly challenged by the onset of flexibility yet remains capable of significantly influencing its future course. On the one hand, flexibility challenges both the technical capacity of law to address problems of inter-systemic co-ordination, together with associated problems of political efficacy and democratic accountability, and also its symbolic capacity as an independent source of power and as a means of constructing an authoritative image and discourse of the political order and cultural community it seeks to represent.[14] The fragmentation of legal orders problematises what previously was taken for granted—the unassailable authority of any particular order—and so poses new technical challenges to find acceptable and mutually validated forms of communication and co-ordination between systems. Equally, the new flexible configuration of authority, because it is not a planned or consensual development, offers little scope for the construction of a grand constitutional image and discourse to undergird its identity and bolster its legitimacy. Further, the technical and symbolic deficiencies may be mutually corrosive. Where there is no unified order and so no mechanically identifiable intra-systemic technique available,[15] how, without begging the question, do we identify an acceptable constituency and method to construct an authoritative version of the new political order? Equally, where there is no legitimating trans-systemic canopy, how do we arrive at acceptable technical solutions to co-ordinate the legal, institutional and democratic orders of the different and contested systems?

On the other hand, the very circumstances that challenge and dilute the problem-solving capacity and symbolic authority of law guarantee that it remains a precious currency. The problems of co-ordination and legitimacy of the new flexible order are on such a scale that law, with its traditionally vast regulatory potential, will inevitably continue to be invoked as a means of containing and resolving crises. Moreover, as a deeply-layered and richly-resourced repository of traditional and cultural meanings, the legal form retains a "legitimacy credit" and a versatility even in the face of new and apparently discontinuous contexts of political organisation and regulation.[16]

To assert the indispensability and resilience of law is not, it should be emphasised, to commit the lego-centric error of viewing law as the only or predominant guarantor of the new order. Fertilised by the rich soil of strategic, sectoral and geopolitical considerations, economic or security-based or other pragmatic

[14] R. Cotterrell, "Some Aspects of the Communication of Constitutional Authority" in D. Nelken (ed.), *Law as Communication* (Aldershot: Dartmouth, 1997) 129–51.

[15] As, for example, in constitution amendment clauses.

[16] Cf. D. Nelken, "Is There a Crisis in Law and Legal Ideology?" (1982) 9 *Journal of Law and Society* 177–90.

discourses of justification may become prominent, and so a legal crisis does not necessarily portend a crisis of the entire order. Just as constitutions in state polities evolve conventions and customs to smooth over crises, or contrive abeyances and leave silences to avoid them,[17] so this may also be true of a more fragmented legal order. Yet there are limits to this. Custom, convention, soft law and various other para-legal forms are lent shape and coherence by the formal legal order. Bargaining in the shadow and in the interstices of a legal framework depends, finally, upon the resilience, relevance and threshold legitimacy of the legal framework.[18]

The Treaty of Amsterdam is instructive of the dual role of law—as both victim of upheaval and restabilising influence—in circumstances of incipient multidimensionality. In its treatment of flexibility, Amsterdam is both *instrumental* and *reflexive*. It both adds to the unplanned architectural sprawl of flexibility, particularly in documenting the latest compromises over Schengen and the Third Pillar,[19] and begins to reflect upon, learn from and impose a certain design and a certain set of ordering principles upon the flexible arrangements already in place or newly provided for, particularly in respect of so-called "enhanced co-operation".[20] This dualism—which fits a broader pattern of retrospective or incremental constitutionalization within the EU Treaty framework[21]—suggests how law, and in particular the ideal of legal uniformity within the EU, can simultaneously exhibit both vulnerability to wider political forces and an independent capacity to make a positive difference to the prospects of the European polity. The vulnerability of the legal form is exposed where the Treaty-makers, *qua* bearers of sectoral, national-strategic and other partial interests, have influenced negotiations in the IGC in the direction of further *ad hoc* flexibility in Justice and Home Affairs, with attendant problems of boundary maintenance

[17] Cf. M. Foley, *The Silence of Constitutions: Gaps, "Abeyances" and Political Temperament in the Maintenance of Government* (London: Routledge, 1989).

[18] For discussion of the formidable challenges posed to the legitimacy and efficacy of the legal order of the single European currency, see P. Beaumont and N. Walker, "The Euro and European Legal Order" in P. Beaumont and N. Walker (eds.), *Legal Framework of the Single European Currency* (Oxford: Hart, 1999) 169–94.

[19] Cf. N. Walker, "Justice and Home Affairs" (1998) 47 *International and Comparative Law Quarterly* 236–45.

[20] For the general framework of enhanced co-operation, see Arts. 43 and 44 TEU; for its application to the First and Third Pillars, see Art. 11 (5a) EC Treaty and Art. 40 TEU respectively. For discussion, see references at n. 2, *supra*.

[21] This can be seen, for example, in the belated recognition given to the European Council in the Single European Act, long after it had become an institutional fact; or, arguably, in the development of a general concept of subsidiarity in the Treaty of Maastricht, after many years of executive and, to an even lesser extent, legislative practice and procedure which paid uneven attention to the logic of subsidiarity. This type of constitutional reflexivity is also commonly found in state constitutions, but arguably it is more pronounced at the EU level precisely because of the ambiguous status of its foundational documentation. Originating as an international treaty rather than a self-styled constitution, it retains much of the detailed legislation typical of Treaty law. Consequently, it has a more pronouncedly two-tier internal structure than many state constitutions, more likely to contain both the detailed instruments of governance and—often as a later addition—principled reflection on these instruments.

and co-ordination, political efficacy, democratic accountability and social legitimacy. But where the Treaty-makers, *qua* guardians of the integrity of the European legal order, reflexively develop general principles of enhanced co-operation, there law reasserts itself as an active agent engaging—even pre-empting—some of the governance problems associated with incipient multi-dimensionality.

If the schizophrenic approach of the law-makers to the EU's claims to sovereign authority reflects the contested legitimacy of the European order within a multi-dimensional framework, Amsterdam also demonstrates how the introduction of flexible premises into a legal order can undermine its technical puzzle-solving capacity in a fundamental manner. Capacities which we take for granted within a unitary framework are lost or fail to be generated in a more fragmented legal environment. For instance, Amsterdam fails to provide a settled rule of adjudication in favour of the EU's supreme court, the ECJ lacking comprehensive or even uniform jurisdiction in the Third Pillar.[22] If this example seems to flow naturally from the concerns of the treaty-makers to preserve national claims, then even where a greater loyalty towards the European order prevails, the accommodation of flexible premises can undermine technical capacity. For instance, the basic intra-systemic assumption that competing principles can be balanced on a common scale in the resolution of a particular dispute is confounded in the formulation of the terms of enhanced co-operation under the general enabling clause of the Amsterdam Treaty.[23] Where a determination falls to be made whether a particular flexible initiative should go ahead under that clause, how are we to weigh the value of the principle of non-interference by participating states either with the *acquis communautaire* or with "the competences, rights, obligations and interests" of the non-participating states, on the one hand, against the value of the competing principle of non-prejudice by non-participating states of the implementation of closer co-operation by participating states on the other? There is not one but two answers, depending upon the perspective of which of the two groups—participating or non-participating states—is privileged in assessing costs and benefits, and there is no objective way within a fragmenting legal order of adjudicating between these two perspectives.

3. BUILDING A METACONSTITUTIONAL FRAME

So flexibility poses a great challenge to law, and not one we can wish away by making law redundant. Flexibility asks new and difficult questions of law, but does so in conditions where it also threatens law's legitimacy and technical capacity. How should law respond to this challenge? My answer is, for the moment, highly schematic. It is also by no means exclusively concerned with the

[22] Art. 35 TEU; cf. P. Tuytschaever, *Differentiation in European Union Law* (Oxford: Hart, 1999) 95–6.

[23] Art. 43 TEU. Cf. Walker, n. 5 *supra*, 386–7.

particular problems of flexibility. Rather, as we shall see, it involves excavating a deep seam of difficulties, with issues of flexibility situated at the rock face.

This excavation involves developing a new way of framing non-domestic law of the public sphere, a new legal discourse which I will call *metaconstitutionalism*. Semantically, the prefix "meta" stands in relation to the activity denoted by the concept prefixed as "a higher science of the same nature but dealing with ulterior problems".[24] Metaconstitutionalism relates to constitutionalism, therefore, as metaphysics does to physics or as metaethics does to ethics. Metaconstitutional rules—or norms or axioms—are rules *about* constitutional rules. Their subject-matter is ultimately the same but they claim within their own authoritative terms a higher or deeper constitutional authority than constitutional rules.

In the definition of key terms, one further refinement is required. Legal philosophy is already familiar with what might be labelled *state-centred*, or *domestic* metaconstitutionalism.[25] This refers to the internally generated and agreed rules and assumptions about what is to count as the constitution and as fundamental law within a state, whether, to take two examples, this metaconstitutional background is conceived of in terms of the Hartian rule of recognition or of the Kelsenian grundnorm. We are not here concerned with this local form of excavation but, instead, with *cosmopolitan* metaconstitutionalism. This refers to a type of legal discourse which has the same general object of reference as constitutional law, namely the fundamental framework of public authority, but which, unlike constitutional law, is not nested in the state and does not look to the state as its fundamental source of validity. Rather, metaconstitutional discourse, notwithstanding the often inconsistent and competing claims made on behalf of the state through its traditional constitutional discourse and representations of sovereignty,[26] always claims a higher or deeper normative authority. The nature of its claims are reflected in the way in which it characterises its relationship with state law. It may purport to authorise, instruct, influence, supplement or supplant state law, or any combination of these. Whatever the case, in no circumstances does it concede the normative superiority of state law. Metaconstitutionalism always conceives of its own authority as original and irreducible.

Why does cosmopolitan metaconstitutionalism provide a useful way of thinking about contemporary non-domestic public law in general and about flexibility and the emerging multi-dimensional configuration of legal authority in particular? Before we can address that question, we must fill out the conceptual bare bones of cosmopolitan metaconstitutionalism as follows. First, we

[24] *The Shorter Oxford English Dictionary.*

[25] Cf. R.S. Kay, "Preconstitutional Rules" (1981) 42 *Ohio State Law Journal* 187–205; L. Alexander, "Introduction" in L. Alexander (ed.), *Constitutionalism: Philosophical Foundations* (Cambridge: CUP, 1998) 1–15. See also n. 36 *infra*.

[26] On sovereignty as a means of representing a unity of political power within a polity, see H. Lindahl, "The Purposiveness of Law: Two Concepts of Representation in the European Union" (1998) 17 *Law and Philosophy* 481–507.

examine the conditions which have made possible, indeed inevitable, the emergence of a type of law which may be conceptualised in metaconstitutional terms. Secondly, we catalogue the various forms taken by metaconstitutional law, and investigate the relationship between these forms.

A. Context of Emergence

Metaconstitutional discourse becomes possible with the passing of the Westphalian one-dimensional global order of sovereign states. State sovereignty in this context conveys the double sense of *internal sovereignty*—the idea of the exclusive and unrivalled legal authority of the state within a particular territorial space—and *external sovereignty*—the idea of the state as the only significant legally recognised player on the stage of global decision-making.[27] In such a world order there was no scope for the development of metaconstitutional law. Constitutional law *simpliciter* was the primary structure in the legal architecture of the international order, precisely *because* constitutional law was a product of the state and the state was internally and externally unrivalled as a source of authority. Under this framework—and despite the views of the early Kelsen[28] and of others of an idealist or liberal internationalist persuasion—international law occupied a secondary position within the global legal architecture. Internally, it did not challenge the authority of the state as master of its own polity. Externally, granted, international law did "regulate" relations between states, but only in the voluntarist sense[29] that it was the product of agreement between states as formally free and equal parties. International law was not and is not the ultimate regulator of states, but rather their regulatory tool.[30]

In the post-Westphalian world, as state sovereignty loses its hegemony in the face of the challenge of globalisation, so too its two legal handmaidens—constitutional law and international law—are no longer adequate or sufficient to fill the regulatory space available in the sphere of public authority. For some commentators, notably modern systems theorists such as Teubner,[31] the most significant upshot of this has been the development of legal innovations at the social peripheries rather than in the political centre, and taking the form of new

[27] Cf. Walker, n. 5 *supra*, 356–60.

[28] For the early view, see H. Kelsen, *Introduction to the Problems of Legal Theory* (Oxford: Clarendon, 1992, tr. B. and S. Paulson) 120. For a later recognition of the possibility of an alternative state-centred monistic order, see H. Kelsen, *The Pure Theory of Law* (Berkely and Los Angelos, Cal.: University of California Press, 1967) 333–9. For a stimulating discussion, cf. C. Richmond, "Preserving the Identity Crisis: Autonomy, System and Sovereignty in European Law" (1997) 16 *Law and Philosophy* 377–420, especially at 410 ff.

[29] On voluntarism, or consensualism, as the dominant theory of international law, see O. Schachter, *International Law in Theory and Practice* (Dordrecht: M. Nijhoff, 1991) ch. 5.

[30] Thus under international law, the parties to a treaty may revoke or change it at any time, and may even disregard treaty provisions which establish a special procedure to be followed: see Vienna Convention on the Law of Treaties (1968).

[31] G. Teubner, " 'Global Bukowina': Legal Pluralism in the World Society" in G. Teubner (ed.), *Global Law Without a State* (Aldershot: Dartmouth, 1997) 3–30.

types of state-transcending regulation in those discrete sectors of civil society served, for example, by commercial law (*lex mercatoria*), environmental law and even international sports law. But while such developments are significant, they are not at the expense of public frameworks of governance. Rather, there have been, and continue to take place, significant institutional developments in the public as well as the private sphere. Enter metaconstitutional law.

B. The Forms of Metaconstitutionalism

Metaconstitutional law comes in a wide variety of forms which cannot be easily distinguished nor neatly classified. Nevertheless, we may identify five main types, which are ordered below in terms of their level of abstraction from the constitutional state.

First, there is legal discourse which seeks to reshape the traditional intra-constitutional law sphere of the structural relations between different groups within the state—whether defined by nation, ethnicity, territory, religion, language or other cleavage—in a manner which goes beyond those forms of legal "identity politics",[32] such as claims to mutual respect, to multicultural citizenship or to distinct political institutions, which can be accommodated within the existing framework of state authority. Instead, it proceeds to question and challenge the constitutional integrity of the state itself through secessionist or quasi-secessionist claims. For the most part this is a *counterfactual* legal discourse. Unlike the forms of metaconstitutionalism considered below—and so, incidentally, making it the most complex metaconstitutional discourse to characterise—it is not anchored within an institutional site or sites which can make a plausible current claim to possess fundamental law-making authority. On the other hand, this form of metaconstitutionalism may be sustained and supported through its relationship to these other, more state-removed metaconstitutional sites which do possess plausible claims to fundamental legal authority.[33] Yet as long as the integrity and internal distribution of authority of the state which it challenges remain intact, then, *ex hypothesi*, secessionist or quasi-secessionist discourse can be no more than aspirational. That does not mean, however, that it is merely a form of constitutional law-in-waiting. It is *meta*constitutional in the sense that while its ultimate purpose may be the creation of a new state, and thus a new constitutional order, the process by which the transformation is

[32] Cf. J. Tully, *Strange Multiplicity: Constitutionalism in an Age of Diversity* (Cambridge: CUP, 1995); "Identity Politics and Freedom: The Challenge of Reimagining Belonging in Multicultural and Multinational Communities", paper to Conference on Reimagining Belonging, Aaalborg, May 1999.

[33] Think, for example, of the way in which minority national movements may be protected by international human rights regimes, or, in the context of the EU, may be sustained and legitimated by the representational or resource-allocation possibilities of association with or membership of the supranational organisation. Cf. M. Keating, n. 3 *supra*. See also 'Beyond the Unitary Conception of the UK Constitution?' *Public Law* (forthcoming).

sought addresses matters of fundamental political authority through arguments—historical, ethical or pragmatic[34]—which refuse to defer to the existing state constitutional order as a definitive and irreducible "power map",[35] and in so doing necessarily poses a challenge to the *general* claim of constitutional law to ultimate authority.[36]

This type of counterfactual metaconstitutionalism may also have an indirect impact upon existing state constitutional law. In the moulding of primary constitutional discourse, political prudence may demand or dialogic openness may encourage the taking into account of secessionist or quasi-secessionist discourse, and often with consequences which escape the intentions of those who make the accommodation. The fluid narrative of constitutional reform in the multinational state of the UK is an apt current example. British constitution-builders should bear in mind that institutions to which they have recently applied the official constitutional *imprimatur*, such as devolved assemblies and local referenda, may have a meaning and a role within alternative metaconstitutional discourses. So, for instance, the new Scottish Parliament is on one view the cement of the Union, on another a stepping-stone to independence.[37] The referendum which preceded it is on one view a healthy exercise in local democracy within an increasingly federalist constitutional pattern, on another a prefigurative assertion of the popular sovereignty of the Scottish people. And if, as, for example, has often been the case in processes of decolonisation, the structural transformation from old to new polity develops critical momentum, metaconstitutional discourse may become more than the catalyst for constitutional shadow-boxing. It may become the form of communication between rival plausible claims to constitutional authority.[38]

[34] See, for example, the rich mix of arguments used on behalf of the secessionist case in the Quebec Secession Reference; *Reference by the Governor of Canada pursuant to s53 of the Supreme Court Act, concerning the secession of Quebec from Canada* [1998] 2 SCR 217. Cf. M.D. Walters, "Nationalism and the Pathology of Legal Systems: Considering the *Quebec Secession Reference* and its Lessons for the United Kingdom" (1999) 62 *Modern Law Review* 370–95.

[35] I.D. Duchacek, *Power Maps: Comparative Politics of Constitutions* (Santa Barbara, Cal., and Oxford: Clio Press, 1973).

[36] It should also be noted that insofar as these arguments are the sorts of jurisprudential arguments used to justify the constitutional identity of states (as opposed to constitutional discourse proper, which *presupposes* the constitutional identity of the state), although in this case it is an alternative vision of constitutional statehood that it is sought to justify, such arguments are of the same order as those found within domestic or state-centred metaconstitutionalism. In this first form of cosmopolitan metaconstitutionalism, therefore, there is a distinct overlap with state-centred metaconstitutionalism. See n. 25 *supra*.

[37] Cf. Scotland Act 1998; See also C.M.G. Himsworth and C.R. Munro, *The Scotland Act 1998* (Edinburgh: Greens, 1999); N. Walker, "Constitutional Reform in a Cold Climate: Reflections on the White Paper and Referendum on Scotland's Parliament" in A. Tomkins (ed.), *Devolution and the British Constitution* (London: Key Haven, 1998) 61–88.

[38] As, for example, in the classic exchange between the Rhodesian High Court and the UK-based Judicial Committee of the Privy Council over the validity of Rhodesia's unilateral declaration of independence. The Rhodesian court held it to be valid, while the court of the original imperial power took the opposite view: *Madzimbamuto* v. *Lardner-Burke* 1968 (2) SA 284; [1969] AC 645; cf. G. Marshall, *Constitutional Theory* (Oxford: Clarendon, 1971) 64–72.

In some cases, the interlocking of constitutional order and metaconstitutional possibility can be even closer. Exceptionally, metaconstitutional reflection upon the challenge to the integrity of a state may be provided for, or at least made possible, within the constitutional procedures of the state itself. So, for example, the reference procedure of the Canadian Supreme Court has recently allowed it to think what for a constitutional court is normally unthinkable—namely whether the unilateral secession of Quebec, and the consequent fragmentation of the Canadian state, is legally competent.[39] Moreover, the court felt equipped to address this question both as a matter of domestic constitutional law, the logic of which predictably quickly disposed of the unthinkable in accordance with the unambiguous direction of the constitutional text, but also as a matter of international law, where the answer, although not structurally pre-ordained, turned out, for that national court at least, to be the same. Nevertheless, this kind of state-centred metaconstitutional reflexivity is not doomed merely to reinforce the *status quo ante*, as demonstrated by the court's strongly argued opinion that, while there was no right to secede, the federal and other provincial governments were under a legal duty to engage with Quebec in *bona fide* negotiations over the terms of its possible secession.

A second type of metaconstitutional discourse seeks to shape and instruct the traditional intra-state constitutional law sphere of the basic rights and duties of the individual *vis-à-vis* the state. The paradigm case here is "international" human rights law.[40] Mainly through Treaty law promulgated at both regional and local level, but backed by peremptory norms of international law (*ius cogens*) and the more general framework of international customary law, this area of law expanded exponentially in the wake of the Second World War. It is a movement that has challenged the premise of untrammelled state sovereignty which prevented the traditional framework of international law from addressing individuals as well as states themselves as the subjects, rather than the mere objects, of its legal rules. As well as the development of a substantive state-transcendent human rights jurisprudence,[41] this form of metaconstitutionalism has been increasingly underscored by a constellation of non-state courts and tribunals within which such rights may be vindicated. The brightest star in this constellation is undoubtedly the European Court of Human Rights,[42] but it is

[39] *Quebec Secession Reference*, n. 34 *supra*; see also Walters, n. 34 *supra*.

[40] Cf. H.J. Steiner and P. Alston, *International Human Rights in Context; Law, Politics, Morals* (Oxford: OUP, 1996).

[41] This jurisprudence is increasingly influential in national courts even of those states, such as the UK, which retain a basically dualist approach to international law, and so for the most part remain reluctant to endorse international law as domestic law without domestic legislative instruction. A landmark decision in this regard is *R.* v. *Bow Street Metropolitan Stipendiary Magistrate, ex parte Pinochet Ugarte (Amnesty International intervening (No.3)* (1999) 2 W.L.R. 827, in which the House of Lords, drawing upon both domestic law and customary international law, held that a former head of state enjoys no immunity in extradition or criminal proceedings brought in the UK in respect of the international crime of torture; cf. H. Fox, "The Pinochet Case No.3" (1999) 48 *International and Comparative Law Quarterly* 687–702.

[42] Cf. B. Dickson (ed.), *Human Rights and the European Convention* (London: Sweet & Maxwell, 1997).

joined by an array of permanent and *ad hoc* tribunals at regional and global level, with the new International Criminal Court a key development at the global level.[43]

A third type of metaconstitutional discourse shapes relations between states in ways which supplement and modify the internal constitutional structure of those states. The current metaconstitutional conversation between Britain and Ireland provides a good example.[44] Under the 1998 Belfast Agreement, constitutional amendments were required in both jurisdictions to recognise more fully the principle of popular consent in shaping the future status of Northern Ireland.[45] More pertinent to the development of sites of metaconstitutional authority, the Agreement also provides for a new permanent institutional complex embracing both East–West structures (British–Irish Council and British–Irish Intergovernmental Conference[46]) and a North–South Ministerial Council[47] as a means to endorse and to stabilise an element of power-sharing between the two states.

This type of arrangement shades into a fourth type of metaconstitutional authority, which in addressing relations between states develops an institutional structure with sufficient depth and scope of authority to constitute a non-state polity. Of course, the extent to which an institutional structure constitutes a separate polity is a matter of degree. Clearly the Good Friday structures, for now at least, fall short, but the GATT/WTO structure and the North American Free Trade Association, to take but two examples, are less clear-cut cases, as also are some of the regional international organisations.[48] At the other end of the spectrum is the supranational legal framework of the EU. Originally conceived of as a means to regulate certain fundamental economic relations between states and designed with the orthodox tools of international law, the EU gradually developed its own claim to sovereign authority within a limited sphere. Indeed, as the EU has attracted a complexity of institutional structure and a range of legal competences which begins to rival those of the state, then it has come to represent a particularly developed form of metaconstitutional law; such an organisation becomes, so to speak, a meta-state.

Fifthly, and at the highest level of abstraction from paradigmatic intra-state constitutional law, metaconstitutionalism embraces a further set of relations between polities—both states and non-state polities (including meta-states)—in the more complex multi-dimensional configuration of authority which charac-

[43] Rome Statute of the International Criminal Court, 17 July 1998, A/CONF. 183/9, 1999 37 ILM 999.

[44] *Agreement reached in the Multi-Party Negotiations*, Cm 3883 (London: HMSO, 1998); cf. B. O'Leary, *The British-Irish Agreement: Power-Sharing Plus* (London: Constitution Unit, 1998); B. Hadfield, "The Belfast Agreement, Sovereignty and the State of the Union" [1998] *Public Law* 599–616; D. O'Donnell, "Constitutional Background to and Aspects of the Good Friday Agreement—A Republic of Ireland Perspective" (1999) 50 *Northern Ireland Legal Quarterly* 76–89.

[45] *Constitutional Issues*, Annexes A and B.

[46] *Strand Three*.

[47] *Strand Two*.

[48] Cf. B. Laffan, *Integration and Co-operation in Europe* (London: Routledge, 1992).

terises the post-Westphalian order. At this "meta-meta" level we are concerned, in the first place, with the relations between EU and its Member States, in particular with the judicial conversation between constitutional courts[49] and the political conversations in successive IGCs[50] and in the EU institutions through which these relations are negotiated. Then, at an even higher level of abstraction, the issues of flexibility and fragmentation which provided our initial focus come finally into view. Here we are concerned with relations between different non-state polities; that is, between the EU meta-state and the other emergent polities of our fragmented order, whether conceived within the EU (e.g. Schengen, Euroland) or beyond (e.g Council of Europe, GATT/WTO). And, finally, to relocate these relations in their proper three-dimensional context, we are also concerned with the multi-tiered relations amongst the sites of authority located both at these different meta-tiers and also at the state tier.

4. THE VALUE OF METACONSTITUTIONALISM

We are now in a better position to explore the value of cosmopolitan metaconstitutionalism as a framework for thinking about the various forms of non-domestic public law, and, in particular, the flexible arrangements associated with the EU.

Thus far, the case for treating metaconstitutional legal discourse as a meaningful unity has been implicit and limited A stipulative definition has provided a broad umbrella. This has been linked to a multi-factorial historical movement away from the constitutional state as the exclusive or primary unit of political authority. Yet this is a negative form of cohesiveness. It merely asserts that metaconstitutional rules are those rules other than constitutional rules that operate in the area of the primary legal constitution of public authority once, but no longer, exclusively or predominantly occupied by constitutional rules. And, arguably, the sense that the coherence of metaconstitutionalism is a negative coherence is reinforced when the sheer range of categories of rules which we have attempted to fit into the metaconstitutional category is considered. What is more, most of the types of legal rules and processes referred to under the aegis of metaconstitutionalism are already recognised under other familiar categories. Thus, some of what we have discussed can, in terms of an only modestly

[49] The most significant recent contribution to this conversation was that of the German Constitutional Court in *Brunner* v. *The European Union Treaty* [1994} 1 CMLR 57: Cf. M. Everson, "Beyond the *Bundesverfassungsgericht*: On the Necessary Cunning of Constitutional Reasoning" (1998) 4 *European Law Journal* 389–410; A. Stone Sweet, "Constitutional Dialogues in the European Community" in A-M. Slaughter, A Stone Sweet and J.H.H. Weiler (eds.), *The European Court and National Courts—Doctrine and Jurisprudence: Legal Change in its Social Context* (Oxford: Hart, 1998) 303–30; B. de Witte, "Direct Effect, Supremacy and the Nature of the Legal Order" in P. Craig and G. de Búrca (eds.), *The Evolution of EU Law* (Oxford: OUP, 1999), 177–213.

[50] On the IGC negotiations prior to the Treaty of Amsterdam, see G. de Búrca, "The Quest for Legitimacy in the European Union" (1996) 59 *Modern Law Review* 349.

revisionist institutional analysis, be fitted into the familiar paradigm of international law, or, in the case of the non-state polities, the newer but now well-established paradigm of supranational law. Alternatively, much of the range of law discussed can be broken down into equally recognisable functional categories—human rights law, currency law, the law of free movement, trade law etc.

Yet none of this argues against the development of a new framework of analysis. Granted, much of the legal discourse discussed can be described under well-established taxonomies, although arguably even this is not true of the "meta-meta" level of legal communication between polities with overlapping and contested jurisdictions within a multi-dimensional order. Yet none of these categorisations and the discourses which they frame exhaust the significance of the legal phenomena that they describe, as the very fact that they are amenable *both* to an institutional and to a functional analysis would suggest. In particular, the institutional categorisation—constitutional, international, supranational—is fundamentally positivist in character, suggesting that the salient distinguishing features of legal rules or sets of legal rules are these discrete sources and jurisdiction. Arguably, however, such a conception is most appropriate to a world in which sources and jurisdiction in general, and these ones in particular, are clearly delineated and stable over time, as in the established Westphalian order, and that where precisely this is brought into question the need for some additional conceptual tools becomes urgent.

This point is underscored if we acknowledge that our conceptual inheritance bears at least some responsibility for the rather inflexible tramlines within which contemporary debate about the adaptability of constitutional values to the non-state sphere takes place. Many commentators who have viewed, often with considerable perspicacity, the drift away from the constitutional state as the centre of legal authority seem to have lacked the language to advance the debate, whether in explanatory or normative terms, in a way which captures what is happening and what might happen, other than by reference to what has ceased to happen. In one variant, for example, the liberal internationalist tradition of Kant and Bentham—the loss of constitutional discourse from the state can only be redeemed by its relocation writ large at the level of the constitution of world society in the form of hegemonic international institutions.[51] The flipside of this constitutional idealism is, of course, the pessimism associated with the assessment of this project as unfeasibly utopian or as undesirably imperialist.[52] In turn, this negative assessment of the prospects for global governance may be linked to one of two attitudes: to an ostrich-like refusal to view the ebbing of

[51] Cf. L.Ferrajoli, "Beyond Sovereignty and Citizenship: A Global Constitutionalism" in R. Bellamy (ed.), *Constitutionalism, Democracy and Sovereignty: American and European Perspectives* (Aldershot: Avebury, 1996) 151–60.

[52] Niklas Luhmann, for example, comments that "the structural coupling between law and politics via constitutions has no correspondence on the level of world society": *Das Recht der Gesellschaft* (Frankfurt: Suhrkamp, 1993), quoted in G. Teubner, n. 31 *supra*, 6.

state constitutionalism as anything other than a temporary blip on a horizon still dominated by the Westphalian order;[53] or to a profound fatalism, which acknowledges both the depth of the challenge to the state and the vulnerability of a constitutionalism adrift from its state anchor, and so fears the prospect of "the end of constitutionalism"[54] in any shape or guise.

More pertinently for present purposes, a similar rigidity of view tends to affect those who focus instead on the intermediate, non-state polities which have emerged, such as the EU. Notwithstanding the early and sustained "constitutionalising" efforts of the Court of Justice,[55] for a long time many commentators continued to regard the language of constitutionalism as untranslatable into the terms of the European polity. Instead the European polity was seen as *sui generis*, its supranational legal order equally unique. Increasingly, however, attempts have been mounted to view the European polity through the prism of constitutionalism, but again this tends to take the form of a direct translation from the paradigm of the state. In its more rigorous versions, this tends to involve an institutionally specific comparative evaluation. So the ECJ is analysed as a constitutional court; the Member State–EU tiering as a "federal" or "confederal" division; the Council, Commission and Parliament as the functional equivalent of the traditional organs of the state-centred constitutional democracy. In its less rigorous versions, it is simply assumed that the language of constitutionalism, notwithstanding its statist origins, can without distortion or loss of relevance be translated to the supranational polity and to its quite different institutional carapace and context of legitimisation. Similarly, and from an even more state-removed starting-point, there has been a marked tendency to analyse the trends towards flexibility and multi-dimensionality in terms of an outmoded constitutionalism.[56] In turn, these various assumptions and preconceptions surrounding the EU constitutionalism debate creates parallel poles to those which frame the world governance debate. There is a tendency to treat the language of constitutionalism dichotomously—either it translates fully to the higher level or not at all. Of course, many commentators recognise *in principle* that the answer is more subtle, more nuanced than this, but they are still often trapped within a register of debate which forces them at best to see the legal authority framework of the EU as more or less like the constitutional authority framework of the state.[57]

[53] Cf. J. Hutchinson, *Modern Nationalism* (London: Fantana, 1994); A.S. Milward, *The European Rescue of the Nation-State* (London: Routledge, 1992).

[54] For a thoughtful exploration of this and other positions, see C.M.G. Himsworth, "In a State no Longer: The End of Constitutionalism?" [1996] *Public Law* 639–60.

[55] Cf. J.H.H. Weiler, *The Constitution of Europe* (Cambridge: CUP, 1999) ch. 2.

[56] Cf. A.G. Toth, "The Legal Effects of the Protocols Relating to the United Kingdom, Ireland and Denmark" in T. Heukels, N. Blokker and M. Brus (eds.), *The European Union after Amsterdam: A Legal Analysis* (The Hague: Kluwer, 1998) 227–52). Arguably, the idea of constitutionalism is doubly distorted and doubly diluted in this type of analysis; the incipient "meta-meta" constitutional sites of flexibility being evaluated in accordance with the values associated with the metaconstitutional site of the uniform EU, but still using the language of plain constitutionalism.

[57] This is arguably true even of much of the best work in the field, including work based on explicitly pluralist assumptions about European legal authority; see, for example, the "mixed

The language of metaconstitutionalism may help to overcome these rigidities and limitations. It does not merely gesture towards the uncharted seas beyond the constitutional state. It also offers a set of co-ordinates to plot the navigation of those seas, and in so doing offers new conceptual, explanatory and normative insights. Conceptually, the language of metaconstitutionalism presents a way to acknowledge a number of important truths simultaneously, and in balance. First, unlike some forms of liberal internationalism—and more emphatically than the new "postnational constitutionalism",[58] it acknowledges the lasting importance of the constitutional state, as the entity to which metaconstitutional discourse is ultimately directed and from which it is ultimately derived. Secondly, unlike state revivalism and myopic state constitutionalism, it acknowledges the depth, scale and durability of the challenge to the authority of the constitutional state, as evident in the claims of normative superiority implicit in the metaconstitutional discourse emanating from the growing range of metaconstitutional sites. Thirdly it acknowledges both the continuities *and* the discontinuities between the public law discourses of the state sphere and the non-state sphere. On the one hand, it offers a clear statement that there is an internal relationship between the two discourses; that metaconstitutionalism seeks to address at one or more removes the problems of public authority originating within and still much centred around state constitutionalism. On the other hand, its eschewal of the language of constitutionalism *simpliciter* announces its insistence that the state–constitution coupling is necessary and exclusive rather than empirical and contingent, and that the discourse of the non-state public law sphere is ultimately of a different order from the discourse of the state public law sphere. Let us now begin to address how these conceptual credits might be cashed in explanatory and normative currency.

In explanatory terms, our classification of the various forms of metaconstitutionalism illustrates that, historically, non-state public law emerges from state public law. There is a self-generating dynamic at work between constitutional and metaconstitutional sites, and between metaconstitutional sites at different

commonwealth" thesis introduced by Neil MacCormick in "Democracy, Subsidiarity and Citizenship in the 'European Commonwealth' " (1997) 16 *Law and Philosophy* 331–56; and subsequently endorsed and developed by Richard Bellamy and Dario Castiglione in "Building the Union: The Nature of Sovereignty in the Political Architecture of Europe" (1997) 16 *Law and Philosophy* 421–45. Although the institutional versatility of the mixed commonwealth matches its polyarchic power structure, in my view the use of an undifferentiated language of constitutionalism to refer to every level and centre of power militates against an examination of the often difficult relational dynamics between different authority sites (see main text at notes 62–71 below) and, in the final analysis, encourages the retention of an inappropriately (and perhaps complacently) holistic vision of the overall "constitutional order".

[58] Cf. D.M. Curtin, *Postnational Democracy* (Utrecht: Universiteit Utrecht, 1997); J. Shaw, "Postnational Constitutionalism in the European Union" (1999) 6 *Journal of European Public Policy* 579–97; J. Shaw, present volume. This work is in fact amongst the most sensitive to the reflexive reworking of national constitutionalism in the age of non-state public law. Yet the "postnational" label (as with similar terms such as "post-sovereign") is somewhat confusing and misleading, suggesting that state constitutionalism has been eclipsed or transcended rather than, as is the case, continuing to provide one pole of an ongoing relationship between different types of institutional site.

levels, with the more rarefied categories of metaconstitutionalism, including the development of meta-states and juridical relations between polities within a multi-dimensional configuration, predicated upon the less rarefied categories, including structural relations between states, direct relations between international organisations and state citizens, transformative metaconstitutional rhetoric within states, and, of course, state constitutionalism itself.

This structural progression from constitutional to metaconstitutional sites provides the enabling context for a similarly patterned discursive continuity. State constitutionalism and, indeed, its external complement, the traditional Westphalian framework of international jurisprudence,[59] provide a substantial reservoir of ideas and techniques to draw upon in the discursive elaboration of metaconstitutional sites, and, similarly, the more abstracted metaconstitutional sites may draw from the less abstracted. Moreover, the flow is not merely one way, and not just because of the normative authority claims of metaconstitutional sites. Since, despite their different starting points, constitutional and metaconstitutional sites co-exist at the same historical juncture, there is ample scope for constitutional sites to learn new tricks from metaconstitutional sites,[60] or to rediscover old ones.

A more detailed analysis of the sources and dynamics of the discursive relationship between constitutional and metaconstitional sites shows that it is structured by their respective authority claims but not limited thereto. As we have noted, metaconstitutional authority sites are distinguished by their claims to ultimate authority, and thus also, where that authority claim overlaps with the claim of a constitutional site or a lower metaconstitutional site, to a normative superiority over those other sites. Yet in the post-Westphaliam world of public law pluralism, where the sovereign claim of the metaconstitutional authority is challenged by the authority claim made at the other site, then if the bridging mechanisms between sites developed to prevent or resolve conflict are insufficient or are themselves challenged,[61] there is no independent mechanism to ensure that the claim of the higher metaconstitutional authority will ultimately prevail. In turn, this encourages an associated type of relation between sites which is not *determined* by authoritative norms but in which the authoritative

[59] A point which Bruno de Witte helpfully reminded me of.

[60] Putting to one side the more typical case, considered in the text below, where one site is instrumental in authorising or influencing another site, there may be circumstances in which one site is influenced or inspired by the example of another without there being any active engagement or transaction between sites. For example, it is arguable that the development of a formal procedure for referring "devolution issues" which arise in lower courts to higher domestic courts for preliminary resolution under Sched. 6 to the Scotland Act 1998, a technique not otherwise practised in UK domestic law, is influenced by the ECJ's well-known preliminary reference procedure for important questions of EU law; Art. 234 (ex Art. 177) TEU.

[61] Thus the German Constitutional Court in the *Brunner* case, in challenging the final authority of the EU treaty framework as interpreted by the ECJ, also implicitly challenged the integrity of the preliminary reference procedure as a key bridging mechanism transmitting the authority of the treaties and the Court to domestic law. See references in n. 49 *supra*.

resources of each site are used as strategic counters by the representatives of these sites as they bargain and compete in pursuit of their different interests.[62]

The absence of a final trans-systemic authority and a definitive framework for dispute resolution also stimulates the pursuit of a type of relation between legal orders quite different from the hierarchical and authoritative or strategic. Space opens up for a more heterarchical and dialogic approach, and this is positively reinforced by the close functional interdependence of different constitutional and metaconstitutional sites and the significant overlap of their key officials. Lacking the comprehensive internal jurisdiction of the Westphalian states, the various levels of constitutional and metaconstitutional order within the post-Westphalian system have governance projects which are seamlessly connected, their institutions intermeshed and their norms interlocked; so much so that, the most myopic visions apart, the overall conception of political community imagined from these various sites tends to be multi-dimensional.[63] So, for example, the meta-state (European) dimension remains highly relevant to the normative vision and strategy developed by many of the most nationalist Eurosceptic actors within the intra-state meta-constitutional debate about the future, or futures, of the various Member State polities. Equally, the state dimension remains relevant even to most committed Eurofederalists in the debate over the future of the EU. The overlap of key officials or official interest representation between state, state oppositional, inter-state, meta-state and "meta-meta" polity sites underlines the scope for reciprocity of perspective, mutual accommodation and reflexive learning between these various sites and their legal orders.

If we now reintroduce the two key normative features of legal discourse—technical capacity and authority—which are challenged by non-state public law in general and the rarefied atmosphere of flexibility and differentiated integration in particular, we can see how a metaconstitutional frame highlights both the difficulties involved and the opportunities presented. The basic pattern of structural and discursive continuity and progression acknowledges the *chronological* primacy of constitutions and constitutionalism over metaconstitutions and metaconstitutionalism, yet that does not gainsay the *normative* primacy of metaconstitutionalism in its own terms. Metaconstitutionalism may draw from the pre-existing tool-kit of constitutionalism and international law, but it must adapt these tools and techniques to its own site-specific purposes and to its reciprocal efforts to exercise normative influence over constitutional sites, while at

[62] To take another, but earlier, example from the German Constitutional Court, the development of its approach between the two *Solange* cases, from a commitment to intervene to protect fundamental national rights in a Community context to an arm's-length approach which would normally defer to European jurisdiction, reveals the success of a competitive strategy to persuade the ECJ to take national constitutional rights seriously: *Internationale Handelsgesellschaft (Solange I)* [1974] 2 CMLR 540; *Wünsche Handelsgesellschaft (Solange II)* [1987] 3 CMLR 265. See also references in n. 49 *supra*.

[63] Cf. D. Archibugi, D. Held and M. Kohler (eds.), *Reimagining Political Community: Studies in Cosmopolitan Democracy* (Cambridge: Polity, 1998).

the same time discovering and asserting the legitimate grounds for its own authority.

As regards technical capacity, we should note that in the constitution of public authority, whether at state or metaconstitutional level, we are invariably confronted with three types of rules; with the regulatory triptych of polity generation (constitution-building), substance (content of prescriptive constitutional norms) and structure (institutional architecture).[64] In each of these areas, the intersection of the different dynamics associated with relations between sites—hierarchical and authoritative or strategic on the one hand and heterarchical and dialogic on the other—affects how effectively technical capacity translates to the demands of a particular site. Yet the relationship between dynamic and outcome is complex. Dialogic relations between sites do not necessarily, or even generally, lead to indisputably positive outcomes in terms of overall quality of governance, just as authoritative or strategic relations do not necessarily, or even generally, lead to indisputably negative outcomes.

At the level of polity generation, for example, where because of the fundamental identity-constituting nature of the rules there tends to be no determinative authoritative relationship between sites, relations may instead be strategically competitive or dialogic. But the strategic relation, where attempts are made to bolster the relative legitimacy and authority of a particular site over another, is as likely to lead to emulation of or improvement upon generation rules, say through the call for referenda or use of constitutional conventions as a form of "democratic baptism"[65] of a new polity, as is the dialogic relation. And it is equally true that in both cases—strategic and dialogic—the concern with the *relative* merits or example of the other can lead to a narrow set of aspirations and limit the scope for *absolute* improvement. At the level of substantive rules, whether the relationship between sites is authoritative, strategic or dialogic, similar difficulties and dilemmas apply and advantages present themselves. To take the example of human rights discourse, the transcendence of cultural particulars and the universalisation of standards may be promoted through an authoritative relationship between sites,[66] or through strategic bargaining or competition between sites,[67] or even, if less likely, through an open

[64] Cf. N. Walker, "European Constitutionalism and European Integration" [1996] *Public Law* 266–90; R.S. Kay, "Substance and Structure as Constitutional Protections: Centennial Comparisons" [1989) *Public Law* 428–39.

[65] A. Weale, "Democratic Legitimacy and the Constitution of Europe" in R. Bellamy, V. Bufacchi and D. Castiglione (eds.), *Democracy and Constitutional Culture in the Union of Europe* (London: Lothian Foundation, 1995) 103–20, 115.

[66] For example, the combination, first, of the rule of national law of many of the signatories to the European Convention of Human Rights that the Convention, in accordance with a monist conception of international law, should be automatically received into national law, and, secondly, of general domestic acceptance of the compulsory jurisdiction of the European Court of Human Rights creates an authoritative relationship in favour of the Council of Europe site.

[67] See the *Solange* cases, discussed at n. 62 *supra*. Consider also the possible consequences of the strategic rivalry presently developing between two metaconstitutional sites, the Council of Europe and the EU, over the protection of rights, and the landmark decision of the ECJ in Opinion 2/94: *Re the Accession of the Community to the European Human Rights Convention* [1996] 2 CMLR

dialogue.[68] On the other hand, the price of an authoritative relationship, typically perceived as the best prospect for universalism, might be the retention of national margins of appreciation, textual qualifications, derogations and reservations, as in the European Convention of Human Rights, all of which features qualify universalism. In any event, complicating the relationship between form of transaction and outcome still further, compromise[69] and respect for cultural difference should not necessarily be seen as inferior to inflexible normative universals. Finally, at the level of structural rules also, none of the three types of relations—authoritative, strategic or dialogic—is obviously superior to the others. As noted earlier, metaconstitutional sites and constitutional sites in the post-Westphalian world tend to be incomplete sections of wider governance projects, and so their institutional designs should ideally complement one another in terms of desiderata such as democratic accountability and functional compatability. Yet each inter-site dynamic has its strengths and weaknesses. An authoritative relation has the advantage of a distinct author, but the weakness of partial and perhaps partisan vision. A dialogic relation has the strength of a more inclusive vision, but the disadvantage of weak steering capacity. A strategic relation has the potential disadvantage of the defensive protection of vested interests and institutional reputations,[70] and the potential advantage of mutually and generally beneficial institutional specialisation.[71]

What these arguments suggest is that in a multi-dimensional configuration of European and global legal authority, there is no one template of relations between metaconstitutional and constitutional sites which is or ought to be endorsed in all cases. Metaconstitutional technique may draw extensively upon the resources of constitutional sites, which in turn will be reflexively influenced by metaconstitutional sites, but there is no one best way of metaconstitutional

265; cf. P. Beaumont, "The European Community Cannot Accede to the European Convention on Human Rights" (1997) 1 *Edinburgh Law Review* 235–49.

[68] Thus the African Charter on Human and Peoples' Rights, which entered into force in 1986, differs from the other regional human rights instruments in that it does not possess a court authorised to settle disputes between states and to rule on individual grievances. Instead, it relies more heavily on dialogic methods—reconciliation and consensus—as a way of settling disputes. However, at least at this early stage of its development, it is also commonly regarded as the least effective of the instruments in securing universal regional standards; cf. Steiner and Alston, n. 40 *supra,* 689–705; S. Davidson, *Human Rights* (Buckingham: Open University Press, 1993) ch. 7.

[69] On the virtues of compromise, see M. Benjamin, *Splitting the Difference: Compromise and Integrity in Ethics and Politics* (Lawrence, Kan.: University of Kansas Press, 1990).

[70] For example, the so-called democratic deficit of the EU is in some measure due to the reluctance of national institutions to allow their EU level counterparts the same democratic respectability. This may be spiced with a degree of bad faith, as it is often those nationalists least inclined to allow supranational institutions democratic respectability who are then most critical of its absence; cf. Walker, n. 64 *supra*, esp. 278–9.

[71] For example, it is part of MacCormick's argument for a mixed commonwealth that some institutional sites are better suited to one form of governance (in particular, the European Commission and Council to oligarchy) and some to another (in particular, institutions of the nation state to democracy). Insofar as it is to the strategic advantage of both sites to sustain this division, then arguably this balance of mutual advantage sustains a reasonable equilibrium between the two forms of governance; n. 57 *supra,* esp. 342–7.

sites making use of their technical legal resources. When we turn, however, to the issue of authority and legitimacy—and recall that technical capacity and legitimacy are closely interwoven, the circumstances in which new metaconstitutional sites are required to authorise themselves, in particular those sites which are emerging within the new flexible, multi-dimensional architecture, offer some hope for the renewal of legal authority.

The paradigm form of the state constitution tends to be traditionally legitimated, difficult to amend or overhaul except through solemn and often formidable procedures, and protected by a monistic conception of authority which assumes the exclusive jurisdiction of the state within a particular territorial space. That is to say, the context in which state constitutions tend to be legitimated and sustained is highly self-referential. They pull themselves up by their own positivist bootstraps, drawing upon resilient sources of symbolic capital and institutional strength. The Westphalian world order may be in transition, but its most significant institutional legacy, the state constitution, remains securely embedded. Dworkin may lovingly reconstruct the American constitution as a liberal utopia,[72] or Ackerman narrate its history and sketch its potential in civic republican terms,[73] but constitutional practice has its own dynamic and little concern for such deep normative reflexivity.

Metaconstitutional sites have none of these "advantages". They lack tradition, well-defined and well-respected rules of amendment, and live in the shadow of a pluralist conception of authority which shares and challenges their jurisdiction in every functional and territorial corner. Metaconstitutional sites may be necessary institutional incidents of the post-Westphalian order, but they lack the ideological niche carved out by their more venerable state counterparts. Their legitimacy is much more precarious, and this is a double-edged sword. On the one hand, it may encourage the preservation of the practice of vicarious legitimisation of these nascent political forms through national institutions, an option which in any case is favoured by proponents of Europe *à la carte* and other shallow intergovernmentalist versions of flexibility. And insofar as this approach is contested and the pressure towards a deeper flexibility is too strong and multi-faceted to resist, the challenge of legitimacy may be avoided through a more coercive and oppressive mobilisation of power.[74] On the other hand, these problems may also encourage fuller and more open processes of legitimisation in the fields of polity generation, substance and structure, drawing upon the tool-kit of state constitutionalism, and perhaps more than the largely self-referential state constitutions themselves, on the rich discourse of political

[72] See, e.g., R. Dworkin, *Law's Empire* (London: Fontana, 1996).

[73] See, e.g., B. Ackerman, *We the People: Foundations* (Cambridge, Mass.: Harvard, 1991).

[74] Arguably, the history of Schengen, one of the key putative polities of the flexible era, has been of an entity which seeks to justify its growing authority by reference not to a matching transparency, accountability and popular mandate, but instead to the gravity and urgency of its internal security mission—a rhetoric which threatens not only to marginalise but even to reject as inappropriate the broader "constitutional" virtues: Cf. M. Anderson, M. den Boer, P. Cullen, W. Gilmore, C. Raab and N. Walker, *Policing the European Union* (Oxford: Clarendon, 1995).

community associated with constitutionalism. The more precarious the legitimacy of a particular metaconstitutional site or context, the greater the danger of failure, but, equally, the greater the opportunity for innovation. And, to return to the technical domain, a more broadly legitimated internal metaconstitutional structure, if delivered, provides a more favourable context for relations with other constitutional sites and lower metaconstitutional sites, *regardless* of whether the dynamic is authoritative, strategic or dialogic. A more legitimate metaconstitutional order is likely to exert more effective authority, to exhibit more broadly-conceived strategic interests and engage in more challenging strategic competition or bargaining, and display a greater propensity to open intersystemic dialogue than would otherwise be the case.

That is why, in conclusion, the putative forms of flexibility growing within, emerging from or circulating around the body of the EU provide such an intriguing challenge to our frameworks of legal and political authority. If, as the resurgence of Euroscepticism after Maastricht indicated, the metaconstitutional order of the original meta-state of the EU, about to embark on its fifth decade, was beginning to show some of the self-referential complacency—the narrow legitimacy—of the Westphalian order of states from which it sprang, the new forms of flexibility promise a loud and intriguing wake-up call. They remind us that innovation in political form and the reimagining and reconfiguration of legal authority are the norm rather than the exception in the more fluid post-Westphalian order. They demonstrate to us that the metaconstitutional logic of such innovation means that existing legal sites should, ideally, be the subject of constant challenge and constructive critique from new sites of putative legal authority. They suggest to us that, as ever, the crisis of legal authority can only be addressed through a process of internal renewal, but one which, in a post-Westphalian order, is achieved across and between institutional sites rather than within one.

3

Old-fashioned Flexibility: International Agreements between Member States of the European Union

BRUNO DE WITTE

1. INTRODUCTION

THE ACT ON the Accession of Austria, Finland and Sweden to the European Union contains a Declaration No. 28 on Nordic Co-operation which states that Finland and Sweden intend to continue, "in full compliance with Community law and the other provisions of the Treaty on European Union, Nordic Co-operation amongst themselves as well as with other countries and territories".[1] The Declaration confirms (as declarations tend to do) two rather evident things: (a) intergovernmental co-operation between a limited number of Member States of the EU is perfectly possible, but (b) membership of the EU imposes certain legal constraints on the scope and content of such co-operation. The new framework for closer co-operation, as provided by the Treaty of Amsterdam, should not be seen as changing this picture fundamentally and as excluding henceforth the possibility of two or more Member States pursuing closer co-operation among themselves outside the framework of EU law. They may continue to pursue such closer co-operation through the instruments provided by international law, chiefly through the conclusion of an international agreement. I have called this, in the title of my chapter, "old-fashioned flexibility", so as to indicate that the intergovernmental route has allowed states to pursue the same objectives as those to be pursued under Amsterdam-style closer co-operation a long time before the recent Treaty amendment, namely right from the beginning of the European Communities' existence. If one examines the full picture of the legal relations between the Member States, then flexibility is not new at all, but has always been there. The really novel thing, which was tentatively introduced by the Treaty of Maastricht, and then amplified by the Treaty of Amsterdam, is the effort of the Member States to discipline their own behaviour by attempting to bring inside

[1] Accession Act, Declaration No. 28 [1994] OJ C241/392. The reference to Norway in this Declaration was later deleted.

the EU structure certain activities which used to take place outside the four corners of EU law[2] and within the wider framework of public international law.

Indeed, the threat of *inter se* agreements[3] was very present in the background of the flexibility discussion, particularly in the early stages of the most recent Inter-Governmental Conference (IGC). In the words of a close observer of the IGC, hiding under the pseudonym "Helmut Kortenberg":

> If such a solution [i.e.: the closer co-operation of Article 43 EU Treaty] had not been found, there was a serious risk of further instances of co-operation along the Schengen model, outside the framework of the Community treaties; and, if these examples of co-operation became numerous, there was a risk that a schism would progressively emerge in the Community, with competition from instances of intergovernmental co-operation developing outside the common institutional framework.[4]

I will come back, in the conclusion of this chapter, to the question whether the new regime established by the Treaty of Amsterdam has effectively succeeded in averting this risk.

When the EEC Treaty was concluded, back in 1957, it was clear to all that the new Community institutions (and those of the other two Communities) would not provide the exclusive framework for the relations between the six Member States. None of the existing bilateral or multilateral treaties was terminated by the EEC Treaty. During the negotiation of the EEC Treaty, and in the period immediately afterwards, several *inter se* agreements were concluded, also on matters not unrelated to those covered by the EEC Treaty. In addition, that Treaty itself referred to international agreements being concluded between Member States. Article 233 (now Article 306) stated that the EEC Treaty did not preclude "the existence or completion of regional unions between Belgium and Luxembourg, or between Belgium, Luxembourg and the Netherlands". In addition, Article 220 (now Article 293) instructed the Member States to enter into negotiations with each other (presumably, with a view to concluding agreements) on specified matters, such as the abolition of double taxation and the recognition and enforcement of judicial decisions.

The text of Article 220 did not specify whether the agreements could be agreements among only *some* Member States, or whether they necessarily had to involve *all* Member States. The latter interpretation was adopted in practice,

[2] Throughout this chapter, the term "EU law" includes EC law. This accords with the view of the nature of the EU legal order which I defended in B. de Witte, "The Pillar Structure and the Nature of the European Union: Greek Temple or French Gothic Cathedral?" in T. Heukels, N. Blokker, M. Brus (eds.), *The European Union after Amsterdam* (The Hague: Kluwer, 1998) 51.

[3] I will frequently use, in this chapter, the term "*inter se* agreements" for agreements concluded between two or more Member States of the European Union. This is the term traditionally used in international law for agreements concluded between some, but not all, parties to an earlier agreement. Also, I will indiscriminately use the terms *agreement*, *treaty* and *convention* for one and the same legal reality, in accordance with the liberal approach to terminology adopted by the Vienna Convention on the Law of Treaties (Art. 2.1(a)).

[4] Helmut Kortenberg, "Closer Cooperation in the Treaty of Amsterdam" Vol. 35 (1998) *CMLRev.* 833, at 835.

and the various Article 220 conventions adopted over the years were concluded between all the Member States. Article 220 was, thus, *not used as an instrument of flexibility* in the "Amsterdam" sense, that is, as an instrument allowing for the participation of only some Member States to the exclusion of others. Yet, the possibility of having recourse to the instrument of an international agreement between all Member States, as an alternative to an EC or EU act, introduces flexibility of a different kind, because it allows the Member States to escape from the formal and procedural requirements of Community law. For this very reason, these agreements *inter omnes* are sometimes viewed with suspicion, and it is debatable whether the Member States are allowed to conclude such agreements outside the fields for which their use is expressly permitted by the founding Treaties in (mainly) Article 293 of the EC Treaty and Article 34(2)(d) of the EU Treaty. But I will not consider these questions in the present chapter, and rather focus on the practice and legal problems of the agreements concluded by only *some* Member States, as they constitute the closest equivalent to Amsterdam-type flexibility. Within this category, one can make a distinction between "genuine *inter se* agreements", to which only some Member States are parties, and "*inter se* agreements *cum tertiis*", concluded between some of the Member States and one or more *third states*. The latter group of agreements must be taken into consideration, because their *differentiating effect in the mutual relations between Member States* may be equally important. These agreements *cum tertiis* are today much more numerous than "pure" *inter se* agreements, and their legal regime presents some important differences.[5]

I will first present a schematic typology of the state practice with respect to *inter se* agreements. This will set the scene for the central part of my contribution, which will deal with the constitutional constraints affecting this choice for the inter-governmental method of co-operation. It will be shown that membership of the European Union involves certain constraints on the discretion of states to conclude international agreements among themselves (with or without third parties). Despite these constraints, *inter se* agreements continue to offer to the Member States the means to practise closer co-operation "outside" EU law. Such old-fashioned flexibility may be more attractive than closer co-operation "inside" EU law, as organised by the Treaty of Amsterdam, for at least two reasons: (i) the legal conditions for taking the "outside" route are less onerous than the conditions set for intra-EU closer co-operation; and (ii) Member States preserve, when acting under international law, complete control over the negotiation process and almost complete control over the implementation and enforcement of the obligations which they accept in the agreement.

[5] Here again, I will not consider agreements with third countries to which *all Member States* are a party (with or without the EC itself), as these agreements do not cause differentiation of rights and obligations between Member States.

2. A SMALL TYPOLOGY OF *INTER SE* AGREEMENTS

As was mentioned above, *inter se* agreements were a normal feature of diplomatic relations in the early years of the European Communities. The European integration process had given rise, in the course of the 1950s, to various organisational efforts, of which the ECSC was merely one, and even the EEC was, at the time of its foundation, only one organisation among many, which only gradually acquired the hegemonic position which the EU has today. Of these hundred "European flowers" planted in the 1950s and early 1960s, quite a number survive in the shadowy parts of the European garden.[6] Only a few of them are pure *inter se* organisations (for instance, the Western European Union[7]), whereas most of them involve third countries; examples include the Central Rhine Commission[8] and the Rhine Protection Commission, the European Conference of Postal and Telecommunications Administrations, the European Patent Organisation, Eurocontrol, the European Space Agency and, of course, the Council of Europe with the many conventions adopted within its framework.

In addition, the Member States of the Communities continued, even after 1958, to develop their network of bilateral (and occasionally trilateral) treaty relations. Some random examples from the early years of the EEC are: the Treaty establishing the Benelux Economic Union, concluded on 3 February 1958, that is, one month after the entry into force of the EEC Treaty[9]; the Agreement on Frontier Workers and the Agreement on Social Security for Migrant Workers, both concluded on 27 March 1958 between France and Italy[10]; the Convention on double taxation concluded between France and Luxemburg on 1 April 1958[11]; and a similar agreement between France and Germany of 21 July 1959.[12]

Despite the large number of *inter se* agreements, there never was, until the early 1990s, a serious danger that a sub-system of states would develop into a rival organisation of the European Communities, or that new regimes of intergovernmental co-operation would be set up alongside the EC.[13] The most effec-

[6] There is an annual survey of membership and activities of a selected number of European organisations in the *Annuaire européen/European Yearbook* (The Hague: Kluwer).

[7] Today, although only EU states are full members of the WEU, non-EU states are closely associated with its work, as *associate members* (Iceland, Norway and Turkey) or *associate partners* (10 Central Eastern European countries, of which three will become associate members after their accession to NATO). For a short description of this WEU brand of "flexibility", see M. Weller, "The European Union within the 'European security architecture'" in M. Koskenniemi (ed.), *International Aspects of the European Union* (The Hague: Kluwer, 1998) 57, at 65–6.

[8] This one is, in fact, much older than the others and has been called "the first true supranational organization": F. Meißner, "Rhine River", *Encyclopedia of Public International Law* (1990) xii, 310, at 310 (North-Holland: Amsterdam).

[9] 381 *UNTS* 165.

[10] 305 *UNTS* 387; 305 *UNTS* 409.

[11] 842 *UNTS* 163.

[12] 770 *UNTS* 325.

[13] The resilience of the Community system is shown by what happened in one of its "marginal" fields, namely education and culture. In 1987, the French government proposed to develop co-operation in the field of education and culture on an intergovernmental and *à la carte* basis: see

tive sub-system within the EC was the Franco-German bilateral alliance, which has a formal basis in the so-called Elysée Treaty of 1963[14]; yet, rarely, if ever, did they develop important initiatives on their own, or did they threaten to establish a major co-operation regime outside the common European framework. This alliance rather acted as a source of initiatives for the development of the European Communities themselves.[15]

The creation of the Schengen co-operation system in the late 1980s, coupled with the various forms of flexibility provided by the Treaty of Maastricht, and the fundamental disagreement between Member States on the future of European integration in the post-Maastricht period, rekindled the academic and political interest in intergovernmental agreements between Member States. The theme was prominent, though only implicitly, in the period leading up to the Intergovernmental Conference on the revision of the EU Treaty. The *Europe of concentric circles* sketched by the French prime minister Balladur, and the *Europe à la carte* recommended by the British prime minister Major, both seemed to assume recourse to *inter se* international agreements for organising the proposed variable geometry. The legal instruments to be used for creating the *core Europe* envisaged in the Schäuble/Lamers paper of 1994 are less clearly identifiable.[16] However, by the time the IGC effectively started, it had become clear that the model of differentiation to emerge from the negotiations would be firmly situated *within* the EU legal order, and would not involve the creation of extra facilities for international agreements between Member States.

The loss of interest in the matter, which has been noticeable since 1996, reflects the modest practice of such *inter se* agreements in recent years. In fact, a cursory study of the international treaty practice of one particular Member State over the last few years shows that new *inter se* agreements have become few and far between. The example chosen is that of the Netherlands, a country with, probably, an average propensity to conclude *inter se* agreements: it is centrally located within the EU, so that EU countries are its "natural partners", but, on the other hand, the scope for transfrontier co-operation is limited by the fact that it has land borders with only two EU countries (against five for France).

J. Vergès, "La voie intergouvernementale: le 'Livre Bleu' français" in B. de Witte (ed.), *European Community Law of Education* (Baden Baden: Nomos, 1989) 135. The other states ignored the idea; instead, culture and education were incorporated into the EC Treaty a few years later.

[14] Co-operation Treaty between France and Germany of 22 Jan. 1963, 821 *UNTS* 323.

[15] See the assessment of the Franco-German sub-system made by Ph. de Schoutheete, "The European Community and its Sub-systems" in W. Wallace (ed.), *The Dynamics of European Integration* (London: Pinter Publishers, 1990) 106, at 108–11. This author concluded, in more general terms (at 122): "[a]t no time has any sub-system sought to replace the Community. On the contrary, they all take the Community as their point of reference."

[16] For a discussion of these various plans, in the political and legal context of the time, see A.C.-G. Stubb, "A Categorization of Differentiated Integration" [1996] *Journal of Common Market Studies* 283; C.-D. Ehlermann, "Increased Differentiation or Stronger Uniformity" in J. Winter, D. Curtin, A. Kellermann and B. de Witte (eds.), *Reforming the Treaty on European Union—The Legal Debate* (The Hague: Kluwer Law International, 1996) 27.

An examination of the international treaties recorded in the *Tractatenblad* (the official treaty gazette of the Netherlands) in the years 1995, 1996 and 1997 reveals very few important bilateral agreements with other EU states. With Belgium, the Netherlands in 1996 concluded a treaty on the delimitation of the territorial sea and one on the continental shelf, as well as a treaty on the construction of a high speed railway link between the two countries; with the Flemish Community,[17] it concluded in 1995 a general cultural co-operation agreement which entailed the partial termination of the old cultural agreement with Belgium; with the Flemish Region, agreements were concluded on the outlets of Meuse water in the border area and on the widening of the Scheldt channel. Several minor agreements were concluded with Germany, dealing with educational co-operation and (trans)frontier matters. One convention on the avoidance of double taxation was concluded with Denmark and another one with Finland, as well as a small amendment to a double taxation convention with the United Kingdom; with the remaining nine Member States, *not a single new international agreement* is on record for those three years, with the exception of the bilateral agreements on the immunity of national liaison officers posted to Europol, required by the Europol Convention itself.[18] In addition to the bilateral agreements, a fairly large number of Benelux agreements are on record, but they carry little weight and the shadow of the EU is clearly visible here as well: two external Benelux trade agreements (with Tunisia and Morocco) were terminated because they had been made obsolete by EC law, and protocols were adopted to amend the Benelux treaties on uniform patent and design law, so as to adapt them to WTO and EC requirements. Finally, accession treaties to the Schengen Agreement and Convention were signed with eight states, all of them Member States of the European Union. For the sake of comparison, one may note that, over the same years, the *Tractatenblad* recorded, under the heading "European Union", a much larger number of "non-flexible" treaties to which *all* EU states are parties: mixed agreements concluded between the EC, its Member States and third countries, the accession treaties of three states to the EU itself, and intergovernmental agreements concluded between EU states only, mainly within the framework of the third pillar of the European Union.

To complement this description of the treaty practice of one Member State in one particular three-year period, I will now provide a more general, and necessarily rather impressionistic, survey of the forms and fields of international co-operation between the Member States of the European Union in recent years.

The first form of *multilateral co-operation* is regional co-operation within a sub-system of the EU. There are, in fact, only two sub-systems in which binding

[17] In Belgium, treaty-making powers have been shared, since the constitutional reform of 1993, between the central State, the Communities and the Regions, each of them exercising treaty-making powers in the matters falling within their internal competences.

[18] Convention based on Art. K.3 of the TEU, on the establishment of a European Police Office (Europol Convention) [1995] OJ C316/2, Art. 41(2).

international agreements are concluded on a regular basis, namely Benelux and Nordic Co-operation. In many fields, the Benelux or the BLEU (Belgium–Luxembourg Economic Union) played a pioneering role in the early days of the EC and continued to run ahead of the EC until the late 1980s for customs co-operation, common commercial policy, freedom of establishment, and monetary association (in the latter case, within the BLEU only).[19] Today, the derogation granted in Article 306 of the EC Treaty (formerly Article 233) has run its course. Most Benelux agreements concluded in recent years have, in fact, been protocols amending earlier agreements in order to bring them into line with EC law developments (see the examples above). Therefore, Benelux agreements are, more often than not, used as an instrument for the *joint implementation* of EC law, rather than as a competing co-operation regime. Nordic Co-operation is, on a closer inspection, not a genuinely *inter se* sub-system, because Nordic conventions involve the third countries of Norway and Iceland.[20]

A second form of multilateral *inter se* agreements is those organising co-operation in *special fields*.

—An old example, which has attracted renewed interest in recent years, is the Treaty establishing the Western European Union, mentioned above.
—The Schengen co-operation regime is, politically, the most prominent example,[21] though it will now be transformed almost entirely from an international law into an EU law regime.[22]
—The Agreement on Social Policy annexed to the Treaty on European Union formally qualifies as an *inter se* agreement. Yet, the acts adopted under this Agreement belong, by virtue of the Social Policy Protocol, to EC law. This qualification was contested by some authors at the time the Maastricht Treaty was adopted, but is generally accepted today, and it was implicitly confirmed by the European Court of First Instance when it found the parental

[19] See the global assessment made by Louis in 1987: J.V. Louis, "Article 233" in J. Mégret *et al.*, *Le droit de la Communauté économique européenne* (Brussels: Editions de l'Université de Bruxelles, 1987) xv, 510.

[20] For example, the Nordic double taxation convention (Helsinki, 1983) and the Nordic cultural co-operation convention (Göteborg, 1971).

[21] Its *inter se* character is affirmed by Art. 140(1) of the Convention: "[e]very Member State of the European Communities may become a Party to this Convention".

[22] The *incomplete* nature of this transformation results, in my view, from the Protocol on Denmark, attached to the Treaty of Amsterdam. This Protocol oddly states that Denmark may agree to be bound by EU measures building on the Schengen acquis, but on the *basis of international law*. Obviously, all Member States are bound by all parts of EU law "on the basis of international law"; so, either this reference in the Denmark Protocol is legally redundant (there is an illustrious precedent for solemn redundant statements in the Decision on Denmark adopted at the Edinburgh summit in 1992), or it assumes that the Schengen Agreement and Convention will continue to exist as international agreements, separate from the EU Treaty, governing the relations between Denmark and the other 12. Does that also mean that the EU Council will, through some strange *dédoublement institutionnel*, act as the Schengen Executive Committee as far as the relations with Denmark are concerned?

leave case to be admissible.[23] Therefore, social policy measures adopted between 1993 and 1997, among fourteen Member States (without the participation of the UK) should be qualified as intra-EU closer co-operation rather than extra-EU intergovernmental co-operation.

—A final example of a multilateral agreement is that signed on 9 February 1994 between Belgium, Denmark, Germany, Luxembourg and the Netherlands on the introduction of a common road tax system; interestingly, this agreement was made on the basis of an express authorisation given by an EC directive,[24]and within the substantive limits traced by it.[25]

Most *bilateral co-operation* agreements between Member States of the EU fall into one of the following categories: transfrontier co-operation agreements,[26] agreements on the use and protection of common river resources,[27] conventions for the avoidance of double taxation,[28] cultural and educational co-operation agreements[29] and special political treaties.[30] An additional, relatively new, category is the agreements concluded for the *implementation of EU obligations*.[31] They are either required by an act of EU law or concluded by Member States on their own initiative.

Agreements *cum tertiis* are much more numerous nowadays. There is, first of all, a large, and increasing, number of *open multilateral treaties*. These are open to all states of the world (in the case of United Nations conventions) or all states of the European region (in the case of Council of Europe conventions). All Member States of the EU have a vocation to accede to these treaties, but as they

[23] Case T–135/96, *Union Européenne de l'Artisanat et des Petites et Moyennes Entreprises (UEAPME)* v. *Council* [1998] ECR II–2335.

[24] Dir. 93/89 [1993] OJ L279/32.

[25] For a description, see D. van Vreckem, "Accord relatif à la perception d'un droit d'usage pour l'utilisation de certaines routes par des véhicules utilitaires dans le cadre de la directive 93/89/CEE du 25 octobre 1993" in C.-D. Ehlermann (ed.), *Multi-Speed Europe—the Legal Framework of Variable Geometry in the European Union* (Bonn: Bundesanzeiger, 1999) 67.

[26] For instance, the Convention on transfrontier co-operation between local authorities, concluded between France and Italy on 26 Nov. 1992 ([1996] Journal Officiel de la République Française 227).

[27] For instance, the Agreements of Charleville-Mézières of 26 Apr. 1994, concluded between France, the Netherlands, and the Regions of Flanders, Wallonia and Brussels, on the environmental protection of the Meuse and Scheldt (French text in [1997] Revue belge de droit international 161).

[28] See the examples from French and Dutch state practice mentioned above. At present, all Member States of the EU have concluded such double taxation conventions with almost all other Member States.

[29] For instance, the Treaty between the Netherlands and the Flemish Community on co-operation in the field of culture, education, science and welfare (Antwerp, 17 Jan. 1995; [1995] Tractatenblad 52); the Treaty on the European cultural channel between France and Germany of 2 Oct. 1990 (the basis of the ARTE television station) [1991] Revue générale de droit international public 509; the Agreement between France and Germany on the creation of a Franco-German University (Weimar, 19 Sept. 1997), Journal officiel de la République française, 1 Oct. 1999.

[30] For instance, the "Good Friday" Agreement between the United Kingdom and Ireland (1998) 37 International Legal Materials 751.

[31] For instance, the bilateral protocols concluded, in application of the Europol Convention, between the Netherlands and the other Member States on the privileges and immunities of national liaison officers to Europol (see n. 18, *supra*).

do not all sign and ratify them (or, at least, not at the same time), differentiation between Member States' rights and duties arises. This is, perhaps, the most prominent form of flexibility through international agreements today. It is not going to disappear as long as the EC/EU has not entirely expropriated the Member States' external relations competences (see the discussion of pre-emption, below at paragraph A). However, some methods are being used in order to reduce the legal differentiation which this causes within the EU. One method is for the European Community to insist on being a co-contracting party to a proposed multilateral agreement, and then to try and synchronise EC and Member State ratification of the agreement. Alternatively, the EC, without itself being a party to the agreement, may request all its Member States to ratify it, so as to achieve legal uniformity among themselves.[32] Preventive moves are also possible, such as the formulation, in the EU framework, of a common negotiating position to be followed by the Member States in a multilateral forum,[33]or the adoption of a uniform treaty model to be used by Member States in bilateral negotiations with third countries.[34] There is, thus, a noticeable practice of the European Union institutions aimed at reducing the differentiating effect of international agreements concluded between Member States and third states.

To be distinguished from these open multilateral treaties are *closed multilateral treaties* involving third states. Here, membership of the system is reserved *ab initio* for some Member States only and the accession of others is impossible because of the subject matter of the treaty or it would, at least, require an amendment of the initial agreement. Examples of this category include: the Rhine Navigation Convention (Mannheim, 1868, amended several times since) to which some Member States are party, together with Switzerland; the Co-operation agreement between the Schengen states and Norway and Iceland (Luxembourg, 19 December 1996); the Convention on the Protection of the Alps; and the various agreements within the framework of the *Francophonie*.

3. THE LEGAL REGIME OF INTER SE AGREEMENTS

It is sometimes wondered "whether it is actually open to a group of Member States to enter into an agreement on a matter which would appear to fall within

[32] An example of such a request is the Commission Recommendation of 27 May 1998 on the ratification of the ILO Convention No 177 on home work of 20 June 1996 [1998] OJ L165/32.

[33] An example is the Common position of the Council of 6 Oct. 1997 on negotiations in the Council of Europe and the OECD relating to corruption [1997] OJ L279/1 (followed by a second common position [1997] OJ L320/1). This mechanism for steering the external activities of the Member States is of particular use for matters falling within the "second" and "third" pillars, due to the perceived absence of treaty-making powers of the European Union (as opposed to the European Community) under the Treaty of Maastricht. Under the Treaty of Amsterdam, things may be different, following the new Art. 38 EU Treaty, in combination with Art. 24.

[34] An example is the Council Recommendation of 30 Nov. 1994 concerning a specimen bilateral readmission agreement between a Member State and a third country [1996] OJ C274/20.

Community or Union competence".[35] In general terms, the answer must be positive. *Inter se* agreements are allowed, for the simple reason that to hold otherwise would be a drastic curtailment of the Member States' treaty-making competences that cannot be assumed to have taken place in the absence of any clear indication in the founding treaties. The Benelux/BLEU clause of Article 306 EC (formerly Article 233) cannot be interpreted *a contrario* as outlawing all *inter se* agreements other than those mentioned there. The clause was included because of the close similarity between the aims of the EEC and those of BLEU and Benelux, namely economic integration. The Benelux countries insisted on the "safeguard" clause so as to prevent their own integration efforts being held up by the expectedly slower progress within the EEC.

The fact that *inter se* agreements are permissible in principle is also confirmed by language used in other parts of the founding Treaties. The Maastricht Treaty incorporated some unmistakable hints that the extension of the fields of EC co-operation, which took place then, did not eliminate the Member States' competence to conclude treaties among themselves. The best known example was Article K.7, the "Schengen clause", stating that "[t]he provisions of this Title shall not prevent the establishment or development of closer co-operation between two or more Member States in so far as such co-operation does not conflict with, or impede, that provided for in this Title". This Treaty Article is no longer there since Amsterdam, and the consequences of its disappearance will require some comment further on in this chapter. Other relevant provisions of the Maastricht Treaty are to be found in the description of the new EC competences in respect of education, culture and health; in each of these areas, the Community is instructed to, first of all, encourage "co-operation between the Member States", and, only in the second instance, to "support their action" by the adoption of Community acts. Although co-operation between states does not necessarily involve the conclusion or application of treaties, this latter instrument is certainly covered by the words of the EC Treaty.

Yet, as was expressly stated with respect to Nordic co-operation in the Accession Act of 1994 (see the first lines of this chapter), co-operation between Member States must be "in full compliance with Community law". In the following pages, I will try to list the various legal parameters which, together, form the EC law standard (or, rather, the EU law standard) with which the Member States must comply. The old Article K.7, quoted above, makes an interesting distinction in this respect, where it states that intergovernmental co-operation should "not conflict with, or impede" EU co-operation. Intergovernmental co-operation can, indeed, *impede* EU policy-making, even where there is no substantive incompatibility between the two. Therefore, the legal parameters include a substantive conflict rule (the principle of the *primacy* of EC law), but also (and first of all) the doctrine of *pre-emption* which is about "impediments"

[35] J.A. Usher, "Flexibility and Enhanced Co-operation" in T. Heukels, N. Blokker and M. Brus (eds.), *The European Union after Amsterdam—A Legal Analysis* (The Hague: Kluwer Law International, 1998) 253, at 260.

rather than actual conflicts. The principle of *subsidiarity* may also affect the conditions for making use of intergovernmental agreements, in one direction or the other; and, finally, the consequences of the regime of intra-EU *closer co-operation* established by the Treaty of Amsterdam need to be examined. I will discuss these four legal doctrines and principles in turn. The legal differences between pure *inter se* agreements and agreements *cum tertiis* will be discussed along the way.

A. Pre-emption of the States' Treaty-making Competence

One knows that the drafters of the EEC Treaty did not address the question whether the allocation of powers to the EEC or the exercise of these powers by the Community institutions could have the effect of removing altogether the power of the states to legislate, or to conclude international agreements, on the same matters. Pre-emption, this "quintessential federalism issue, . . . did not fit into the framers' original international law paradigm".[36] The doctrine was slowly developed through a number of, not always consistent, judgments of the European Court of Justice.

It is appropriate to consider, first, the implications of the doctrine of pre-emption with regard to agreements that *do not involve participation of third states*. If one assumes that *inter se* co-operation between Member States is subject to the same pre-emption standard as unilateral action of these Member States, then the importance of the pre-emption would seem rather limited. There are only a few "blocks" of Community policies that might be considered as the EC's exclusive preserve[37]; thus, bilateral trade agreements between Member States, which were a favourite area of intergovernmental co-operation in the 1950s, are no longer allowed and do no longer occur. For areas of non-exclusive competence, that is, practically all areas of Community policy, pre-emption requires "occupation of the field" by means of Community acts, a situation which is to be assessed on a case-by-case basis,[38] but should not lightly be assumed to exist.[39]

There could be reasons, though, for using a special, more severe pre-emption standard with regard to *joint action* between Member States, as compared to

[36] G. Bermann, "Taking Subsidiarity Seriously: Federalism in the European Community and the United States" (1994) 94 *Columbia Law Review* 331, at 358.

[37] The ECJ has recognised the existence of two fields of exclusive competences "by nature", namely the common commercial policy and the conservation of biological resources of the sea.

[38] See the "pre-emption checklist" proposed by A. Furrer, "The Principle of Pre-emption in European Union Law" in G. Winter (ed.), *Sources and Categories of European Union Law* (Baden Baden: Nomos, 1996) 521, at 532.

[39] I agree with N. Bernard, "The Future of European Economic Law in the Light of the Principle of Subsidiarity" (1996) *CMLRev*. 633, at 663: "one has to conclude that pre-emption has a fairly narrow field of application and concerns primarily the common organizations of agricultural markets . . . Even there, pre-emption analysis must be handled with caution and the limits of the field being occupied must be defined with care."

their *unilateral action*. If Member States want to co-operate in *any* of the fields of EC competence (whether exclusive or shared), should not the EC be the proper place for such co-operation, rather than an *ad hoc* intergovernmental framework? A distinction must be made here between genuinely *parallel* treaties, that is, conventions between *all Member States* on matters within the competence of the EC and the EU, and *partial* agreements among only some Member States. As mentioned in the introduction, I do not intend to deal with the former category of treaties here, but it is clear that they should be viewed with suspicion, as they could allow the Member States to "switch" from the EC or EU track to the international law track, while by-passing the institutional balance established by the founding Treaties. That concern does not apply with the same force to *partial* agreements among only some Member States. If one were to prohibit such agreements altogether, then the veto of one state, in matters for which the EC must act unanimously, would stop the Community from acting, without leaving to those willing to co-operate any alternative means outside the Community structure.

In the literature, this matter has been discussed primarily in relation to the Schengen Agreement and Convention. The Schengen co-operation regime was started at a time when a general consensus on abolishing the controls on persons at the intra-Community borders could not be reached (as it still cannot today). The Schengen instruments were expressly presented as an interim arrangement in preparation of a final regime at the level of the European Community, rather than as a separate and rival co-operation regime.[40] The same reasons which justified the rule of Article 233 of the EEC Treaty, whereby the Benelux countries could adopt more advanced measures of integration, can be applied here.[41] Yet, in the course of the years, there grew the concern that Schengen was changing from a laboratory into a stable institutional regime functioning alongside the European Union, but with important deficits in terms of transparency and judicial protection. The legal limit to Member State action of this type is to be found, not in the doctrine of division of powers, but perhaps in the duty of sincere co-operation of the Member States, as codified in Article 10 EC Treaty. This principle implies that states are not allowed to use intergovernmental co-operation which they have established among themelves as an argument for impeding the development of a European Union policy. This is, of course, a rather vague standard which the ECJ would have difficulties in applying. In view of the incorporation of the Schengen system in the EU framework, this question may (momentarily?) have lost practical interest.

[40] C. Timmermans, "Free Movement of Persons and the Division of Powers between the Community and its Member States—Why do it the Intergovernmental Way?" in H. Schermers *et al.* (eds.), *The Free Movement of Persons in Europe* (Dordrecht: Martinus Nijhoff, 1993), 352, at 362.

[41] Schengen is, in some respects, an extension of the Benelux co-operation. Belgium, Luxembourg and the Netherlands concluded the Schengen Agreement and Convention as the "Governments of the States of the Benelux Economic Union", because border controls had already been abolished between them on the basis of an earlier *inter se* agreement; the Schengen Executive Committee grew out of the earlier Ministerial Working Group of the Benelux.

Finally, one could conceivably consider Article 293 of the EC Treaty (formerly Article 220) to be a *special pre-emption rule*. By providing for negotiations between *all* Member States on the matters listed there,[42] it might at the same time exclude the possibility of *partial agreements* between those states. Practically speaking, the fact that the elimination of double taxation is one of the subjects listed in Article 293 might mean that bilateral double taxation conventions are no longer admissible and should be replaced by an EC double taxation convention. Although there might be good policy reasons for adopting such an EC convention,[43] the existence of a legal duty to do so is uncertain, and certainly does not seem to be accepted by the Member States.[44]

With reference, now, to agreements concluded with *third states*, the pre-emption issue plays a more prominent role. In the field of commercial policy, taken in the narrow sense of Article 133 of the EC Treaty (ex Article 113), Member States are no longer allowed to conclude treaties with third states, although a derogation regime has been put in place by the Council.[45] In other areas of external relations, the implications of the Court's case law on the exclusive external powers of the EC, and on EC occupation-of-the-field along the lines traced in the ERTA judgment[46] and confirmed in Opinion 2/91,[47] preoccupied the Member States so much that they sought, in all major Treaty revisions since ERTA, from the Single European Act to the Treaty of Amsterdam, to preserve their treaty-making powers in express terms. The recognition of the EC's power to conclude international environmental agreements was accompanied by the affirmation of the states' continued power to do so as well (Article 174 EC). A similar formulation was used for development co-operation (Article 181 EC) and monetary policy (Article 111(5) EC).[48] In all three cases, the remaining

[42] That, at least, is the accepted interpretation of Art. 293.

[43] See D.W. Williams, *EC Tax Law* (London: Longman, 1998) 17–19; T. Scherer, *Doppelbesteuerung und Europäisches Gemeinschaftsrecht* (Munich: C.H. Beck, 1995) 82–7; W. Vermeend, "Tax Policy in Europe" [1998] *EC Tax Review* 151, at 157.

[44] Already in 1968, a draft Convention on the elimination of double taxation, based on Art. 220 EC Treaty, was put on the table, but never got very far. In 1990, the Member States agreed on a multilateral convention for the elimination of double taxation in a very limited context (the "Arbitration Convention"), but both before and after that date they have continued to conclude general double taxation conventions on a bilateral basis.

[45] The Council regularly allows Member States to renew or maintain in force a long list of trade agreements with third countries; the latest such derogation, valid until 30 Apr. 2001, was adopted in 1997 (Council Decision 97/351 [1997] OJ L151). This practice was admitted by the ECJ in Case 174/84, *Bulk Oil (Zug) AG* v. *Sun International Limited and Sun Oil Trading Company* [1986] ECR 559, para. 23.

[46] Case 22/70, *Commission* v. *Council* [1971] ECR 263.

[47] *Opinion 2/91* [1993] ECR I–1064, para. 9: "[t]he exclusive or non-exclusive nature of the Community's competence does not flow solely from the provisions of the Treaty but may also depend on the scope of the measures which have been adopted by the Community institutions for the application of those provisions and which are of such a kind as to deprive the Member States of an area of competence which they were able to exercise previously on a transitional basis".

[48] For a discussion of the residual external competences of the Member States that have adopted the single currency, see C. Zilioli and M. Selmayr, "The External Relations of the Euro Area: Legal Aspects" Vol 36 (1999) *CMLRev*. 273, at 317 ff. A legally different point is that individual Member States may be authorised to negotiate and conclude external monetary agreements *on behalf of the*

powers of the Member States were declared to be subject to the "principles in the judgment handed down in the AETR case".[49] In Amsterdam, the express grant of an EC competence in relation to the crossing of the external frontiers was accompanied by a Protocol confirming the states' competence to conclude international agreements on border-crossing.[50]

These statements, by being restricted to particular fields of external relations, still leave considerable uncertainty in other fields. One major area of controversy is *transport policy*. In respect of transport by inland waterways, the Council expressly stated, in the preamble to the relevant 1996 Regulation, that it fell "within the Community's field of competence",[51]thereby accepting a pre-emptive effect for external agreements, and the Commission recently started infringement proceedings against two Member States which had concluded bilateral inland waterways agreements with third countries, on the ground that this was a matter exclusively for the Community.[52] Another area of transport policy, that of civil aviation, presents a much more complicated picture. The Commission had argued for many years that the EC's competence to deal with the commercial aspects of air transport was an exclusive one, so that Member States were no longer allowed to conclude bilateral international agreements on traffic rights with the United States or other countries.[53] The WTO Opinion of the European Court established that external transport policy was not included in common commercial policy, and that the EC's external power in this field, was an implied one, based on its internal competences under the Transport Title of the EC Treaty.[54] This means that the states' treaty-making competences may be pre-empted through the adoption of internal EC transport legislation. The Commission argues that this is indeed the case, and is currently conducting infringement proceedings against no fewer than ten Member States on the ground that they have concluded open skies agreements with the United States which, on some points at least, impinge on the Community's exclusive powers.[55]

EC, an original construction adopted recently for monetary relations with Monaco, San Marino and Vatican City (see the three Council Decisions 1999/96, 1999/97 and 1999/98 [1999] OJ L30/31 ff.).

[49] Declaration No. 9, annexed to the Final Act of the SEA (with reference to environmental protection); Declaration No. 10, annexed to the Final Act of the Treaty of Maastricht (with reference to all three areas).

[50] Protocol No. 8 of the Treaty of Amsterdam, annexed to the EC Treaty.

[51] Council Reg. 1356/96 of 8 July 1996 on common rules applicable to the transport of goods or passengers by inland waterways between Member States with a view to establishing freedom to provide such transport services [1996] OJ L175/7.

[52] Sixteenth Annual Report on Monitoring the Application of Community Law 1998, COM (1999) 301 of 9 July 1999, 62.

[53] See COM(90)17 of 23 Feb. 1990.

[54] *Opinion 1/94 (re WTO Agreement)* [1994] ECR I–5267, paras. 48–53.

[55] The evolution of the "open skies" competence conflict is presented and discussed by P. Eeckhout, *The European Internal Market and International Trade—A Legal Analysis* (Oxford: Clarendon Press, 1994), ch. 3. Reference to the pending infringement proceedings is made in the Sixteenth Annual Report on Monitoring the Application of Community Law 1998, COM (1999) 301 of 9 July 1999, 66. It may be noted that these legal actions are also seen by the Commission as a way of eliciting from the Council an authorisation to start negotiations for a Community air traffic agreement with the United States, which would replace the existing bilateral ones. For an analysis

A new controversial area of external EC competence was brought into being by the transfer of former "third pillar" matters to the new EC Treaty Title on visas, asylum, immigration and other policies related to free movement of persons. Immediately after the entry into force of the Treaty of Amsterdam, the Commission requested from the Council an authorisation to conduct negotiations with third states on readmission agreements, arguing that distortions could arise because of the existing practice of bilateral readmission agreements with third states. Thereupon, the Council expressly stated its view that the Community's competence in this matter was not exclusive and developed the following "guidelines" which nicely and accurately render the present complexity of the pre-emption doctrine:

> A Member State can continue to conclude readmission agreements with third States provided that the Community has not concluded an agreement with the third state concerned or has not concluded a mandate for negotiating such an agreement. In individual cases Member States may also conclude bilateral agreements after the conclusion of a Community agreement or after the opening of negotiations, for instance where the Community agreement or the negotiating mandate contains only general statements on readmission but one or more Member States require more detailed arrangements on the matter. The Member States may no longer conclude agreements if these might be detrimental to existing Community agreements.[56]

A final question is whether the breach by Member States of their duty to abstain from concluding international agreements in the field occupied by the EC can give rise to special *remedies*. The Commission can, obviously, start its usual infringement action. As far as remedies by national courts are concerned, it has been argued that they should treat national law which, from the Community point of law, is *ultra vires*, as null or void rather than simply non-applicable,[57] but I do not see sufficient ground for accepting that EC law *imposes* on the states the creation of such a far-reaching federal-type remedy. In my view, the remedies under national law are the same here as for breach of the principle of supremacy, a principle to which I now turn.

B. Primacy of Community Law

This is undoubtedly the heart of the legal matter. In view of the modest limits to the Member States' treaty-making competence, described above, the central legal issue is usually that of the *substantive* compatibility between existing (or projected) *inter se* agreements and rules of Community law.

of the debate from the Commission's perspective, see O. Jankovec, "La politique commune des transports aériens" [1999] *Revue du marché unique européen* nr 2, 145, at 215–24.

[56] Press Release on the meeting of the Council of Justice and Home Affairs, 27/28 May 1999.

[57] N. Neuwahl, "Shared Powers or Combined Incompetence? More on Mixity" Vol 33 (1996) *CMLRev*. 667, at 672.

The leading conflict rule is the principle of the primacy of Community law, as developed in the case law of the ECJ. Yet, to the extent that the application of an(other) international agreement is involved, the general conflict rules of international law may also come into play.[58] From the perspective of the European Court of Justice, the only exception to the supremacy of EC law over conflicting norms contained in international agreements of the Member States is the rule of Article 307 of the EC Treaty (ex Article 234), which preserves the rights of *third countries* deriving from agreements made by Member States before they were part of the European Community, i.e. before 1 January 1958 for the original Six, and before the respective dates of accession for the other nine Member States.[59] This rule reflects the *pacta tertiis* rule of international law, codified in Article 34 of the Vienna Convention on the Law of Treaties, and should therefore be held to apply to the second and third pillars of the European Union as well.[60] The rule implies, among other things, that national authorities and national courts are allowed (provisionally) to apply a measure of national law which conflicts with Community law, to the extent that the measure is required by such a prior international agreement with third states,[61] but the Member State concerned should take all necessary steps to remove this obstacle to the application of Community law.

If, however, the rights of third states are not affected, prior agreements of the Member States (whether concluded amongst themselves or with others) are to be set aside by national courts when conflicting with EC law. This is, again, in accordance with ordinary rules of international treaty law, which state that, in the case of a conflict, a later treaty prevails among the states parties to both treaties.[62] This rule applies where the conflict arises from the provisions of the EC Treaty itself, as the ECJ held in a very early judgment,[63] but also in the, more frequent, cases where the incompatibility arises from some later directive or reg-

[58] On which see W. Karl, "Treaties, conflicts between" in *Encyclopedia of Public International Law* (1984) vii, 467 (Amsterdam: North-Holland).

[59] The latter specification was inserted into the text of Art. 307 by the Treaty of Amsterdam.

[60] One recent application of this rule in "third pillar" practice can be found in the Convention on Jurisdiction and the Recognition and Enforcement of Judgments in Matrimonial Matters ([1998] OJ C222/1), Art. 38(2)(a): Denmark, Finland and Sweden are granted the option of declaring that the Nordic Convention of 6 Feb. 1931, concluded between these three countries, Iceland and Norway, will apply in their mutual relations in place of the rules of the new EU Convention. One may note that the Commission's recent draft which proposes to transform this Convention into an EC Reg. under the "first pillar" retains the same rule (see COM (1999) 220 of 4 May 1999, Art. 38(2)).

[61] Case C–158/91, *Criminal proceedings against Jean-Claude Levy* [1993] ECR I–4287, paras. 11–12; Case C–124/95, *R.* v. *HM Treasury & Bank of England, ex parte Centro-Com* [1997] ECR I–81, paras. 56–7; Joined Cases C–364/95 and C–365/95, *T. Port GmbH & Co.* v. *Hauptzollamt Hamburg-Jonas* [1998] ECR I–1023, paras. 59–61.

[62] Vienna Convention on the Law of Treaties, Art. 30(3). For a detailed study of the conflict rules in Art. 30 of the Vienna Convention, see E. Roucounas, "Engagements parallèles et contradictoires" 206 *Hague Recueil* (1987, VI) 9, at 77–103.

[63] Case 10/61, *Commission* v. *Italy* [1962] ECR 1, at 10: "by virtue of the principles of international law, by assuming a new obligation which is incompatible with rights held under a prior treaty a State *ipso facto* gives up the exercise of these rights to the extent necessary for the performance of its new obligations".

ulation.[64] On rare occasions, the new Community act specifies the consequences of its enactment for prior international agreements concluded amongst the Member States.[65]

The case law of the European Court of Justice departs from the ordinary canons of international law in a third hypothesis, namely that of agreements concluded between Member States *after* they became members of the EC/EU. International law adopts the rule of relative validity: a bilateral tax treaty between, say, France and Italy which conflicts with the EC Treaty would overrule the EC Treaty in the mutual relations between these two countries, but the rights which the other Member States derive from the EC Treaty must be preserved.[66] The ECJ does not accept this doctrine of relative validity "within the inner circle" and posits instead the absolute supremacy of EC law: *inter se* agreements must yield to EC law in the same way as purely national laws must, so that diverging *inter se* regimes, even where they do not directly affect the rights of other Member States, are in breach of EC law and should be disapplied (except, of course, when the EC act itself allows for an *inter se* derogation).

The limited evidence available on this question seems to show that the national courts have accepted this EC-specific conflict rule which requires them to set aside a later international treaty.[67] In countries such as the UK, Germany and Italy, where Community law is generally granted a different, and higher, status than ordinary international law, there is no difficulty in this respect. In other countries, whose constitutional law recognises the primacy of *all* international treaties (such as France, Belgium and the Netherlands) there could be a theoretical problem (on what grounds should they base their preference for an agreement—the EC Treaty—which was concluded earlier than the other one?), but I am not aware of any practical difficulties. Where the parties foresee possible conflicts, they may insert a conflict rule into the agreement itself, conceding priority to EC law in an eventual conflict. A good, and important, example, is Article 134 of the Schengen Convention of 1990: "[t]he provisions of this Convention shall apply only in so far as they are compatible with Community law".

The fourth hypothesis, that of a conflict between EC law and a later agreement between Member States and *third states* is less straightforward. Occasionally, an EC or EU act specifies that it takes precedence over earlier

[64] See, for instance, the *Matteucci* case, discussed below (the text at note 72).

[65] E.g. EC Reg. 574/72, implementing Reg. 1408/71 on social security co-ordination, expressly states that it replaces bilateral conventions on the matter, but it also has an annex listing those provisions of bilateral conventions which remain in force (updated version [1983] OJ L230/86, Art. 5 and Annex 5).

[66] Vienna Convention on the Law of Treaties, Art. 30(4).

[67] E.g. in Case C–3/91, *Exportur SA* v. *Lor SA et Confiserie du Tech* [1992] ECR I–5529, the referring French court assumed that Art. 30 of the EEC Treaty (today, Art. 28 EC) would prevail, in the case of a conflict, over the bilateral convention concluded in 1972 between France and Spain (this convention, though originally one concluded between an EC member and a third state, had become an *inter se* agreement by the time of the dispute).

multilateral agreements to which (some of) its Member States are parties,[68] but such a statement obviously cannot bind the third states concerned, for whom the EC Treaty and secondary Community law is a *res inter alios acta* which is not supposed to affect their rights. At least on one occasion, the European Court of Justice bluntly affirmed a duty for national courts to give priority to EC acts over conflicting (and earlier) international obligations of the state concerned.[69] But it is far from certain that a national court in a monist Member State will take the same view. When confronted with such a conflict, the national court will have to choose between giving priority to the later international agreement, thereby triggering the state's responsibility under EC law, or giving priority to EC law, thereby triggering the responsibility of the state under international law.

So far for the discussion of the *formal* parameters of supremacy. I will now consider in somewhat closer detail the most obvious *substantive* point at which international agreements concluded by the Member States may enter into conflict with Community law. A central principle of substantive EC law that can be affected by *inter se* agreements is that of *non-discrimination on grounds of nationality*. This may seem almost inherent in the existence of agreements to which some states participate and others not. In the context of the new EC Treaty provisions on closer co-operation (where the non-discrimination principle is expressly repeated[70]) Helmut Kortenberg states:

> In fact, any co-operation is discriminatory, since it establishes different regimes in different Member States. Thus what is prohibited is the reservation of benefits flowing from closer co-operation to nationals of participating Member States from the moment that nationals of other Member States fulfil the necessary conditions to enjoy such benefits.[71]

The word "discriminatory", in the first phrase of the quotation, is used in a loose political sense (expressing the concern that closer co-operation may disrupt the solidarity or equal conditions of competition among Member States), and not in its technical legal meaning of an invidious distinction against certain persons on the ground of their nationality. If, say, Belgium, France and the

[68] For instance, Art. 39 of the recent EU Convention on Matrimonial Matters, cited above, claims precedence for the Convention over a list of multilateral conventions of private international law adopted after 1958 (mainly in the framework of the Hague Conference).

[69] Case 181/80, *Procureur Général* v. *Arbelaiz-Emazabel* [1981] ECR 2961, para. 31, where the Court held, in response to a question posed by a French court, that "Spanish fishermen may not rely on prior international agreements between France and Spain in order to prevent the application of the interim regs. adopted by the Community in the event of any incompatibility between the two categories of provisions" (the agreements concerned had been adopted after 1958, so that the conflict rule of the (then) Art. 234 EC did not apply). For a detailed commentary on this case and some related cases, see R.R. Churchill and N.G. Foster, "European Community Law and Prior Treaty Obligations of Member States: The Spanish Fishermen's Cases" [1987] *International and Comparative Law Quarterly* 504.

[70] Art. 11(1)(c) of the EC Treaty.

[71] Helmut Kortenberg, "Closer Cooperation in the Treaty of Amsterdam" Vol 35 (1998) *CMLRev*. 833, at 848.

Netherlands conclude a treaty for the protection of the river Meuse against pollution, they establish closer co-operation which does not affect in any adverse way the rights of nationals of other Member States, and therefore does not constitute discrimination in the sense of Article 12 of the EC Treaty. The problem of discrimination, in the *legal* sense of the word, arises (as is, indeed, indicated by H. Kortenberg' second sentence) only for those agreements granting reciprocal benefits to the citizens or residents of the contracting states. Examples thereof are agreements on educational and cultural exchanges, air traffic agreements and, most notoriously, bilateral tax agreements. If, for instance, Belgium and Germany conclude a cultural co-operation agreement on the basis of which they grant education scholarships to each other's nationals, then the citizens of the 13 other Member States of the EU are excluded from the benefit of such a scholarship. Is this in breach of the EC Treaty principle of non-discrimination?

The European Court of Justice had to consider this precise question in *Matteucci*.[72] Miss Matteucci was an Italian national who was born in Belgium and had received her entire education there. She was a teacher of "rhythmics" in Namur and applied for a specialisation scholarship in order to study singing and voice-training in Berlin, under the cultural co-operation agreement concluded between Belgium and Germany in 1956. The competent authority in Belgium refused to pass on her application to the German authorities, on the ground that she was not Belgian and thus did not comply with the nationality condition contained in the co-operation agreement.[73] The Court of Justice held that Matteucci, as an EC migrant worker in Belgium, had the right to equal treatment with Belgian nationals in respect of all social advantages, in accordance with Article 7(2) of Regulation 1612/68 on the free movement of workers. The scholarship scheme for advanced training in Germany was held to be a social advantage,[74] so that Matteucci could not be barred from applying for a scholarship. The fact that the exclusion did not result from a unilateral Belgian measure, but from a bilateral agreement with Germany, was held to be irrelevant by the Court: "the application of Community law cannot be precluded on the ground that it would affect the implementation of a cultural agreement between two Member States".[75]

In its observations in the *Matteucci* case, the French government warned the Court: "[c]ase-law which came to regard the provisions of such an agreement as

[72] Case 235/87, *Annunziata Matteucci* v. *Communauté française of Belgium et al.* [1988] ECR 5589.

[73] Art. 4 of the 1956 agreement provides that "each Contracting Party shall grant to *nationals* of the other party scholarships to enable them to undertake or continue studies or research in the other country" (emphasis added).

[74] The notion of "social advantage" has been given a very broad interpretation by the Court of Justice; see, prior to *Matteucci*, D. O'Keeffe, "Equal Rights for Migrants: The Concept of Social Advantages in Art. 7(2) of Regulation 1612/68" [1985] *Yearbook of European Law* 93; for more recent accounts, see P. Craig and G. de Búrca, *EU Law. Text, Cases and Materials* (2nd edn., Oxford: OUP, 1998) 699–703; and S. Peers, "Social Advantages and Discrimination in Employment: Case Law Confirmed and Clarified" Vol 22 (1997) *ELRev*. 157.

[75] *Matteucci* case, n. 72 *supra*, para. 14.

discriminatory would have an adverse effect upon the development of that class of agreements and might jeopardise the pursuit of legitimate objectives of bilateral co-operation".[76] The European Court was not stopped by such considerations, and, as the French government stated, it is really only one particular "class" of bilateral agreements which is directly affected by *Matteucci*. The *Matteucci* ruling is limited by the facts of the case to the situation of EU migrants and their families, who reside in one of the countries that have concluded the bilateral agreement: this class of persons is entitled to the benefits available under the agreement, whether these benefits consist of scholarships or tax advantages.[77] This equal treatment right is not limited to workers and their families (it now extends to every EU citizen who lawfully resides in the country),[78] but the right of equal treatment does not imply that Italian citizens living in Italy can apply for a scholarship under the Belgo–German cultural agreement, or can generally benefit from tax arrangements under the Belgo–Dutch double taxation treaty.

Taxation is, in fact, the main area in which the *Matteucci* principle may wreak damage to the existing bilateral relations of the Member States. The extent to which Member States may legitimately differentiate between residents and non-residents for tax purposes has been the object of some controversial ECJ judgments over the last decade.[79] Double taxation agreements are precisely intended to improve the position of non-residents, as they try to avoid persons being taxed in two countries for the same income, and therefore they correspond to EC policy objectives. If, however, the bilateral agreement between Member States A and B uses other tax allocation rules than the agreement between A and C, then the nationals of country B may find themselves being treated worse by the tax authorities of A than the nationals of country C. In such a situation, can one say that state A is discriminating (in the sense of the EC Treaty) against the nationals of state B? Does EC law require the states to read an unwritten "most-favoured nation" clause in each bilateral agreement with other EU states, so that, in effect, a multilateralisaton of each of those bilateral agreements occurs? This, according to an expert commentator, "undoubtedly represents the six million dollar question of European tax law".[80] Contrasting answers can be found in the literature,[81] and the ECJ has, so far, not been forced to squarely address this question.

[76] French government's observations, as rendered in the Report for the Hearing, *ibid.*, 5595.

[77] Indeed, Art. 7(2) of Reg. 1612/68 (OJ English Special Edition 1968 (II) 475) mentions social and tax advantages in one breath.

[78] Case C–85/96, *María Martínez Sala* v. *Freistaat Bayern* [1998] ECR I–2691, para. 63.

[79] See the survey by J. Wouters, "The Case-Law of the European Court of Justice on Direct Taxes: Variations upon a Theme" [1994] *Maastricht Journal of European and Comparative Law* 179. See, with specific reference to the possibly discriminatory effects of bilateral agreements, Case C–307/97, *Compagnie de Saint-Gobain, Zweigniederlassung Deutschland* v. *Finanzamt Aachen-Innenstadt*, Opinion of Mischo AG of 2 Mar. 1999, paras. 75 to 92.

[80] P. Farmer, "EC Law and National Rules on Direct Taxation: A Phoney War?" [1998] *EC Tax Review* 13, at 29.

[81] See the contrasting views of J. Schuch, "Most Favoured Nation Clause in Tax Treaty Law" [1996] *EC Tax Review* 161, and E. Kemmeren, "The Termination of the 'Most Favoured Nation

After this discussion of the non-discrimination principle, as the central (though not exclusive) *locus* of conflicts between EC law and international agreements of the Member States, I will conclude this section with some general considerations on the *enforcement* of the principle of primacy. Primacy is not only directed at the courts. It also entails a duty for governments and parliaments to modify existing laws and regulations conflicting with Community law and to refrain from enacting such laws and regulations. In the case of international agreements between Member States, compliance with the principle of supremacy is more complicated than where "purely" domestic law is incompatible with EC law, because joint action by the Member States involved in the *inter se* agreement will be required. Such joint action may not be strictly necessary in countries such as Germany or the UK where the primacy of international treaties over a later Act of Parliament is not recognised; there, a brutal "treaty override" through the adoption of national legislation contrasting with an earlier international agreement would be enough to restore compatibility with Community law. But other Member States, where the higher authority of international treaty obligations is constitutionally recognised, will need to enter into negotiations with their co-contracting parties so as to eliminate the incompatibility with EC law.[82] This process may be facilitated by including a clause in the *inter se* agreement committing the parties to do so, on the model of the following provision in the tax treaty between France and Italy:

> If the clauses of this Convention become incompatible with the provisions decreed by the bodies of the European Communities, both States shall, after consultation between their competent authorities, settle by mutual agreement, through diplomatic channels, the terms and conditions under which such clauses shall cease to apply.[83]

This provision can be seen as a good expression of what all Member States should do, on the basis of their *duty of sincere co-operation*. This duty, which is formulated in Article 10 of the EC Treaty (ex Article 5), is a *general* principle of which the principle of primacy is the main embodiment. The operative scope and practical importance of the general principle depend on one's definition of primacy. If primacy is defined, as I defined it above, as a source of obligations not just for national courts but also for national parliaments and governments, then the added value of the general principle of sincere co-operation is rather

Clause' Dispute in Tax Treaty Law and the Necessity of a Euro Model Tax Convention" [1997] *EC Tax Review* 146. A balanced view is taken by C. Tietje, "Die Meistbegünstigungsverpflichtung im Gemeinschaftsrecht" [1995] *Europarecht* 398, who argues that selective benefits for some EU nationals only constitute *prima facie* discrimination, but that they may be justified by public interest requirements.

[82] The same, obviously, applies to treaties with third states, where the practical difficulties will be even greater.

[83] Point 17 of the Protocol to the Treaty between France and Italy for the avoidance of double taxation with respect to taxes on income and capital and the prevention of fiscal evasion and fraud (Venice, 5 Oct. 1989). I owe the reference to G. Maisto, "Residence of Individuals and the Italy-France Tax Treaty" [1999] *European Taxation* 42, at 43.

limited. Yet, the particular context of the problem at stake here (namely, the tension between an *inter se* co-operation framework and the general requirements of Community law) highlights the separate importance of the duty of co-operation. To the extent that unilateral action by individual Member States is insufficient to ensure full compliance with Community law, the states have a duty to co-operate among each other (*horizontal co-operation*) in the light of their duty of loyalty towards the Community (*vertical co-operation*). The Franco-Italian clause mentioned above should therefore be read into all *inter se* agreements concluded between Member States. One might even think that, due to the broad expansion of Community policies, such a standard clause should *systematically* be included in all new *inter se* agreements.

Horizontal co-operation between Member States is not only required for eliminating occasional legal conflicts with Community law, but also, and increasingly, for contributing to the smooth implementation of Community acts. As was seen above, a number of agreements between Member States are nowadays concluded simply to facilitate the application of Community law, and are therefore completely within the EU orbit.

C. The Principle of Subsidiarity

Whereas the doctrines of pre-emption and primacy, examined above, act as limits to the Member States' discretion in making international agreements, the principle of subsidiarity, in contrast, could be seen as a limit to the discretion of the European Community in adopting acts that would affect earlier international agreements between the Member States, or that would occupy the field so as to preclude the adoption of such agreements in the future. In fact, subsidiarity has rarely been seen from this angle. In legal documents and in the vast literature on subsidiarity, discussion of the principle is nearly exclusively focused on the question whether the Community should act, or rather its Member States *on their own*. But it is not clear whether *co-operation between Member States* outside the Community framework is or is not an option which is supported by the Community principle of subsidiarity.

There is no trace of this question in the Conclusions on subsidiarity of the European Council in Edinburgh, nor in the Protocol on subsidiarity and proportionality annexed to the Treaty of Amsterdam, where subsidiarity is systematically presented as a choice between Community action and *unilateral* Member State action. The "international" option is referred to only in the early Commission document on subsidiarity of 1992, in which that institution stated:

> particular attention should be paid to the possibility in certain cases of achieving the objectives set out in the Treaty *through international agreements rather than via an internal instrument*, for subsidiarity surely also means not legislating at Community

level when action is already being taken at international level and proving just as effective as Community action.[84]

This statement, which was not taken very seriously by the Commission itself,[85] leads to two observations, or rather two distinctions. A first distinction to be made is, once more, that between international agreements with and without third states. The Commission's statement seems to refer, albeit implicitly, to the former category. And indeed, concluding an agreement with third countries may often be more effective than internal Community law, depending on the scale of the problem addressed. Thus, regulation of transport on the Rhine cannot effectively be accomplished on the basis of internal EC acts, but requires an agreement with Switzerland, due to the geographical situation of that country and its acquired rights. The same reasoning does not apply to *inter se* agreements without the participation of third countries. Here, the added value of intergovernmental co-operation is highly debatable. Consider, for example, another set of rivers, namely the Meuse and Scheldt, whose basin is entirely contained within the borders of the European Union countries. The need for a comprehensive regulatory regime had for many years been recognised by the riparian states, but international negotiations had been dragging on. When, finally, the Agreements of Charleville-Mézières were concluded in 1994, many of the questions that were on the earlier ambitious agenda had been left aside.[86] River transport rules and environmental emission standards were not included, as the contracting parties considered that these matters were sufficiently taken care of within the framework of the European Community. What was left was, essentially, the creation of two international river commissions entrusted with environmental management and control tasks. The states correctly recognised the priority of Community regulation in all matters in which the Scheldt and Meuse are similar to other rivers in the EU, and concentrated on some more specific executive tasks, for which they are better equipped.

This example leads to a second distinction implied by the wording used in the Commission document of 1992, namely that between cases in which international action "is already being taken" and cases where the choice between the Community and the international track is still entirely open. Thus, it might be politically and legally advisable for the European Union to respect certain well-worn frameworks of intergovernmental co-operation, such as the Hague system

[84] Commission Communication of 27 Oct. 1992, *Bull. EC* 10–1992, 116, at 123 (emphasis added).

[85] The Commission conveniently forgot to mention this option once the TEU had come into force. In its report to the European Council on the application of the subsidiarity principle in 1994 (COM(94)533 of 25 Nov. 1994), it discusses (at 12) various "alternative approaches" to straightforward Community legislation, but the conclusion of international agreements between the Member States is not mentioned.

[86] For a description of the negotiation process and the content of the agreements, see A. Gosseries, "The 1994 Agreements Concerning the Protection of the Scheldt and Meuse Rivers" [1995] *European Environmental Law Review* 10; P. d'Argent, "L'évolution du statut juridique de la Meuse et de l'Escaut: une mise en perspective des accords de Charleville-Mézières du 26 avril 1994" [1997] *Revue belge de droit international* 133.

of private international law conventions, the World Intellectual Property Organisation and, above all, the Council of Europe convention system. The principle of subsidiarity would not prevent the EU institutions from co-ordinating the action of the Member States within these larger fora, or from replacing the Member States in some of these fora, but it would act as a limit to EU initiatives aimed at displacing existing, and well-functioning, legal regimes adopted within these larger international contexts. When proposing a "rival" Community instrument, the Commission should do more than emphasise the "natural" superiority of Community law, and indicate in a detailed way why the international legal regime fails to meet policy objectives of the European Union, such as the smooth functioning of the internal market or the adequate protection of the environment.

The general point made by the 1992 document of the Commission, that intergovernmental action may prove "just as effective", must, therefore, be qualified. The point rings true where the question to be dealt with requires, by its nature, the involvement of third states or concerns, by its nature, only two neighbouring Member States (say, transfrontier co-operation between local authorities). It is also true where a relatively well-functioning international regime is in place, and enacting a separate EC regime would only cause havoc. But if those conditions are not met, then, I submit, intergovernmental action should generally be considered as "less effective", and therefore the enactment of EC law should be preferred *in the name of subsidiarity*. The decisive reason is what could be called, in a summary fashion, the special qualities of Community law (and even non-Community EU law) compared to ordinary international law.[87] This includes such elements as the more open and transparent nature of the decision-making process, the efficiency of that decision-making process, its usually more democratic nature,[88] the existence of a more effective compliance system, and a greater capacity for adaptation to changing circumstances. This would lead to the conclusion that, where action within the framework of the European Community is, in view of the scale of the problem, marginally less appropriate than international co-operation between either more or fewer than 15 states, EC action should nevertheless be preferred to the conclusion of an international agreement. It is only where the EC framework is *clearly* less adapted than the rival option of intergovernmental co-operation that EC action would be precluded in the name of subsidiarity. This general guideline may, however, be sup-

[87] See, generally, C. Timmermans, "Free Movement of Persons and the Division of Powers between the Community and its Member States—Why do It the Intergovernmental Way?" in H. Schermers *et al.* (eds.), *Free Movement of Persons in Europe* (Dordrecht: Martinus Nijhoff, 1993) 353, at 364–7.

[88] See the judicious remarks by Craig and De Búrca to the effect that the democratic character of EC decision-making should be evaluated in the light of the even less democratic character of the many *ad hoc* international agreements which states would have to conclude if the EC were not there: P. Craig and G. de Búrca, *EU Law—Text, Cases and Materials* (2nd edn., Oxford: OUP, 1998), 157–8). This assessment is hardly affected by the formal circumstance that international agreements generally require approval by the national parliaments of the contracting states, whereas Community legal acts do not.

plemented by specific subsidiarity regimes for certain fields. Thus, in the fields of education, culture and public health, the EC Treaty itself concedes priority to "co-operation between the Member States".

D. The Amsterdam Regime of Closer Co-operation

I stated in the introduction to this chapter that the elaborate regime of closer co-operation within the four corners of EU law, as established by the Treaty of Amsterdam, should not be seen to imply a prohibition for Member States to continue or develop closer co-operation under international law. Where the text of Article 43 of the EU Treaty holds that "Member States which intend to establish closer co-operation between themselves may make use of the institutions", the use of the word "may" could be read to imply that states may also establish closer co-operation in other ways, not provided by the EU Treaty itself.[89] A different view is taken by Constantinesco, who proposes a distinction between intergovernmental co-operation in fields not falling within the competence of the EU and EC, which continues to be allowed, and intergovernmental co-operation in matters coming within the competence of the EU and EC, which, after Amsterdam, would no longer be allowed. He emphatically states:

> *dans le champ d'application des traités communautaires, les Etats membres ne disposent plus—en dehors de la "co-opération renforcée" offerte par le traité d'Amsterdam—d'autres possibilités d'engager des actions collectives.*[90]

There is one intriguing element in the recent Treaty revision which might seem to add support to this radical view, namely the deletion of the former Article K.7 which expressly allowed for closer co-operation outside the framework of the Third Pillar. The deletion could be seen to imply that such closer co-operation is now prohibited as far as the revamped third pillar area is concerned; and even, by extension, that intergovernmental agreements are banned altogether, across the various EU pillars and treaties.

Yet, a more obvious explanation for the deletion of Article K.7 is that it might have seemed superfluous to the negotiators of the Treaty of Amsterdam. The Article had been enacted at Maastricht with a specific view to the Schengen regime that had just been set up between some of the Member States; now that the Treaty of Amsterdam incorporates the Schengen *acquis* in the EU structure, there may be no need for Article K.7 any longer. Furthermore, international conventions on third pillar matters are a generally accepted instrument of EU

[89] See G. Gaja, "How Flexible is Flexibility under the Amsterdam Treaty" [1998] *CMLRev. Vol 35; RMUE* 855, at 870; C.-D. Ehlermann, "Différenciation, Flexibilité, Coopération renforcée: les nouvelles dispositions du traité d'Amsterdam", *Revue du Marché Unique Européen* (1997), Nr 3, 53, at 66.

[90] V. Constantinesco, "Les clauses de 'coopération renforcée'. Le protocole sur l'application des principes de subsidiarité et de proportionnalité" [1997] *Revue trimestrielle de droit européen* 751, at 755.

law itself and, contrary to the position before Amsterdam, they do not necessarily require ratification by all Member States for their entry into force (new Article 34(2)(d) of the EU Treaty).[91] Such third pillar conventions need not even be *concluded* unanimously, since the system of closer co-operation of Article 40 of the EU Treaty applies to all third pillar instruments, including therefore the adoption of conventions. The limit to this intergovernmental flexibility is that the conventions must involve at least eight Member States. So, a new "Schengen" system could now be enacted under the EU Treaty itself.

Despite this new flexibility inside the EU framework, I do not think that one should legally exclude the possibility of *inter se* agreements (outside the EU framework) being concluded in matters of police and judicial co-operation.[92] The mere deletion of the former Article K.7 is not, in the absence of a positive prohibition, a sufficient ground for denying to Member States the possibility of concluding *inter se* agreements on police and criminal justice co-operation. Article 39(5) of the Schengen Convention refers, with regard to police co-operation, to "more detailed present or future bilateral agreements between Contracting Parties with a common border". There is no plausible reason why such agreements should no longer be admissible in the future, even in the absence of an express permission, as long as the states envisaging such agreements inform and consult the other EU states.[93]

If this conclusion is true for the third pillar, it should *a fortiori* be true for the first pillar. In contrast with Constantinesco's view, I take it that *inter se* agreements on EC-related matters remain possible after Amsterdam. Closer co-operation under Article 11 EC refers to fields in which the Treaty has given the EC a competence to act; it does not add new powers[94] and, consequently, does not affect the Member States' existing power to conclude international agreements. That conclusion not only applies to *inter se* agreements concluded among fewer than eight Member States, but also, I submit, to agreements concluded among more than eight states. Imagine that a proposal to introduce a Union-wide carbon tax is approved by 13 states but meets with the stubborn opposition of two states, and that the susbsequent proposal to introduce such a tax by using the closer co-operation mechanism is, again, vetoed, by the two "outsiders". Then the 13 states would arguably preserve the power, which they already have now, to enact such a tax unilaterally through national legislation.

[91] Note, however, that some flexibility already existed before Amsterdam. See, e.g., the Convention on extradition of 1996 [1996] OJ C313/12: whereas it will enter into force only after ratification by all Member States, its Art. 18(4) allows for provisional application between those ratifying states declaring their willingness to apply it.

[92] This is also the position taken by H. Bribosia, "De la subsidiarité à la coopération renforcée" in Y. Lejeune (ed.), *Le Traité d'Amsterdam—Espoirs et déceptions* (Brussels: Bruylant, 1998) 23, at 83.

[93] Art. 34(1) of the EU Treaty.

[94] See e.g. A. Dashwood, "States in the European Union" (1998) *ELRev*. Vol 23 210, at 214: the closer co-operation mechanism "will not allow action to be taken in matters for which the Treaty does not already provide a legal basis; it will only be available to circumvent the unwillingness of certain Member States to exploit existing powers".

Why, then, should they not be allowed to introduce it on the basis of a joint agreement under international law?

Apart from this general question, there remains the more specific question whether the detailed *conditions* for intra-EU closer co-operation, imposed by the Articles 43 and 40 of the EU Treaty, and by Article 11 of the EC Treaty, also affect the legal regime of intergovernmental agreements between Member States. It is clear, from a simple reading of these new Treaty Articles, that the conditions which they impose are much more onerous than the conditions highlighted above as applying to intergovernmental agreements pre-Amsterdam. There is a good reason for this severe regime: as the closer co-operation mechanism of Amsterdam delivers the keys of the powerful EU/EC engine to a group of Member States, such a move should be allowed less liberally than "old-fashioned" recourse to the more modest instruments of international law. Indeed, these enactments under international law cannot derogate from EU law and can, at any time, be derogated from by measures of EU law. Therefore, I do not think that the "ten commandments" for intra-EU closer co-operation should also be applied to intergovernmental agreements, because that would introduce an unwanted, and undesirable, degree of rigidity to the legal relations between the Member States. I conclude that the legal regime of intergovernmental agreements has not fundamentally changed since the entry into force of the Treaty of Amsterdam.

4. CONCLUSION

One of the paradoxical and possibly unintended consequences of the rigid regime of Amsterdam-style closer co-operation is that the temptation to leave the EU framework and set up a separate *inter se* regime under international law will continue to exist. It is not entirely unthinkable that, in ten years' time, we might come to the conclusion that closer co-operation under the EU and EC Treaties did not work due to its rigid conditions, whereas variable geometry based on international law was flourishing more than ever before. Gaja concludes his analysis of the Amsterdam regime by stating, "one is left to wonder whether in the Treaty of Amsterdam a more flexible general mechanism of flexibility would not have provided a better option".[95] Or better still, could the drafters not have seized the opportunity to spell out in clear terms the scope and legal conditions for *inter se* agreements?

The temptation to use the instruments of international law in order to launch ambitious new forms of European co-operation could well emerge on the occasion of the next Intergovernmental Conference, if there is fundamental disagreement between groups of countries about the future of European integration. In a hearing before the French Senate in June 1999, Jacques Delors

[95] Gaja, n. 89 *supra*, 870.

considered it likely that, in the years to come, a vanguard of countries would lead the way towards closer European integration through the conclusion of one or more "particular treaties" between themselves.[96] This, however, is merely a hypothetical possibility. For the time being, there is no immediate danger of seeing a multiplication of "Schengen" and "Euroland" types of construction or the creation of a "core group" setting up its own integration regime outside the European Union framework. The evolution over the last 20 years seems to show that the states generally find intergovernmental co-operation less attractive than co-operation in the framework of European law. The incorporation of the Schengen acquis and the efforts to allow for intra-EU closer co-operation are the most visible illustrations of this tendency. Apart from the spectacular cases which are often mentioned, such as Schengen and the Social Agreement (which is really much more EC law than international law anyway), *inter se* co-operation has been limited to rather modest matters, and its importance is declining. Even without strict legal compulsion to stop using these alternative routes, the Member States have, on their own account, come to the conclusion that it is advisable to concentrate their efforts and invest their political resources in the complex game of the European Union rather than organising many little side-games. If one takes this into account, then the events of recent years (and particularly the Amsterdam summit) do not signal the disintegration of the Community legal order, but rather reinforce the tendency towards greater legal homogeneity among the Member States of the European Union.

[96] Délégation du Sénat pour l'Union européenne, Audition de M. Jacques Delors sur la réforme des institutions européennes, 16 June 1999, <www.senat.fr/europe/r16061999.html>, 8: "[j]e crois nécessaire une initiative franco-allemande autour d'un projet. Les Etats intéressés pourraient la rejoindre. Elle prendrait la forme d'un traité particulier, compatible avec les traités européens. On peut imaginer divers domaines où cette formule pourrait s'appliquer: le rapprochement des fiscalités, la défense, l'énergie".

4

Flexible Models: External Policy and the European Economic Constitution

MARISE CREMONA

1. INTRODUCTION: FLEXIBILITY AND DIFFERENTIATION

TO WHAT EXTENT do the EC's external relationships demonstrate the flexibility and differentiated integration that we are seeing emerge as characteristics of the constitution of the European Union? This chapter,[1] in raising this question, is intended to provide a framework in which we can analyse the operation of "flexibility" and "differentiation" in the context of external policy. The concepts of flexibility and differentiation are used by the EC in its external policy, and by the wider international community, in distinctive ways. The fundamental question that must be tackled is just what these concepts might mean in this particular context, and here "flexibility" and "differentiation" offer two rather different perspectives.

From one perspective, the factors that condition the type of relationship offered by the EU to third states indicate a highly developed form of *differentiation* between states and groups of states which is at the same time regional, developmental and conditional.

The second perspective focuses on the *flexibility* of the Community as negotiator, in defining the scope and content of specific external agreements so that they reflect the priorities and needs of the negotiating partners. Does the Community in fact offer a package deal which is not so much the result of a complex multilateral multi-staged negotiation (in the style of the Uruguay Round "package") but which is more like the travel agent's package, a standard-form contract requiring adherence to an essentially non-negotiable core of commitments?

The two perspectives are connected: the content of the package offered to a negotiating partner, and the partner's bargaining leverage, will depend in part on that partner's position within the Community's differentiated external

[1] Earlier versions of this chapter were given to the seminar on "The Constitution of the EU: From Uniformity to Flexibility" held at the EUI Florence, 23–24 Apr. 1999, and to the 6th ECSA biennial international conference held in Pittsburgh, 2–5 June 1999. Thanks are due to Gráinne de Búrca, Joanne Scott, Gerrit Faber and participants and fellow panel members at both events for their helpful comments.

policy, whether based on regional or economic criteria or on grounds of political conditionality (or, more likely, on a combination of these). Both the process of differentiation and the nature of the Community's flexibility in negotiations are essentially based on the Community's own assessment of those factors which it has itself identified as important. The idea of a "non-negotiable core" also raises the possibility of a parallel between the core commitments required of third states, and the (putative) common core to which the Member States are committed and which form a unifying set of values and norms holding together a Union which has flexibility built into its post-Amsterdam constitution.

A. Differentiation

Differentiation is increasingly explicitly identified by the Community (and especially the Commission) as a key element in its external policy formation. The implication is often that the need to differentiate is based on objective differences between the Community's interlocutors, for example their different stages of economic development.[2] In fact we find the Community defining its own basis (or bases) for differentiation, making its own assessment of what factors may be relevant, and then using these to delimit the "offer" it is prepared to make to the third state or group of states in question. Differentiation in this sense not only affects the type of agreement a third state may be offered: a reciprocal free trade agreement, an association agreement with or without a recognition of membership aspirations, a "co-operation" or a "partnership" agreement. It also affects autonomous Community measures, such as trade preferences, and financial and technical assistance.

The assessment of "difference" will depend on a number of factors. In what follows these are grouped into three categories:

(i) regional or geopolitical, as the Community develops specifically regional policies towards (for example) south-east Europe, the Euro-Mediterranean region, southern Africa, or the "European" and "Asian" newly independent states (NIS) of the former Soviet Union; these regional policies may be the result of regional integration movements within the regions concerned,[3] or sub-regional distinctions depending on the Community's own differentiation, with south-east Europe, or the NIS, for example.

[2] Edwards and Philippart point out that "differentiation" in the pre-Amsterdam intra-Community context also carried with it an implication that the differences were based on objective factors, whether economic or social: G. Edwards and E. Philippart, *Flexibility and the Treaty of Amsterdam: Europe's New Byzantium* CELS Occasional Paper No 3 (Cambridge: University of Cambridge Centre for European Legal Studies, 1997) at 3, citing C.-D. Ehlermann, "How Flexible is Community Law? An Unusual Approach to the Concept of 'Two Speeds' " (1984) 82 *Michigan Law Review* 1274.

[3] Such as the Interregional Framework Co-operation Agreement with MERCOSUR (Brazil, Argentina, Paraguay, Uruguay) [1996] OJ L69/1; or the Framework Agreement on co-operation with the Cartagena countries (Bolivia, Columbia, Ecuador, Peru, Venezuela) [1998] OJ L127/10.

(ii) differentiation may also be based on economic or developmental characteristics, not only treating developing countries as a group but differentiation between levels of development within the group. This type of differentiation has been stressed by the Commission in the context of the renegotiation of ACP–EU trade relations[4] and is closely connected with, and likely to lead to, flexibility in the structure and terms of agreements and assistance programmes as well as in implementation provisions.

(iii) a third aspect of differentiation is more overtly based on the Community's own assessment of its partners and may be termed "conditional differentiation". By this I mean the way in which conditions (sometimes general, sometimes quite specific) are attached to the development of relations between the EU and its partners. These range from accession conditions, through general "human rights" clauses in trade agreements, to references to specific ILO Conventions in regulations on trade preferences. Distinctions are made on the basis of compliance with specified—usually primarily political—conditions. A particularly fully-worked-out example of this is the Council's Conclusions of April 1997 on the principle of conditionality governing the development of the EU's relations with certain countries of south-east Europe[5] which have been followed through in regular assessments by the Commission and Council. Here we see judgements being made on progress against targets set by the EC itself, resulting in decisions to (for example) renew or not renew tariff preferences. We also see conditions explicitly attached to the progressive development of relations, from tariff preferences, to financial assistance, through to first stage co-operation agreements and ultimately to association agreements.

The next section of this chapter will explore in more detail these three aspects of differentiation, and the way in which they may operate together in a more or less explicit way.

B. Flexibility

Section three of this chapter turns to the degree of flexibility in the Community's approach to external agreements. "Flexibility", in the form of waivers, derogations, safeguard and other exceptional measures, is of course one of the supposed characteristics of GATT 1947 which founded the European Court of Justice's conclusion that "the GATT rules are not unconditional and an obligation to recognise them as rules of international law which are directly applicable in the domestic legal systems of the contracting parties cannot be based on

[4] "Relations between the European Union and the ACP countries on the eve of the 21st century—challenges and options for a new partnership", COM(96)601 final.

[5] Conclusions of Council on the principle of conditionality governing the development of the EU's relations with certain countries of south-east Europe, 29 Apr. 1997, *Bull.EU* 4–1997.

the spirit, general scheme or terms of GATT".[6] One aspect of flexibility thus denotes the extent to which—in crude terms—the EC may be willing to take account of the particular needs of its interlocutors and to depart from strict reciprocity in its agreements, either in formulating the substantive obligations themselves or, where substantive reciprocity is the ultimate objective, in allowing flexible implementation such as asymmetric timetables, special derogations and/or financial support for the transition. Flexibility in this sense is closely connected to ideas of reciprocity, and may have implications for the status of the legal obligations created by agreements.

As the Community's network of international relations, especially its contractual relations, grows ever more complex, we can see the emergence of a number of key, or core, provisions. One of the most obvious of these is the clause which stipulates that democracy and the rule of law and respect for human rights and fundamental freedoms are essential elements of the agreement,[7] but other principles are emerging: first, a move towards reciprocity of trade liberalisation (through free trade agreements) and away from non-reciprocal preferences, together with an extension of the scope of economic agreements to cover services as well as trade in goods; secondly, a concomitant willingness to envisage varying degrees and types of asymmetry in the implementation and phasing of these reciprocal agreements and in the derogations and exceptions permitted; thirdly, an increasing emphasis on regulatory issues, alongside market liberalisation measures, together with an expectation or even requirement of regulatory convergence towards Community standards in certain key related policy areas, such as competition and the protection of intellectual property.

The reasons for these developments are multi-layered, interconnected and not always explicit. In part no doubt we are seeing a reflection of developments at a world trade level, as links are made between trade liberalisation and the adoption of minimum standards, with fierce debate about how far this linkage can and should extend. However this is not only a question of external pressure; there is a rationale for these developments which arises out of the connection within the Community's own economic constitution between market integration and market regulation and which raises questions concerning the extent to which other elements of that constitution (individual rights, judicial review processes, non-discrimination) can and should be exported along with market liberalisation. The final section explores the model of market integration offered by the Community to third states, and the implications of what might be seen as the extension of aspects of the *acquis communautaire* to selected third states. To what extent does adoption of Community norms imply adoption of other aspects of the Community's economic constitution?

[6] Case C–280/93, *Germany* v. *Council* [1994] ECR I–4973, para. 110.

[7] Commission Communication on the inclusion of respect for democratic principles and human rights in agreements between the Community and third countries, 23 May 1995, COM(95)216 final, approved by the Council, 29 May 1995.

2. REGIONAL, DEVELOPMENTAL AND CONDITIONAL DIFFERENTIATION

A. Regional Differentiation

(i) Regional Integration and Regional Differentiation

The Community's external policy has always had a regional dimension,[8] and over the last ten years we have seen the development of this dimension into a way of structuring its relationships and even, one may say, the Community's way of looking at the world. The increasing sense of the Community's own international identity, which is based on a regional identification, has formed the basis for regional initiatives such as the "Europe" Agreements with central and eastern Europe,[9] the Euro-Mediterranean Partnership,[10] the EU–MERCOSUR Framework Agreement,[11] and relations with South-East Asia.[12] It is not only that the EU's regional approach has been strengthened by regional integration initiatives such as MERCOSUR, the Andean Pact, ASEAN, APEC and NAFTA; in fact, the EU has raised regional integration (both economic and political) into an objective of its regional strategies. It is actively encouraging regional integration in the form of initiatives such as the Barcelona process,[13] EU–ASEAN co-operation,[14] within Central and Latin

[8] See generally G. Edwards and E. Regelsberger (eds.), *Europe's Global Links: The European Community and Inter-Regional Cooperation* (London: Pinter, 1990).

[9] Association Agreements concluded with Hungary, Poland, Romania, Bulgaria, Slovakia, the Czech Republic, Estonia, Latvia, Lithuania, Slovenia. For comment see M. Maresceau and Montaguti, "The Relations Between the EU and Central and Eastern Europe: A Legal Appraisal" (1995) 32 *CMLRev*. 1327; M. Cremona, "The New Associations" in S. Konstadinidis (ed.), *The Legal Regulation of the European Community's External Relations after the Completion of the Internal Market* (Aldershot: Dartmouth 1996).

[10] Barcelona Conference Declaration and Work Programme, 27–28 Nov. 1995, *Bull. EU* 11–1995. For comment see M. Cremona, "The Euro-Mediterranean Partnership: A Regional Strategy for the EU" in P. Xuereb and R. Pace (eds.), *The European Union, the IGC and the Mediterranean: State of the European Union Conference 1996* (Malta: EDRC, 1996) Malta; G. Edwards and E. Philippart, "The Euro-Mediterranean Partnership: Fragmentation and Reconstruction" (1997) 2 *EFA Rev*. 465; F. Hakura, "The Euro-Med Policy: The Implications of the Barcelona Declaration" (1997) 34 *CMLRev*. 337.

[11] Interregional Framework Co-operation Agreement with MERCOSUR (Southern Common Market: Brazil, Argentina, Paraguay, Uruguay) [1996] OJ L69/1. For comment see P. B. Casella and E. L. Marques, "European Union—MERCOSUR Relations: A Critical Overview" [1997] 2 *EFA Rev*. 455; J. Dauster, "MERCOSUR and the European Union: Prospects for an Inter-Regional Association" (1998) 3 *EFA Rev*. 447.

[12] The Commission communication "Towards a New Asia Strategy", COM(94)314 final, makes a distinction between three regions within Asia: East Asia, South Asia and South-East Asia: Co-operation Agreement with ASEAN (Indonesia, Malaysia, Philippines, Singapore, Thailand) [1980] OJ L1441. Myanmar, Laos and Vietnam have since acceded to ASEAN and it is intended that Cambodia do so. For comment see J. McMahon, "ASEAN and the Asia-Europe Meeting: Strengthening the European Union's Relationship with South-East Asia?" (1998)3 *EFA Rev*. 233.

[13] Barcelona Conference Declaration and Work Programme, 27–28 Nov. 1995, *Bull. EU* 11–1995.

[14] The ASEM process (Asia–Europe summit meetings) first took place in Bangkok in Mar. 1996, bringing together leaders of ten East and South-East Asian countries and the EU Member States and the European Commission; dialogue covers economic and commercial, cultural and political

America,[15] and in its regional strategy towards the former Soviet Union and south-east Europe. This encouragement towards regional integration works in two ways, in the sense that by strengthening links between certain groupings, it also serves to reinforce the regionally-based differentiation between these groupings, an aspect of the regional approach in south-east Europe which has been resisted by some of the affected states.

The two examples considered below illustrate both these aspects of regional differentiation: the use of regional or geopolitical distinctions by the Union to structure its external policy, and within this, its positive emphasis on support for regional integration.

(ii) The Regional Approach in South-East Europe

The Community has explicitly adopted what it calls a "regional approach" towards the countries of south-east Europe. On 30 October 1995 the Council adopted a set of guidelines for future negotiations with and between the parties to the conflict in former Yugoslavia in which it stated that the EU's long-term relation with the countries of the region should "take the form of agreements in the framework of a regional approach".[16] This regional approach has formed the basis of all further assessments and statements, including the Commission's common principles of October 1996,[17] and the Council Conclusions of April 1997,[18] and has evolved into the "stabilisation and association process" outlined in the Commission's Communication of May 1999.[19]

A "regional approach" in this context has some distinct characteristics. First, the Union makes its own differentiation between states. In contrast to the ACP states, where the Commission has said that "it would, of course, be for the ACP countries themselves to choose the regional structures with which the EU negotiates",[20] in south-east Europe the distinctions are based entirely on the Community's own

issues. See Commission Communication, "Creating A New Dynamic in EU–ASEAN Relations" COM (96)314 final.

[15] For example, in the Economic Partnership, Political Co-ordination and Co-operation Agreement between the EC and Mexico (the "Global Agreement") the parties agree to promote intra-regional trade in Central America and the Caribbean, and to stimulate regional co-operation on the environment and on technological and scientific research (Art 37) [1997] OJ C350/6. The Interregional Framework Co-operation Agreement between the EC and MERCOSUR states that "the Parties shall seek to further the objectives of MERCOSUR's integration process" (Art 18) [1996] OJ L69/1. A similar provision is found in the Framework Agreement on Co-operation between the EC and the Cartagena Agreement (Andean Pact) and its member countries (Bolivia, Colombia, Ecuador, Peru and Venezuela) [1998] OJ L127/11, Art. 26.

[16] Bull EU 10–1995 at 138.

[17] Commission Report, "Common principles for future contractual relations with certain countries in south-eastern Europe (Albania, FYROM, Bosnia & Herzegovina, Croatia, FRY)", 2 Oct. 1996 COM(96)476 final.

[18] Council Conclusions on the principle of conditionality governing the development of the EU's relations with certain countries of south-east Europe, *Bull. EU* 4–1997, 132.

[19] Commission Communication on the Stabilisation and Association Process for countries of South-Eastern Europe, 26 May 1999, COM(99) 235.

[20] COM(97)537 final at sect. 5.2.

assessments. Thus the "regional approach" in this specific sense covers only those states of the region which are *not* part of the group of associated (applicant) states. These latter states form a separate grouping, with their own sub-division into those which have been found to be close enough to compliance with primary accession criteria to have started negotiations (currently Slovenia), and those which have not yet done so (currently Bulgaria and Romania[21]). For the other states in the region, to which the "regional approach" applies, the Community distinguishes between Albania and the former Yugoslav Republic of Macedonia (FYROM) on the one hand, and on the other Croatia, Bosnia and Herzegovina (BiH) and the Federal Republic of Yugoslavia (FRY), partly because the former already have "first generation" agreements with the EC, and partly on the ground that the latter are party to the Dayton/Paris peace agreements.[22]

Secondly, the EU is adopting an approach towards these vulnerable states which is based on "common principles" but which treats each state individually depending on its economic and political progress and its compliance with explicit conditions at each stage. Thirdly, among these conditions is a "regional approach" in the sense that regional openness and co-operation are an important element. In its 1995 Guidelines the Council stated that the fostering of reconciliation and establishment of open and co-operative relations between the states should be one of the purposes of future agreements with countries in the region, and they should "have an element of clear political and economic conditionality"; willingness to engage in regional co-operation (as well as political and economic reform) will determine their future relations with the EU. This is spelled out further in the Council Conclusions adopted in April 1997, and also in the FYROM Preferential Co-operation Agreement itself.[23] The agreement contains clauses encouraging co-operative and good-neighbourly relations with other countries in the region, underlining the importance of these co-operative relations for future development of relations with the Union. Similar clauses are likely to feature in any future agreement with the countries of the region. In its recent Communication on the stabilisation and association process, the Commission emphasises the common aspirations (closer relations with the EU) and economic interdependence of the countries of south-east Europe and the consequent need for bilateral, multilateral and regional co-operation:

> Assistance to them must also have a regional perspective, encouraging and requiring the countries concerned to work together, as well as with their neighbours in the wider region and with the EU, to further their economic development. In particular, the multilateral dimension of the existing approach must be enhanced, to avoid the risks of concentrating solely on a policy of selective bilateralism to the detriment of a truly regional strategy.[24]

[21] The European Council held in Helsinki, Dec. 1999, decided to open negotiations with these states in February 2000.

[22] COM(96)476 final; COM(99)235 final.

[23] Council Decision 97/831 [1997] OJ L348/1; the Agreement came into force on 1 Jan. 1998.

[24] N. 19 *supra*. See also the Stability Pact for South-Eastern Europe, Cologne, 10 June 1999, which there is no space to discuss here.

In practical terms this means that the conditions to be attached to the "incentives" of association agreements and other assistance will place "increased emphasis on the need for regional co-operation".

(iii) Differentiation in Relations with the New Independent States

Differentiation on a regional basis is also clearly evidenced in the EC's relations with the states of the former Soviet Union, although it is far less clearly articulated. The first and greatest distinction in a twofold differentiation[25] is between those States which have association agreements with the EC in the form of Europe Agreements, have applied for membership of the EU and are now part of the pre-accession process (the Baltic states) and those (the New Independent States or NIS) which have Partnership and Co-operation Agreements (PCAs).[26] In its May 1995 Communication on Russia,[27] the Commission stated that since accession to EU is "not in the EU's view, an option for [the NIS countries], the network of PCAs . . . must provide the framework which will allow the bridging of the political and economic gap between those countries acceding to the EU and their neighbours to the East".

However, a regionally-based difference has also been made between the so-called "European" NIS (Russia, Ukraine, Moldova and Belarus) and "non-European" NIS (Kyrgyzstan, Kazakhstan, Georgia, Armenia, Azerbaijan, Uzbekistan and Turkmenistan). More recently, in its Agenda 2000 documentation, the Commission has stressed the fact that the post-enlargement EU will have borders with Russia, Ukraine, Belarus and Moldova; these states will become its nearest Eastern neighbours.[28]

The overall effect of this distinction, which is not explicit in the PCAs themselves, is that the European PCAs hold out at least the prospect of a relationship with the EU that is closer to, though not the same as, that found in the Europe Agreements with the countries of central and eastern Europe (CEES), possibly leading ultimately to an association. The non-European PCAs are closer to Trade and Co-operation Agreements,[29] although with additional elements such as the provision for political dialogue. The most obvious manifestation of the difference is the so-called "evolutionary clause" that is present in the agreements with the European NIS. As far as trade relations are concerned, all the PCAs have as their immediate objective the establishment of non-preferential MFN-based trade relations, effectively putting in place some of the elements of WTO

[25] A term used by Hillion, n. 26 *infra*, at 401.

[26] PCAs have been signed with Russia, Ukraine, Moldova, Belarus, Kyrgyzstan, Kazakhstan, Georgia, Armenia, Azerbaijan, Uzbekistan and Turkmenistan, although they are not all in force. For comment see C. Hillion, "Partnership and Cooperation Agreements between the EU and the New Independent States of the Ex-Soviet Union" (1998) 3 *EFA Rev*. 399.

[27] Commission communication on EU and Russia: the future relationship, COM(95)223 final.

[28] Agenda 2000 "For a Stronger and Wider Europe", COM(97)2000, *Bull. EU* Supp. 5/97.

[29] As they come into force for each state, the PCAs will replace the Trade and Economic and Commercial Co-operation Agreement concluded with the USSR in 1989 [1990] OJ L68/1.

membership for these states.[30] The "European" PCAs also include a clause committing the partners to consider the prospect of negotiating a free trade agreement (with, however, no commitment on the start of negotiations). The objectives of the PCA with Russia include:

> to create the necessary conditions for the future establishment of a free trade area between the Community and Russia covering substantially all trade in goods between them, as well as conditions for bringing about freedom of establishment of companies, of cross-border trade in services and of capital movements.[31]

There are other differences; for example, the European PCAs contain provision for the co-ordination of social security provision similar to the social security clauses in the Europe Agreements,[32] a clause not found in the non-European PCAs.

In its Explanatory Memorandum to its proposal for a new TACIS regulation to provide economic and technical assistance to the NIS and Mongolia, the Commission emphasises differentiation between the NIS, although this is articulated in terms of their differing levels of commitment to economic transition and progress towards democratic systems, rather than geopolitical factors. Again, although the Commission does say that a number of the NIS partners themselves advocated a more differentiated approach, the process of differentiation depends on the Community's own assessment and its results are built into the Regulation, which is an autonomous instrument not subject to negotiation. The Commission says that it considered the possibility of accommodating regional differentiation through the adoption of a number of separate regulations, but, "in the interests of flexibility", decided to propose one overall regulation. Within the draft Regulation, differentiation is spelt out, identifying the "differing needs and priorities of the principal regions covered by the regulation".[33]

The other aspect of regionalism—promotion of regional co-operation—is also present in both the PCAs with the NIS and the new TACIS Regulation. The PCAs contain preambular statements asserting that regional co-operation is an objective of the agreement, and one of the objectives of the PCA with Russia is "to provide an appropriate framework for the gradual integration between Russia and a wider area of co-operation in Europe".[34] One practical effect of this is that although an MFN obligation forms the basis of the bilateral PCA

[30] Eventual membership of the WTO is recognised as a mutual objective in the preamble to the PCAs and, under Art. 4 of the PCA with Russia, the parties agree to consider changes that may be necessary in the light of eventual WTO accession by Russia.

[31] The PCA with Russia [1997] OJ L327/1, Art. 1. Art. 3 further provides: "[t]he Parties undertake to consider development of the relevant Titles of this Agreement, in particular Title III [on trade in goods] and Article 53 [on competition policy], as circumstances allow, with a view to the establishment of a free trade area between them".

[32] *Ibid.*, Art. 24.

[33] Commission proposal for new TACIS Reg. for 2000–2006, COM (98) 753 final, [1999] OJ C37/5 Art. 2(4). The Regulation was adopted on 29 Dec. 1999.

[34] This objective is also stressed in the EU's Common Strategy on Russia, adopted under Art. 13 TEU on 4 June 1999, 1999/414/CFSP, OJ [1999] L 57/1.

trading relationships, the PCA allows the NIS partners to preserve existing preferential arrangements *inter se*, at least for a transitional period. It is worth noting an added incentive here: to the extent that Russia (for example) enters into treaty-based free trade agreements within the NIS, these will be excepted in the same way as the EC's existing preferential and free trade agreements (such as the Europe Agreements), by analogy with GATT Article XXIV.[35] The Commission views regional and inter-state co-operation as "fundamental instruments" in promoting stability as well as economic development[36]; the draft TACIS Regulation places regional co-operation among the key aims of the assistance programme:

> The programme shall aim to promote inter-state, inter-regional and cross-border cooperation between the partner states themselves, between the partner states and the Union and between the partner states and Central and Eastern Europe.[37]

B. Differentiation and Economic Development

The distinction between the associated "Europe Agreement" states of central and eastern Europe (including the Baltic states) and the European and non-European NIS, with differing levels of partnership agreements is based on economic development as well as geographic and geopolitical factors. None of the NIS are yet members of the WTO, and the PCAs reflect this; they are all still treated by the EC as "non-market economy" states for the purpose of anti-dumping policy. In a somewhat different way economic status also affects the Community's relations with the developing countries.

The idea of differentiation based on the developmental status of the partner states is inherent in the special provisions for developing countries found in the GATT (and now WTO). In the Preamble to the Marrakesh Agreement establishing the WTO the parties refer to their "different levels of economic development" and recognise that there is a need "for positive efforts designed to ensure that developing countries, and especially the least developed among them, secure a share in the growth of international trade commensurate with the needs of their economic development". Part IV of GATT 1947 (which forms part of GATT 1994) contains specific provisions on trade and development, such as Article XXXVI(8) allowing for less than full reciprocity in trade negotiations between developed and less-developed contracting parties. Other examples among the Multilateral Agreements on Trade in Goods in Annex 1A include

[35] The PCA with Russia [1997] OJ L327/1, Art. 10(2). There is an explicit reference to GATT Art. XXIV which is typical of the way in which the PCAs "shadow' GATT disciplines. The exception to MFN treatment covers free trade and customs union agreements and also "advantages granted to particular countries in accordance with the GATT and with other international arrangements in favour of developing countries".

[36] Explanatory Memorandum to the Commission proposal for a new TACIS Reg. for 2000–2006, COM(98) 753.

[37] Commission proposal for a new TACIS Reg. for 2000–2006, COM(98) 753, Art. 2(5).

Article 4 of the Agreement on Trade-Related Investment Measures (TRIMS), and Article 12 of the Agreement on Technical Barriers to Trade, on special and differential treatment of developing country members, which includes time-limited exceptions. The GATS also contains in Article IV a specific provision designed to increase developing country participation in trade in services.

This approach has formed the basis of the Community's development policy, and in particular the Lomé Convention, which offers a degree of non-reciprocal preferential trade to the ACP states with special provision for the least-developed, landlocked and island states.[38] In the Commission's words:

> The EU used [this] policy (involving non-reciprocal trade preferences) in the Yaoundé and now Lomé Conventions, as an instrument of development, and to provide an economic dimension to its assistance to former dependent territories.[39]

The "graduation" mechanism adopted in the more recent GSP Regulations is a specific example of Community policy differentiation between developing countries.[40] Here I would like only to highlight the extent to which differentiation has become a key concept for the EC in defining its approach to the renegotiation of Lomé, incorporating differentiation *between the ACP states* (as opposed to differentiation between developed and developing states) on a dual basis: regional and economic.

In its Communication on guidelines for the negotiation of new co-operation agreements with the ACP countries, the Commission proposes that the ACP states should continue to be treated as a group (reflecting their own wishes) but that within this framework:

> there is a need for differentiation reflecting the regional dimension of economic and trade cooperation, the increasing role of regional integration as a factor for development and, more generally, the need to adjust to the facts of life and the specific circumstances of the ACP group's various components by conducting dialogue and cooperation activities at the most appropriate level.[41]

Thus the proposal is for the negotiation of a new overall EU–ACP partnership agreement, to be followed by differentiated regional or subregional economic co-operation and partnership agreements linked to the overall agreement. The initial partnership agreement would establish as an overall objective the conclusion of economic co-operation agreements with the ACP regions, specifying

[38] The Fourth Lomé Convention was signed at Lomé, Togo, 15 Dec. 1989 [1991] OJ L229/3; a revised text of Lomé IV following mid-term review was signed in Mauritius on 4 Nov. 1995, Council and Commission Decision of 27 Apr. 1998 [1998] OJ L156/1.

[39] Commission report, "WTO Aspects of EU Preferential Trade Agreements with Third Countries" presented to the General Affairs Council in Apr. 1997 and to the European Council at Amsterdam, June 1997.

[40] The graduation mechanism takes account of developmental and specialisation criteria; the GSP Reg. also gives greater preferences to the least developed countries. See most recently Council Reg. 2820/98 of 21 Dec. 1998 applying a multiannual scheme of generalised tariff preferences for the period 1 July 1999 to 31 Dec. 2001 [1998] OJ L357/1.

[41] COM(97)537 final.

the regional subgroups and countries, the general framework and overall timetable for the economic co-operation or partnership agreements to be negotiated during the second stage.

These regionalised agreements (for West Africa, Central Africa, southern Africa, East Africa, Caribbean and Pacific Regions) will develop co-operation in a number of areas and as the Commission states "an approach aimed at enhancing the economic partnership would obviously have to take account of each partner's level of development, constraints and capacities". These include not only the economic development of partner countries or groups of countries, but also the extent to which the existing subregional groups have achieved a sufficient degree of economic integration to make negotiation of agreements with the EU feasible. We are therefore seeing differentiation based on regional and economic considerations, within an overall framework coming under the rubric of a "partnership".

C. Conditional Differentiation

In the previous section we have seen an approach (in the context of the ACP states) in which the level of economic integration envisaged by regionally-based agreements may deepen over time as a result of the economic development of the partner states. In contrast, we can now return to south-east Europe, and an example of "conditional differentiation" in which progress towards greater economic integration with the EU depends on political as well as economic progress.

In EU policy towards south-east Europe generally, the "regional approach" to relations has been expressly linked to conditionality. In reviewing the position of the Western Balkans in December 1998, the European Council stressed "the importance it attaches, in the EU's relations with all these countries, to conditionality in the framework of the EU's regional approach".[42]

The Guidelines adopted in 1995 by the Council made it clear that Community assistance with reconstruction and regional economic development was to be conditional.[43] The specified conditions included implementation of the peace agreement, respect for human rights, minority rights and the right to return of refugees and displaced persons, respect for the principles of market economy, co-operation with the international war crimes tribunal, and—with respect to FRY (Serbia and Montenegro)—the granting of a large degree of autonomy for Kosovo.

These conditions form the basis of the "common principles for future contractual relations with certain countries in South-Eastern Europe" adopted by the Commission in October 1996.[44] The Commission is quite open in stating

[42] Conclusions of the European Council, Vienna, Dec. 1998, para. 108.

[43] *Bull. EU* 10–1995 at 138.

[44] COM(96)476 final.

that the EU has a great interest in peace and stability in the region, and "given the three republics [Croatia, FRY, BiH] interest in forging closer ties with the EU, the establishment and content of contractual relations with them does also represent an effective tool in bringing about the desired stability".[45]

What is particularly interesting about these conditions is that they are more than purely rhetorical: it is possible to trace their concrete application in the more detailed Council Conclusions on conditionality adopted in April 1997,[46] and subsequent regular reports and assessments by Commission and Council.

The Council Conclusions of April 1997 were based on a strategy paper by the Commission of February 1997 and establish conditions which are both general and specific to individual countries. The Council adopts a graduated approach, which means that different degrees of conditionality will apply to (in ascending order) trade preferences, financial assistance and economic co-operation (under PHARE), and contractual relations. Contractual relations themselves will also be graduated, in the sense that the start of negotiations will require less progress than their conclusion, and an initial first stage trade and co-operation agreement may lead on to an association agreement. The general conditions include free and fair elections, independent media, and compliance with the GFAP (General Framework Agreement for Peace). In addition, the Council specifies criteria for judging compliance with these conditions under the heads of democratic principles, human rights, rule of law, respect for and protection of minorities and market economy reform.

Since 1997 assessments have been made on a regular basis by the Commission (April 1998, November 1998, May 1999) and Conclusions on future policy adopted by the Council. As a result, each state is in a different position and these five countries illustrate a range of different stages of relation with the EU, as well as being drawn together in the so-called "regional approach" with its explicit political and economic conditionality. FYROM has a second stage agreement granting preferential trade conditions, with political dialogue included within the agreement, and an evolutionary clause in the agreement itself; financial and technical assistance is granted via the (autonomous) PHARE instrument. The Council has now agreed to open negotiations with FYROM for an association agreement and draft negotiating directives have been prepared.[47] Albania has a first stage agreement establishing essentially basic MFN trade conditions, together with autonomous trade preferences renewed annually and PHARE assistance.[48] BiH has no agreement, but benefits from trade preferences, and from PHARE assistance although the latter is limited to assistance linked to the implementation of the peace plan. Croatia has no agreement or PHARE

[45] *Ibid.*, at 4.

[46] *Bull. EU* 4–1997, 132.

[47] Council Conclusions of 19 July 1999; on 8 Sept. 1999 the Commission adopted draft negotiating dirs. for an SAA with FYROM , IP/99/656. See further n. 51 *infra*.

[48] [1992] OJ L343/1. The existing trade preferences were upgraded in the wake of the Kosovo crisis in a new Reg. adopted on 29 July 1999 (Reg. 1763/99/EC [1999] OJ L211/1).

assistance, but benefits from autonomous trade preferences renewed annually. FRY has no agreement, no trade preferences (although it enjoyed these briefly for a period of a few months in 1997) and no PHARE assistance; on the contrary it is subject to economic sanctions such as the freezing of funds held abroad and prohibition of new investment.[49] The Community has difficulty differentiating between Serbia and Montenegro within FRY: the Commission in its reports differentiates between them, but all the measures covered by the regional approach (trade preferences, PHARE, negotiation of agreements) can only apply to states and therefore FRY is treated as a whole.[50]

The EC claims that progress for all these states up (or down) the ladder of trade preferences, financial assistance, and first and second stage agreements with a goal of association status, is subject to compliance with specific conditions, on the basis of regular assessments by the Commission. The most recent events in Kosovo have also indicated that progress in relations with the EU may be offered as a "reward" for helping with the immediate crisis and, longer term, maintaining a stance which conforms to western European political priorities (such as the EU position on Serbia), with a view—according to the EU—to promoting greater stability in the region.[51] The new stabilisation and association process, offering the possibility of association agreements for these states, as a "higher incentive" forming part of an enhanced approach, will also require compliance with "more demanding conditions, both political and economic".

Other examples of both positive and negative conditionality are easy to find, although in other cases we tend to see a one-off reaction to a particular situation, rather than a sustained policy such as that towards south-east Europe. For example, in early 1997 the EC reacted to the constitutional crisis in Belarus in terms which were closely tied to its relations with the EU: having expressed doubt about "the declared willingness of the Belarusian Government to work constructively with the EU and relevant international organisations towards establishing a political system which respects the internationally accepted

[49] An arms embargo has been in place since 1996, when the general economic sanctions against Serbia and Montenegro were lifted: Common Position 96/184/CFSP [1996] OJ L58/1. In March 1998 a Common Position on economic and political sanctions was adopted: 98/240/CFSP [1998] OJ L95/1; a number of measures threatened in the Common Position have now been adopted, including Reg. 926/98/EC [1998] OJ L130/1 implementing economic aspects.

[50] Although see Joint Action 98/301/CFSP in support of Montenegro [1998] OJ L138/1, intended to provide immediate assistance to the new government to continue economic and political reform. In addition in Jan. 1999 the Montenegrin national airline was exempted from the flight ban imposed on Yugoslav carriers in Sept. 1998.

[51] In Apr. 1999 the Special General Affairs Council in its Conclusions on Kosovo, noted the help being given to the refugees by Albania and held out the possible "reward" of upgraded relations as well as technical and financial advice and assistance. The Council adopted a very similar conclusion in relation to FYROM, and this message was endorsed by the Political Dialogue meetings between the EU and Albania and FYROM respectively, both held on 27 Apr. 1999. In June 1999 the Council invited the Commission to prepare a report on the feasibility of opening negotiations for a Stabilisation and Association Agreement with Albania. Following the Commission's positive report of 16 June on FYROM (COM(99)300), accepted by the Council on 19 July 1999, negotiating directives were adopted by the Council on 24 Jan. 2000, Press: 10-Nr 5046/00.

norms for human rights and political freedoms" the EU stated that "cooperation between EU Member States and institutions and Belarus cannot proceed in the absence of convincing efforts to establish such a system".[52] Later in 1997 the Council deplores the Belarusian authorities' "non-constructive, indeed obstructive, attitude to its relations with the European Union" and concludes that neither the EC not its Member States can yet formally conclude the Partnership and Co-operation Agreement (nor the interim trade agreement).[53] Implementation of Community technical assistance programmes (under TACIS) was halted, "except in the case of humanitarian or regional projects or those which directly support the democratization process"; and this led to the adoption of a TACIS programme for the development of civil society in Belarus, which might be seen as a positive measure designed to bring about an improvement in the conditions which had led to the negative refusal to conclude the PCA.[54]

The position taken towards Belarus was founded on the conditions attached to the PCAs, most notably respect for democracy, the rule of law and protection of human rights. Nevertheless we can see a differentiation between Russia and Ukraine (whose PCAs are now in force) on the one hand, and Belarus on the other, which is not simply founded on a refusal to conclude the PCA with a state which was not observing these "essential elements". The relative importance to the EU of the partners is clearly crucial. The 1995 war in Chechnya, although it caused some heart-searching, did not ultimately block the conclusion of either the interim agreement or PCA with Russia. While issuing statements deploring what was happening in Chechnya, the EU was also careful to stress that it "attaches importance to its relations with Russia . . . is concerned at the possible consequences of the crisis" and "that these relations must be based on the shared principles of the United Nations and the OSCE, as confirmed in the Partnership Agreement".[55]

Ward has suggested an even more substantial differentiation in the operation of the most obvious form of conditionality, the Community's insistence (or not) on including a "human rights" clause in its agreements: a differentiation based in part on the importance of the relationship from the Community's perspective, and in part on an unstated distinction which appears to be drawn between developing and industrialised countries.[56] Contractual relations between the EC and industrialised countries such as the USA and Australia are largely based on

[52] General Affairs Council, 29 Apr. 1997: Council Declaration on Relations with Belarus.

[53] General Affairs Council 15 Sept. 1997: Council Conclusions on Belarus.

[54] Council Decision 98/1/EC of 18 Dec. 1997 on a TACIS Civil Society Development Programme for Belarus for 1997 [1998] OJ L1/6.

[55] Presidency Statements on Chechnya, Brussels (17 Jan. 1995)—Nr. 4215/95 (Presse 11) CFSP: 2/95, and Brussels (23 Jan. 1995)—Nr. 4385/95 (Presse 24)—CFSP : 7/95. The importance of Russia for the EU is underlined by the fact that the first ever Common Strategy, adopted on 4 June 1999 under Art.13 TEU (as amended by the Treaty of Amsterdam) was on Russia.

[56] A. Ward, "Frameworks for Cooperation between the European Union and Third States: A Viable Matrix for Uniform Human Rights Standards?" (1998) 3 *EFA Rev*. 505. See also K. Smith, "The Use of Political Conditionality in the EU's Relations with Third Countries: How Effective?" (1998) 3 *EFA Rev*. 253.

sectoral agreements, and these have escaped the EC's policy of including human rights clauses in all trade and co-operation agreements.[57] Can one then argue that there is a policy of differentiation between developed and developing countries, whereby the Community will insist on an element of conditionality in its contractual relations with the latter—an element which itself forms a basis, as we have seen, for further differentiation?

It is hard to deny some element of differentiation here, and by its nature conditional differentiation is most effective when it is directed at states which are likely to be influenced by the incentives offered by the Community. We have also seen that economic and regional factors as well as conditionality form a basis for Community differentiation and that these are often linked: conditionality may be economic as well as political, for example. Differentiation in Community external policy is not simply a matter of treating developed and developing countries differently, or even differentiation between the more or less economically or politically powerful. Nor, while it takes account of some objectively assessable factors, is it simply a matter of the objective application of some kind of scale. It represents a highly nuanced relation to third states, based on the interplay of a number of objective and subjective factors, including the historical relationships of the Member States, their (various) current interests, the desire of the Community and—especially—the Union to forge an international identity and to assert its presence in its near neighbourhood. The Union is more than a large trading *bloc* and its agenda is wider, but one of its most potent instruments is still the trade/economic agreement offering market access (and in some cases financial and technical assistance). It is hardly surprising if trade relationships not only reflect but are instrumental in defining an emergent foreign policy.

The Community emphasis on sectoral agreements, rather than on general trade agreements, with the industrialised world has another dimension: the external constraint imposed by the GATT—and now WTO. In examining just what this means we will be moving on to a consideration of the different treaty options that are open to the Community and the flexibility shown by the Community in negotiating their substantive provisions.

3. FLEXIBILITY

A. Trade Provisions and Reciprocity

The most fundamental distinction in the possible options for the trade provisions within agreements is that between reciprocal and non-reciprocal preferential agreements. As an international institution which is bound by the GATT,

[57] Commission Communication on the inclusion of respect for democratic principles and human rights in agreements between the Community and third countries, 23 May 1995, COM(95)216 final; approved by Council on 29 May 1995.

and which is now a WTO contracting party, the EC is bound in its external economic relations by the basic MFN obligation found in Article 1 of the GATT 1947. Developing countries benefit from special exemptions under GATT rules which allow a developed member (such as the EC) to grant trade preferences without insisting on reciprocity.[58] Where, on the other hand, trade preferences are granted to a developed member, in order to comply with GATT these (i) will have to be based on reciprocity and (ii) will either have to be offered to all other GATT parties under the MFN obligation, or will need to fulfil the GATT conditions for free trade areas and customs unions which operate as an exception to the MFN obligation.

A fully reciprocal trade preference bilaterally negotiated and then offered to all other parties under MFN is not a viable proposition, so as between developed countries the effective choices are (i) a trade relationship based on MFN tariffs bound under GATT; or (ii) a GATT-compliant free trade (or customs union) agreement. The latter are by no means unknown, of course, having been concluded by the EC with the industrialised states of Europe, first as bilateral FTAs with the EFTA states, and then extended within the multilateral European Economic Area Agreement. It is noticeable, however, that these examples relate to countries within Europe. As the Commission points out in the context of notifications to GATT under Article XXIV, "the WTO Secretariat data contains very few examples of recent free trade agreements being concluded between parties which are not geographically contiguous or linked by other regional arrangements".[59]

The alternative to a full free trade area (which to satisfy GATT conditions must cover "substantially all" the trade between the parties and should not exclude any sector completely) is therefore to conduct trade on an MFN basis, with specific agreements designed to reduce non-tariff barriers such as (for example) mutual recognition of standards and conformity assessment and customs co-operation. So, for example, although in the early stages of the New Transatlantic Agenda agreed with the USA in 1995 there was discussion of a possible free trade agreement, the Transatlantic Economic Partnership (TEP) launched in May 1998 and the Action Plan adopted in November 1998 are based (as far as trade in industrial goods is concerned) on a common initiative to encourage further reductions of MFN tariffs within the multilateral context of the WTO. The Commission discussion document which preceded the TEP is clear about the reasons for this. In addition to the need to be seen to be supporting and not undermining the multilateral trading system, there is much more to be gained, in terms of EC–USA trade, by using the combined weight of these trading *blocs* to lever a generalised reduction in tariffs:

[58] See e.g. Art. XXXVI(8) GATT 1947.

[59] Commission report, "WTO Aspects of EU Preferential Trade Agreements with Third Countries", n. 39 *supra*. The EC's Global Agreement with Mexico is an exception here.

> much greater gains will accrue from the elimination of industrial tariff barriers on an MFN basis involving a broad range of other countries . . . the EU and the US will make a joint commitment that, in future multilateral negotiations, they will eliminate all industrial tariffs by 2010 if a critical mass of trading partners (understood in terms of volume of trade and/or numbers of countries) do the same. A bilateral preferential deal is thus ruled out.[60]

The TEP does not make an explicit joint commitment in quite this form, and limits itself to joint initiatives designed to reduce industrial tariffs multilaterally. But the reasoning behind a multilateral rather than bilateral approach in the case of major industrial trading partners is clear.

This tendency towards multilateralism is also evidenced in the reciprocal free trade agreements which have formed the basis of economic relations within the "wider Europe": with the EFTA states (the EEA and FTA with Switzerland), with Turkey, Malta and Cyprus (the Association Agreements and Customs Union), with the countries of central and eastern Europe (the Europe Agreements), south-east Europe (the Stabilisation and Association Agreements) and the Mediterranean states (the Euro-Med Agreements). Of these, only the EEA is in itself multilateral, but the others form part of a network of similar agreements, including horizontal agreements between the EC's partners, encouraged by the EC as part of its policy of promoting regional integration referred to earlier:

> the EU's preferential agreements do serve to open markets by pushing forward a pattern of tariff disarmament in partner countries, helping them to prepare for further multilateral liberalisation. . . . The EU has also been encouraging partners to join the WTO if they had not done so.[61]

The Partnership and Co-operation Agreements represent another network of agreements, with the emerging economies of the former Soviet Union. These are not (yet) free trade agreements. They are reciprocal but non-preferential agreements, establishing MFN treatment as far as tariffs are concerned and abolishing quantitative restrictions on industrial goods, so bringing these non-members of the WTO into a trading relationship with the EC on a par with its GATT-based multilateral framework. We have already noticed that it is the PCAs with the European states (Russia, Ukraine, Moldova, Belarus) which envisage the possibility (though without commitment) of a free trade agreement, thus supporting the conclusion that the general objective for trade relations within the "wider Europe" is based on free trade (and customs unions).[62]

[60] The New Transatlantic Marketplace, Communication of Sir Leon Brittan, Mr Bangemann and Mr Monti, 11 Mar. 1998.

[61] Commission report, "WTO Aspects of EU Preferential Trade Agreements with Third Countries", n. 39 *supra*.

[62] This reflects what the Commission has called the "strategic" dimension to preferential agreements, "to provide an economic dimension to wider agreements with neighbouring countries, with which more general co-operation was envisaged"; Commission report, "WTO Aspects of EU Preferential Trade Agreements with Third Countries", n. 39 *supra*.

Non-reciprocal preferential agreements—that is agreements which offer preferential access to the Community market in return for MFN treatment for Community goods—are fast becoming scarce. With the exception of the current agreement with FYROM, which is likely to replaced in the near future by an association agreement with the ultimate objective of reciprocal free trade, the most important is the Lomé Convention with the developing ACP states. It is worth noting that countries which might be eligible for preferences but which do not yet have agreements with the EC (such as Croatia), or whose agreements do not offer trade preferences (such as Albania, India or Brazil), are in general covered by autonomous trade preferences such as the General System of Preferences or the special regulations for former Yugoslavia. The Commission has suggested that ACP states deciding not to be part of the move toward reciprocity envisaged in the proposals for new co-operation agreements will continue to benefit from trade preferences within the GSP system.[63] Thus, unilateral non-reciprocal preferences are increasingly autonomous measures, not contractual obligations.

A tendency is becoming clear: a tendency to move towards greater levels of reciprocity in trade agreements. The old-style co-operation agreements with the Mediterranean states, such as Algeria or Morocco, which were non-reciprocal preferential agreements, are being replaced by the newer Euro-Med Agreements which envisage eventual reciprocal free trade. Even the Lomé Convention, the flagship of non-reciprocity for the developing countries, looks likely to be replaced with agreements which, although certainly not insisting on any fixed timetable for full reciprocity, are designed to lead in that direction. The Commission in its policy paper on guidelines for the negotiation of new co-operation agreements with the ACP countries states that the EU–ACP economic partnership must abandon "the traditional approach to trade" centred on a system of unilateral preferences, in favour of "a more balanced approach characterised by a genuine partnership and taking account of the parties' mutual interests".[64]

The model being proposed by the EC to the ACP includes regional agreements which may be either economic co-operation agreements (which although not totally reciprocal would contain an element of reciprocal treatment for EU exports with provision for further liberalisation) or economic partnership agreements (which would provide for the gradual establishment of reciprocal WTO-compliant free trade areas). Their trade provisions would establish differing degrees of reciprocity and appropriate timetables. The timing and length of the transitional periods, during which the (non-reciprocal) *status quo* in trading terms would be maintained, is proving to be a contentious issue in the negotiations which have now got under way. A waiver under Article IX WTO and/or Article XXIV(10) of the GATT would be required both to maintain existing

[63] COM(97)537 at sect. 5.4.
[64] COM(97)537 at sect. 5.1.

preferences during the negotiating period and for the non-reciprocal economic co-operation agreements. The long-term objective for the EU appears to be to achieve WTO-compliant free trade agreements with each of the ACP regions.[65] To the extent that non-reciprocal trade preferences survive, this will take the form of autonomous measures, in particular the GATT-compliant GSP system.

A highly significant precedent has been set with the signing earlier this year of a new trade, development and co-operation agreement with South Africa.[66] Existing EC relations with South Africa operate at a number of levels. South Africa has been a qualified member of the Lomé Convention since April 1997,[67] participating in the Lomé institutions but ineligible for both non-reciprocal trade preferences and access to funding from the European Development Fund (EDF).[68] There is also a 1994 co-operation agreement[69] which will be complemented by the new Free Trade Agreement, as well as sectoral agreements on science and technology, wine and spirits, and fisheries.

The new bilateral trade agreement has the ultimate objective of the establishment of a free trade area, complying with WTO rules, and covering the free movement of goods in all sectors, the ultimate liberalisation of trade in services, and the free movement of capital. The agreement will also cover economic co-operation, including trade and investment promotion and cross-border initiatives facilitating regional trade and investment. At the end of the transitional period the FTA will cover the bulk of trade[70] between the parties, with an element of differentiation between the two parties. Liberalisation will be asymmetric, with the Community proceeding more quickly, and South Africa able to exclude sensitive products to a greater extent than the EC, including products which are sensitive within Botswana, Namibia, Lesotho and Swaziland (BNLS

[65] "In the long run, the harmonisation of the preferences offered by the EU to all LLDCs and a proliferation of economic co-operation agreements compatible with the WTO, and in particular GATT Article XXIV on free-trade areas, would ultimately mean that the EU's future trade arrangements were perfectly in line with WTO provisions and require no exceptions": COM(97)537 at sect. 5.5.

[66] See "The European Union and South Africa: An Overview of the Relationship in the Light of the Conclusion of the Trade, Development and Cooperation Agreement", European Commission, Apr. 1999.

[67] Council Decision 97/535/EC on Decision 1/97 of the ACP–EC Council of Ministers approving the Protocol governing the accession of South Africa to 4th Lomé Convention as revised in Mauritius [1997] OJ L220/1.

[68] Instead, financial assistance is provided through autonomous Community regs.: Council Reg. 2259/96 on development co-operation with South Africa [1996] OJ L306/5; see also Reg. 213/96 on EC investment partners financial instrument (ECIP) for Latin America, Asia, Mediterranean, South Africa [1996] OJ L28/2.

[69] [1994] OJ L341/62. This Agreement is based on both the trade and development co-operation provisions of the EC Treaty (Arts. 133 and 181 (ex Arts. 113 and 130y) EC), and provides the basis for normalisation of EC—South Africa relations post-apartheid. It does not contain specific measures on trade but provides a basis for further negotiation.

[70] Agricultural products will be included although the Community proposes exceptions for products totalling about 39% of the EU's current agricultural imports from South Africa.

countries), with whom South Africa has a customs union (the Southern Africa Customs Union—SACU).[71]

One former Commissioner has referred to the objective of this Agreement as being to create a "Developmental Free Trade Area", "not just an old fashioned Free Trade Zone",[72] the difference apparently lying in the level of flexibility—the account that can be taken of South Africa's own developmental needs—and also the account taken of South Africa's relationship with its regional partners. The Commission sees the FTA as an instrument that will encourage regional economic integration (and thus fit into its priorities for the revised Lomé Convention). The projected Free Trade Agreement with South Africa will thus represent an interesting attempt to bring together WTO-compatible reciprocal free trade with differentiation and developmental objectives.

It is also possible to see this move towards reciprocity of trade liberalisation in the most recent EC agreement with Mexico. The Economic Partnership, Political Co-ordination and Co-operation Agreement between the EC, its Member States and the United Mexican States[73] is intended "to strengthen commercial and economic relations by means of the liberalization of trade in conformity with the rules of the WTO". The trade provisions of the agreement are designed to achieve "a bilateral and preferential, progressive and reciprocal liberalization of trade in goods and services, taking into account the sensitive nature of certain products and service sectors and in accordance with the relevant WTO rules" (Article 4). The Joint Council set up by the agreement will by decision establish the procedures and timetable for this progressive liberalisation.[74] The "relevant WTO rules" include Article XXIV of the GATT, so the ultimate objective is intended to be at least an Article XXIV-compliant free trade area, although the timetable for achieving this is left to the Joint Council to determine. Likewise for services, the Joint Council is to decide on the arrangements for a progressive and reciprocal liberalisation of trade in services, in accordance with the relevant WTO rules, in particular, Article V of the GATS. The Joint Council, consisting of the EU Council of Ministers, the

[71] According to the Commission, the EU will liberalise 95% of its South African imports within 10 years, whereas South Africa will liberalise 86% of its EU imports within 12 years. Under the terms of the SACU Treaty the BLNS countries will have to approve the FTA before it can enter into force: Commission paper of Apr. 1999, see above n. 66 *supra*. The BNLS countries are also fellow members of the Southern Africa Development Community (SADC) which in Aug. 1996 adopted a Trade and Development Protocol, designed to lead, within 8 years to the establishment of a free trade area. For an overview of the various regional integration agreements in Southern Africa, see Mörner, "Regional Integration And Trade Liberalisation In Southern Africa—An Overview" [1999] 2 *ITLQ* 85.

[72] João de Deus Pinheiro, former European Commissioner, "Building a New Framework for Trade and Co-operation with South Africa and the Other Countries in the Southern African Region", European Conference on Southern Africa, Maastricht, 17 Apr. 1997.

[73] [1997] OJ C350/6, COM(97)527.

[74] The decision of the Joint Council will deal with customs duties and charges having an equivalent effect, quantitative restrictions and measures having equivalent effect, the prohibition of fiscal discrimination, customs co-operation, technical regulations and standards, mutual recognition of conformity assessment, and exceptions and safeguard measures including anti-dumping (Art. 5).

European Commission and Members of the Government of Mexico, will have the power to take binding decisions and the speed at which trade liberalisation actually occurs will of course depend largely on the degree of commitment shown in the Joint Council and willingness to implement its decisions.[75]

What are the reasons behind the discernible move towards reciprocity and free trade not only within the wider Europe but further afield? Both the Agreements which have been signed (with South Africa and Mexico) and those that are projected as part of the renegotiation of Lomé put great emphasis on compliance with WTO rules, and there is no doubt that this is a factor. GATT rules on free trade have been tightened up to some extent by the Uruguay Round Agreements, especially in terms of the timetable for achieving a free trade area or customs union,[76] and are being taken more seriously, in part because there are so many more of them. The EC has an interest in its trading partners, which are increasingly entering into preferential agreements of their own, complying with WTO rules and is giving greater emphasis to doing so itself.

A further factor, which also lies behind the WTO approach to trade and development, is the (contested) view that developing countries will derive most benefit from full integration into the global economy. This emerges clearly in the Commission's statements on the renegotiation of the Lomé Convention.[77] Although, as we have seen, the Commission emphasises differentiation in the new agreements, particularly in order to take account of the needs of the least developed states (LLDCs), this should not rule out reciprocal liberalisation, in the context of regional integration, altogether: "[t]he benefits of taking part in an area of enhanced economic co-operation with the EU should outweigh any interim costs of liberalisation".[78] This "no gain without pain" attitude does however also recognise that reciprocity would require a "greater adjustment effort" from the LLDCs and these efforts "would have to be taken into account when assessing their needs and give rise to extra help in the form of flanking measures (transition aid, macroeconomic assistance, sectoral assistance etc.)".[79] Likewise, in discussing the new agreement with South Africa, the Commission recognises that the BNLS states within the SACU customs union will suffer "adjustment costs" as a result of opening up their markets to competition with EU producers, as well as a reduction in revenue from the lowering of tariffs. Nevertheless, the Commission states that "in the long term" the agreement will have a net positive effect for the BNLS countries.[80]

[75] Draft Decisions of the Joint Council were approved by the Commission on 18 Jan. 2000, see COM (2000) 9.

[76] The Understanding on the Interpretation of Art. XXIV in GATT 1994 states at para. 3 that the "reasonable length of time" by which a customs union or free trade area should be achieved "should exceed 10 years only in exceptional cases".

[77] For further discussion of the extent to which the proposed FTAs are likely to benefit the ACP states, see Faber, "Free Trade Areas as a Model for Future EU–ACP Relations", paper given at the Sixth ECSA Biennial International Conference, Pittsburgh, 2–5 June 1999 (on file with the author).

[78] COM(97)537 at sect. 5.3.

[79] *Ibid.*, at sect. 5.3.

[80] Commission paper of Apr. 1999, see n. 66 *supra*.

B. Flexibility and Asymmetry

Having identified a tendency, or even a policy, on the part of the EC which looks increasingly for reciprocal trade liberalisation from its partners, both bilaterally and multilaterally, we should now ask what degree of flexibility is, or can be, incorporated into these aspects of the EC's economic agreements. Flexibility in practice appears in two forms: first in relation to the timing of commitments, sometimes including an asymmetry in the timetable, and secondly in the levels of coverage and exemption and derogation allowed.

Flexibility as to timing operates in a number of ways. At one level, provision can be made to move from one type of commitment to another by means of staged new agreements: the evolutionary clause in the "European" PCAs, for example, or the current agreement with FYROM. The proposed new regional agreements with the ACP states would fall into this category too, specifying the period after which to assess the progress made towards liberalisation and to establish a timetable for subsequent stages, including the move towards regional economic partnership agreements which would provide for the gradual establishment of a free trade area. The Agreement with Mexico relies on a timetable to be established by the Joint Council, without giving a deadline. Clearly, there is a great deal of scope for flexibility here in terms of the timetable, although one should bear in mind that once a free trade agreement is concluded, the Article XXIV of the GATT time period expectation of ten years comes into play. Flexibility in timing can also include asymmetric timetables in the agreement itself, as is the case in both the Europe and Euro-Med Agreements and the prospective FTA with South Africa. Under this approach, the EC will dismantle its tariff barriers more quickly than the partner (often immediately), within the overall timetable and deadline.

Flexibility also appears in the level and types of exemption and derogation permitted by an agreement, and these may also be asymmetric. For example, the Europe and Euro-Med Association Agreements[81] both contain "infant industry" clauses allowing for the increase or re-introduction of customs duties by the partner state (not the EC) in derogation from the staged elimination of tariffs envisaged by the Agreements.[82] These are seen as exceptional measures and are subject to conditions including time limits and consultation requirements, but prior consent is not a requirement, underlining the element of flexibility here.

Although free trade agreements must cover substantially all trade between the parties in order to comply with GATT, they may be flexible in their treatment of sensitive products, either through differential timetables, or through exemptions and derogations. In the Euro-Med Agreement with Tunisia for example, although the EC is to remove all tariffs on industrial products immediately,

[81] With the exception of the Association Agreement with Israel.

[82] See e.g. Art. 14 of the Euro-Med Agreement with Tunisia, Art. 28 of the Europe Agreement with Poland.

Tunisia is to abolish duties on industrial goods according to a graduated timetable which varies according to the category of products listed in the Annexes. In the Agreement with Mexico, the Joint Council, in establishing the trade liberalisation programme, is to establish coverage and transitional periods, taking into account "the sensitive nature of certain products". The FTA with South Africa also contains derogations for products which are sensitive to the EC, to South Africa and to South Africa's customs union partners in SACU.

EC agreements have special provisions for agricultural products and normally do not envisage full liberalisation. This of course reflects both the historical difficulty of applying GATT disciplines to agricultural products and the particular history of the extreme sensitivity of the EU Member States to the idea of open competition and free trade in agricultural markets. The Commission has defended this stance as one of "careful liberalisation":

> GATT Article XXIV has never envisaged that a free trade area or customs union would require entirely free trade in all products between the participating members. . . . a more restrictive regime in agriculture remains possible in a manner consistent with Article XXIV provided the sector is itself covered and provided there is real liberalisation within that sector over the transitional period.[83]

Here, therefore, the EC's move has been away from complete exclusion of the sector (as was the case for example with the original FTAs with EFTA states) towards a commitment to negotiate further liberalisation on a product-by-product basis (a "positive list" approach), with plenty of scope for flexibility in terms both of timing and indeed the ultimate goal. The FTA with South Africa represents the most ambitious initiative so far in this respect, in that it would include agricultural products in the ultimate objective of free trade, subject to a "negative list" of sensitive products[84] (the negative list however comprising around 45 per cent of South African agricultural exports to the EC). Not surprisingly, the negotiations on agriculture have proved the most contentious aspect of the agreement (and others, such as the Euro-Med Agreement with Egypt). The fact remains that the flexibility for agricultural products in EC free trade agreements, while possibly defensible under current GATT rules, is generally more of a benefit to the EC than to its partners and sits uneasily with the EC position on the benefits of trade liberalisation for developing economies.

C. Liberalisation of Services

One further aspect of trade liberalisation should be mentioned. Increasingly, the EC defines trade to include trade in services as well as goods. Countries negotiating trade agreements with the EC can expect to find the liberalisation of

83 "The place of agriculture in free trade agreements", sect. IV of Commission report, "WTO Aspects of EU Preferential Trade Agreements with Third Countries", n. 39 *supra*.

84 *Inter alia* oranges and orange juice and wines.

services on the agenda, and the clauses on services are fairly standardised: a commitment framed in terms of GATS-based MFN treatment,[85] with the prospect of negotiated liberalisation in the light of future developments within GATS. These developments have been (and will be) to a great extent sector-based (financial services, telecommunications, information technology, maritime services etc.) and future bilateral negotiations are likely to reflect this aspect of services liberalisation, although this does not of course rule out "package deals" encompassing a number of sectors. Where the other party is a WTO member, the services provision will typically be phrased as a reaffirmation of existing GATS commitments (for example, the Euro-Med Agreement with Tunisia, the Europe Agreement with Poland). Where the party is not a WTO member, the clause will seek to achieve a broadly similar level of MFN obligation (for example, the Euro-Med Agreement with Jordan, the PCA with Russia). The Global Agreement with Mexico goes (potentially) further than most in providing—by means of decisions to be adopted by the Joint Council—for "a progressive and reciprocal liberalization of trade in services", in accordance with the relevant WTO rules, in particular, Article V of the GATS.

This increasing attention to services is clearly partly—indeed largely—the result of the GATS and sectoral negotiations within the GATS framework. However it is also evidence of a different phenomenon which we will explore more fully in the next section: the extension of external economic policy[86] beyond the customs union into other aspects of the internal market. The external dimension to the internal market was perhaps rather late in being recognised but its implications can no longer be ignored.[87] Leon Brittan has said that his "own instinct is that the current process of liberalising trade in services is not very different from the early steps to liberalise trade in goods".[88] We should not then be surprised at the rather cautious nature of the EC's position in relation to services, and its policy of maintaining a high degree of flexibility in its bilateral contractual commitments. However in practice this means that the EC's position bilaterally is effectively GATS-driven, following the position it is taking within multilateral GATS negotiations. While the EC does not show any sign of being keen to enter into full-scale bilateral liberalisation of services ahead of global liberalisation, negotiating partners which are not yet members of the WTO are likely to find that they are expected to make at least reciprocal MFN commitments to the EC in the services sector.

[85] The GATS-based MFN obligation is unconditional and not based on reciprocity; national treatment (full non-discrimination) is based on individual country commitments contained in schedules.

[86] Using this term in a more general sense which is not tied to Art. 133 (ex Art. 113) EC.

[87] See P. Eeckhout, *The European Internal Market and International Trade: A Legal Analysis* (Oxford: OUP, 1994); M. Cremona, "External Relations and External Competence: The Emergence of an Integrated Policy" in P. Craig and G. de Búrca (eds.), *EU Law: An Evolutionary Perspective* (Oxford: OUP, 1999).

[88] Leon Brittan, "WTO and Services: The Current and Future Agenda", Geneva, 24 June 1997.

D. Market Integration and Market Regulation

To further this discussion of flexibility within EC external economic policy, and particularly within economic agreements, we need to return to the question of the external dimension to the internal market, and its implications. Within the Community itself, market integration has been accompanied by—or rather has led to the need for—market regulation. Dismantling of trade barriers has led to the need for common policies on (*inter alia*) technical standards, certification systems, regulatory policies and competition rules. What I believe we are now seeing is a recognition by the EC that the already identified increased emphasis on reciprocal free trade leads to a need for a regulatory dimension to its external policy. To some extent this approach has been driven by the development of relations with the applicant states of central and eastern Europe. Alignment of their regulatory policies in relation to standards, competition, intellectual property, services etc. was an obvious part of their pre-accession preparation.[89] But the principle is a broader one, and covers agreements with states which have no prospect or desire for accession. The link between market integration and market regulation, including the issue of the level at which regulation should take place (international, regional, national etc.), is a question with which both the EC legal order and the WTO system have had to contend, and as we know the answers that have been given have not always been the same. This is not the place for a proper comparison of these approaches.[90] What we will do, however, is attempt to gain an impression of the EC approach to the link between liberalisation and regulation in the specific context of its external agreements. Our aim will be to see whether the EC is developing a policy stance in these areas which sets up (at the least) a presumption as to substantive content when negotiating agreements with third country partners.

One of the most striking features of Community agreements concluded within the last decade has been the inclusion of provisions on harmonisation or approximation of laws. In many cases a general clause is accompanied by provisions dealing with harmonisation of specific laws such as (for example) technical standards, competition or intellectual property protection. The most well known of such clauses are perhaps those found in the Europe Agreements. Here the parties declare that the major precondition for economic integration of the associated state into the Community is the approximation of existing and future legislation to that of the Community,[91] particularly in (among others) the fields

[89] E.g., Commission Communication on approximation of laws COM(94)391 final, 16 Sept. 1994; Commission "White Paper" COM(95)163 final, 3 May 1995.

[90] See e.g., J. Scott, "On Kith and Kine (and Crustaceans): Trade and Environment in the EU and WTO", Jean Monnet Working Paper 3/99. For a discussion of how the EC and WTO models have influenced each other, see S. Woolcock, "The European Acquis and Multilateral Trade Rules: Are they Compatible?" (1993)31 *JCMS* 539; P. Holmes and A. Young, "Exporting Rules: The European Union as Model for International Regimes?", paper given to the ECSA 6th Biennial International Conference, Pittsburgh, 2–5 June 1999 (on file with author).

[91] Art. 68 of the Europe Agreement with Poland.

of customs law, company law, banking law, intellectual property, financial services, consumer protection, indirect taxation, technical standards and the environment.[92] There are then further specific provisions among those dealing with economic co-operation dealing with, for example, intellectual property rights, the acceptance of EC industrial and agricultural standards, and protection of health and safety of workers. However there are also approximation clauses in the Euro-Med Agreements,[93] in the PCAs,[94] and very specific approximation commitments in the customs union agreement with Turkey.[95] In (almost[96]) every case, it is a matter of approximation to Community norms. As I have argued elsewhere, there is a real sense in which acceptance of Community standards is becoming a condition of liberalised market access, for services as well as goods.[97]

One reason for this is linked to the problems that may arise under WTO rules where states seek to impose their own standards on imports. As far as technical standards are concerned, the WTO rules are based on the principles of MFN and national treatment (subject to exceptions); these principles do not in themselves remove the barriers to trade caused by a multiplicity of different national standards, and the compatibility of even non-discriminatory standards with (for example) the WTO Agreement on the Application of Sanitary and Phytosanitary Measures (SPS Agreement)[98] is itself a problematic issue.[99] Within the EC such non-discriminatory barriers have been attacked by the twin weapons of mutual recognition and harmonisation, based on the Treaty itself and secondary legislation. A parallel approach is possible in international trade, within WTO rules. As the Commission has said in the context of EC–USA negotiations:

> two areas for bilateral (non-MFN based) co-operation exist . . . First, mutual recognition. . . . Members may bilaterally recognise the competence of their respective certification bodies. . . . Second, harmonisation. All Members are free to determine the specifications that products must meet, within certain general rules. Nothing prevents two countries from harmonising such specifications, provided that these are applied to other Members in a non-discriminatory manner.[100]

[92] *Ibid.*, Art. 69.

[93] Art. 52 of the Euro-Med Agreement with Tunisia. This is the general provision; there is also a specific reference to the "promotion" within Tunisia of Community technical rules and European standards for industrial and agri-food products and certification procedures, with the possibility of concluding agreements for the mutual recognition of certification: Art. 40.

[94] Art. 55 of the PCA with Russia.

[95] Turkey Customs Union Agreement [1996] OJ L35/1. Art. 52 is the general provision; specific provisions include Art. 37 on competition, and Arts. 12 and 26 on customs, anti-dumping and commercial defence measures.

[96] Art. 55 of the Association Agreement with Israel is an exception.

[97] See M. Cremona, "The European Union as an International Actor: Issues of Flexibility and Linkage" (1998) 3 *EFA Rev.* 67 at 86.

[98] [1994] OJ L336/40.

[99] See e.g. the WTO Appellate Body decision, *EC Measures Concerning Meat and Meat Products (Hormones)* which can be found on the WTO website at http://www.wto.org/wto/dispute.

[100] The New Transatlantic Marketplace, Communication of Sir Leon Brittan, Mr Bangemann and Mr Monti, 11 Mar. 1998.

Harmonisation is one way, therefore, of extending trade liberalisation bilaterally in conformity with WTO MFN obligations. But (as with reciprocity) there is more to it than this. In proposing a new partnership with the ACP states, the EU links enhanced co-operation "extended into a series of trade-related areas" to "integration in the world economy". In making the link, the Community is engaged not only in a market opening exercise for its own benefit and—as it sees it—for the benefit of the partner countries, it is also concerned to underpin this liberalisation with an open-market-based economic and legal infrastructure, just as an "open market economy with free competition" provides the basis for the Community's integration policies.[101] "Trade-related areas" include compliance with technical, health and safety standards, basic labour rights, environmental measures, investment protection, protection for intellectual property rights, trade in services, competition policy, consumer policy and access to public procurement.[102] The Community sees harmonisation of laws affecting trade in goods and services as part of the process of global economic integration which will benefit emerging economies and developing countries. As such it argues that harmonisation to EC standards is not only good for the EC in the sense that it diminishes "regulatory competition" on export as well as domestic markets, but regulatory convergence is good for the partner countries as well. The Commission has even argued that regulatory convergence towards EC norms will benefit third countries in that they will then benefit from any mutual recognition agreements that the EC concludes with major importers such as the USA.[103]

Competition policy provides a good example of this regulatory convergence and the imposition of Community norms within trade agreements, to differing degrees depending on the level of integration envisaged. International agreements may deal with competition policy in a number of different ways. First, there may be provisions solely concerned with competition as it affects trade between the contracting parties, and/or provisions concerned with competition within the domestic market of each party. Secondly, the provisions themselves may do any or all of the following (a) lay down certain core substantive principles, (b) provide for effective domestic enforcement of competition rules, (c) provide for technical assistance in developing regulatory capacity, (d) provide for co-operation between national (or Community) competition authorities, including provision for negative and positive comity.[104]

[101] Art. 4(1) (ex Art. 3a(1)) EC.

[102] COM(97)537 at sect. 5.1.

[103] "The New Transatlantic Marketplace", Communication of Sir Leon Brittan, Mr Bangemann and Mr Monti, 11 Mar. 1998, at sect. B(6). The EC has concluded MRAs with the USA, Canada, Australia, New Zealand, Switzerland and Israel, although the two latter agreements are not yet in force.

[104] These elements are often present in the provisions relating to intellectual property, which there is no space to examine here. In the case of intellectual property, however, the promotion of "regulatory discipline" will often include references to, or even a commitment to sign up to, international conventions (which do not so far exist for competition): see e.g. Art. 54 of the PCA with Russia, Art. 12 of the Global Agreement with Mexico.

The early FTAs with the EFTA states declared certain uncompetitive practices incompatible with the agreement in terms based on the language of the EC Treaty Articles 81 and 82 (ex Articles 85 and 86).[105] Enforcement was inter-state in nature, via the institutional dispute resolution procedures set up by the agreements. While these clauses laid down core principles (based on Community norms), they only applied to practices which affected trade between the parties in the context of the agreement. They did not seek to establish common harmonised competition rules at a domestic level, or even establish mechanisms for co-operation between competition authorities, and indeed the very different approaches of some of the EFTA states to competition policy issues was one of the attractions for the EC in drafting the competition provisions in the EEA. The EEA, at the other extreme, establishes a full-scale application of EC competition policy within the EEA territory, although by parallel enforcement agencies (the EC Commission and the EFTA Surveillance Authority).[106] The EEA, with its explicit attempt to create a "dynamic and homogeneous" area, is a special case of harmonisation. However, again within the last decade, the Community has adopted an approach which both links competition to economic integration and emphasises harmonisation. Devuyst has pointed out that the EC has been "very active in extending its own competition policy model to countries that do not yet have a tradition in the enforcement of antitrust rules. The instrument used to achieve this goal has been linkage with preferential and non-preferential trade agreements".[107]

Among the preferential trade agreements referred to by Devuyst the Europe Agreements are the pioneers. In its *Twenty-second Report on Competition Policy* (1992), the Commission stated:

> The Europe Agreements . . . do not envisage the same degree of economic integration and therefore do not contain the same ambitious rules as the EEA Agreement. However because the Europe Agreements aim at achieving greater economic integration than the Agreements concluded with the EFTA countries in 1972, their competition rules go beyond those contained in the latter.

The rules in the Europe Agreements "go beyond" the EFTA agreements of the 1970s by imposing a two-fold obligation on the partner countries, covering domestic competition policy as well as competition issues related to trade between the contracting parties. As with other trade agreements, provisions containing the principles of Articles 81, 82 and 87 (ex Articles 85, 86 and 92) EC

[105] E.g., see EEC–Swiss FTA [1972] OJ L300/188, Arts. 23 and 27.

[106] EEA [1994] OJ L1/1, Arts. 53–60 and Protocols 21–27; Agreement between EFTA States on establishing EFTA SA and EFTA Court [1994] OJ L344/1. For comment see Diem, "EEA Competition Law" (1994) 5 *ECLRev*. 263.

[107] Y. Devuyst, "The International Dimension of the EC's Antitrust Policy: Extending the Level Playing Field" (1998) 3 *EFA Rev*. 459 at 469. See also A. Jacquemin, "The International Dimension of European Competition Policy" (1993) 31 *JCMS* 91; J. Bourgeois, "Competition Policy and Commercial Policy" in M. Maresceau (ed.), *The EC's Commercial Policy after 1992: The Legal Dimension* (Dordrecht, Kluwer, 1993).

with reference to trade between the parties are included.[108] But, in the interests of consistency in the application of the rules, these provisions go further by making explicit reference to the EC Treaty Articles: assessment of practices contrary to these provisions shall be made on the basis of "criteria arising from the application" of Articles 81, 82 and 87 EC.[109] Implementing rules are drawn up by Association Council decision, establishing enforcement mechanisms and procedures which (taking place at national level by national competition authorities) are likely to be more effective than the inter-state mechanisms of the early free trade agreements.[110] The implementing rules that have been adopted also contain provision for co-operation between enforcement agencies similar to that found in the co-operation agreements concluded by the EC in cases where the EC's trading partner already has a fully functioning competition policy and harmonisation is not an issue.[111] The second level of obligation imposed by the Europe Agreements on the partner country is the obligation to align its own competition laws with those of the Community, including the establishment of effective enforcement agencies.[112] The Europe Agreements thus contain elements of each of the four aspects of competition policy provision mentioned above. The Euro-Med Agreements contain almost identical provisions in relation to the application of competition rules modelled on Community rules to trade between the parties; the harmonisation provision is less specific but capable of encompassing competition policy.[113]

The Turkey Customs Union Agreement, envisaging a closer degree of economic integration with the Community, imposes even more stringent competition policy requirements. It contains substantive copies of Articles 81, 82 and 87 EC including, significantly, an actual prohibition of anti-competitive conduct as opposed to a mere declaration of incompatibility, and also including the equivalent of Article 81(2) EC, so that prohibited agreements are automatically void (the EEA is the only other agreement to do this). The Turkey Agreement also contains very specific approximation of laws provisions with respect to competition policy: Turkey was to pass a competition law modelled on that of the EC (including block exemption regulations and "the case law developed by the EC

[108] Art. 63(1) of the Europe Agreement with Poland. Industrial products and services are covered; exclusions operate for agricultural and fisheries products and coal and steel products (the latter are dealt with in a separate protocol).

[109] *Ibid.*, Art. 63(2).

[110] *Ibid.*, Art. 63. Implementing rules were adopted by the EC–Poland Association Council [1996] OJ L208/24. For comment see Van den Bossche, "The International Dimension of EC Competition Law: The Case of the Europe Agreements" (1997) 18 *ECLR* 24.

[111] See in particular, the EC–USA Agreement on competition [1995] OJ L95/45; the Agreement between the EC and the USA on the application of positive comity principles in the enforcement of competition laws [1998] OJ L173/26; see also the proposal for a Council and Commission Decision concluding the Agreement between EC and Canada regarding the application of their competition laws, COM(98)352 final.

[112] Art. 69 of the Europe Agreement with Poland.

[113] Arts. 36–38 of the Euro-Med Agreement with Tunisia establish the primary obligation. Art. 52 provides that "cooperation shall be aimed at helping Tunisia to bring its legislation closer to that of the Community in the areas covered by this Agreement".

authorities"), and establish a competition authority, before the entry into force of the customs union.[114] As a corollary, there is the possibility of reviewing the trade defence mechanisms, especially the anti-dumping clause, in the light of an effective enforcement of competition rules, a provision which links trade liberalisation to effective regulatory mechanisms in an unusually explicit way.[115] Neither the Europe Agreements nor the Euro-Med Agreements contain such undertakings.

As we have seen, the Global Agreement with Mexico envisages the eventual establishment of a free trade area in both goods and services, and so one would expect extensive competition provisions. In keeping with the style of this agreement, however, the enactment of substantive provisions is left to the Joint Council. The Council is to "establish mechanisms of cooperation and coordination among their authorities with responsibility for the implementation of competition rules", a co-operation procedure similar to that in the specific co-operation agreements with the USA and Canada. However the Joint Council also has within its remit the adoption of rules relating to practices covered by Articles 81 and 82 as well as mergers, state monopolies and public undertakings.[116]

Among the non-preferential agreements, the competition provisions in the PCAs provide a good example of differentiation. In keeping with the fact that they are not free trade agreements, the provisions on competition are more limited, and they do not use the terminology of Articles 81, 82 or 87 in their reference to anti-competitive practices. In the "European" PCAs, such as that with Russia, the parties agree "to work to remedy or remove through the application of their competition laws or otherwise, restrictions on competition by enterprises or caused by State intervention insofar as they may affect trade between the Community and Russia". This "work" will include ensuring that the parties "have and enforce laws addressing restrictions on competition by enterprises within their jurisdiction"[117] and "rules on competition" are among the areas covered by the approximation of laws provision: "Russia shall endeavour to ensure that its legislation will be gradually made compatible with that of the Community".[118] Restrictions and distortions of competition will be dealt with by consultation within the institutions set up by the Agreement (no implementing rules are envisaged). The provisions in the "non-European" PCAs are more

[114] Art. 37 of the Turkey Customs Union Agreement, which came into force on 1 Jan. 1996. Turkish legislation on competition has been adopted: see Law No. 4054 on Protection of Competition, Official Gazette 22140, 13 Dec. 1994; Law No. 97/9090 on Appointment of the Competition Board, Official Gazette 22918, 27 Feb. 1997. See WTO Secretariat Report and government policy statement for WTO Trade Policy Review Body in Oct. 1998, available at http://www.wto.org/wto/reviews/turkey.htm.

[115] Art. 42 of the Turkey Customs Union Agreement. The EEA makes a similar link: under Art. 26 and Protocol 13, anti-dumping measures are prohibited between the EEA parties, but only as regard those areas in which the *acquis communautaire* is fully accepted.

[116] Art. 11 of the Global Agreement with Mexico. See Annex XV of the draft decision of the Joint Council, COM(2000) 9.

[117] Art. 53 of the PCA with Russia. This Art. also includes provision for state aids, state monopolies and public undertakings.

[118] Art. 55 of the PCA with Russia.

embryonic: competition is included in the provision on approximation of laws, together with technical assistance from the Community, and "the Parties agree to examine ways to apply their respective competition laws on a concerted basis in such cases where trade between them is affected".[119]

What conclusions can we draw from this range of agreements? As is evidenced also by the Commission's efforts in the multilateral framework of the WTO, the Community is concerned that trade liberalisation should be accompanied by more effective regulatory disciplines, and preferably commonly agreed principles. The Commission has argued for "a close connection between competition law and policy and the WTO market opening objectives"[120] and more generally that "further liberalisation in the WTO should be underpinned by multilateral rules bringing not only transparency, fairness and predictability, but also promoting sustainable development and other concerns".[121] In this global, multilateral context, the Commission has stressed the flexibility of its approach to establishing common rules and has emphasised, alongside effective enforcement and international co-operation between regulators, the need for core principles based on the existing WTO values of non-discrimination and transparency. In all current bilateral trade agreements some degree of commitment to the principles of free competition is expected, with the commitments being more rigorous and—importantly—more clearly based on the Community model in the case of countries with which a high degree of integration is envisaged (free trade and customs union agreements).

This is not merely a question of a closer economic relationship requiring a greater degree of convergence. Community competition policy is specifically designed to operate within a context of commitment to cross-border market integration and the appropriateness of its approach to issues such as vertical restraints may be open to question outside this context.[122] There is evidence, then, not only that trade liberalisation will carry with it a need for regulatory measures, but also that the EC regulatory model, having been designed with market integration as its leading objective and having developed (unlike the regulatory systems of a unitary state) within a system of multi-level governance, appears an obvious starting point especially in a bilateral context. As Holmes and Young point out, the EC institutions (courts as well as legislature) have had considerable experience in developing strategies for resolving "the tension

[119] Art. 44 of the PCA with Kazakhstan [1999] OJ L196/1.

[120] "The EC Approach to Trade and Competition", preparation for the Seattle Third Ministerial Conference (30 Nov.–3 Dec. 1999), available on http://europa.eu.int/comm/dg01/newround/sea-comp.htm. See also Commission Communication of 17 June 1996, "Towards an International Framework of Competition Rules", COM(96)284; Singapore Ministerial Declaration, WTO Ministerial Conference, 13 Dec. 1996.

[121] Commission Communication "The EU Approach to the Millennium Round", 5, available on http://europa.eu.int/comm/dg01/dg1newround.htm.

[122] "Community competition policy therefore, unlike competition policy of Member States or our trading partners, has not only had to take account of the need for a system of undistorted competition but also the market integration objective": Commission Green Paper on Vertical Restraints in EC Competition Policy COM(96)721 at 1.

between trade liberalisation and regulatory sovereignty". They argue, in the context of multilateral liberalisation, that "[t]he EU's strength as a potential model for the world system is its history of seeking to create a regulated balance between open markets for their own sake and the right of governments to safeguard legitimate public policy objectives".[123] However the emphasis—in Community agreements—on the export of substantive norms and standards underplays a significant element of the Community approach: the importance of procedure and process in achieving the "regulated balance". The multi-player, multi-level nature of the system is a crucial factor in the regulatory outcome. In the next section we will explore some of the implications for external policy of this characteristic of the European economic constitution.

4. THE ECONOMIC CONSTITUTION

This chapter has, so far, set out two connected arguments: first, that differentiation of an increasingly developed kind between its trading partners is a noticeable feature of current EC and EU external policy, and this will affect the type of relationship "offered" to the third country and the consequent level of economic integration envisaged. "Partnership", "cooperation", "association", "developmental", "framework" and even now "stability" are a few of the terms used. Partnership is often used where a close relationship is desired, either within the wider Europe or as part of development policy; framework agreements are used as the basis for more extensive commitments that are not (yet) on a partnership level. These categories are becoming more important than the legal base-founded categories of association and "simple" trade agreements. This differentiation depends on geographic and geopolitical priorities, as well as political and economic status (or conditionality), and is by no means static, in that third countries can and do "progress" from one kind of relationship or agreement to another.

Secondly, we have established a number of substantive priorities in the conclusion of economic integration agreements by the EC. First is the move towards reciprocal free trade, and away from non-reciprocal preferences. Second is the emphasis on establishing a degree of "regulatory discipline" which may involve harmonisation or approximation to Community models, and which covers broadly trade-related issues including technical standards, competition policy and intellectual property. The emphasis on the Community model will be stronger where a greater degree of integration is envisaged, and/or where the

[123] P. Holmes and A. Young, n. 88 *supra*, 26. The Commission has also pointed to the relevance of the Community model in the WTO context: "[t]he experience of the EU itself has demonstrated that further liberalisation (through both the creation of a single European market and through multilateral obligations), underpinned by policies aimed at improving social conditions and sustainable development, can be carried out in a way that optimises the benefits of globalisation, mitigates negative effects, and creates net welfare gains": Commission Communication, "The EU Approach to the Millennium Round", n. 121 *supra*, 4.

agreement is envisaged as supporting a major economic and legislative reform programme in the partner state.

Both these factors impose a constraint, or a lack of flexibility, in the EC's negotiations with its trading partners. To a considerable extent, the EC will offer a package of provisions that fits its own conception of differentiation and its own views of what level of integration is desirable, and will "tailor" the regulatory provisions accordingly.

We shall now turn, rather more briefly, to a final question. At the risk of greatly over-simplifying, the Community's model of economic integration may be characterised as "constitutional", with its "essential characteristics" such as primacy over national law, the creation of individual rights, and institutionalised decision-making and judicial review procedures, operating not merely alongside but as a part of its economic law provisions. Where the EU makes demands, or creates expectations that its trading partners will conform to Community standards (political as well as technical) and regulatory disciplines, we speak of the Community (or Union) "model" but this does not necessarily imply that the relationship with the partner state will share the characteristics of the Union's constitution. To put it another way, could the spill-over effect which leads from market integration to market regulation lead further down the path of economic constitutionalism? The Union itself represents a multi-dimensional system within which inter-connected legal orders reflect differentiated integration.[124] Are we seeing, in the partial extension of the "Community acquis" to some third states, the boundaries of the Community legal order becoming more porous so that the distinction between being "in" or "out" is blurred?

Whether or not this may happen in the future, the evidence is that it has not happened yet. This is not just a matter of content, of "gaps" in the essential elements of the Community *acquis* in even the most integrationist agreements, such as the fact that horizontal or flanking policies such as environmental policy and social policy are barely touched upon: the substantive content of the Community's economic constitution will always be contested. Even where rules are adopted which follow the Community model, in relation to tariff and non-tariff barriers for example, their interpretation will not necessarily mirror that of the equivalent EC provisions: the Court has said that Community agreements are an "integral part" of the Community legal order,[125] but equally similarity of terms does not by itself imply identical interpretation, as terms need to be read in the context of their objectives and the framework within which they are designed to operate.[126] Interestingly, one of the reasons given for this conclusion in the *Polydor* case (in the context of a free trade agreement with then non-

[124] N. Walker, "Sovereignty and Differentiated Integration in the European Union" (1998) 4 *ELJ* 355.

[125] Case 181/73, *Haegeman* v. *Belgium* [1974] ECR 449, para. 5.

[126] Case 270/80, *Polydor Ltd. and RSO Records Inc.* v. *Harlequin Record Shops Ltd. and Simons Records Ltd.* [1982] ECR 329, paras. 14–18.

member Portugal) was the absence in the agreement of an institutional structure capable of achieving a balance between market integration and market regulation:

> the instruments which the Community has at its disposal in order to achieve the uniform application of Community law and the progressive abolition of legislative disparities within the common market have no equivalent in the context of the relations between the Community and Portugal.[127]

This institutional structure is not only a mechanism for creating common principles or harmonised norms. It is a means of reconciling conflicting and competing interests, a key element of the constitutional process that is itself a key to the Community's legal and political order. Community agreements with third countries are far from possessing even the necessary infrastructure for such a constitutional model of integration. To the extent to which third states are expected to conform to Community regulatory norms, neither they nor their citizens have any real involvement in the decision-making processes, legislative or judicial, which give rise to those norms and which have to undertake the concomitant complex balancing of interests. Arrangements for consultation are included in the EEA and Turkey Customs Union Agreement, and are a *de facto* part of the pre-accession partnership but the decision-making autonomy of the Community legal order has never really been compromised.[128] The conditionality, both political and economic, which plays an increasingly important part in Community external policy, requires third states to conform to standards, principles and objectives (such as increased regional integration) set by the Community itself. Neither does forming an integral part of the Community legal order necessarily imply that the nature and structure of an agreement are such as to give rise to the creation of directly enforceable individual rights.[129] In the *Hermès* ruling the Court is more concerned with its interpretative jurisdiction and the preservation of uniformity of interpretation (and thereby the integrity of the Community legal order) than with the issue of individual rights.[130] The position of nationals of third states within the Community legal order, even in the context of economic integration agreements, is still precarious.

[127] *Ibid.*, para. 20.

[128] On decision-making within the EEA, see *Opinion 1/91: Re the Draft Agreement on a European Economic Area* [1991] ECR I–6079, and M. Cremona, "The 'Dynamic and Homogeneous' EEA: Byzantine Structures and Variable Geometry" (1994) 19 *ELRev*. 508. On the Turkish Customs Union Agreement, see S. Peers, "Living in Sin: Legal Integration under the EC-Turkey Customs Union" (1996) 7 *EJIL* 411.

[129] Cases 22–24/72, *International Fruit Company NV & Others* v. *Produktschap voor Groenten en fruit* [1972] ECR 1219; Case 104/81, *Hauptzollampt Mainz* v. *Kupferberg* [1982] ECR 3641; Case 12/86, *Demirel* [1987] ECR 3719; Case C–280/93, *Germany* v. *Council (bananas)* [1994] ECR I–4973. It goes without saying, perhaps, that any decision of the ECJ on the direct effect or otherwise of a Community agreement is operative only within the Community legal order, not that of the other Contracting Party/ies.

[130] Case C–53/96, *Hermès International* v. *FHT Marketing Choice BV*, [1998] ECR I–3603. Tesauro AG does however put forward an interesting argument which links reciprocity of obligation with direct effect at paras. 32–33.

And yet neither does this absence of participation in the institutional framework and unilateral adoption of Community norms fit the classic "WTO model" of economic agreement based on mutually advantageous reciprocity of rights and obligations.[131] Community agreements may be designed to comply with WTO criteria, but the degree of differentiation and (lack of) flexibility in the Community's external economic policy sits somewhat uneasily with WTO concepts of non-discrimination and mutuality. In discussing the export of Community norms in a multilateral context Holmes and Young rightly point out that "where one jurisdiction (whether the EC or the US) succeeds in persuading others of the desirability of adopting their system as a model, the price of this exporting of the system is that it can take on a life of its own in the outside world".[132] The WTO model is, despite arguments supporting its constitutionalisation,[133] one which as yet "merely" creates rights and obligations between the Contracting Parties; although it may be moving in that direction it is still some distance away from the EU's "constitutional charter based on the rule of law".[134] Nevertheless, within the WTO the EC is having to come to terms with the dynamism of a system with an increasingly independent and judicialised dispute settlement procedure.

Outside the multilateral (WTO) context however, the absence of reciprocity in the regulatory process, as opposed to increased reciprocity in relation to substantive obligation, is a striking feature of Community external policy. If one aspect of the debate surrounding flexibility in the post-Amsterdam Union concerns the extent to which it is possible to identify a core of essential commitments within the economic constitution and thus beyond any opting out or in, and the procedures necessary to safeguard Member States' interests in the exercise of "closer co-operation", the integration model which the Community is offering to third countries appears to combine a set of standardised commitments with the absence of both procedural transparency and the processes needed to underpin a constitutional project.

131 Admittedly also an ideal more than reality.

132 P. Holmes and A. Young, n. 88 *supra*, 24.

133 See e.g. U. Petersmann, *The GATT/WTO Dispute Settlement System. International Law, International Organisations and Dispute Settlement* (The Hague: Kluwer Law International, 1997) The Hague.

134 Cf. *Opinion 1/91: Re the Draft Agreement on a European Economic Area* [1991] ECR I–6079. See also Case C–149/96 *Portugal* v. *Council*, judgment of 23 Nov. 1999.

5

Flexibility and the European Court of Justice

CAROLE LYONS*

1. INTRODUCTION

THE PURPOSE of this chapter is to discuss the ways in which the Amsterdam Treaty changes on "flexibility" (enhanced or closer co-operation) will affect the role of the European Court of Justice. It is about the functioning of the Court as an institution in the new institutional architecture of the differentiated Union. The objective is to offer an insight into the potential impact of the co-operation provisions on the approach of the Court and to explore how the operation of flexibility may in practice affect the Court's role and function. The argument focuses on some aspects of the restructured judicial architecture which result from the Treaty changes as they relate to flexibility. In addition, the discussion makes tentative suggestions as to how the flexibility provisions may be affected by the Court's perspective.

Concern about the role of the Court inevitably leads to questions about the role of law in a differentiated or multi-speed European Union. This concern manifested itself loudly at the time of the Maastricht Treaty, especially in the context of the Social Policy Agreement and the UK "opt-out", a primitive form of closer co-operation which emerged as result of IGC negotiation stalemate. The impact of this opt-out on the nature of EC law was a primary concern of legal writers after the Treaty.[1] Much of the writing at the time was dedicated to understanding how the uniformity of EC law was affected by the Maastricht Treaty having created a level of EC law which would not apply to all of the Member States. However, as many of the chapters in this collection demonstrate, the idea that all EC legislation applied equally to all Member States was

* Many thanks go to Gráinne de Búrca, Joanne Scott and Neil Walker for helpful advice and comments.

[1] See, e.g., J. Shaw, "Twin-Track Social Europe—the Inside Track" in D. O'Keeffe and P. Twomey (eds.), *Legal Issues of the Maastricht Treaty* (London: Wiley Chancery, 1994) and C.-D. Ehlermann, "Increased Differentiation or Stronger Uniformity" in J.A. Winter *et al.*, (eds.), *Reforming the Treaty on European Union, The Legal Debate* (The Hague: Kluwer, 1996). On another system of opt-outs under the Maastricht arrangements for EMU see generally P. Beaumont and N. Walker (eds.), *Legal Framework of the Single European Currency* (Oxford: Hart, 1999).

not new even at the time of the TEU.[2] Similar concerns arise in relation to the EMU opt-outs. Nonetheless, there is a significant difference between the kind of unequally applied law referred to in these chapters and the social policy development under the TEU. The development of European Union social policy is seen by many to be at the heart of European integration in terms of commitment to Treaty objectives and a more general reflection of Member State attitudes to a vision of a "social Europe". Politically, this form of flexibility was far more significant than, for example, disequilibrium in the application of EC law in various extra-European territories of the Member States. Another significant difference is that the role of the Court and, importantly, the status of the law in question, are clearly regulated or pre-established in the case of the forms of differentiated integration which occurred before Maastricht. Under the TEU, in contrast, the Member States were feeling in the dark towards some workable form of differentiation on social policy development, IGC compromise being prioritised over a coherent and recognisable judicial system for the EU. The provisions on flexibility which have been placed in the Treaties after Amsterdam are the product of considered reflection on some of the defects of the cruder system which emerged from the Maastricht IGC. In so far as the ECJ is concerned, its role has been taken into account in the closer co-operation framework and outlined in the Treaties. The identification of formal changes in the Court's institutional role, although the primary focus of this chapter, is not the main concern in coming to an understanding about how flexibility will be judicially affected. Of deeper significance is the question of how properly institutionalised flexibility will affect the "traditional" role of the ECJ as the constitutional court of a relatively uniform EU.

The ToA "has introduced what one may call a principle that derogates from the traditional canons of unity and uniformity of Community law".[3] A significant (though obvious) remark in this respect is that the introduction of flexibility into this Treaty does not mean that the Court's role has been made more flexible. In fact the opposite is true, and the various modalities of variable geometry and flexibility which have been introduced into the Treaties under the ToA have a globally constraining effect on the ECJ, arguably limiting its autonomy and placing limits on its jurisdiction. Increasing the potential for flexibility in the EU is the general aim of the ToA, but the closer co-operation and variable geometry provisions, as well as the various opt-ins and opt-outs and how they impact on the ECJ, lead to complexity and confusion concerning its role.

In many ways, the fact that such a discussion is far from being the sole or primary focus of a work dedicated to an analysis of flexibility is indicative of the location of the flexibility changes at another level of constitutional development of the EU. The impact of closer co-operation on the Court of Justice was not the

[2] See Chs. 3 and 6 in this collection and also H. Kortenberg, "Closer Cooperation in the Treaty of Amsterdam" (1998) 35 *CMLRev.* 833 and C.-D. Ehlermann, "Differentiation, Flexibility, Closer Co-operation: The New Provisions of the Amsterdam Treaty", (1998) 4 *ELJ* 246.

[3] G. Gaja, "How Flexible is Flexibility under the Amsterdam Treaty?" (1998) 35 *CMLRev.* 855.

primary concern of the Treaty negotiators at Amsterdam. Nor was the flexible future of the EU considered primarily as a legal issue. Understanding the full impact of flexibility can be aided through observing the changes to the Court's jurisdiction, but these changes are not central to the redefined institutional mosaic. In providing for future flexibility under the ToA, the role of the Court was not centre stage.

The chapter attempts to expose the issues arising from the fundamental changes in the role of the Court brought about by the Amsterdam Treaty. Article 220 (ex Article 164) EC is now far from adequate as a basic indication of the Court's jurisdiction. The expansion and diversification of the Court's role across the Treaties was a process which began under the TEU. The Social Policy Agreement and the primitive flexibility which that entailed specifically affected the scope of the Court of Justice to review the effect of SPA derived law on the non-participating UK. Secondly, the establishment of the pillars and the creation of the potential for EU law, closely bordering EC law but not subject to the power of the Court, led to ambiguity surrounding the Court's role and to a specific limitation of the Court's role in this respect (as detailed under the then Article L TEU). The Amsterdam Treaty has rendered the situation much more complex but subject to less ambivalence, in that the Court's jurisdiction is now more precisely delineated and defined. The question is, do these fundamental changes represent "[u]ne régression de contrôle juridictionnel"[4] or can these crucial alterations to the judicial branch be seen as a positive development?

The chapter is structured in the following way: part 2 deals with ways in which the Treaty of Amsterdam changes impact generally on the ECJ but focuses specifically on the way in which a differentiated judicial role results from these changes. Part 3 looks at the enhanced co-operation provisions and the role of the Court within the new framework for managing differentiation in the Union. Part 4, finally, analyses these changes in terms of the likely impact on the approach and function of the ECJ, making a series of observations and indicating potential areas of particular interest as to the possible future position of the Court under the closer co-operation regime.

2. THE COURT IN A DIFFERENTIATED LEGAL ORDER

Before the changes introduced by the Amsterdam Treaty, Article L (now Article 46) TEU outlined the framework for judicial input into EU law and policy-making. The amended Article L, now Article 46, TEU is the starting point for the observation of the Court's role in the post-ToA EU in general, but also for the specification of its power over closer co-operation provisions. The boundaries of the Court's functions are more blurred after the Amsterdam amendments and the system of jurisdiction much more complex. The new position of

[4] H. Labayle, "Le Traité d"Amsterdam. Un espace de liberté, de securité et de justice"(1997) 33 *RTDE* 851 at 862.

the limits of ECJ jurisdiction after Amsterdam resembles a very patchy structure,[5] in which the amended Article 46 TEU offers the first indication of the scope of the Court's powers. There are several ways in which the general jurisdiction of the Court of Justice has been altered or affected by the terms of the Amsterdam Treaty.[6] These are: the conditional extension of the Court's jurisdiction to rule on matters covered by the (restructured) Third Pillar,[7] on matters of fundamental human rights,[8] jurisdiction over the flexibility framework (Title VII TEU) as well as limited jurisdiction over the new Title on visas, immigration and asylum under the EC (Title IV EC) and over the related Protocols.[9] Furthermore, the Court's jurisdiction can also alter and expand in a differentiated manner outside the context of Treaty amendments, through instruments such as Conventions between Member States, for example, the Brussels Convention or the Europol Convention.[10]

The alterations to the Court's role reflect the widespread concerns expressed after the Maastricht Treaty about the limited function of the Court in the adjudication of measures arising then under the Third Pillar and also the shallowness and hypocrisy of the relatively meaningless declaratory character of the non-justiciable fundamental human rights clause.[11] Comments at the time were rooted in concern about the development of EU policy and legislation without the effective judicial supervision of the ECJ. In respect of these changes therefore, the Amsterdam negotiations can be said to have taken account of the defects concerning the role of the Court. There is in the new Treaty system, in other words, a commitment to have the Court involved as an institutional actor in the new policy developments of the EU and to have some text based representation of the ECJ role in the fundamental rights sphere.

The Maastricht Treaty had heralded a new era for the Court of Justice, in terms of its jurisdiction being excluded from significant areas of EU activity. To an extent, the Amsterdam Treaty has remedied this by a combination of "communitarisation" (bringing some third Pillar areas within the remit of the EC pillar) and also the extension of the Court's jurisdiction under other changes made

[5] R. Dehousse, "European Institutional Architecture after Amsterdam: Parliamentary System or Regulatory Structure?" (1998) 35 *CMLRev*. 595 at 596.

[6] Art. 46 TEU (ex Art. L TEU) defines the new limits of the Court's jurisdiction. The Court's powers are stated to apply only to the EC Treaty (and ECSC and Euratom Treaties), the provisions of Title VI TEU (but subject to the conditions laid out thereunder in Art. 35 TEU), the provisions of Title VII TEU, under the conditions provided for by Art. 11 EC and Art. 40 TEU and, finally, Art. 6 TEU. See A. Albors-Llorens, "Changes in the Jurisdiction of the European Court of Justice under the Treaty of Amsterdam" (1998) 35 *CMLRev*. 1273 for comprehensive treatment of the Court's general position after Amsterdam.

[7] Art. 35 (ex Art. K.7) TEU.

[8] Art. 6(2) (ex Art. F) TEU.

[9] Protocol on the position of the UK and Ireland, Protocol on the position of Denmark and Protocol integrating the Schengen Acquis into the framework of the EU.

[10] See further P. Beaumont, "European Court of Justice and Jurisdiction and Enforcement of Judgments in Civil and Commercial Matters" (1999) 48 *ICLQ* 223.

[11] See, generally, D. O'Keeffe and P. Twomey (eds.), *Legal Issues of the Maastricht Treaty* (London: Wiley Chancery, 1994).

by the ToA. Amsterdam developments in respect of the Court of Justice in general represent a significant revision of the role of and respect for law in the newly structured European Union. The Maastricht negotiators chose to expand the Community and establish the Union without the involvement of the judicial branch and were castigated for this, and this situation has been at least addressed if not fully resolved under Amsterdam.

The Court's jurisdiction's prior to the ToA changes was essentially confined to the EC Treaties and the final provisions of the TEU. Thus, the position prior to Amsterdam was at least not overly complex. It suggested that there were very clear boundaries to the Court's jurisdiction, namely that there should be no Court "interference" in the Second and Third Pillar matters and the Court could rule only on the EC Treaties and the final provisions of the TEU. This reflected the distrust of the Court's interpretative powers which some Member States would have had in respect of issues of national security or immigration policy. However, even though the Court had been effectively excluded from ruling upon Third Pillar matters, this had not prevented it taking the opportunity to consider its jurisdictional borders. Both the ECJ and the Court of First Instance have confirmed their willingness to declare that their jurisdiction extends to Third Pillar-related issues, despite the absence of specific jurisdiction in this regard.[12] These cases are suggestive of the Court's willingness to interpret its jurisdictional scope beyond the confines of Article 46 TEU. It will be interesting to observe to what extent the ECJ position may change in this respect post-Amsterdam with the Article 46 amendments now providing the possibility of judicial input into the Pillars, albeit in a limited manner.

The main provisions of the new jurisdiction can be summarised as follows; first, Article 46 TEU is amended to extend the Court's jurisdiction to Third Pillar (Title VI TEU) matters (police and judicial co-operation in criminal matters), according to the provisions set out in Article 35 (ex Article K.7) TEU. Here a special kind of Third Pillar specific form of jurisdiction has been designed for the Court, namely a restricted form of preliminary rulings, direct action and actions against Member States[13]. Member States are required to make a declaration accepting the jurisdiction of the ECJ in this regard. This is an instance of discretion-based jurisdiction, exposing some Member State citizens to the possibility that their state will not opt for jurisdiction and leading to a lack of uniformity in interpretation here with nationals of different Member States enjoying different levels of protection. Despite the strict rules surrounding jurisdiction in this regard it is a major development that the Court is to have a say in Third Pillar matters, remedying a situation much decried after Maastricht from a civil liberties perspective. The EU Member States had manipulated for themselves an

[12] See Cases C–170/96 *Commission* v. *Council* [1998] ECR I–2763, T–174/95, *Svenska Journalistfurbundet* v. *Council*, [1998] ECR II–2289, T14/98, *Hautala* v. *Council*, 19 July 1999.

[13] Albors-Llorens, n. 6 *supra*, at 1278 ff., and M. de Boer, "Justice and Home Affairs in the Treaty on European Union: More Complexity Despite Communautarization" (1997) 4 *MJECL* 310 and N. Walker, "Justice and Home Affairs" (1998) 47 *ICLQ* 236.

extra-parliamentary zone of activity where important decisions on all the matters within the then remit of the Third Pillar would escape judicial supervision, both at national and supranational level. This situation is now remedied by both communitarisation and this new possibility of limited jurisdiction over the Third Pillar. However, it is significant in this regard, that Article 35 TEU expressly denies direct effect to the measures emanating from the Third Pillar.

The communitarisation of immigration, visa and asylum matters has given the Court of Justice extended jurisdiction over an area of EU activity previously falling under the Third Pillar and declared to be outside the scope of the Court's jurisdiction.[14] But the role of the Court under Title IV EC is not the same as it is under the EC Pillar in general. There is a limited preliminary reference procedure (just as there is also a limited, but different, preliminary reference system under Title VI TEU), and measures relating to the maintenance of law and order and internal security are stated to be outside the scope of the Court's powers (Article 68(2)). There is, also, a special advisory procedure under the new Title which will allow Member States to seek a ruling of interpretation from the Court, without it becoming a subject of legal proceedings (Article 68(3)). Strictly speaking, these revisions of the Court's jurisdiction are not related to closer co-operation, *per se*. However, these specific changes introduced under Title IV EC and Title VI TEU contribute significantly to the overall picture of a differentiated judicial space in the European Union. The limitations on the role of the Court under Title IV EC can be criticised in that the opportunity has been missed to create a common judicial area under this Title, the "justice" in the name not being reflected in the provisions themselves.[15]

The pattern of conditional extension to jurisdiction evidenced above is repeated in respect of the integration of the Schengen Agreement into the EC Treaty system. There are limitations on the Court's jurisdiction in respect of this particular form of agreed enhanced co-operation, relating to the areas of the Schengen Agreement which are now consigned to Title IV EC.[16] According to Article 2(3) of the Schengen Protocol, the ECJ shall have no jurisdiction on measures or decisions relating to the maintenance of law and order and the safeguarding of internal security. This reflects the position also expressed in Article 68(2) concerning the jurisdiction over Title VI EC matters in general but is wider, in that Article 68(2) refers just to preliminary rulings and not to Article 230 jurisdiction. In essence, these various new formulations of preliminary reference (in Title IV EC, Title VI TEU and the Schengen Protocol) limit the scope which national courts have to participate in or to use this procedure, restricting

[14] For a lengthy discussion of the new Title IV EC see K. Hailbronner, "European Immigration and Asylum Law under the Amsterdam Treaty" (1998) 35 *CMLRev*. 1047 and den Boer, n. 13 *supra*.

[15] J. Monar, "Justice and Home Affairs in the Treaty of Amsterdam: Reform at the Price of Fragmentation" (1998) 23 *ELRev*. 321 at 323.

[16] E. Wagner, "The Integration of Schengen into the Framework of the European Union", 2 1998 *LIEI* 1 at 24.

the power to courts of last resort only. Under the Third Pillar regime there are two stages restricting the possibility of a preliminary reference action occurring in this area; the Member States have explicitly to accept the Court's competence in this regard and they may further specify which courts in their legal systems are to allowed to use the new procedure.[17] Furthermore, the ECJ is confined in respect of the acts over which it may have preliminary jurisdiction under this procedure, and these do not encompass the provisions of Title VI itself. To sum up, in any case arising in a national court which has a migration or immigration dimension the scope for use of Article 234 will never be very clear and will lead to confusion in national courts, and of course may not even be available in some national courts. This "proliferation of new solutions"[18] will be rendered even more complex in the future by the fact that under Article 67 EC, once the transitional period is over, new provisions relating to the powers of the ECJ may be adopted by the Council. The general trend relating to the new, differentiated preliminary reference system has been to restrict both the courts which may avail of the Article 234 procedure and also the scope of the ECJ itself in this regard. But complexity and restraint at what price? If reduced workload is the goal, is it justifiable to have such a pragmatic perspective towards EC Law? The ECJ itself has recently highlighted the problems relating to preliminary references under the current system.[19] The delays in the system and effects on the rights of individuals are underlined. Yet, the Court itself supports the restriction of preliminary rulings in specialised areas to specific national courts.[20]

None the less, the crucial risk of divergent interpretations of Community acts in the area of migration is a serious consideration. The new terms on variegated forms of preliminary ruling which will prevail under Title IV EC and Title VI TEU will result in significant differences in both the use of this procedure throughout the EU and in respect of the uniform application of EU law. Under Title IV EC, the Member States may choose to submit themselves to the Court's preliminary ruling jurisdiction. Under the Third Pillar, States may also so choose[21] and, furthermore, select which courts will be able to avail of the preliminary reference possibility. These two jurisdictional scenarios will result in considerable divergence of EC/EU law pertaining to the areas concerned. In some Member States (those which do not opt for jurisdiction), none of the courts may be permitted to resort to Article 234 (ex Article 177) in respect of, say, an asylum matter, whereas in others the full scope of EC law and the ECJ will be available in all courts. Furthermore, the position of the courts in the

[17] Art. 35 TEU.

[18] Wagner, n. 16 *supra*, at 3.

[19] *The Future of the Judicial System of the European Union: Proposals and Reflections* (Luxembourg: ECJ Publications, 1999).

[20] *Ibid.*, 23.

[21] "On the occasion of the signing of the [ToA] only six Member States declared to accept preliminary rulings by the Court [under Title VI TEU]", Austria, Belgium, Germany, Greece, Luxembourg and the Netherlands: J. Monar, "Justice and Home Affairs in the Treaty of Amsterdam: Reform at the Price of Fragmentation" (1998) 23 *ELRev*. 320 at 331.

non-participating states in respect of the use of a relevant ECJ interpretation or declaration of validity is uncertain and will at any rate result in potentially uneven application of EC and EU law throughout the EU. This level of differentiation poses serious issues in terms of citizens and their effective participation in the EU legal order, given, especially, that immigration and asylum matters inherently concern individuals' free movement and residence rights. In addition, the coherence and relative comprehensibility of the law pertaining to the EC/EU migration regime is fundamentally affected by the differentiated applications of Article 234 envisaged under the new rules for the Court in the reformatted immigration and asylum system after Amsterdam.

The opt-in possibilities for Member States in relation to the new forms of preliminary reference will result in an application of variable geometry in this regard with unequal use of the procedure in the EU. The principal and primary aim of the Article 234 procedure is uniformity of interpretation. These new procedures pose a serious threat in this regard. There is a paradox here, as the teleological essence of the procedure is destroyed by the new regimes. Will national courts without the power to refer still be able to use ECJ interpretations or, more importantly, invalidity declarations? There has been erosion of uniformity or attachment to uniformity in this regard in favour of a more pragmatic perspective.

Therefore, as can be seen, rather than neglect the role of the ECJ at Amsterdam, the ToA negotiators paid careful and precise attention to the exact position of the ECJ in respect of all the developments under this Treaty. One might suggest even too careful attention, seeming to ascribe a belt and braces approach to the Court, not allowing it to escape from the confines of these tight descriptions of jurisdiction deriving from Article 46 TEU. This approach is flawed in designing a web of jurisdiction that is difficult to grasp but also and more fundamentally because the Court itself will not readily see its interpretative functions so easily controlled and limited. At one level, though, this political attempt to box in the Court is an interesting development. Although the Court's jurisdiction has been expanded beyond the limits set by the Maastricht Treaty, on one view this is a very guarded and protected expansion, one which allows limited scope for the Court to develop an expansive interpretation of the provisions. On another view, providing an extensive range of textual references for the Court's jurisdiction gives that institution a more constitutionally valid basis for its functioning, no longer being vulnerable to criticism for radical and wild forays of interpretation.

3. THE CLOSER CO-OPERATION FRAMEWORK AND THE COURT

The new closer co-operation regime introduced under the Amsterdam Treaty preserves the dynamism but not the sense of collective enterprise in European integration in providing for some of the Member States to develop an area of policy for and within the EU without the collaboration of all other Member

States. Integration progresses but is territorially confined. As many of the chapters in this collection discuss, this approach towards the future of the EU is not new but it has received a more legally grounded dimension under the ToA, being now constitutionally embedded in the Treaties. There are two levels of pronouncements on flexibility in the ToA: the general provisions (Title VII TEU, i.e. Articles 43–45 TEU) and the specific provisions, Article 11 EC and Article 40 TEU, the latter providing for the operation of flexibility within the First and Third Pillars respectively.[22]

Kortenberg usefully categorises the various levels of closer co-operation provided by the Amsterdam Treaty.[23] These are: closer co-operation *predetermined* by the ToA itself (such as the integration of the Schengen Agreement and the various arrangements under Title IV EC), *undetermined* closer co-operation which will be governed by general enabling clauses and specific conditions laid out in both the First and Third Pillars, and, finally, co-operation on a *case-by-case basis*, as in the Second Pillar.[24] (This last level is less significant from the Court's perspective.) In other words, past, present and future closer co-operation were all catered for at Amsterdam.

The route to appreciating where and how exactly the Court may intervene in matters concerning flexibility begins with Article 46 TEU, which refers to Court jurisdiction under Title VII TEU (Articles 43–45, the general enhanced co-operation clauses), but under the conditions laid out in the specific applications of that Title in both the EC Treaty and the TEU. These Articles (Article 11 EC and Article 40 TEU) are the two gateways to flexibility in the First and Third Pillars[25] and Title VII TEU the "mother clause" or general enabling provision. There are differences between the two "gateway" provisions; the list of conditions is longer in Article 11, Article 40 does not provide that closer co-operation should not concern citizenship,[26] and the procedures applicable in the two situations of flexibility are also different. Under Article 11 EC the Commission plays a central role in the process and the Council is the sole decisive actor under Article 40 and the resulting instruments are also different. As Shaw points out, closer co-operation itself is never defined in any of these provisions.[27]

Both the enabling provisions and the specific applications of flexibility are well documented and have attracted important commentary.[28] Obtaining, however, a clear perspective on the precise role of the Court in this system is not

[22] For an account of the background to the introduction of flexibility at Amsterdam see J. Shaw, "The Treaty of Amsterdam: Challenges of Flexibility and Legitimacy" (1998) 4 *ELJ* 63–86.

[23] H. Kortenberg, "Closer Cooperation in the Treaty of Amsterdam" (1998) 35 *CMLRev*. 833. See also G. Edwards and E. Phillipart, *Flexibility and the Treaty of Amsterdam: Europe's new Byzantium*, CELS Occasional Paper, 1997, No 3 who also use this type of catergorisation and N. Walker, "Sovereignty and Differentiated Integration in the European Integration" (1998) 4 *ELJ* 355.

[24] *Ibid*., at 835.

[25] Monar, n. 15 *supra, at* 333.

[26] A surprising omission, see *ibid*.

[27] Shaw, n. 22 *supra,* at 71.

[28] See Kortenberg and Ehlermann, n. 2 *supra,* and N. Walker, "Sovereignty and Differentiated Integration in the European Union" (1998) 4 *ELJ* 355.

immediately obvious from the face of the provisions. The starting point, again, is Article 46(c) TEU which provides that the Court shall have jurisdiction over "the provisions of Title VII [TEU], under the conditions provided for by Article 11 of the [EC] Treaty and Article 40 [TEU]". Looking first, therefore, at the "mother" clause therefore in Title VII TEU; this provides both a positive and negative list of general conditions for the application of closer co-operation, all of which are, according to Article 46, subject to the interpretative jurisdiction of the Court. There is no actual mention of the role of the Court in the wording in Title VII. As for the specific rules governing future flexibility, Article 11 EC lays out a list of negative conditions for closer co-operation under the First Pillar and specifies procedures and institutional roles. Once again, there is no specific mention of the Court under this provision, though there is indirect indication under Article 11(4).[29] Finally, Article 40 TEU, which will govern closer co-operation under the Third Pillar, does mention specifically the position of the Court. Article 40(4) states that "the provisions of the [EC] Treaty concerning the powers of the Court of Justice . . . and the exercise of those powers shall apply to [closer co-operation under Article 40]". Overall, this constitutes a byzantine and complex web of provisions which do not clarify or precisely illuminate the position of the Court. There is also widespread speculation that these provisions are too confining and complex to induce the Member States to make regular use of them.[30]

The Court's jurisdiction on enhanced co-operation is a power to review decisions to operate such co-operation to determine their compliance with the general co-operation provisions in Title VII TEU. This power of the Court is itself then subject to the different conditions found in the specific co-operation clauses in the two Pillars concerned (i.e. Articles 11 EC and 40 TEU). This means that, for example, in the case of any enhanced co-operation under the First Pillar, the Court has, according to Article 11 EC, jurisdiction to review both the decision to operate enhanced co-operation and any implementing legislation resulting therefrom. In contrast, the Court's power in relation to Third Pillar enhanced co-operation is confined to the decision to establish that process in the first place; in other words, the general provisions of the EC Treaty concerning the Court will apply *only* to the initial decision to operate flexibility under the Third Pillar. Finally, as regards judicial supervision of the outcome of any such co-operation in Third Pillar policy areas, Article 35 TEU is the applicable provision. As discussed above, the Court's jurisdiction in respect of any such implementing legislation and the action of participating Member States will be limited in the way specified in that provision. That, therefore, is the general position of the Court within the closer co-operation regime.

Judicial control of the EC Treaty closer co-operation provisions[31] could

[29] "The acts and decisions necessary for the implementation of cooperation activities shall be subject to all the relevant provisions of this Treaty . . .".

[30] See further, Kortenberg, n. 2 *supra*, and S. Weatherill, Ch. 11, in this collection.

[31] See F. Tuytschaever, *Differentiation in the European Union* (Oxford: Hart Publishing, 1999) at 61.

encompass the ECJ being called upon to rule on, first, the conditions for authorisation set out in Article 11 EC itself. Secondly, it has been suggested that the Court may have a role in adjudicating a refusal by the Commission to submit a proposal to the Council concerning authorisation for closer co-operation.[32] In terms of the justiciability of such a refusal, it has been suggested that this is limited to the formal compliance by the Commission with the requirement to give reasons for the decision and not as regards the content of the refusal itself.[33] The Commission appears to have discretion under Article 11 to refuse to submit a proposal to the Council but it is suggested here that there may be limits to these powers. The suggestion concerns the possible interpretation by the Commission of the meaning of exclusive competence. Moving on from Article 11 EC, Shaw also suggests that Article 43(2), a statement of loyalty, which being broadly modelled on Article 10 (ex Article 5) EC, is capable of extensive interpretation by the Court. Article 11 EC is characterised by Shaw as containing "a set of five supplementary commandments".[34] However, confusion is introduced here as some of them replicate Article 43 but some also add extra and more precise conditions for the application of enhanced co-operation under the EC Pillar. She suggests a reordering of the five conditions in order to highlight their relative importance. Article 46 TEU states that the powers of the ECJ shall apply to Article 43 under the conditions laid out in Article 11—a circuitous route to understanding the scope of the jurisdiction, but Article 11 does not put any conditions on the exercise of the ECJ power. Tuytschaever suggests that the ECJ powers do not extend to interpreting the Article 43 criteria for authorisation, or to decisions to establish closer co-operation and instead only to application to one of the specific fields of policy or implementation of that decision.[35] Was it the intention of the IGC to ensure that the full powers of the ECJ extend to all matters within the framework of co-operation under the EC Treaty? If this is indeed the case then being able to submit Article 43 to the Court's jurisdiction will mean that the notion of "*acquis communautaire*" would, for the first time, be possibly subject to the Court's interpretation, with potentially interesting implications for example in the new accessions context.

The specific provisions in Article 11 EC contain a negative list of the fields in which co-operation will not be permitted.[36] There will be much room for interpretation here. A Member State may oppose the decision on closer co-operation to be taken by QMV in the Council for stated and important reasons of national policy. In this case no vote will be taken so no legal act will result, and therefore no jurisdiction of the ECJ will result. But the Council then by QMV may ask the European Council to arbitrate. This however could arguably result in a legal

[32] *Ibid.*

[33] J. Shaw, "The Treaty of Amsterdam: Challenges of Flexibility and Legitimacy" (1998) 4 *ELJ* 63 at 75.

[34] *Ibid.*, at 72.

[35] Tuytschaever, n. 31 *supra*, at 63.

[36] See Kortenberg, n. 2 *supra*, at p 848.

act, an act of the Council (rather than of the European Council which of course is not subject to the jurisdiction of the Court) bringing it within the jurisdiction of the ECJ under Article 230 EC. The Court will generally review the conditions for resorting to closer co-operation under both Title VII TEU and Article 11 EC and then review the product of that closer co-operation once authorised. It has been pointed out however that it would be difficult for the Court to be given the opportunity to review the existence of important reasons of national policy as here also no act will exist to be subjected to the Court's review.[37]

It is worth nothing that concerns have been expressed about the justiciability of the closer co-operation provisions, with comparisons being made with subsidiarity under Maastricht.[38] It is true that interpreting co-operation clauses will necessitate the Court ruling on difficult questions such as whether an area chosen for enhanced co-operation falls within the exclusive competence of the EC. But the complexity of these issues does not render them *per se* non-justiciable. Nor, it is submitted, would the fact that a decision to activate enhanced co-operation is a political decision, make the Court shy of proffering an interpretation in any given instance.[39] In particular, in so far as the EC Pillar is concerned, the ECJ will be required to determine whether a particular application of enhanced co-operation is or is not within an area of exclusive competence. In this way, such potential for adjudication will involve the Court in a similar exercise as that also envisaged under Article 5 (ex Article 3b) on subsidiarity, where the determination of exclusive and non-exclusive competence is also implied and no less complex.[40]

The judicial appreciation of co-operation measures will also involve review of the position of non-participating Member States and the impact of co-operation provisions on nationals of these states. This situation is similar to the post-TEU queries about the Social Policy Agreement. In particular, questions about the meaning of EU citizenship in a fragmented polity will necessarily be implicated in this context.[41] The ultimate output or product of closer co-operation will not affect non-participating states (Article 43(1)(f)). This results in a situation whereby that which is treated as Community law by some Member States is not equally regarded by others (i.e. the non-participating states). This is a serious and fundamental erosion of the uniform nature and tradition of EC law, bol-

[37] Gaja, n. 3 *supra,* at 865.

[38] See further Albors-Llorens, n. 6 *supra,* at 1284.

[39] See further, G. Edwards and E. Phillipart, "Flexibility and the Treaty of Amsterdam: Europe's New Byzantium" (1997) CELS Occasional Paper, No 3.

[40] See generally G. de Búrca, "Reappraising Subsidiarity's Significance after Amsterdam" (1999) Harvard Law School, Jean Monnet Working Papers, on http://www.law.harvard.edu/Programs/JeanMonnet/papers/99/9990701.html and also G. de Búrca, "The Principle of Subsidiarity and the Court of Justice as an Institutional Actor" (1998) 38 *JCMS* 217.

[41] On this subject and for a relevant analysis of Case 235/87, *Annunziata Matteucci* v. *Communauté française de Belgique et al.* [1988] ECR 5589, see also Bruno de Witte, Ch. 3, this collection.

stered by the Court raising issues similar to those raised in the debate about the social policy agreement law after TEU. [42]

There is a distinction between the provisions setting out the management of future flexibility as opposed to elements of flexibility which were in fact provided for at the time of the ToA. These occur under the new Title IV EC and in the related opt-outs of the UK, Ireland and Denmark, and also to the integration of the Schengen *acquis* into the framework of the European Union. It is also specifically provided that the closer co-operation under Title IV EC will not result in legal obligations for the non-participating states.[43] This is a specific application of flexibility, along the model adopted at the Maastricht Treaty, but one which is more sophisticated and takes into account the criticisms of that kind of simplistic opting-out for which that Treaty provided. The Court of Justice has a different role in relation to Treaty negotiated flexibility than it does in relation to the potential Article 43 type closer co-operation envisaged in the future. For a start, the former is much easier to organise, without formalised institutional input and without having to resort to the rigours of the flexibility clauses now in the Treaties. The Member States concerned not to participate in a new area of, or an extension of, EC competence negotiate this at the time of the IGC, specifying precisely their position. Mention should, finally, be made of the Schengen protocol in this regard. It is the best example of the kind of closer co-operation *outside* the framework of the European Union,[44] in fact precisely the kind of closer co-operation which is envisaged now to be covered by the new flexibility provisions, thus allowing the EC institutions, and in particular the Court, an input into such initiatives. Steps were taken at Amsterdam to integrate this pre-existing form of flexibility, the Schengen *acquis* Protocol. These provisions are quite complex in themselves. For our purposes here in appreciating the full range of the Court's jurisdiction in relation to flexibility, it can be observed that under the Schengen protocol, the 13 signatory states are authorised to establish a form of closer co-operation among themselves within the scope of the Schengen Agreement to be conducted within the institutional and legal framework of the EC.

It can be observed, therefore, that a very complex network of Treaty provisions governs the judicial appreciation of flexibility and its potential outcome. This appears to introduce a significant amount of confusion into the realm of ECJ jurisdiction. It also has important implications for citizenship understanding of the closer co-operation system. These concerns are now addressed in the next Part.

[42] See further D. Curtin, "The Constitutional Structure of the Union: A Europe of Bits and Pieces" (1993) 30 *CMLRev.* 17.

[43] Protocol on the position of the UK and Ireland.

[44] See further B. de Witte, Ch. 3, this collection.

4. THE FUTURE OF THE RESTRUCTURED JUDICIAL ARCHITECTURE

Amsterdam has produced a complex network for flexibility and a new system is envisaged with a redefined and restricted role for the Court. What other general reflections and questions may be raised in attempting to analyse the implications of enhanced co-operation on the functioning and role of the ECJ in the differentiated polity which will result? A general preliminary remark is that the new co-operation regime has led to a situation in which the Court has seen both a significant restriction in its powers as a Court and also an expansion of its jurisdiction. Much criticism can be made of the complicated jurisdictional space which emerged from Amsterdam. Nonetheless, it has given cause for reflection on the role of the Court. This institution would have been far from being the prime consideration of those drafting new provisions for a flexible Union but judicial issues were not ignored under this Treaty. There is a suggestion of a pattern emerging here perhaps with the Court function becoming more tightly prescribed at IGC negotiations. This pattern, of increasing control over the Court resulting from the IGC process, may lead to an incremental change in the nature of the relationship between the Court and the Treaties it is charged with interpreting. One possible consequence is a restructured jurisdiction for the judicial branch as it becomes more controlled by the political branch. Is this a kind of revenge at last? Alternatively, it may promote a more mature and structured role for the Court leading to a new phase where it will not have the freedom of its glory days to interpret EC law into new dimensions, a phase in which the Court becomes a more constrained agent but under which it may be granted a different kind of freedom to act within clearer and more obvious confines, thus freeing it from charges of excessive abuse of its powers.

As Shaw says, the process of identifying and interpreting the key features of the EC/EU's constitutional core and the irreducible minimum of a single legal order is the primary task of the lawyer.[45] She also asserts that "[t]he future role of the Court of Justice and its likely approach to the new challenges remain moot points but are of considerable interest nonetheless".[46] Here I make a series of observations about that role of the Court, or attempt to expose some of the dilemmas of co-operation for the Court, from the perspective of understanding the constitutional core of the legal order.

The question of how the Court will police the fragmentation of Community law arising from closer co-operation is fundamental. The handling of the review of the operation of enhanced co-operation will be an extremely delicate exercise at many levels. It will reveal the longstanding uncertainties embedded in the Treaty system, fundamental concepts of the EC/EU legal order the meaning of which is still uncertain, such as exclusive competence and *acquis communautaire*. The new provisions, therefore, while far from complex, present the Court

[45] Shaw, n. 33 *supra*, at 70.
[46] *Ibid.*, 80.

with a valuable opportunity and scope for expansive interpretation in the future. They also raise fundamental questions about the role of law in a differentiated polity. Furthermore, the complexity of the system post-Amsterdam is a threat to the coherence and understanding of EU law for citizens and national courts alike. The interaction of citizen and the EU judicial system is hindered by the new rules.

A second important issue concerns the extent to which the new architecture affects the internal coherence of EC law. If there was something special about the nature EU law, residing in fundamental principles developed by the Court and its allegiance to uniformity, has this now been affected by embedding the judicial system in all of these complex rules and partitions of jurisdiction? EC law had a special mode of reasoning, relating to ALL Member States and national courts, and this is now affected by the changes in terms of the specific closer co-operation and the general system of flexibility. The function of EC law, uniform law, concerned connections between all Member States, and although this may at times have been narrowly located in the preservation of the common or single market,[47] it constituted the uniqueness of the supranational system which risks being eroded by ToA closer co-operation changes.

Flexibility is a political initiative and compromise and it is difficult to see how something so instrumentally inspired translates into the judicial realm. We need to consider how the Court can work with and within this political compromise. There is a legal and political concept of the constitution of the EU, and closer co-operation lies at the heart of this tension, with the political pursuing flexibility as the optimum route for integration and the legal concept intimately allied to one of flexibility's conceptual opposites, uniformity.[48] The political constitution, as formed and reformed by the IGC process, produces a different outcome to that which the legal concept of constitution emerging from the Court's jurisprudence does, with the latter traditionally attached to uniformity. The Court is not merely an institution which might be at the service of closer co-operation as an aspect of European integration. It is has always seen itself as and acted as far more than that, as a constitutional court standing above the Treaty order. But its constitutionalist tendencies may have been usurped by the Amsterdam changes. The ECJ was responsible for shaping European identity to a large extent, and this may be fundamentally affected by the fragmentation of the legal order inherent in closer co-operation. The original goal was the common market and related uniformity of the legal order. Closer co-operation (and the jurisdictional variable geometry produced by the ToA changes) is a challenge to the interpretative autonomy which the Court had fashioned for itself over the years. A related question is has what might be termed "the autonomy of EU law" itself been affected by the flexibility initiatives?[49] This autonomy lies

[47] E.g., Case 44/79, *Hauer* v. *Land Rheinland-Pfalz* [1979] ECR 3727, at para. 14.

[48] See Shaw, Ch. 15, this volume.

[49] On the autonomy of EU law, see further, H. Lindahl and B. van Roermund, "Law without a State? On Representing the Common Market", Z. Bankowski and A. Scott (eds.), *The European Union and Legal Theory* (Blackwells, 2000).

in the interpretation of the objectives in Articles 2 and 3 EC, and this is not affected by flexibility. In fact, the conditions laid out in Title VII TEU and in Article 11 EC and Article 40 TEU contribute to preserving the autonomy of EC law in this respect. Would the autonomy of the Court now be found in the interpretation of "ever closer Union" and, if so, what might be the relationship between that and closer co-operation since, on one reading, the latter is a direct contrast to closer Union?

The overall restructuring of the Court's jurisdiction might be justified if closer co-operation can be said to advance a political community for the EU or enhance citizenship of this community. However, as discussed above, both the complexity and lack of coherence in the flexibility provisions render citizen participation in the legal order more difficult. In particular, the specific manifestations of closer co-operation under the ToA in the sphere of immigration and asylum have the potential seriously to impede citizenship access to justice. Would support for the developing concept of citizenship mean that the Court would have to take into account Articles 17–22 EC (on citizenship of the Union) when considering a flexibility issue? Article 11(1)(c) expressly prevents closer co-operation concerning citizenship, but a wider and more significant consideration is the extent to which citizens of a given Member State (and, therefore, EU citizens) may input into a decision to participate or not in a closer co-operation development.

Much of the specific or predetermined flexibility concerns justice and home affairs. The EU Member States are still skating awkwardly around how to handle a common immigration policy. The particular rules under Title IV EC have attracted criticism as they go the root of ECJ jurisdiction under the First Pillar whereas other developments are outside the borders of that pillar. In other words, the much called-for communitarisation was not accompanied by full ECJ jurisdiction, rather a kind of special, confined, intra-First Pillar variety of jurisdiction has been created. A consideration arising therefrom is whether or not this pattern is likely to be repeated, or, in other words, will the practice of special case jurisdiction even under the EC pillar become the norm for the future. If there are concerns such as these arising from the ToA changes, from a more positive perspective, it may also be envisaged that flexibility may encourage a more developed debate and rejuvenation in the discussion of the Court's role. Flexibility under the ToA reflects an honest acceptance of the internal divisions in the EU. It lifts the veil on uniformity and provides a new lens through which to view the EU legal and political system. It is a sign of a mature polity to be able to divide without fundamental rupture. But the Court's role in adjudicating this diversity is therefore essential. The Court may be a kind of unitary overall constitutional arbiter, even if the system has become a fragmented and diverse one.

The future role of the Court in a multi-dimensional juridical space cannot be guessed at. The Court is profoundly affected by closer-co-operation but, even more than the political institutions, it also has the power profoundly to influence its future. The role of the ECJ in a fragmented legal order will emerge over time as it regulates the multiple speeds at which the EU now operates.

5. CONCLUSION

The Amsterdam Treaty was a reflective moment in the process of European integration. European integration consists of such a process as well as the concrete development of a polity. The IGC system is a fundamental part of that process, and though its procedures may seem like playground politics as each state fights its corner, this is the core of the political constitution of the EU. The lack of sophistication of the IGC process which produced flexibility might be criticised but this process forces out preferences and the ToA puts this practice on a more reasoned footing. The introduction of flexibility has forced a level of honesty or reality about the nature of the integrative process; "we Europeans"[50] do not have to do everything together outwith the common market core.[51]

Political unity has no determined or determinable end[52] and closer co-operation is part of its current manifestation and a feature of dynamic integration. In other words dynamic integration can and must encompass differentiated integration. It is a constitutional continuum,[53] which does not mean that closer co-operation will distort the main goals or risk negating the progress of the integration process. The analysis of the Court also has to be seen in this light. Flexibility provides a new and different phase for the Court, not necessarily a worse or better one.

Closer co-operation can be viewed from both a constitutional and a substantive perspective. The revised role of the Court too can be viewed from both of these angles. The rules and new divisions of jurisdiction create a complex substantive set of sources for seeing where the limits of Court jurisdiction are. But the appreciation of this structure is more significant than the *ad hoc* or arbitrary gathering of these pockets of varied jurisdiction. The overall, global impact on the Court as a constitutional actor has to be appreciated. Flexibility establishes a system to mediate and manage governance of the EU, but it is also subject to and will affect the judicial ordering, the legal order of the Union and more specifically the institution at its heart, the Court of Justice.

As with previous phases of fundamental reform of the EU, the impact of enhanced co-operation on the "constitution" of the EU is now partly within the power of the Court. In a European Union with a divided power system[54] and a

[50] *Ibid.*
[51] See further, G. de Búrca, Ch. 7, this collection.
[52] N. 49 *supra*, at 12.
[53] H. Lindahl, "European Integration: Sovereignty and the Politics of Boundaries", research paper presented at Aberdeen Law School 1999, forthcoming (2000/2001), at 18.
[54] I. Pernice, "Multilevel Constitutionalism and the Treaty of Amsterdam: European Constitution-making Revisited" (1999) 36 *CMLRev*. 703 at 707.

fragmented legal order it is likely that, however complex and developed the flexibility regime, in its challenge to the very idea of a uniform legal order, uniformly adjudicated, it will, paradoxically, allow the adjudicator a significant role in forging a new conception of legal order.

6

Flexibility in the Geographical Scope of EU Law: Diversity and Differentiation in the Application of Substantive Law on Member States' Territories

JACQUES ZILLER

1. INTRODUCTION

THIS CHAPTER'S main argument[1] is that the EC/EU constitution has always acknowledged flexibility—or to put it into French language terms *l'Europe à géométrie variable*—ever since the adoption of the Treaties of Rome: the differences in the geographical scope of the different European Communities and European Union legal systems are at the root of differentiation as a general phenomenon in EU law. A second argument is that the constitutional issues involved are major ones as well on the basis of their content but also because of the fact that they have led to a major, although very little publicised, constitutional controversy between the ECJ on one side, the other institutions and the Member States on the other.

It was clear even before the first enlargement—on the basis of an early version of the *acquis communautaire* argument—that there was no option to adhere to only one or two of the three Communities. The mere fact that none of the three Communities had the same territorial scope of application clearly stresses, however, that they were conceived as legally independent systems. When it was decided to merge their institutions in 1965, the definition of the territorial scope of the treaties was left untouched, although the end of de-colonisation could have been a good reason to suppress these differences. This underlines the fact that flexibility/differentiation was a major component of the system set up for the economic integration of European countries. Neither the Maastricht Treaty in 1992 nor the Amsterdam Treaty in 1997 has changed this situation. On the

[1] My special thanks go to Carole Lyons and to Grainne de Búrca for their very useful comments on the first drafts of this paper. For more details on the geographical scope of EU/EC law, see: J. Ziller, "Champ d'application territoriale du droit communautaire" in *Juris-Classeur Europe, fasc. No 470.* (Paris: Editions du Juris-Classeur Europe, 1998). The arguments developed here are however new ones for the main part.

contrary they have added a difference between TEC and TEU to the existing differences between the Paris and Rome treaties. Even within the EC Treaty, substantial differences in the territorial scope of application are to be found, as a quick look at Article 299 (ex Article 227) shows (see Annex A). This will be demonstrated by an analysis of the different Treaty provisions defining their geographical scope.

A supplementary dimension is added to this issue by the mere fact that one of the most significant provisions which introduced a differentiation in the geographical scope of EC law has undergone dramatic changes in interpretation and formulation from Rome 1957 to Amsterdam 1997. Indeed paragraph (2) of Article 227 of the EEC Treaty (now Article 299 TEC) has mainly been a source of exclusion of the relevant territories from the Common Market—with exemptions—from 1958 until 1978. From 1978 onwards, without any change in the wording of the Treaty, but simply because the ECJ adopted a different interpretation of the same provisions, it has meant an ever closer inclusion of the same spaces into the Common/Internal Market, reducing step by step the differences with other parts of its territory. This lasted until the Member States amended the relevant Article in the Amsterdam Treaty in order to set limits to this evolution. This issue—the status of Community outermost regions—is one of the clearest examples of the use of their respective constitutional powers by the institutions and the Member States in order to shape the future of the Union.

Even if the population and spaces concerned are both very far away from the European continent and rather small, the legal, economic and political elements of this phenomenon have significance in terms of EU constitutionalism, which is far from being at the fringe. Moreover, the problems that have arisen in relation to these Treaty provisions have involved the ECJ, the Commission and the Member States in a way that might provide some interesting lessons for the newer forms of differentiation and closer co-operation.

2. FLEXIBILITY IN THE SCOPE OF THE TREATIES: A UNION WITHOUT A TERRITORY

Behind the discussion on the European constitution lies the question of the nature of the EU/EC, and especially its differences when compared with the classical state concept. Flexibility and differentiation in applicable law are not alien to federal states or even unitary states.[2] However, in the case of the EU, flexibility in space underlines a very specific feature which differentiates it from any type of state: neither the EU nor the ECs have a territory of their own. Although the significance of this flexibility seems to vary from one Member State to the

[2] Both the United Kingdom (even before devolution) and France since the end of World War II have shown significant differentiation of the law applying to different parts of their territories: see J. Ziller, *Administrations comparées* (Paris: Montchrestien, 1993), 75 ff.

next, the constitutional intricacies that are linked to this phenomenon should be considered as highly relevant by all of them.

A. The EU Lacks Two of the Classical Components of a State in International Law

According to the classical definition in international and constitutional law, a state is made up of three non-dissociated elements: a territory, a population and a set of governing institutions. Neither the EU nor the Communities can be deemed to possess a territory, as the issues linked to the definition of the territorial scope of application of EU law clearly show.

Contrary to the solution adopted in the Paris and Rome Treaties, the Treaty of Maastricht does not specify its territorial scope of application. A closer look to the issues involved shows that the different pillars of the Union do not seem to involve the same territories. Applying the classical rules of interpretation of international treaties as laid down in the Vienna Convention on the Law of Treaties, the rules of the TEU should in principle apply to the entire territory of all Member States. However the ECSC, EC and Euratom Treaties establish exemptions to this rule by reducing the geographical scope of application of the first pillar. The subject matter of the second pillar escapes a territorial definition, as foreign policy—and even partly defence[3]—is potentially affecting foreign countries, that is territories that are not under a Member State's jurisdiction. Thus, as the TEU does not foresee exemptions to its geographical scope of application contrary to the first pillar treaties, and as the second pillar is hardly relevant to this issue, one could argue that only the third pillar normally applies to the entire territories of Member States: it is not possible to say that the territory of the Union, if it existed, would equal the sum of all the Member States' territories.

The definition of the territorial scope of each of the three Communities differs and is clearly limited by the principle of speciality. Euratom has the broadest geographical scope of application, as Article 198 of the relevant Treaty specifies that it applies to the entire territory of all Member States: "European territory" as well as "non-European territories within their jurisdiction", with selected exceptions for Danish and United Kingdom territories (i.e. the Faeroe Islands and Greenland, British sovereign zones on Cyprus, and there is only a partial application to the Channel Islands and Isle of Man). The EC already has a much smaller territorial scope: according to Article 299 (ex Article 227) the TEC normally applies to the entire territory of all Member States, but with a variable intensity (see section 2) and with a specific position of Overseas Countries and Territories (OCTs), which means in practice their exemption

[3] It is specially striking that the second pillar does not include a principle of mutual assistance, for which the definition of the relevant territory would be most important.

from the major part of EC law. Furthermore, the EEA agreement can be analysed as a partial extension of the territorial scope of the Internal Market, thus showing a clear discrepancy between the territory of the Internal Market and that of the EU Member States. The ECSC has a much narrower territorial scope of application, as Article 79 of the relevant Treaty limits its application to "European" territories of Member States, thus excluding all territories which are not geographically speaking European. One should remember that the ECSC Treaty is programmed to expire on 23 July 2002, thus automatically in theory expanding the scope of EC rules to products formerly covered by the ECSCT Treaty.[4]

As such the existence of different geographical scopes of application for different sets of legal rules is not unknown to modern states, but in the case of the EU, the definition of the "territory" is not in the hands of the Union itself. Two aspects are to be taken into account. As for all other Articles of the Treaties, unanimity is necessary in order to change the definition of the territories to which the law applies. Thus, in order to exempt Greenland from the application of EC law, Denmark had to negotiate a treaty amending the Communities Treaties from 1982 to 1984.[5] This could underline the competence of the "masters of the treaties" in defining the territory of the EU, something not so different from statal constitutions. But there is a second aspect, which has proven much more important in practice. The territorial scope of application of EU law can be changed unilaterally by a Member State giving independence to (decolonisation) or incorporating a territory. De-colonisation has not meant a dramatic change for numerous territories, because of the definition of the territorial scope of the Treaties: in the greatest number of cases, association on the basis of the EC Treaties themselves (as an OCT) has been replaced by association on the basis of a treaty between the EC and newly independent states (Yaounde/Lomé conventions). But increase in a Member State's territory has clearly shown where the competence lies in delimiting the EC territory: the re-unification of Germany, which legally speaking needed no approval whatsoever of EC institutions and Member States, was the sole decision of one Member State and led to an increase by 4.66 per cent in the territory submitted to EC law, with a population of 16.5 million. This clearly differentiates the EU from any federation.

This latter issue shows a certain consistency in the links between the EU and state components: in the same way as the size of the EU "population" relies on Member States' unilateral decisions because of the link between citizenship of

[4] Although there are no academic sources to confirm it, the lack of relevance of the ECSC Treaty for non-European parts of EU Member States' territories seems to be due not only to legal reasons but also to the lack of relevant products in those territories: the issue at stake would be highly abstract.

[5] France did not do the same in the case of Saint-Pierre-et-Miquelon, which should have remained an OCT, but were considered as part of EC territory between 1976 and 1985 by the EC institutions and Member States only because of changes in French law. The precedent however seems irrelevant, as the other Member States and the Commission did not object to this unilateral change, and as the ECJ never had to give its view.

the Union and citizenship of a Member State, the size of EU "territory" relies on Member States' unilateral decisions. Once again, it shows that the EU lacks at least two of the three major components of a state: it has no territory and no population of its own and no unilateral control over these two.

B. The Perspective on this Issue Varies from one Member State to Another

European legal literature has paid little attention to the issue of the territorial scope of EC law. This is not too surprising as its relevance varies from one Member State to another. Since the early 1990s, it has been mainly French literature that has shown a real interest in the topic.[6] The difference in points of view is linked to the existence of different categories of Member States in this respect.

For eight Member States, the national territory coincides entirely with the scope of application of undifferentiated EU/EC law: Belgium, Germany, Greece, Ireland, Italy, Luxembourg, Austria and Sweden. It is only natural if lawyers and scholars from those countries show little interest in the issue of territorial differentiation and even less understanding of the underlying political economic and social issues, which may appear to them to be a strange residue of colonialism.[7] The diversity of the territories for the other Member States concerned and the diversity of their legal status should however show that the issue goes far beyond that of post-colonialism.

On the brink of the twenty-first century, seven Member States exercise sovereignty over territories which partially or entirely escape the application of EU/EC law: Denmark (Faeroe Islands and Greenland), Spain (Canary Islands, Ceuta and Melilla), France (overseas departments and territories), the Netherlands (Dutch Antilles and Aruba), Portugal (Azores, Madeira[8]), Finland (Åland Islands, and,

[6] See especially: D. Dormoy, "Association des pays et territoires d'outre-mer (PTOM) à la Communauté européenne" 573 *Juris-Classeur Europe, fasc. 573* ; D. Custos, "Champ d'application territorial du droit communautaire—Départements d'outre-mer " in *Juris-Classeur Europe, fasc.* 572; J.-L. Dewost, "L'application territoriale du droit communautaire. Disparition et résurgence de la notion de frontière" in *La frontière, colloque S.F.D.I. (*Paris: Pedone, 1980), 253 s.; M. Dony, "Territoire communautaire" in A. Barav and C. Philip (eds.), *Dictionnaire juridique des Communautés européennes* (Paris: PUF, 1994), 1070 s.; J. Groux, " 'Territorialité' et droit communautaire" [1987] *Revue trimestrielle de droit européen* 5 s; S. Karagiannis, "A propos du règlement des conflits d'intérêts entre les territoires dépendant d'Etats membres et les Communautés européennes" [1998] *Revue de Droit International et de droit comparé* 330; F. Neri, *Le champ d'application du droit communautaire en matière de libre circulation des travailleurs* (Milan: Franco Angeli, 1982); I. Omarjee, "Le Traite d'Amsterdam de l'avenir de la politique de différenciation en faveur des départements français d'outre-mer" (1998) 34 *Revue trimestrielle de droit européen*, 515; D. Perrot and F. Miatti, "Les Lapons et les îles Åland dans le quatrième élargissement—Contribution à l'étude de la différenciation juridique au sein de la Communauté européenne" (1997) 413 *Revue du Marché commun et de l'Union européenne* 670 s; A. Rigaux, "Territoire communautaire" in *Répertoire communautaire* (Paris: Dalloz, 1995); as well as J. Ziller, n. 1 *supra*.

[7] In the case of Belgium and Italy, this could be reinforced by the fact that those two countries still had overseas dependencies in the 1950s, but not more since the early 1960s.

[8] Macao, even before its return to China at the end of 1999, was considered as a third country without any special link to the EC, like Hong-Kong until July 1998.

to a certain extent, "Lapland" as far as some specific rights of their traditional population are concerned) and the United Kingdom (Channel Islands and the Isle of Man, Crown colonies and territories etc.). The constitutional standing of these territories varies considerably from one Member State to another and can evolve in time with the potential of new difficulties in the relationship between EU/EC law and domestic law. The main difference is between the UK territories on one side, which are not legally speaking part of the British state, and whose inhabitants do not normally benefit from UK citizenship—except for Gibraltar and the Falklands—and the other countries, whose dependencies are part of the state even if substantially autonomous, and whose inhabitants benefit from EU citizenship. This constitutional difference as such has important consequences for the scope of European citizenship (see below at 2.C).

The Member State with the greatest diversity of territories in terms of EU status happens to be France. Comparing the European and national constitutional status of overseas "departments" (French West Indies, French Guiana and Réunion), which are highly integrated from a constitutional and social point of view, and that of "overseas territories" which may enjoy a very important degree of autonomy (it is the case of New Caledonia and French Polynesia) raises an unresolved question. On one side the neutrality of EU/EC law towards the internal constitutional organisation of Member States leaves untouched the essential attribute of sovereignty which permits giving independence to a territory or incorporating a new one: this issue is not governed by EU/EC law. However there is a severe constitutional constraint on Member States as regards the possibility of subtracting part of their territory from the application of EU/EC law: contrary to classical international law, where this is usually dealt with by unilateral reservations, unanimity of the Member States is necessary by way of a revision of the founding Treaties. The case of the territorial scope of *Schengen* is particularly complex: the French overseas departments, which are part of EC territory, have been excluded from the Schengen area by Article 138(1) of the relevant convention, and a declaration of the French government, annexed to the Amsterdam Treaty perpetuates this exclusion. The question could arise whether this exclusion has a constitutional basis in the *Schengen acquis*, or is based on a French unilateral declaration.[9]

C. Even in the Case of EC Law Strictly Speaking there is a Highly Complex and Differentiated Set of "Territories"

Contrary to the Maastricht Treaty, the Treaties of Rome and Paris defined their territorial scope; but they proceed in different ways. Adding to the complexity

[9] In my view, the answer is very simple: the *Schengen acquis* is based on the wording of the convention unless stated otherwise in the Amsterdam Treaty. But why then did the French government deem the abovementioned declaration to be necessary, if not for the purpose of emphasising an obvious legal point?

of having a different scope for each of the three Communities, even the EEC Treaty defined a highly complex and differentiated set of "territories". With the enlargement of the EC and the revisions of the Treaties, this complexity has constantly grown, and never has been seriously questioned.

In principle, the Treaty applies to the whole territory of all Member States (Article 299(1)) as "primarily defined by reference to [their] constitution" (*Hansen* case,[10] point 10), with clearly stated exceptions. The Treaty expressly provides for the exclusion of certain territories (Article 299(3); second sentence and (6)). The OCTs are submitted to a specific set of rules (Article 299(3) combined with Annex II (ex Annex IV) TEC). Outermost regions follow special rules allowing for an evolving differentiation (see the third part of this chapter). This diversity of regimes is as such a most obvious exemplification of flexibility in EC law.

The special regime of OCTs is a system of association, mainly based on non-reciprocal conditions of access to the market. However the combination of this special regime with other EC law provisions is subject to differentiated interpretation, and is as such an unresolved issue in EU constitutional law. There could be a contradiction between the geographical scope of application and the personal scope of application of EC law in the case of Danish, French and Dutch OCTs. There are very delicate problems for the application of free movement of workers to OCTs: the limitation of the territorial scope of EC law involves limitations for the free movement of persons, whereas the territorial origin of citizens of a Member State on the territory of the state should have no consequence according to the constitutional principles of non-discrimination which is embodied in all the written constitutions of Member States and could thus be easily considered as a general principle of law common to Members States. Giving priority to the territorial scope, as many scholars do, would infringe upon the most basic principles of Member States' constitutional law, namely the exclusion of discrimination between citizens according to their origin.

This is to be linked to an unresolved dispute on the applicability to OCTs of Treaty provisions other than those of Part IV (Association of The Overseas Countries and Territories). Whereas the ECJ and most scholars seem to limit applicable Treaty provisions to Part IV (Provisions on OCTs) and the Articles formally referred to in this part, I maintain that only Part III (internal market) is not applicable to OCTs and in particular that parts I (general principles), II (citizenship), V (institutions) and VI (general and final provisions) must apply to those territories unless part IV foresees exemptions. The case law of the ECJ on this issue has not always been clear-cut: while in *Kaefer and Procacci*,[11] the Court clearly avoided answering the question which could have been relevant, in *Leplat*[12] it insisted very much on the fact that "failing express provisions, the

[10] Case 148/77, *Hansen* v. *Hauptzollamt Flensburg*, [1978] ECR 1787.

[11] *Kaefer* v. *The French State*, *Procacci* v. *The French State*. Cases C–100/89 and C–101/89, [1998] ECR 4647.

[12] Case C–260/90, *Leplat* v. *Territory of French Polynesia*, [1992] ECR I–643.

general provisions of the Treaty do not apply to the countries and territories" (point 10). However, the Maastricht Treaty was not applicable to the case, and it should be taken into account that it reorganised the structure of the TEC in order to give special prominence to Part II on Citizenship. There can be no argument that the rules on citizenship do not apply to OCTs; on the contrary they obviously apply to all but the British OCTs because of the national constitutional principle of equality between citizens. The CFI in *Antillan Rice Mills*[13] seemed to follow this latter line of argument,[14] but the Court still constantly quotes its sentence in *Leplat*, even after the entry into force of the Maastricht Treaty.[15] My view is that the Court, not having had to solve an issue about citizenship (part 2) or general principles (part 1), has had no opportunity better to formulate its position.

As noted earlier, whereas the Member States may unilaterally include or exclude a territory from the EC scope of application through giving it independence or incorporating it, unanimity of all Member States is required to give a special status (like that of OCTs or outermost regions) to specific territories. The precedent of Greenland in 1984 should be seen as prevailing over the seemingly illegal precedent of Saint-Pierre-et-Miquelon between 1976 and 1985. The apparent contradiction between those two possibilities demonstrates the lack of relevance of classical concepts such as sovereignty or the opposition between monism and dualism in order to resolve EU constitutional issues. The solution of such issues relies on a mix of national unilateral decisions and multilateral treaty provisions based upon unanimity: flexibility in space depends mainly on EC Member States individually or collectively, as "masters of the treaties".

3. FLEXIBILITY WITHIN THE INTERNAL MARKET: MASTERS OF THE TREATIES *V.* ECJ?

In the restricted framework of the EC Common/Internal Market, the case of the so-called outermost regions (Azores, Canary Islands, Guadeloupe, French Guiana, Madeira, Martinique and Réunion) is as such an interesting case of flexibility: flexibility in space, as the application of EC law in those regions undergoes specific variations, but also flexibility in time, due to the dramatic changes in the interpretation *and wording* of the relevant Treaty provision, Article 299(2) (ex Article 227(2)) TEC. As a matter of fact, the case of Community outermost regions may be considered as a unique example of constitutional struggle between the "masters of the Treaty" and the ECJ.

[13] Cases T–480/93 and T–483/93, [1995] ECR II–2305.

[14] However, as theCFI seems to have misinterpreted *Hansen* in this decision, it seems difficult to rely on its argument in that case. The Court neither followed nor condemned the relevant formulation in its 1999 decision, quoted in n. 15 *infra*, in the same case.

[15] See especially Case C–390/95 *Antillan Rice Mills* v. *Commission*, 11 Feb. 1999, not yet reported, point 36, and Ruiz-Jarabo Colomer AG's Opinion of 1 June 1999 in Case C–17/98, *Emesa Sugar*, point 29.

A. Article 227(2) of the Rome Treaty: A Paradoxical Evolution of the ECJ Case Law?

When the Treaty of Rome was drafted it was decided to set up a special association regime for the colonial empires/overseas dependencies of Belgium, France, Italy and the Netherlands in Part IV of the EEC Treaty (Association of the Overseas Countries and Territories). As these territories were not fully integrated in the domestic market of the relevant countries, this was most logical. Most of them have become independent states; the remainder still have the status of OCTs. An exception, however, had to be made for Algeria and the French overseas departments (DOM: *départements d'outre-mer*). Contrary to other European overseas dependencies, the four "old colonies" of Guadeloupe, French Guiana, Martinique and Réunion and their inhabitants enjoyed the same legal status (with very few exceptions) as the European territory of the French Republic. They had participated in the French Revolution, especially when slavery was abolished in 1794. The reintroduction of slavery by Napoleon in 1802 had led to the independence of Saint-Domingue, becoming the Republic of Haiti in 1804. Slavery's definitive abolition in 1848 led to the total assimilation of the entire population of these colonies, as the former slaves—of African descent—enjoyed French citizenship on an equal footing with Europeans. This was particularly important in the context of the French Republican school system from 1880 onwards, as it led to a very high degree of cultural assimilation in all classes of society. Eventually the local political class asked for total legal assimilation of the four "old colonies", which were transformed into "*départements*", while the other elements of the Empire kept a special legal status and were called Overseas Territories (*territoires d'outre-mer*—TOM), with the exception of Algeria which had its own special status until independence in 1962. There were thus constitutional and political arguments to support the request for a specific treatment of those territories in the Treaty of Rome. Article 227(2) EEC provided for a partial immediate integration in the Common Market, as far as its core principles were concerned, and for a special adaptation mechanism for other Treaty provisions.

Although these adaptive measures had to be adopted before 1 January 1960 according to the Treaty, almost nothing had been done at that date (due to the war in Algeria). In the 1960s and 1970s the Commission and the Council, with full agreement of the French government, progressively introduced a series of adaptations for the DOM. However it was clear that the institutions did not feel bound by the time limit set in Article 227(2). Treaty provisions that were not quoted in this Article were considered as not applicable to the DOM, unless duly specified in secondary EC legislation. The core provisions and principles of the Common Market and Customs Union, as listed in Article 227(2), were applicable, but common policies were only partially applicable. The situation remained unchanged until the late 1970s, when local politicians and the French government started to question the appropriateness of this regime.

German importers of alcoholic beverages were quicker, as they gave rise to a preliminary ruling of the ECJ. In the *Hansen* case of 1978,[16] the question at stake was whether rum produced in Guadeloupe should be exempted from German taxes like other French products, or whether Guadeloupe should be considered as outside of Common Market for the purpose of taxation. Article 95 EEC was not quoted in the list of Article 227(2) and secondary legislation did not mention the applicability of tax provisions in the DOM.[17] While the Commission stuck to the interpretation that had prevailed since 1960, and insisted that only the provisions quoted and the relevant secondary legislation were applicable, the Court made an unprecedented[18] move. It asked the French government, which had obviously not noticed the interests at stake in the request which originated from a German court, to express its views. As this request coincided with a revision of the Chirac/Giscard d'Estaing government's policy on the evolution of French overseas dependencies,[19] the French government followed a rather new line. It claimed that after expiration of the time limit set in Article 227(2), the whole EEC Treaty was applicable to the DOM, unless specified otherwise in secondary legislation—thus applying the same principles to French and EC legislation. Advocate General Capotorti, and later the Court, took up the views of the French government—even formally quoting its position. This led to a radical change of the EEC legal regime of DOM. It clearly seemed that the Court wanted to acknowledge the choices made by a Member State on the basis of a relevant Treaty provision.

According to the Court's interpretation in the *Hansen* case, the time limit set in Article 227(2) only meant a period during which the provisions not quoted would not apply unless specified by delegated legislation. However, once this deadline was reached, all the provisions of the Treaty would become applicable as on the rest of Common Market territory, but the Council kept the possibility of adapting them through delegated legislation in order to enable "the economic and social development of these areas".[20] During the 1980s the EC institutions as well as academia, local politicians and the French government stuck to the following interpretation of *Hansen*, supported by a strict reading of the decision's wording: the DOM had to be considered as an integral part of the Common Market, but they could be exempted from the application of specific aspects of legislation by unanimous decision of the Council. Thus EC legislation could be adapted, as long as the purpose of adaptation was social and economic development. But no difference was to be made between the core provisions

[16] See n. 10 *supra*.

[17] On the contrary, they benefit from exemptions from certain aspects of VAT and other tax regimes.

[18] It was unprecedented at that moment.

[19] The general idea was to suppress the category of *territoires d'Outre-mer* perceived as a remainder of colonisation, either by bringing them to independence—as in the case of Djibouti or the Comores—or by changing them into *départements*, like Saint-Pierre-et-Miquelon.

[20] Art. 227(2) EEC last sentence, quoted by the ECJ in the *Hansen* case, n. 10 *supra*.

listed in Article 227(2) line 2 and other provisions of the Treaty: they were all eligible for adaptation.

On the basis of this line of interpretation, the Commission prepared a series of special measures in view of the achievement of the internal market, which were ready at the end of 1988. They took the form of two Council decisions of December 1989[21]: POSEIDOM, which contained specific framework principles for the DOM but made no exceptions to Treaty provisions, and a decision on the "dock dues" (*octroi de mer*), a taxation regime specific to the DOM, which clearly provided for a series of exemptions. With the accession of Portugal and Spain, three other Member States' regions shared the same type of geographic, economic and socio-cultural characteristics as the French DOM. Some specific provisions had been put in the accession Treaties, but they had not been mentioned in Article 227. In the framework of the regional policy it was decided to apply the same set of standards to these so-called "outermost regions". POSEIDOM served as a model for two other framework programmes POSEIMA[22] and POSEICAN.[23] The three framework programmes led to a whole series of regulations and decisions.[24] In addition, lobbying from local politicians at the end of the 1991 Inter-Governmental Conference (IGC) led to the drafting of a declaration (see Annex C) which had to be adopted together with the new Treaty, clearly a restatement of the *Hansen* doctrine, in favour of all seven outermost regions.

Everything seemed clear until 2 November 1991, when Advocate General Jacobs' Opinion in a case on the dock dues opened the way to a much more restrictive interpretation of Article 227(2). In his conclusions in the *Legros* case,[25] where the dock dues regime before December 1989 was at stake, the Advocate General indicated—outside the scope of the actual request for preliminary ruling—that the Council did not have the power to make the type of exemptions foreseen in the dock dues decision of December 1989. The Council therefore made an intervention, which led to a second Opinion from Advocate General Jacobs a few months later, a very rare event. Contrary to the Advocate General the Court said nothing on the 1989 decision—this would have been an illegal *ultra petita* statement—but it clearly indicated that the exemption power of the Council was to be limited to the provisions not quoted in Article 227(2) line 2. This was confirmed by the *Lancry* decision of 1994,[26] which invalidated the part of the December 1989 decision on dock dues which—on the basis of Articles 227 (now Article 299) and 235 (now Article 308) TEC—allowed France to maintain a derogatory taxation regime in the DOM until December 1992.

[21] Council Decisions 89/687/EEC POSEIDOM (p. 39) and 89/688/EEC dock dues arrangement of 22 December 1989, [1989] OJ L399/46.

[22] Council Decision 91/315/EEC of 26 June 1991 [1991] OJ L171/10 for Madeira and the Azores.

[23] Council Decision 91/314/EEC of 26 June 1991 [1991] OJ L171/5 for the Canary Islands.

[24] See Custos, n. 6 *supra*.

[25] Case C–163/90, *Legros* [1992] ECR I–4685.

[26] Case C–363/93, *Lancry S.A.*, [1994] ECR I–3978.

The court seemed not only to change its case law,[27] but also to be aiming at a restriction of the Commission's and Council's powers as stated in the Declaration on outermost regions. If a narrow view was to be taken the adaptations for the outermost regions could barely differ from the common flexibility provided by the application of the principle of equality, i.e. applying differing rules to differing situations.

For those scholars who would like to see an evolution of the ECJ to a less activist attitude after 1992, it should be stressed that at the end of the 1970s (in *Hansen*) the Court followed a Member State's view in accepting a wide application of flexibility, whereas from 1992 on, it took a view which was much narrower than the official line of the Member States acting in an IGC, the Commission, Council and Parliament. In this case, activism seems rather to be a feature of the post-1992 ECJ case law. In order to understand the clear tendency towards market orthodoxy revealed by the *Legros–Lancry* doctrine, one should however stress that, while drafting his conclusions in the *Legros* case, Advocate General Jacobs also had to examine the status of OCTs, with a case of local taxation showing some similarities with the dock dues regime at stake in the *Legros* case. His conclusions for the *Leplat* case[28] show that he had to compare in some way or other the regime of OCTs and that of outermost regions. It is most probable that he, and the Court, wanted to underline that flexibility within the internal market should not lead to situations identical to association[29]: either a region is fully integrated, with some flexibility, and it accepts both the benefits and burdens linked to the internal market, or the relevant governments should start to negotiate an association status for the region in question, as Denmark has done for Greenland.

In any case academia and politicians in France, Portugal and Spain often criticised the Court's decisions in the *Lancry* case for reverting to simplification and to priority of economic considerations over socio-political ones and for ignoring the clear will expressed at the 1991 IGC in the Declaration on outermost regions by reducing the scope of flexibility.

B. Article 299 TEC: The Member States Setting Limits to the Constitutional Supremacy of the ECJ?

Since the beginning of the 1990s local politicians in the outermost regions have started lobbying their governments in order to obtain a revision of Article

[27] Contrary to the statement made by the Court itself in point 37 of the *Lancry* decision, I still think, together with other scholars, that the *Hansen* decision clearly made no difference between provisions that could be adapted and others that could not. See also D. Perrot, "A propos de l'arrêt Legros, réflexion sur le statut communautaire des départements d'outre-mer" in [1993] *Revue du Marché Commun*, 427 s.

[28] See n. 12 *supra*.

[29] There is a great temptation to quote this line of reasoning of the Court as the *jurisprudence Legros-Leplat* , i. e. if translated from the French the *Fatman/Flatman doctrine*.

227(2), considered as obsolete in its formulation and not sufficiently safeguarding these regions' interests. However this lobbying started quite late, *inter alia* because it took quite some time for the French politicians in the DOM to realise that their interests lay in common action with the Portuguese and Spanish regions. Thus the Treaty of Maastricht proceeded to only a very minor revision of the EC Treaty itself—the deletion of the word Algeria—accompanied by a declaration without legal consequences. The new course of the ECJ since the *Legros* case probably helped to achieve in the Amsterdam revisions what had not been done in those of Maastricht (see Annexes B and C).

Apart from the French, Portuguese and Spanish governments, the other Member States could be at best indifferent, if not hostile,[30] to special status for the outermost regions. But during the 1995–7 IGC several other governments—including the German and British governments—shared a latent hostility towards the Court. This was probably the most favourable environment in order to draft a new formulation of Art. 227(2) which would reaffirm the standard *Hansen* doctrine as a response to the perceived escalation in the ECJ case law shown in *Legros* and *Lancry*. A new request (*Chevassus-Marche*) for a preliminary ruling directly questioning the core of the December 1989 Council decision on the dock dues was under way, leading to some anxiety in the relevant government departments and outermost regions. This led to the adoption of the new text, of Art. 299(2), which obviously draws on proposals put forward by representatives of the outermost regions during the period of the IGC.[31]

As there is no written evidence and no testimony of the IGC negotiations, I can only put forward a personal hypothesis, which seems to me a highly interesting hypothesis from the point of view of constitutional powers. The argument could be the following: in its case law from 1992 to 1994 (*Legros* and *Lancry*), the ECJ seemed to ignore the common will of the Commission, the Council and the Parliament as expressed in the 1989 POSEIDOM and dock dues decisions and—probably worse—the clear will of the unanimous Member States as expressed in the Declaration on outermost regions annexed to the Maastricht Treaty in 1992. This attitude of the Court started to be expressed (in Advocate General Jacobs' Opinion) at the time when the draft text of the 1992 Declaration was already published, and was confirmed in the period following the Danish and French referenda of 1992. As a reaction five years later, Member States used their powers as "masters of the treaties" by putting into the text of the TEC what formerly was expressed only in a declaration. Only a few months later the Court had to decide on the validity of the core part of the 1989 Council decision on the dock dues regime based on Articles 227 and 235 EC, allowing for a special new regime of dock dues for the period after 1 January 1993. To the

[30] It is largely the Outermost regions which are at stake in the conflict on bananas.

[31] See: Propostitioon de modification de l'article 227–2 du Traité de Rome, adoptée à Point-à-Pitre le 29 mars 1995 and Déclaration des présidents des régions ultrapériphériques—Funchal, 14 mars 1996, both in L. Grard and A. de Raulin (eds.), *Le développement des DOM et la Communauté européenne* (Paris: La Documentation Française, 1998), 173.

surprise of interested officials and scholars, the Court accepted the validity of the 1989 Council decision. I am inclined to argue that with this decision in the *Chevassus-Marche* case,[32] the Court wanted to acknowledge the signal sent by the IGC, i.e. by the Member States acting as "masters of the treaties".

From the point of view of flexibility however, it is very difficult to appreciate whether Article 299(2) of the Amsterdam Treaty is a step forward or backward.[33] The new text no longer includes a list of automatically applicable provisions. This means on one hand that adaptation is no longer limited to certain provisions only, but can apply in principle to the whole of the Treaty and secondary legislation—a return to the classical *Hansen* doctrine. On the other hand, the very complicated formulation of Article 299(2) is not a mere reproduction of the final sentence of Articles 277 (now 299) and 235 (now 308): flexibility does not allow for "undermining the integrity and the coherence of the Community legal order". Here is a new formulation of the core of EC law: who other than the ECJ could draw the limits? Could the other institutions take the lead in indicating more precisely what Article 299's substance should be? At the end of the day there is a supplementary lack of clarity in the text of the TEC—for worse or for better.

4. CONCLUSIONS

The Amsterdam IGC acknowledged the necessity "to reformulate the association arrangements by February 2000".[34] I hope to have demonstrated the need of a reformulation of the relevant provisions of the TEC, at least marginally. Nothing is mentioned in the conclusions of the Cologne Council, but the Commission, *inter alia*, is still in a position to put the point on the agenda, as it can indeed be argued that the issue is fully separate from those which should preferably be discussed with the future new members. One of the important things to do would obviously be to clarify that Part IV and the association arrangements are replacing Part III of the Treaty as far as OCTs are concerned, but that the other parts of the TEC are applicable to the whole territory of Member States, including OCT's if necessary, but for the exceptions provided for in Art. 299(3) *et seq*. Moreover, if the IGC were to deal with fundamental rights, the geographical and personal scope of that part of EC law should also be clarified.

Is there also a need to reformulate Article 299? This partly depends on the evolution of the ECJ case law in a context of closer attention to the needs and limits of flexibility. As far as these regions are concerned, the first step however has been taken by the Member States, at the Cologne Council of 3 and 4 June

[32] Case C–212/96, *Chevassus-Marche* [1998] ECR I–743.

[33] See Omarjee, n. 6 *supra*.

[34] Declaration no 36 on Overseas Countries and Territories, annexed to the Treaty of Amsterdam.

1999.[35] The need for legal stability rather pleads for keeping the issue of outermost regions out of the next IGC.

ANNEX A. ARTICLE 299 (EX ARTICLE 227) TEC

"1. This Treaty shall apply to the Kingdom of Belgium, the Kingdom of Denmark, the Federal Republic of Germany, the Hellenic Republic, the Kingdom of Spain, the French Republic, Ireland, the Italian Republic, the Grand Duchy of Luxembourg, the Kingdom of the Netherlands, the Republic of Austria, the Portuguese Republic, the Republic of Finland, the Kingdom of Sweden and the United Kingdom of Great Britain and Northern Ireland.

2. The provisions of this Treaty shall apply to the French overseas departments, the Azores, Madeira and the Canary Islands.

However, taking account of the structural social and economic situation of the French overseas departments, the Azores, Madeira and the Canary Islands, which is compounded by their remoteness, insularity, small size, difficult topography and climate, economic dependence on a few products, the permanence and combination of which severely restrain their development, the Council, acting by a qualified majority on a proposal from the Commission and after consulting the European Parliament, shall adopt specific measures aimed, in particular, at laying down the conditions of application of the present Treaty to those regions, including common policies.

The Council shall, when adopting the relevant measures referred to in the second subparagraph, take into account areas such as customs and trade policies, fiscal policy, free zones, agriculture and fisheries policies, conditions for supply of raw materials and essential consumer goods, State aids and conditions of access to structural funds and to horizontal Community programmes. The Council shall adopt the measures referred to in the second subparagraph taking into account the special characteristics and constraints of the Outermost regions without undermining the integrity and the coherence of the Community legal order, including the internal market and common policies.

3. The special arrangements for association set out in Part Four of this Treaty shall apply to the overseas countries and territories listed in Annex II to this Treaty.

This Treaty shall not apply to those overseas countries and territories having special relations with the United Kingdom of Great Britain and Northern Ireland which are not included in the aforementioned list.

4. The provisions of this Treaty shall apply to the European territories for whose external relations a Member State is responsible.

[35] See the Presidency Conclusions, point 38: "[t]he European Council invites the Commission to submit to the Council by the end of 1999 a report identifying a package of measures to implement the provisions of Article 299(2) of the EC Treaty with regard to the outermost regions".

5. This Treaty shall apply to the Åland Islands in accordance with the provisions set out in Protocol No 2 to the Act concerning the conditions of accession of the Republic of Austria, the Republic of Finland and the Kingdom of Sweden.

6. Notwithstanding the preceding paragraphs:

a. this Treaty shall not apply to the Faeroe Islands;
b. this Treaty shall not apply to the Sovereign Base Areas of the United Kingdom of Great Britain and Northern Ireland in Cyprus;
c. this Treaty shall apply to the Channel Islands and the Isle of Man only to the extent necessary to ensure the implementation of the arrangements for those islands set out in the Treaty concerning the accession of new Member States to the European Economic Community and to the European Atomic Energy Community signed on 22 January 1972."

ANNEX B. ARTICLE 227(2) OF THE ROME TREATY (BEFORE AMSTERDAM)

"2. With regard to [Algeria and[36]] the French overseas departments, the general and particular provisions of this Treaty relating to:

the free movement of goods;
agriculture, save for Article 40(4);
the liberalisation of services;
the rules on competition;
the protective measures provided for in Articles 109h, 109i and 226;
the institutions,

shall apply as soon as this Treaty enters into force.

The conditions under which the other provisions of this Treaty are to apply shall be determined, within two years of the entry into force of this Treaty, by decisions of the Council, acting unanimously on a proposal from the Commission.

The institutions of the Community will, within the framework of the procedures provided for in this Treaty, in particular Article 226, take care that the economic and social development of these areas is made possible."

ANNEX C. DECLARATION ON THE OUTERMOST REGIONS OF THE COMMUNITY (MAASTRICHT, 1992)

"The Conference acknowledges that the Outermost regions of the Community (the French overseas departments, Azores and Madeira and Canary Islands) suffer from major structural backwardness compounded by several phenomena (remoteness, island status, small size, difficult topography and climate, eco-

[36] Those two words were deleted by the Maastricht Treaty.

nomic dependence on a few products), the permanence and combination of which severely restrain their economic and social development. It considers that, while the provisions of the Treaty establishing the European Community and secondary legislation apply automatically to Outermost regions, it is nonetheless possible to adopt specific measures to assist them inasmuch and as long as there is an objective need to take such measures with a view to the economic and social development of those regions. Such measures should have their aim both the completion of the internal market and a recognition of the regional reality to enable the Outermost regions to achieve the average economic and social level of the Community."

ANNEX D. STATISTICAL INFORMATION

NB: most astonishingly in the era of the internet, simple data such as the updated population of all Member States including their outermost regions and OCTs are not directly available. The following data are taken from the *Encyclopaedia Britannica Book of the Year 1998*, or from my own calculations based upon several sources (marked **).

Composition of the "EU territories"

*European territory of the three Communities (total of 2,321,132 km² 370,147,000 inhabitants**)*

Belgium	30,528 km²	10,189,000 in.
Denmark	43,094 km²	5,284,000 in.
Germany	356,974 km²	82,143,000 in.
Greece	131,957 km²	10,541,000 in.
Spain	497,510 km²	37,923,000 in. **
France	543,965 km²	56,616,000 in.
Ireland	70,285 km²	3,644,000 in.
Italy	301,309 km²	57,511,000 in.
Luxembourg	2,586 km²	420,000 in.
The Netherlands	41,526 km²	15,619,000 in.
Austria	83,858 km²	8,087,000 in.
Portugal	89,003 km²	9,243,000 in.
Finland	338,145 km²	5,145,000 in.
Sweden	449,964 km²	8,863,000 in.
United Kingdom	244,110 km²	58,919,000 in.

These data include the Åland Islands which are part of the EC, but neither the Faeroe Islands (1 399km²; 43 800 in.) nor the Isle of Man (572 km², 69 600 in.**), the Channel Islands (194 km², 152 600 in.**), or Gibraltar (5,8 km², 28 100 in.**) which are submitted to a diversity of association regimes.

*Non-European territory of the EC internal market i.e. outermost regions (part of the EURATOM territory but not of the ECSC territory) total of 102,203 km², 3,974,000 inhabitants***

Spain	7,273 km²	i.e. :
Canary Islands	7,242 km²	1,530,000 in. **
Ceuta and Melilla	31 km²	69,000 in. **
France	91,887 km²	i.e.:
Guadeloupe	1,780 km²	434,000 in.
French Guiana	86,504 km²	152,000 in.
Martinique	1,091 km²	399,000 in.
Réunion	2,512 km²	681,000 in.

Clipperton and Indian Ocean Spare Islands (the latter disputed by Mauritius and Madagascar) ± 50 km² no inhabitants.

Portugal	3,043 km²	i.e.:
Azores	2,247 km²	300,000 in. **
Madeira	796 km²	400,000 in. **

Overseas Countries and Territories (associated to EC, part of Euratom territory, not ECSC territories) 2,296,904 km² 995,850 inhabitants (among which 927,500 are citizens of an EU Member State):

Denmark (Greenland)	2,175,600 km²	56,300 in. (Danish citizens)
France	529,799 km²	571,100 in.** (French citizens) i.e.:
New Caledonia	18,567 km²	201,000 in.
French Polynesia	4,200 km²	220,000 in.**
French Austral and Antarctic Territory (without claims on the Antarctic, "frozen" by the relevant multilateral treaty)	7,600 km²	no permanent inhabitants
Wallis-and-Futuna Islands	280 km²	16,000 in.**
Mayotte	374 km²	128,000 in.**
Saint-Pierre-et-Miquelon	242 km²	6,100 in.**
The Netherlands	993 km²	298,200 in. (Dutch citizens) i.e.:
Aruba	193 km²	84,200 in.

Federation of the Netherlands Antilles (Bonaire, Curaçao, Saba, Saint Eustache, Saint Martin)	800 km^2	214,000 in.

Under UK sovereignty 17,200 km^2 70,250 in.**, amongst which fewer than 2,000 are British citizens, i.e.:

Anguilla	91 km^2	7,300 in.
British Antarctic Territory (without claims on the Antarctic, "frozen" by the relevant multilateral treaty)	5,320 km^2	no permanent inhabitants
British Indian Ocean Territory	60 km^2	no permanent inhabitants
British Virgin Islands	153 km^2	12,700 in.
Cayman	264 km^2	25,900 in.
Falkland Islands	12,173 km^2	1,900 in. (British citizens)
Montserrat	102 km^2	600 in.
Pitcairn:	4.5 km^2	50 in.
Saint Helena and Dependencies	159 km^2	7,300 in.
Southern Sandwich Islands and Southern Georgia	4,000 km^2	no permanent inhabitants
Turks and Caicos Islands	193 km^2	14,500 in.

Bermuda Islands (54 km^2, 61,000 in.) are not included in OCT's, as the Association decision is not applicable although on the list of annex II.

7

Differentiation within the Core: The Case of the Common Market

GRÁINNE DE BÚRCA*

1. INTRODUCTION

THE AIM OF this chapter is twofold. It seeks first to examine the nature and extent of certain kinds of legislative differentiation which have existed over the years between Member States of the European Community, focusing specifically on differentiating provisions within harmonisation directives in the internal market sphere. Secondly, it seeks in so doing to explore what kind of "core" commitment or set of commitments might be said to characterise European Community, now European Union, membership and effectively to limit the nature and extent of differentiation which ought to take place.

The recent moves to institutionalise general provisions on differentiation and closer co-operation within the EU Treaties focus a number of questions about the aims and aspirations of the EU as a political entity. Over the years, the value of uniformity in the application of and adherence to Community law and policy has been institutionally asserted as one of the central tenets of the enterprise. At the heart of the original move towards the creation of the European Communities was a desire to pool some of the resources and capacities of nation states within Europe and to create a central supranational level of government responsible for enabling, in the first place, a market-place in common to exist between those states. The deeper reasons for the creation of this common market have always remained open to debate: whether, as a first step towards a European political union, to ensure greater peace and stability within Europe, to augment the capacities of the individual states to act on both domestic and international issues, or to create a united trading *bloc* capable of rivalling other world trading powers. But it is indisputable that what constituted the first major step in the process of shaping a European political entity, and what remains today as the central plank of the European Communities and Union, is the set of norms and policies making up what has variously been called the common, single or internal market.

* I am very grateful to Madeleine de Leeuw for her research assistance, and to Joanne Scott, Neil Walker and the participants at the workshop held in Florence in Apr. 1999 for their comments and advice.

To this extent, the common market can be said to be at the centre of the EC and the EU, and commitment to the norms and policies which underpin it has always been essential to membership.[1] And while it is evident that the apparent changes in the EU's constitutional framework, as reflected in the expanding language of flexibility, variable geometry, closer co-operation etc. of the post-Maastricht era, have relevance for newer, less established and more contentious or peripheral areas of Community and Union policy competence, it is less clear whether or how they may affect essential areas of the internal market.[2] On the one hand, the future-oriented Amsterdam Treaty provisions on closer co-operation endeavour to place the entire package of Europe's past policies securely beyond reach by declaring that the *acquis communautaire* must not be affected.[3] On the other hand, not only is this unavoidably vacuous stipulation likely to be loosely interpreted in practice, but the newer kind of primary, Treaty-based differentiation contemplated by these provisions is not the only way of permitting states to adopt different positions in relation to Community policies, or to opt out from parts of those policies. Apart from the *ad hoc* Maastricht Treaty-sanctioned differentiation for EMU and Social Policy, as well as the Irish protocol on abortion and the Danish second-homes protocol, there was a longer established Community practice of permitting certain kinds of differentiation between Member States even within the most hallowed parts of the EC's supposedly uniform and shared internal market *acquis*, and a somewhat sanitised formulation of this practice was subsequently enshrined by the Single European Act in what was then Article 8c (now Article 20)[4] of the EEC Treaty.[5]

[1] H. Wallace and W. Wallace, *Flying Together in a Larger and More Diverse European Union* (Netherlands Scientific Council for Government Policy, Gravenhage W 87/1985): "by convention the single market and the four freedoms, complemented by the rules of competition and the common commercial policy, comprise the founding core of the EC model and its key policy goals. These are the elements that cannot be stripped away, being deeply embedded in the treaties and subsequent legislation". "It is generally argued that this cluster of commitments must be accepted by all members states on the same basis and that other countries should not be admitted until and unless they are able to undertake the full range of commitments." And they acknowledge that although reality is more nuanced than this and that there is significant legislative differentiation, nonetheless "the notion that full acceptance of the single market is a *sine qua non* of full EU membership is strongly held".

[2] See the analysis of M. Dewatripont, F. Giavazzi, J. von Hagen, I. Harden, T. Persson, G. Roland, H. Rosenthal, A. Sapir and G. Tabellini, *Flexible Integration, Towards a More Effective and Democratic Europe* (London: Centre for Economic Policy Research, 1995) identifying the single market as a common base.

[3] To use W. Wessels' description in "Flexibility, Differentiation and Closer Co-operation: The Amsterdam Provisions in the Light of the Treaty Report" in M. Westlake (ed.), *The European Union Beyond Amsterdam: New Concepts of European Integration* (London: Routledge, 1998) 76, 78, "the impression given is of a fortress being built around . . . areas considered sacrosanct".

[4] "When drawing up its proposals with a view to achieving the objectives set out in Article 8a [now Art. 18], the Commission shall take into account the extent of the effort that certain economies showing differences in developments will have to sustain during the period of establishment of the internal market and it may propose appropriate provisions.

If these provisions take the form of derogations, they must be of a temporary nature and must cause the least possible disturbance to the functioning of the common market."

[5] For a very helpful and comprehensive account of differentiation in the EC and EU over the years, see F. Tuytschaever, *Differentiation in European Union Law* (Oxford: Hart Publishing, 1999).

2. THE NOTION OF "CORE"

There is a certain ambiguity in the term "core", which tends to be used in the EU context to refer to a number of different issues.[6] Labels such as "core" and "periphery" are either used to indicate groups of states which are considered central in a geographic sense or, more figuratively, to describe states which have historically been at the centre of the drive towards integration and which continue to be closely involved in the formulation and promotion of all key policies. Another sense in which it is used is to indicate a general "core commitment" required for membership of an organisation, including matters such as compliance, participation in accordance with agreed rules, and attitudes towards key obligations and norms. Steve Weatherill, for example, in discussing the notion of *acquis communautaire*,[7] argues for some kind of constitutional "hard core" in the EC legal order which is not readily capable of transformation and which represents the essential characteristics of the system. As far as substantive policy is concerned, the term "core" generally refers to one of the original and foundational areas of action provided for in the EEC Treaty, such as the establishment of the common market, or a number of others, such as the common commercial policy and competition policy. This chapter combines a number of these ideas of core, in assessing the past practice of Member States within the Council who have secured differentiating treatment for themselves, when adopting what were intended to be harmonising or approximating directives in the internal market field.

The notion of "core" is thus being used here to explore the idea that, within a polity such as the EU which is considerably more than a traditional intergovernmental order of states, there must be certain limits to flexibility and to differentiation, some minimum degree of commitment to a basic and shared set of policies. This notion of commitment combines the idea of acceptance of both the content of particular policies and the specific legal and constitutional characteristics of such measures. The examination of a range of internal market legislation containing differentiating provisions helps to exemplify, within a key policy area which of its nature aims at producing a degree of uniformity amongst states, what the specific exceptions suggest about the states' commitment to this core common policy, and whether there appear to be *de facto* and not just *de jure* limits to the kind of exceptions permitted. While the formal legal position—articulated by the Court of Justice amongst others—is that the grounds on which Member States may enjoy differential treatment must be temporary and must reflect objective socio-economic differences rather than

[6] Wallace and Wallace n. 1 *supra*, 33, for example, distinguish between core policies, core countries and core institutions.

[7] "Safeguarding the Acquis Communautaire" in T. Heukels, N. Blokker and M. Brus (eds.), *The European Union after Amsterdam* 153–178 (Europa Institute of Leiden, 1998) The Hague, ch. 8.

subjective political preferences,[8] examination of legislative practice suggests a considerably more blurred picture. It is partly the case, of course, that the distinction between objective and subjective grounds is an exaggerated one, but it is also undoubtedly true that Member States have opted out, sometimes for longer and repeatedly renewed periods of time, from common policies in the internal market sphere, for reasons which seem like little more than the maintenance of a competitive advantage or a fundamental rejection of part of the policy measure in question.

3. LEGISLATING FOR THE COMMON MARKET

The kernel of the EC's common market consists of the four notional freedoms, the free movement of goods, persons, services and capital between Member States. These are institutionalised within the legal framework of the Community in a number of ways: first, in the general Treaty provisions—the "negative integration" norms—which formally require the Member States to remove restrictions from and to guarantee those freedoms, and secondly in the Treaty provisions which envisage EC legislative measures—"positive integration" provisions—being adopted to "approximate" or harmonise the regulatory laws of the Member States, whose differences might otherwise constitute costly barriers to trade between states. The main examples of this second category of Treaty provisions are listed in Article 14 (ex Article 7a, and before being renumbered by the Maastricht Treaty, originally Article 8a) of the EC Treaty, which was first inserted by the Single European Act as part of the attempt to revitalise the entire common market project in the mid 1980s. The first two paragraphs of that Article provide that:

> 1. The Community shall adopt measures with the aim of progressively establishing the internal market (over a period expiring on 31 December 1992) in accordance with the provisions of this Article and of Articles 15, 26, 47(2), 49, 80, 93 and 95[9] and without prejudice to the other provisions of this Treaty.
>
> 2. The internal market shall comprise an area without internal frontiers in which the free movement of goods, persons, services and capital is ensured in accordance with the provisions of the Treaty.

The various Articles listed in this provision cover a range of policy areas in which legislation to further the common market was envisaged, such as the common customs tariff, freedom of establishment and the free movement of persons, transport policy and indirect taxation. A considerable amount of legislation was adopted in the area of the free movement of persons and establish-

[8] See e.g. C.-D. Ehlermann, "How Flexible is Community Law? An Unusual Approach to the Concept of 'Two Speeds' "(1984) 82 *Michigan Law Review* 1274; Wallace and Wallace n. 1 *supra*, 49–52; and F. Tuytschaever, *Differentiation in European Union Law* (Oxford: Hart Publishing, 1999), ch. 4.

[9] Formerly Arts. 7c, 28, 57(2), 59, 84, 99 and 100A.

ment under Article 47(2) (ex Article 57(2)), but Articles 94 and 95 (ex Articles 100 and 100A) have been the most fertile sources of harmonisation or approximation legislation, since those provisions are general in nature. Article 94 requires the Council, acting unanimously, to issue directives "for the approximation of such laws, regulations or administrative provisions of the Member States as directly affect the establishment of the common market", and Article 95 and the amended Article 47(2) (along with a range of other Treaty bases for internal market legislation) were introduced by the Single European Act primarily in order to provide for the possibility of qualified majority voting.[10] Article 95 is slightly different from Article 94, in that it does not refer to the common market, but instead to the adoption of approximating measures (not only directives) "which have as their objective the establishing and functioning of the internal market". Whether the "internal market" is a concept which differs in any significant way from the "common market" remains open to question,[11] but the measures adopted under both of these provisions serve to exemplify the legislative attempts to eliminate regulatory and other differences between Member States which were thought to hinder the setting up of the promised European-wide market.

In examining the kind of "approximating legislation" which has been adopted under these three Treaty provisions—Articles 47(2), 94 and 95 (ex Articles 57(2), 100 and 100A)[12]—the intention is to consider what sort of differentiation has been permitted over the years to take account of different needs and demands of individual Member States. Studies of this kind should provide some insight into the nature of the Community's "common market" core, and into the question of how much flexibility within such central areas seems to have been considered compatible with the notion of a common market. This in turn prompts a more general reflection on whether there is a minimum degree of conformity which states must accept for the EU to maintain an identity as a polity.

[10] At the same time, the SEA added Arts. 8a–c (now Arts. 18–20) into the EC Treaty (specifying 1992 as a date for establishing the internal market), making explicit provision for limited differentiation in what was then Art. 8c (now Art. 20) EC. See n. 4, *supra*. The move to qualified majority voting meant the loss by individual Member States of the bargaining power which was undoubtedly important in making a case for a specific derogation within a given harmonising measure, and the express provision in Art. 20 EC might be seen as some kind of compensation for this.

[11] See K. Armstrong, "Governance and the Single European Market" in P. Craig and G. de Búrca (eds.), *The Evolution of EU Law* (Oxford, OUP, 1999) 745, 747, discussing the views of P. Pescatore on the Single European Act.

[12] The primary focus of the research for this chapter has been Art. 94 (ex Art. 100) EC, based on the assumption that the unanimity requirement would have enhanced the likelihood of finding examples of differentiation under this legal basis. However, searches have also been carried out of Art. 100a (now Art. 95) legislation, but apart from a number of provisions necessitated by German reunification and some outstanding transitional provisions following the earlier accession of Portugal and Spain (which have not been included in the tables), there seemed to be few significant instances of differentiation which did not also appear under the search for Art. 47(2) (ex Art. 57(2)) legislation, since those measures had a dual legal basis. Nor do the results of the legislative search under Art. 100 purport to be exhaustive, since the search methods used were selective. Further, some of the minor examples of differentiation, such as the transitional provisions for newly acceding or recently acceded Member States, have deliberately been omitted.

As the EC and EU continue to widen, to diversify, to multiply in membership, to expand policy competences and to grow in institutional complexity, the risk that proliferating forms of flexibility and differentiation will increasingly undermine its sense of coherence or purpose and fragment its legitimacy and authority, along with its constitutional structures, must become greater. Further, the kind of differentiation which is permitted is also likely to affect the perceived legitimacy of the polity, in the sense that differential treatment on the basis of "domestic partisanship" or political obstructionism,[13] rather than identifiable socio-economic difference, may gradually undermine the idea of commonality which underpins not just the common market core but the Community and the Union also. Thus the question of what, if anything, can be identified as a core constitutional commitment of the EU becomes a more important one.

The focus of the case study is on a specific kind of legislative flexibility, i.e. the provision of clearly acknowledged differential treatment for one or more Member States within Community "approximating directives" in this particular internal market sphere. And although secondary legislative differentiation seems less dramatic and less disruptive to Community aims than the kind of Treaty-based differentiation which has become more common since the Maastricht Treaty amendments, the existence of such a practice is worth examining for at least two reasons. In the first place, it can be scrutinised as an early precedent for the more recent and more constitutionally significant types of flexibility which have emerged, culminating in the closer co-operation provisions of the Amsterdam Treaty, and secondly it took place within the context of a core area of Community policy in which uniformity and harmonisation of differences between Member States have been asserted as important goals.

4. DIFFERENTIATION WITHIN THE COMMON MARKET

The "differentiating" measures being examined in this context are distinct from legislation which is flexible in a more general way, for instance (what might be called micro-flexibility) provisions which leave a broad degree of discretion in implementation[14] or establish general derogations or exceptions, similar to those contained in Article 95(4)[15] and (5) or 39(3) of the EC Treaty, which would permit any Member State to deviate from the requirements of the measure for certain reasons and in accordance with a specified procedure. The body

[13] See H. Wallace and A. Ridley, *Europe: The Challenge of Diversity* (London: RIIA, 1985) 40 and Wallace and Wallace, n. 1 *supra*, 50–3.

[14] See the chapter by J. Scott "Flexibility, 'Proceduralization', and Environmental Governance in the EU" and the examples of flexibility within dirs. and soft law measures given by Catherine Barnard in her chapter, "Flexibility and Social Policy", both in this volume.

[15] For a recent example of Sweden's attempt to obtain a derogation in respect of a foodstuffs dir., and to maintain a differentiated position in national law before the Commission had responded under Art. 95(4), see Case C–319/97, *Criminal proceedings against Kortas*, ruling of 1 June 1999, not yet reported.

of legislation examined here (which could be called "meso-level" flexibility) differs from these examples in that the directives in question do not actually incorporate a degree of flexibility into the definition of the general policy requirements they contain. Rather they expressly exempt a named Member State or States, usually for a specified period but sometimes more open-endedly, from an otherwise fairly concrete, distinct and uniform obligation. They contain specific, individual exemptions which have been negotiated by a Member State or States apparently in order to respond to a particular need of that state.

This type of differentiation also contrasts clearly with that envisaged in the new closer co-operation provisions of the EC and EU Treaty (what we might call macro-flexibility), and indeed also with the previous Schengen-type *ad hoc* arrangements. They differ partly in that some of the newer provisions—particularly those introduced by the Amsterdam Treaty—are positively rather than negatively framed, in the sense of certain states wishing to forge ahead in a particular policy area and being willing to do so without the participation of the remaining states. Thus any onus to "explain" is not on the Member States which choose not to participate, but on those which choose to instigate closer co-operation. The kind of internal market differentiation which has occurred within Community law, by comparison, has not usually been structured in the form of certain Member States forging ahead in a given area without the participation of others who are unable or unwilling, but rather as certain Member States which actually participate in the adoption of a policy measure gaining a specific and normally temporal exemption from the requirements of a policy which will otherwise bind them all in common.

It differs also in certain respects from the individual opt-outs for the UK from the Social Policy Agreement, for the UK and Denmark from Economic and Monetary Union, and for the UK and Ireland from the post-Amsterdam incorporation of "Schengen" policy into the EC Treaty. Most obviously, it has not generally been constitutionally incorporated by being provided for in the Treaties themselves,[16] but rather originates in specific pieces of secondary legislation. For such secondary differentiation to be lawful, on the other hand, it must—unlike the *ad hoc* forms of Treaty-based macro-flexibility—comply with any principles and limits to be found in the Treaties or prescribed by the Court of Justice,[17] although in the case of the bulk of the measures set out in the tables below, there were no specific advance conditions set out in the Treaties. Secondly, this kind of legislative differentiation does not generally entail the non-participation of a Member State (or States) across an entire policy area, but rather exempts a state or states from a specific obligation or requirement contained in a fairly particular policy measure.

16 Although Art. 20 (ex Art. 8c) of the Treaty represents a kind of *ex post facto* constitutional codification of some of the practice of secondary legislative differentiation in the internal market sphere: see n. 4 *supra* and text.

17 See in particular the cases discussed by Ehlermann, n. 8 *supra*, at 1286, and more recently the discussion by Tutyschaever, n. 8 *supra*, ch. 4.

On the other hand, it should also be emphasised that the various distinctions which are drawn between different types of flexibility, differentiation and others—both here and in the literature in general—are relatively fluid, and that many of the various definitions and categorisations share common features and overlap. The distinctive features of the "approximation legislation" in question are deliberately being highlighted here, mainly in order to examine the significance of a particular and not uncommon type of internal market differentiation for an understanding of the EC/EU constitutional framework over time. More generally, however, such differentiation is neither as dramatic nor as significant in constitutional terms as the more recent examples of Treaty differentiation such as the Social Policy Agreement and EMU, since it does not entail the pursuit by different groupings of states of entirely different sets of policies to which others do not commit themselves. Legislative differentiation which permits individual and normally time-limited exceptions for specific Member States within the context of a shared commitment to common policy goals and full participation in the general decision-making process would not seem to threaten an overall ideal of "Community", commonality or unity in the way that it has been feared some more recent and major manifestations of differentiation could do. Nonetheless, the fact that extensive legislative differentiation has existed for a long time in the context of "approximation" legislation adopted under provisions such as Articles 94, 95 and 47 (ex Articles 100, 100A and 57) is significant in the sense that this branch of decision-making has normally been thought to exemplify the classic, traditionally conceived Community aims (admittedly always a regulatory ideal rather than a reality) of integration, harmonisation and unity, in the context of the central task of establishing a common market free of frontiers and sharing the same competitive conditions. This common or internal market is still seen as a common base to which all present and future EU Member States are expected to commit and bind themselves in the same way.[18] The fact that even within this more "protected" sphere of common policy-making, there has been a long-standing acceptance and accommodation of the need for diversity, well before this practice was formally legitimated by the constitutional framework of the Treaties, may suggest that even the established central commitments of EC membership are looser and more fluid than the notion of core might suggest.

5. THE COMMON MARKET AS "CORE"

Any attempt to identify or define the essence or core of the European Community and Union seems likely, in an era when pluralism and postmodernism represent the dominant intellectual trends, to fail. The idea that there

[18] See, for the expectation that would-be Member States shall also adhere, the chapter by Marise Cremona "Flexible Models: External Policy and the European Economic Constitution" in this volume.

may be something fixed or immutable which defines the essence of the polity is at odds with some of the more recent depictions of the EU as an essentially contested project,[19] as one in which there is a multiplicity of voices and objectives, and an inevitable and necessary indeterminacy rather than a fixed end-point or route.[20] In her contribution to this volume, Jo Shaw contrasts a traditional conception of constitutionalism which is founded on the operation of institutions under the rule of law which seek to provide good government and to protect certain rights and values, with a more process- or dialogue-based model underpinned only by the values of mutual recognition, consent and cultural continuity.[21] Her argument is that flexibility in the EU context does not have to be seen as a way of avoiding deeper questions of constitutional democracy. On the contrary, she argues that it could be part of a useful constitutional response to a diverse society, if constitutionalism is conceived of as a continuous process of dialogue in relation to an entity which is constantly in the course of negotiation and renegotiation, rather than as the fixed legal framework within which a previously agreed project of economic and political integration is pursued. From this perspective, the idea of identifying the core commitments of EU membership by analysing the notion of the "common market" could appear as a misguided attempt to define the fixed end of integration or the essential identity of the European polity.

However, this chapter does not advance a normative thesis to the effect that the common market project should form a substantive and largely immutable core of Europe's constitution. Rather it seeks to question, partly through an empirical study of a central sphere of Community policy, whether some minimum degree of commitment to certain shared processes, aims and policies seems necessary for the existence of a polity, and what the content of that commitment appears to be in the EU context. The focus on the common market, rather than merely on institutional structures and norms, brings detailed substantive policy into play, which itself reflects the economic goals at the heart of the EU constitutional framework. Economic norms have been placed at the centre of the constituent treaties, and the common market still remains, despite the expansion of policy competences and the rhetorical move from "Community" to "Union", at the heart of the political project. The single market is not only an important and central part of the EU's political strategy,[22] but it is also presented as the core of the *acquis* to which applicant Member States are increasingly expected to subscribe.[23] The ability of states and other actors to influence the nature and direction of the "common market" through participation, dialogue and argument is

[19] Z. Bankowski and E. Christodoulidis, "The European Union as an Essentially Contested Project" (1998) 4 *ELJ* 341.

[20] I. Ward, *A Critical Introduction to EU Law* (London: Butterworths, 1996) ch. 5.

[21] J. Shaw, "Relating Constitutionalism and Flexibility in the European Union".

[22] See Armstrong, n. 11 *supra*.

[23] See Cremona, in this volume.

another and larger question, and one which is essential to the legitimacy of the EU.[24]

Conceiving and examining the common market as one of the central commitments of EU membership is not necessarily to say that the harmonisation of provisions on the eradication of brucellosis, or of national laws relating to honey (to take some examples from the tables below) in themselves form the constitutional heart of the European polity. However, the single market notion entails a very central and concrete set of substantive policy commitments which has formed the basis for the broad original integrative ideal of "bringing together" Member States within a common political and economic endeavour. It has been argued that the common market concretises and represents the "common good" of the EU as a political unity.[25] Together with the idea of supranational and transnational constitutionalism as an alternative to the international method, commitment to this broad (and ultimately renegotiable) conception of the common good, which leads in turn to a more precisely defined set of basic policies, could be said to form the constitutional core of EU membership.

6. AFTER AMSTERDAM: REVISITING DIFFERENTIATION WITHIN THE COMMON MARKET

Despite the fact that it is now more than 15 years old, the article written by Claus Dieter Ehlermann on "An Unusual Approach to the Concept of Two Speeds" remains one of the most interesting and thought-provoking pieces on the subject of differentiation.[26] While his analysis has lost little of its relevance with the passage of time, developments since then have cast a different light on some of the premises and assumptions underlying the article. He argued that the appeal of flexibility or differentiation lay primarily in the reluctance to have recourse to qualified majority voting at the time, and that this appeal would fade if such voting were to become more popular. However, although the use of qualified majority voting is considerably more common today, both the possibility that a "blocking minority" of states (rather than simply an individual veto) could impede the desired progress of others, and the implications of ever wider policy and geographical expansion have ensured that the notion of differentiated integration remains as salient as ever. Even within the sphere of internal market legislation, Member States continue to negotiate, albeit less frequently, differential positions for themselves even after the introduction of qualified majority voting under Articles 95 and 47(2) of the EC Treaty.

[24] See H. Lindahl and B. Van Roermund, "Law Without a State: On Representing the Common Market", forthcoming, and also H. Lindahl, "The Purposiveness of Law: Two Concepts of Representation in the European Union" (1998) 17 *Law and Philosophy* 481.

[25] Lindahl and Van Roermund, n. 24 *supra*.

[26] N. 8 *supra*.

In the early 1980s, proposals for introducing mechanisms to facilitate a "two-speed Europe" were in circulation, and Ehlermann sought to demonstrate the considerable scope for differentiation which already existed within Community law, albeit subject to certain limits implicit in the non-discrimination principle and subject to some of the fundamental Treaty prohibitions. Amongst the types of flexibility then existing, he listed examples of differentiated application of secondary Community law, many falling within the field of agricultural policy. Building on some of his suggestions, this chapter takes one particular branch of common market legislation in order to analyse a little more systematically the kind of differentiation which has taken place. In highlighting not just the nature of the differential provisions which were permitted, but more specifically the reasons given for these, the study may provide further insights into the permissible limits of diversity within what is acknowledged to be a core part of Community policy. These examples of legislative differentiation can also be contrasted, in an instructive way, with the more recently institutionalised forms of closer co-operation within the Treaties.

Arguably, or at least at first sight, the kind of middle-level differentiation in secondary legislation set out in the tables below and the newer Treaty provisions on closer co-operation have more in common with each other than either has with the cruder, politically negotiated opt-outs of the Social Policy Agreement, EMU, the Irish abortion protocol and the Danish second-homes protocol. This is so even though the latter four examples are, like the Amsterdam provisions, enshrined within the primary Treaties. It can be argued that both secondary legislative differentiation of the kind exemplified below and the closer co-operation provisions function within the context of a broader constitutional commitment, in the sense of an overall shared commitment to the same normative project.

In this sense they are unlike the strongest of the *à la carte* examples above such as the original UK social policy opt-out, or even—despite its minor economic or practical significance—the Danish second-homes protocol. These latter examples actually suggest a more fundamental questioning of some of the most basic assumptions of the EU polity, and of some of the basic principles underpinning the common market concept, such as the non-discrimination principle and the equalisation of the conditions of competition. This fundamental questioning was expressed through a political refusal to participate in or to accept the consequences of some of the Community's central common policies. The differential treatment was bargained for and insisted upon by the Member State in question, at a moment of fundamental, back-to-the-drawing-board renegotiation of the Treaties, as the price for signing up to other proposed Treaty amendments. The reasons for seeking such exceptional treatment were, at best, controversial and, at worst, alleged to be in breach of the fundamental principles underpinning the whole European constitutional order.[27]

[27] On the debate about the legality of the Social Policy Agreement, see P.Watson, "Social Policy after Maastricht" (1993) 31 *CMLRev*. 481 and C. Barnard, "A Social Policy for Europe: Politicians 1 Lawyers 0" (1992) 8 *IJCLLIR* 15.

In contrast, given the requisite overall commitment to the particular legislative policy in question or to the provisions and aims of the Treaties more generally, both the secondary legislative differentiation (at least in so far as can be discerned from the preamble and provisions of some of the legislative measures) and the post-Amsterdam Treaty provisions operate in a relatively structured and procedurally pre-determined way, requiring the involvement of the relevant EC institutions and the participation of the Member States. The two however differ from one another, first in that the legislative exceptions are generally time-limited, thus normally demanding a commitment from the "differentiated" Member State to subject itself ultimately to that particular measure, rather than simply to the general policy aims. This is not true of the new Treaty provisions, except in so far as closer co-operation is only to operate within the existing limits of Community or Union competence, and in this respect all Member States have by definition already committed themselves in a general way to all the principles, aims and objectives of the Treaties. The new mechanisms of flexibility, in other words, operate within the "constitutional embrace" of the Treaties, rather than taking place in the curious vacuum of an intergovernmental conference when the states are in theory free (subject to international law requirements and principles such as that of good faith) to negotiate as the sovereign masters of an international order.

Secondly, there is no apparent requirement for the Member States which choose not to participate in an area of closer co-operation to give reasons for their non-involvement, whereas in most instances of secondary legislative differentiation examined below, some reference (however sketchy and unconvincing) to the reasons for the special treatment is made, and the nature of the reason is important for the legality of the measures. Further, under the terms of Article 11 of the EC Treaty, any form of closer co-operation in Community matters must satisfy the requirement that it does not constitute a discrimination or restriction on trade between Member States nor distort conditions of competition between them. This appears to impose a fairly strong formal limit on the kind of closer co-operation which should occur, so that if co-operation in that particular policy sphere has the effect of distorting the common market e.g. by providing a certain kind of competitive advantage for one state, it would not appear to comply with the Treaty conditions.[28]

On the other hand, some degree of discrimination is necessarily inherent in the notion of differentiation. According to a paper written by the Commission in 1978, differentiation between Member States within secondary Community legislation could in fact be seen as a fulfilment of, rather than a breach of, the non-discrimination principle, since this principle requires that "different cases must be handled in different ways".[29] However, this principle of legitimately

[28] On this and the other criteria for closer co-operation more generally, see S. Weatherill's chapter in this volume. He points out, as others have done, that, if taken very literally, these conditions would make almost any form of closer co-operation extremely difficult.

[29] "The transitional period and the institutional implications of enlargement", *Bull. EC*, Supp. 2/78.

differential treatment is, according to the Commission, subject to certain limits: mainly limits of degree and time. Thus, where harmonising legislation was concerned, the differences existing between Member States ought not to be exaggerated, and secondly the differential treatment should cease "as soon as circumstances permit". These limitations are now reflected in Article 20, in a retrospective legitimation of the practice by the Single European Act's amendment to the EC Treaty. However, even though the tone of the Commission's paper and of Article 20 EC suggests that differentiation is a temporary phenomenon which should reduce over time as the relevant "objective differences" are ironed out, the conditions giving rise to the need or the desire for diversity are likely to continue and possibly to evolve rather than diminish and disappear. As the Commission also pointed out even in the 1970s, the economic and social conditions within the original six Member States were considerably more homogenous than in a larger Community of nine, 12 or 15—let alone 20 or 25. It seems inevitable that the conception of a common market with a single, universally applicable body of rules would not be the same for a Community of six homogenous states as for a much larger and more heterogeneous Community, in particular as the subject matter of EC regulatory harmonisation and approximation (and thus the content and scope of the common market sphere) grows wider. On this basis, it would not be surprising if the attempts to secure differential treatment for particular Member States even in the internal market context did not significantly diminish with the passage of time.

7. ANALYSING THE REASONS FOR LEGISLATIVE DIFFERENTIATION AND THE EXTENT OF COMMITMENT TO THE CORE

The analysis above suggests that the differentiation which occurred within secondary legislation, such as that under Articles 94, 95 and 47 (ex Articles 100, 100A and 57), took place, unlike the Maastricht-era Treaty-based opt-outs, broadly within the framework of an overall constitutional commitment to the same policies and ends, and for the kind of time-limited, objective, socio-economic reasons suggested by the Commission and by Ehlermann, cited above. It is notable too that when, in 1986, the SEA added Article 20 (ex Article 8c) to the EC Treaty, it provided only for a particular kind of temporary, "least disruptive" differentiation and on the basis of only one, albeit broadly conceived, justification, i.e. "the extent of the effort that certain economies showing differences in development will have to sustain". Since this Treaty provision evidently represents the retrospective imposition of a constitutional framework on the sorts of practices which were already in existence, these conditions seem intended to reflect the limits and conditions which that past practice had (or ought to have) respected.

It seems clear, nonetheless, from looking at a range of the examples in the tables below that while quite a number of differentiating provisions are explained by reference to what effectively amounts to a claim of different levels of economic development, this was certainly not the only or even the main reason given for differentiating provisions within internal market legislation. In eight out of 41 (i.e. one fifth of these) directives listed below which were adopted under Article 100, each of which contained at least one differentiating provision, no reason for such differentiation was given in the preamble to the measure or in its actual provisions. Some of these derogations were relatively minor and of short duration,[30] but there are other more significant differentiating provisions for which no reason is given and which are not time-limited. One example is to be found in the exceptions for Greece contained in Directive 83/90, concerning health problems in the Community's fresh meat trade. An equally unexplained and non-time-limited[31] derogation in Directive 85/433 on the mutual recognition of pharmacy qualifications, appears to exempt Greece from the obligation to secure freedom of establishment for self-employed pharmacists.[32]

More generally, it can be seen that many of the reasons cited in the legislative measures themselves are at best rather sketchy, and frequently unconvincing. For example, in Council Directive 85/384 on mutual recognition of formal qualifications in architecture, in which Luxembourg was given an additional two and a half year implementation period, the fear was expressed on Luxembourg's behalf that, being a small country, the sudden move to enable the holders of such qualifications to establish themselves and provide services in other Member States could disturb the organisation of its profession.[33] It has to be admitted that the likelihood of a stampede of architects into one particular Member State such as Luxembourg seems very slight, given the relatively low levels of labour migration, including professional migration, within the EU, and this pattern was certainly evident by the mid-1980s.[34]

There are fairly clear instances, of course, of "objective socio-economic differences" such as the provisional measures for protection against farm animal diseases—e.g. swine fever and brucellosis—which were prevalent in specific regions. And where gradual harmonisation is or was being attempted in policy

[30] For example, the temporary exception for the UK from part of Dir. 76/889 on radio interference caused by electrical equipment. It seems often that where the derogation is a very minor one, or very short in time (e.g. one year or less) no reasons are given. Evidently is felt that no justification is needed for such a limited form of differentiation.

[31] The only limit envisaged was that the Commission would, after 10 years, submit proposals for extending the right of establishment to Greece in this field.

[32] Greece's unwillingness to give even formal legal recognition to the freedom of establishment required by Community law not only is reflected in this kind of insistence on legislative differentiation, but also can be gleaned from the number of cases initiated by the Commission against that state under Arts. 226 and 228 (ex Arts. 169 and 171) concerning the free movement of persons. See also the parliamentary question posed by Markus Ferber concerning Greece's refusal to give effect to the right of establishment of architects, despite the terms of Dir. 85/384 on this subject: Question No 2067/97 [1998] OJ C21/138.

[33] A similar kind of reasoning on Luxembourg's part is to be found in the much earlier Dir. 68/366 on self-employed persons in the food manufacturing industry.

[34] See S. O'Leary, "The Free Movement of Persons and Services" in Craig and de Búrca (eds.), n. 11 *supra*, 377.

areas which are controversial or nationally distinctive, longer derogation periods and more general reasons seem to be the practice.[35] However, other factors which have been claimed by particular Member States to constitute a distinct economic problem concerning them seem to be rather more questionable. The line between the desire to protect a domestic industry or the desire to maintain a national competitive position on the one hand, and the need for recognition and maintenance of a "legitimate" national difference on the other is not a clear one, and the sketchy nature of the reasons given in the legislative measures themselves does not assist in clarification. Ambiguous examples of this kind can be seen in the maintenance, through a series of directives, of tax exemptions for international travel in the case of Denmark and also Greece and Ireland,[36] the permission given in Directive 79/32 to Germany and Denmark to maintain a broader definition of cigars and cigarettes for tax purposes, or the extensive derogations given to Greece in Directive 90/239 concerning the maximum tar yield of cigarettes. Similarly in the case of Ireland's derogation for gas oil in Directive 75/516 and Greece's for marine gas oils in Directive 93/12: certainly these products or industries are important for those Member States in question, but these cases raise questions about how the recognition of differences and the facilitation of differentiation of this kind (what about, for example, the special position of farming in France, banking in Germany, and now perhaps the computer industry in Ireland?) sits with the general commitment to the "common" market core.[37]

In the end, what stands out as being most distinctive about this long-standing form of secondary legislative differentiation is the normal practice of giving reasons for the exempted position of one or more Member States. And if the giving of reasons has the effect of exposing the fact that some of the positions bargained for by Member States call into question the extent of their commitment to the core principles of competitive equality and non-discrimination underlying the single market concept, it nonetheless remains the case that these exemptions were argued for within the confines of the Council where voting was by unanimity or qualified majority, and subject to any other constraints operating within the EC institutional context. Further, since the agreement of at least a substantial majority of the members of the legislature is required for the granting of a derogation in this legislative field, it seems to be the case that, in most

[35] E.g. Dir. 88/357 on direct insurance other than life insurance, and Dir. 90/435 on taxation of parent companies and subsidiaries.

[36] See e.g. Dirs. 76/134, 83/2, 83/651, 85/348 and 87/198.

[37] There is an interesting example of a "special pleading" made by two Member States in an early harmonisation measure adopted in the late 1960s, which resulted in the requested exemption being extended to all Member States equally. In Directive 69/463 on harmonisation of turnover taxes, the preamble declares that both Belgium and Italy had informed the Commission that (for "conjunctural and budgetary reasons" amongst others) they would not be in a position to meet the final date of 1 Jan. 1970 for introducing VAT in accordance with the first VAT Directive of 11 Apr. 1967. Rather than giving the one- and two-year extensions requested to these two Member States, however, Dir. 69/463 instead extended the deadline for introducing VAT by two years for all Member States.

instances, only derogations which are of relatively limited economic significance are permitted where the reasons are not particularly convincing.

In the context of the closer co-operation provisions instituted by the Treaty of Amsterdam, any requirement of reasoning in fact rests on those states which wish to move ahead in developing an area of policy (e.g. to demonstrate that the Treaty conditions for closer co-operation have been met), rather than on those which choose not to participate. Further, these are likely, given the conditions set, to be areas of policy which fall outside any agreed or presumed "core". The reason why the major Maastricht Treaty opt-outs from EMU in particular, but also from the Social Policy Agreement, were seen as especially contentious examples of "unreasoned" differentiation was not only because of their economic significance, but also because they were symbolically very important policy areas more or less closely bound up with the single market concept. The Maastricht opt-outs were therefore seen by many to represent, in quite a sharply defined way, a paradoxical and unacceptable kind of constitutionally incorporated "breach" of some of the fundamental, underlying core commitments of EC and EU membership. In contrast, even though these are also formally unreasoned, both the "Schengen" type of closer co-operation[38] and that envisaged in the general Amsterdam Treaty closer co-operation provisions differ, in that they do not involve key or core areas of Community policy, but rather newer, more sensitive, contested or peripheral areas of EC or EU policy which are being furthered by groups of willing Member States. The Schengen-type and closer co-operation models, in the end, entail an integrative form of differentiation which seeks to push ahead with a previously undeveloped or underdeveloped policy field, whereas the Maastricht-type and secondary legislative models of differentiation entail a negative (disintegrative?) form of refusal to participate in a commonly agreed core policy field.

Thus, placing the practice of internal market legislative differentiation in the context of the various other significant forms of flexibility, what is particularly interesting is the fact that it combines one of the features of the controversial Maastricht opt-outs (i.e. that a Member State is permitted a differentiated position within an area which is important to the common market core) with an implicit, albeit loosely observed, requirement of reasoning and justification. Both the existence and the observation of this obligation on the Member State to proffer a plausible reason for the distinctive position which it claims to need in relation to what should otherwise be a core common policy, which provides some lens, however weak, through which to assess the nature and extent of its commitment to that core.

[38] For further discussion of this and similar types of co-operation between EU Member States, see Bruno de Witte's chapter, "Old Flexibility: International Agreements between Member States of the European Union" in this volume.

8. CONCLUSION

Ultimately, there are a number of lessons to be learnt from the legislative study undertaken here. One perhaps obvious point, which is also evident from a number of the other chapters in this book, is that there is a considerably greater continuity than may generally have been supposed between the kind of differentiation which has recently come to prominence and been the subject of so much debate within the EU, and the practices of the past. While the Amsterdam Treaty has led to the institutionalisation of a certain, circumscribed kind of policy differentiation under the title of closer co-operation, this incorporation within the EU Treaties is partly a reformed version of what was already to some extent happening amongst Member States, rather as the incorporation of Article 20 (ex Article 8c) of the EC Treaty was a reformed version of what had been happening for some years in the field of secondary legislation.

The second point is that the kind of differentiation which represents the greatest challenge to the Community's regulatory ideal of uniformity and commonality is that exemplified by the Maastricht "unconstitutionalised" opt-outs, which were negotiated and took place outside the embrace of the treaties, yet paradoxically were then enshrined within those documents in a kind of formal affront to that ideal.[39] However, it is not only the extra-constitutional nature of the intergovernmental bargaining processes which secured those opt-outs which marked them out in this way, but also the nature of the differentiation established, in the sense that those policy areas constitute or concern important aspects of the single market. In other words, these differentiated positions represented, to many, a rejection of part of the core commitment of Community and Union membership.

Thirdly, what this particular study of secondary legislative practice can be said to have in common with these most problematic Maastricht opt-outs is the fact that the differentiation took place within the context of the Community's internal market core, in the form of derogations from measures which were intended to approximate national laws and policies. And while this occurred ostensibly within the framework of basic Treaty norms and subject to judicial and thus constitutional control, it seems likely from a survey of some of the measures that these constitutional constraints had, at best, a variable impact in practice. Ultimately however, the setting within which this kind of differentiation had to take place, including the institutional framework and the requirement of

[39] A good example of the rhetoric of this ideal of legal uniformity can be found in a recent judgment of the ECJ, in which it discusses the centrality of the competition law provisions of the Treaty: "Article 81 (ex 85) constitutes a fundamental provision which is essential for the accomplishment of the tasks entrusted to the Community and, in particular, for the functioning of the internal market. . . . [I]t is manifestly in the interest of the Community legal order that, in order to forestall differences of interpretation, every Community provision should be given a uniform interpretation, irrespective of the circumstances in which it is to be applied": see paras. 36 and 40 of Case C–126/97, *Eco Swiss China Time Ltd.* v. *Benetton International NV*, ruling of 1 June 1999, not yet reported.

plausible justification, seems to have limited the extent of the encroachment into the core which might have occurred. Clearly, the closer co-operation model of "integrative differentiation" is premised on a different basis from this earlier legislative practice, in seeking to prohibit any "negative" derogation from core parts of the *acquis* or from "exclusive" Community policy, and to promote only a tightly controlled form of positive, differentiated integration. Yet, although the history of secondary legislative differentiation suggests that derogations which may infringe the core principles and commitments of the EU are unlikely to be particularly significant or numerous, the spectre of a future, large-scale, Maastricht-type extra-constitutional exemption from part of the core has not disappeared. Whatever the attempts made to constitutionalise and institutionally constrain the extent and form of differentiation which may take place in the EU context, the reality is that these inevitably remain subject to the possibility that a given state or states, assuming the role of Herren der Verträge, may force a different deal. Whether, however, the gradual attempt to rein in the multiple forms of differentiation within an umbrella constitutional framework may have succeeded in reducing the likelihood of such an outcome remains to be seen.

Table 1

Table of "differentiating" legislation adopted under Article 100 (now Article 94) E(E)C

Directive	*Type of provision*	*Length of differentiation period*	*Member state*	*Reason given*
Council Dir 73/23/EEC, [1973] OJ L77/29 on harmonising MS laws re electrical equipment within certain voltage limits	Extra period for implementation of the obligations in the Dir	3½ years	Denmark	None given
Council Dir 74/409/EEC [1974] OJ L221/10 on harmonisation of MS laws relating to honey	Exemption from the Dir's ban on using the term to describe certain products other than honey	4 years	Denmark and Germany	"immediate implementation of the ban could cause disturbance of the market where the use of [the term in question] is permitted by previous national legislation"
Council Dir 75/106/EEC, [1975] OJ L42/1 on approximation of MS laws re making-up by volume of certain pre-packaged liquids implementation	Authorisation to defer	3½ years	Belgium, Ireland, the Netherlands and the UK	"Too quick a change in the means of determining quantity laid down by national legislation and the organisation of new systems of control and adoption of a new measurement system would present difficulties" for these MS

Table 1 cont.

Directive	*Type of provision*	*Length of differentiation period*	*Member state*	*Reason given*
Council Dir 75/716/EEC, [1975] OJ L307/22 on approximating MS laws re the sulphur content of certain liquid fuels	Deferral of obligation to reduce sulphur content in gas oil	5 years	Ireland	Programme for reducing sulphur content in gas oil raises "particular technical and economic problems for Ireland" (also reassurance that the derogation should not affect the gas oil market other than in Ireland)
Council Dir 76/134, [1976] OJ L21/9 on the derogation for Denmark re rules governing turnover tax and excise duty applicable in international travel	Authorisation to maintain national rules re exemptions applicable to international travellers for certain products	1 year	Denmark (entire Directive is addressed to Denmark)	None given (other than request of Denmark for extension of derogation originally given in Act of Accession 1972)
Council Dir 76/119/EEC, [1976] OJ L24/58 on harmonising MS provisions re outward processing	Extra period for implementing the Dir (Also some transitional provisions for Denmark, UK and Ireland as "new" or recently acceded MS)	18 months	Ireland	"During the period of progressive introduction of the CCT by the new MS, Irish industry will not be able to cope with the reduction of tariff protection re trade with 3rd countries and within the Community"

Council Dir 76/211/EEC, [1976] OJ L46/1 on approximation of MS laws re making-up by weight or volume of pre-packaged products	Extra period for implementing the Dir	2½ years	Belgium, Ireland, the Netherlands and the UK	Same as for Dir 75/106 above
Council Dir 76/889, [1976] OJ L336/1 on approximation of MS laws re radio interference caused by certain electrical equipment	Temporary exception for certain semi-conductor lighting dimmers	1 year	United Kingdom	None given
Council Dir 77/82/EEC, [1977] OJ L23/50 on rules governing turnover tax and excise duty applicable in international travel	As for Dir 76/134 above	1 year	Denmark (entire Directive is addressed to Denmark)	As for Dir 76/134 above
Council Dir 77/805/EEC, [1977] OJ L338 amending Dir 72/464 on taxes, other than turnover taxes, affecting the consumption of manufactured tobacco	Permission to charge an additional excise duty on cigarettes whose tar yield is above a certain level	30 months	UK	The introduction of a harmonised tax system in the UK without any accompanying measures of adaptation might conflict with the health policy applied by the UK Government

Table 1 cont.

Directive	*Type of provision*	*Length of differentiation period*	*Member state*	*Reason given*
Council Dir 78/51/EEC, [1978] OJ L15/32 prolonging derogations re brucellosis and tuberculosis to Denmark, Ireland and the UK	Prolonging derogations	1 year	Denmark, Ireland and the UK	"the time required to provide solutions to basic technical problems" and "in order not to disrupt the traditional trade in live animals between the UK and Ireland"
Council Dir 78/54/EEC, [1978] OJ L16/22 extending derogations re protection against swine fever to Denmark, Ireland and the UK	Extending derogations	1 year	Denmark, Ireland and the UK	Inadequacy of the period laid down for resolving technical difficulties; The need for swine fever eradication measures to be adopted by Council
Council Dir 78/611, [1978] OJ L197/19 on approximating MS laws re lead content of petrol	Derogation from provisions concerning reduction of lead content of petrol	5 years	Ireland	"reduction of lead content of petrol raises specific technical and economic problems in Ireland" (further explanation that derogation is likely to affect Irish market only)
Council Dir 79/9, [1979] OJ L6/27 on eradicating brucellosis, TB and leucosis in cattle	Authorisation of EAGGF payment of higher slaughter premium than for other Member States		Belgium	High incidence of these diseases in certain regions of Belgium

Council Dir 79/32, [1979] OJ L10/8 on taxes other than turnover taxes, affecting the consumption of manufactured tobacco	Permission to treat certain tobacco types as cigars or cigarettes despite more limited definition within the Dir	2 years	FR, Germany and Denmark	"Economic reasons"
Council Dir 79/110, [1979] OJ L29/24 on notification and implementation of plans for accelerated eradication of brucellosis and TB in cattle: exceptional authorisation for Italy	Authorisation to postpone fulfilment of the obligation contained in earlier Dir 77/391/ EEC and 78/52/EEC, to draw up and notify national eradication plan	1 year	Italy	Italian government's official information to Commission that it was "encountering considerable difficulties in drawing up its national eradication plans"
Council Dir 79/111, [1979] OJ L29/26 prolonging certain derogations in Dir 78/54 re brucellosis, TB and swine fever for Denmark, the UK and Ireland	Authorisation to retain national methods for maintaining "tuberculosis-free", and "brucellosis-free" herds	1 year	Denmark, Ireland and the UK	"The time required to provide solutions to basic technical problems" and "in order not to interrupt the traditional trade in live animals between Ireland and the UK"
Council Dir 80/218, [1980] OJ L47/24, prolonging derogations from Dirs 64/432 and 72/461 for Denmark, the UK and Ireland in respect of swine fever	Authorisation to retain national rules on protection against swine fever upon introduction into their territory of swine for breeding, store and slaughter, and to imports of fresh pigmeat	6 months	Denmark, Ireland and the UK	No specific reason given: reference back to derogations in previous Dirs (which were then granted "because of the time required to provide solutions to basic technical problems")

Table 1 cont.

Directive	*Type of provision*	*Length of differentiation period*	*Member state*	*Reason given*
Council Dir 80/607/EEC, [1980] OJ L170/32, prolonging derogations from Dirs 64/432 and 72/461 for Denmark, the UK and Ireland in respect of swine fever	As for Dir 80/218 above	4 months	Denmark, Ireland and the UK	As for Dir 80/218 above
Council Dir 80/1098/ EEC, [1980] OJ L325/11 amending Dir 64/432 on swine vesicular disease and classical swine fever	Authorisation to retain national rules on protection against swine fever upon introduction into their territory of swine for breeding, production and slaughter	Six months (or date when other MS are able to comply with relevant health requirements)	Denmark, Ireland and the UK	These countries are free from classical swine fever and its persistence in other parts of the Community represents a danger to their stock
Council Dir 80/1099/ EEC, [1980] OJ L325/14 amending Dir 72/461 on swine vesicular disease and classical swine fever	Authorisation to retain national rules on protection against swine fever upon introduction into their territory of fresh pigmeat	Six months (or date when other MS are able to comply with relevant health requirements)	Denmark, Ireland and the UK	As for previous Dir
Council Dir 80/1100/ EEC, [1980] OJ L325/16 amending Dir 80/215 on swine vesicular disease and classical swine fever	Authorisation to retain national rules on protection against swine fever upon introduction into their territory of pigmeat products	Six months (or date when other MS are able to comply with relevant health requirements)	Denmark, Ireland and the UK	Persistence of classical swine fever in certain parts of the EC represents a danger for these Member States which are free from the disease

Council Dir 80/1275/ EEC, [1980] OJ L375/76 amending Dir 72/464 on taxes, other than turnover taxes, affecting the consumption of manufactured tobacco	Extension of derogation in Dirs 72/464 and 77/805 above	Six months	UK	None given
Council Dir 83/2/EEC, [1983] OJ L12/48 re the derogation granted to Denmark on the rules governing turnover tax and excise duty on imports in international travel	Permission to apply certain quantitative limits on import of goods by travellers after a stay abroad of less than 24 or 48 hours	3 and 5 years	Denmark (entire Directive is addressed to Denmark)	"The tax system at present applied in Denmark does not yet allow the full application of such rules in Denmark without the risk of serious economic consequences"
Council Dir 83/90/EEC [1985] OJ L176/23 amending Dir 64/433/ EEC on health problems affecting intra-Community trade in fresh meat	Permission to retain national rules concerning frozen meat	No specific time limit (until Council lays down additional requirements for frozen meat)	Greece	None given
	Permission to maintain national controls re the meat of solipeds	Not time limited	Greece	None given
Council Dir 83/648/EEC, [1983] OJ L360/49 on harmonising MS laws on turnover taxes, deferring the introduction of VAT for Greece	Deferral of time limit for obligation contained in earlier VAT Directives	2 years	Greece	For "technical and economic reasons"

Table 1 cont.

Directive	*Type of provision*	*Length of differentiation period*	*Member state*	*Reason given*
Council Dir 83/651/EEC [1983] OJ L370/62 prolonging the derogation for Ireland re the rules on turnover tax and excise duty in international travel	Extension of authorisation to exclude goods of a certain value from tax exemption	6 months	Ireland	"The tax system at present applied in Ireland does not yet allow full application of the tax exemption granted to travellers coming from other MS without the risk of serious economic consequences" (compare the reason given for Danish derogation in Dir 83/2 above)
Council Dir 84/5/EEC, [1984] OJ L8/17 on the approximation of MS laws on insurance against civil liability in respect of using motor vehicles	Extra period given to increase guarantees to specified level	7 years	Greece	The differing situations at the time in those Member States regarding minimum amounts, cover and excesses applicable by the relevant national compensation body (where uninsured vehicle is involved)
	Extra period given to implement required excess	2 years	Italy	
	Extra period given to include compensation for damage to property	4 years	Ireland and Greece	

Council Dir 84/231/EEC, [1984] OJ L117/42, amending Dirs 69/169 and 83/2 on harmonising provisions on exemption consequences from turnover tax and excise duty on imports in international travel	Extra period for carrying out 2-stage increase of value of travellers' exemption	1 year	Greece	None given
	Extension of earlier derogation in re value of tax-free imported goods	Not time-limited, as long as exemption remains at level set in the Dir	Ireland	Economic consequences
	Permission to apply certain quantitative limits on import of goods by travellers after a stay abroad of less than 24 or 48 hours	1 year	Denmark	Risk of serious economic consequences
Council Dir 85/303/EEC [1985] OJ L156/23, amending Dir 69/335/EEC on indirect tax on raising capital (capital duty)	Permission to decide which of certain transactions should be subject to and which exempt from capital duty	Not time limited	Greece	Unlike in other MS, no capital duty existed in Greece at the relevant time
Council Dir 85/348/EEC, [1986] OJ L14/19, amending Dir 69/169 on the harmonisation of provisions on exemption from turnover tax and duty in international travel	Permission to exclude goods of a certain varying values from the exemption	Not time limited	Denmark, Greece and Ireland	"the economic consequences" which might occur in these countries if the tax exemption for travellers from other MSts were authorised
	Permission to apply quantitative limits on import of certain goods to which the tax exemption applies, following a stay of less than 24 or 48 hours in	2 years	Denmark	"the risk of economic consequences"

Table 1 cont.

Directive	*Type of provision*	*Length of differentiation period*	*Member state*	*Reason given*
Council Dir 85/349/EEC, [1985] OJ L183/27 on tax relief on importation of goods of non-commercial character in small consignments	Exemption, for goods of a certain value, from obligation to provide tax relief	Not time limited	Ireland	"The tax system currently in force in Ireland does not yet authorise the full application of tax relief on small consignments of a non-commercial character" within EC
Council Dir 85/361/EEC, [1985] OJ L192/18 on harmonisation of turnover taxes: derogations for German farmers to compensate for removal of MCAs	Authorisation to use VAT in order to grant special aid permitted under earlier Regulation and Decision	6½ years	FR Germany (entire Dir is addressed to Germany)	Germany had been authorised by earlier legislation to grant special aid in order to compensate for the dismantling of MCAs
Council Dir 86/188/EEC, [1986] OJ L137/28 on protection of workers from risks related to noise exposure at work	Extra period given to implement	1 year	Greece and Portugal	None given
Council Dir 86/247/EEC, [1986] OJ L164/27 on harmonising MS laws on	Deferral of time limit for implementation of obligations contained in	1 year	Greece (entire Directive is addressed to Greece)	"economic and technical reasons"

turnover taxes and deferral of introduction of the common VAT system for Greece	earlier VAT directives			
Council Dir 86/653/EEC, [1986] OJ L382/17 on co-ordination of MS laws relating to commercial agents	Extra period for implementation of the obligations	4 years	Ireland and the UK	These three MS have to "make a particular effort to adapt their regulations", especially those concerning indemnity for termination of contract
	Extra period to implement obligation to ensure agent is indemnified after termination of contract	3 years	Italy	
Council Directive 87/21/EEC, [1987] OJ L15/36 amending Dir 65/65 on approximation of provisions relating to proprietary medicinal products	Extra period given to implement	5 years	Greece, Spain and Portugal	They should have extra time to complete the review of old proprietary medicinal products provided for in Dir 75/319/EEC (i.e. before either of the three became member states)
Council Dir 87/198/EEC, [1987] OJ L78/53 amending Dir 69/169 re the derogation granted to Denmark on the rules governing turnover tax and excise duty on imports in international travel	Extension of derogation contained in earlier Directives (see Dir 85/348 above)	2 years	Denmark	Any change of the previous rules "would at present cause serious economic difficulties for Denmark"

Table 1 cont.

Directive	*Type of provision*	*Length of differentiation period*	*Member state*	*Reason given*
Council Dir 90/434/EEC, [1990] OJ L225/1 on the common system of tax applicable to mergers, divisions, transfers of assets and exchanges of shares re companies of different Member States	Temporary exception from the provisions concerning transfer of assets and shares	1 year	Portugal	None given
Council Dir 90/435, [1990] OJ L225/6 on the common system of taxation applicable in the case of parent companies and subsidiaries of different Member States	Exemption from ban on taxing certain profits distributed by subsidiaries to parent companies of other states	Not time limited	Greece	"Nature of its tax system" i.e. Greece does not charge corporation tax on distributed profits
	Exemption from same ban	8 years (with possibility of extension)	Portugal	"budgetary reasons"
	Partial exemption from same ban: permission to levy a compensatory tax on certain profits distributed by subsidiaries to parent companies	6 years	FR Germany	"Nature of its tax system" i.e. FRG charges tax on distributed profits at much lower rate than for retained profits

Council Dir 93/12/EEC, [1993] OJ L74/81 on the sulphur content of certain liquid fuels	Derogation from the prohibition on the marketing of diesel fuels whose sulphur content exceeds a certain level	5 years	Greece	The "specific techical and economic problems" raised for Greece in the context of marine gas oils. [Also explanation that the derogation should affect mainly the Greek market]

Table 2

Table of "differentiating" legislation adopted under Article 47 (ex Article 57) or 95 (ex Article 100A) E(E)C
* signifies a measure adopted under the dual legal basis of Articles 47 (ex Article 57) *and* 95 (ex Article 100A)
** signifies a measure adopted under Article 95 (ex Article 100A) without Article 47 (ex Article 57)

Directive	*Type of provision*	*Length of differentiation period*	*Member state*	*Reason given*
Council Dir 68/366, [1968] OJ L260/12 on transitional measures governing activities of self-employed persons in the food manufacturing and beverage industries.	Commission may authorise Luxembourg to suspend provisions of Dir governing mutual recognition of experience and qualification	To be determined by the Commission	Luxembourg	The risk of "serious difficulties" and the need to "avoid a disproportionate influx" into a state which does not make the taking up of these activities subject to any rules
Council Dir 73/239/EEC, [1973] OJ L228/3 on co-ordinating provisions on the taking-up and pursuit of the business of direct insurance other than life assurance	Permission to maintain a national prohibition on the simultaneous undertaking in its territory of health insurance, credit and suretyship insurance or insurance in respect of recourse against third parties and legal defence	Up to 4 years (pending further co-ordination, which is to be implemented by then)	FR Germany	(In general terms) the absence of adequate co-ordination of national measures for the protection of insured persons
Council Dir 78/686/EEC, [1978] OJ L233/1 on mutual recognition of qualifications of dental practitioners	Extra period for implementing the obligations in the Dir	4½ years	Italy	The dental profession is not yet organised in Italy

Council Dir 78/687, [1978] OJ L233/10 concerning co-ordination of provisions in respect of activities of dental practitioners	As for Dir 78/686	As for Dir 78/686	Italy	"Italy is obliged to create a new category of professional persons entitled to practice dentistry under a title other than that of doctor . . . not only introduce a specific system of training but also set up structures proper to this new profession"
Council Dir 79/267, [1979] OJ L63/1 on co-ordination of provisions relating to the taking up and pursuit of the business of direct life insurance	Exemption from the authorisation requirement of the Dir for certain kinds of undertaking in certain Member States	Not time limited	Certain UK undertakings: (those set up by Royal charter or by private act or special public act)	These already fulfil requirements as to security and other financial guarantees
	Permission for a Member State to maintain its own system of guarantees for technical reserves	1 years "pending co-ordination of legislation on the winding-up of undertakings"	Certain listed Belgian, UK and Italian undertakings. Luxembourg	Member States have different regulations re the simultaneous carrying on of life assurance and other activities
Council Dir 85/384/EEC, [1985] OJ L223/15 on mutual recognition of qualifications in architecture	Permission to suspend application of provisions requiring recognition of non-university diplomas and other qualifications	4½ years	Luxembourg	"the sudden introduction of this provision could, in view of the country's small size, lead to distortion of competition and disturb the organization of the profession"

Table 2 cont.

* signifies a measure adopted under the dual legal basis of Articles 47 (ex Article 57) *and* 95 (ex Article 100A)
** signifies a measure adopted under Article 95 (ex Article 100A) without Article 47 (ex Article 57)

Directive	*Type of provision*	*Length of differentiation period*	*Member state*	*Reason given*
Council Dir 85/433/EEC, [1985] OJ L253/37 on mutual recognition of diplomas, certificates and other evidence of formal qualifications in pharmacy and exercise of right of establishment	Derogation from obligation to recognise qualifications awarded by other Member States, (except for *employed* persons)	Not time-limited (but Commission after 10 years is to submit proposals for extending right of establishment between Greece and other MS)	Greece	None given
**Council Dir 88/295, [1988] OJ L127/1 amending Dir 77/62 on the co-ordination of procedures on the award of public supply contracts and repealing provisions of Dir 80/767	Extension of time period for implementation of the obligations in the Directive	3 years and 2 months	Spain Portugal	Spain and Portugal recently adopted legislation to implement Dir 77/62 and further changes would "adversely affect the adaptation of the private sector" in those countries
			Greece	Greece is in process of adapting to Dir 77/62 and incorporation of further EC rules at this stage would adversely affect

				the public supply contract sector as far as economic stability, transparency and maintenance of trading conditions are concerned
Council Dir 88/316, [1988] OJ L143/26 on the approximation of MS laws relating to the making-up by volume of certain pre-packaged liquids	Permission for permitted certain substances listed in the annex to be marketed in the UK and Ireland, where they do not exceed a specified volume	Not time limited	UK and Ireland	No reason given
Council Dir 88/357/EEC, [1988] OJ L172/1, amending Dir 73/239 on co-ordinating provisions on the taking-up and pursuit of the business of direct insurance other than life assurance	Retention of derogation in Dir 73/239 above	Not time-limited ("pending co-ordination")	FR Germany	Same as Dir 73/239
	Permission to apply different transitory regime to certain risks;	3–5 years	Greece, Spain, Ireland and Portugal	Article 8c (subsequently became 7c, and Art 20 after Amsterdam Treaty) of the EC Treaty, i.e.
	Permission to apply different thresholds	varying for different stages	Greece, Spain, Ireland and Portugal	"to take into account the extent of the effort that certain economies
	Permission to exempt risks situated within these MS from previous Community provisions on co-insurance	5 years	Greece, Spain, Ireland and Portugal	showing differences in *development* will have to sustain during the period of establishment of the internal market"

Table 2 cont.

* signifies a measure adopted under the dual legal basis of Articles 47 (ex Article 57) *and* 95 (ex Article 100A)
** signifies a measure adopted under Article 95 (ex Article 100A) without Article 47 (ex Article 57)

Directive	*Type of provision*	*Length of differentiation period*	*Member state*	*Reason given*
*Council Dir 89/395 [1989] OJ L186/17 amending Dir 79/112 on approximation of MS laws on labelling, presentation and advertising of foodstuffs for consumer sale	Exemption from "durability" labelling requirement for milk and milk products sold in re-usable glass bottles	Not time limited	UK and Ireland	No reason given
Council Dir 89/647/EEC, [1989] OJ L386/14 on a solvency ratio for credit institutions	Exemption of agricultural bank from obligation to maintain a certain ratio level	9 years	Greece (Agricultural Bank of Greece)	None given
	Authorisation to apply a specific weighting to loans on certain types of property	5 years	Greece, Denmark and Germany	None given (but Commission is to investigate whether this causes distortions in competition)
**Council Dir 90/232, [1990] OJ L129/33 on the approximation of MS laws relating to civil liability	Extra time period for implementing the main obligations of the Dir	3 years	Greece, Spain, Portugal and Ireland	Article 20 (formerly 8c) EC Treaty, "the extent of the effort which must be undertaken by certain

insurance re the use of motor vehicles	Extra time period for implementing compulsory insurance for motorcycle pillion passengers	6 years	Ireland	economies which show differences in development"
**Council Dir 90/239, [1990] OJ L137/36 on approximating MS provisions concerning the maximum tar yield of cigarettes	Temporary derogations with regard to four different maximum tar limit values	1 year, 7 years, 9 years and 15 years respectively	Greece	"the introduction of maximum tar yields would result in particular socio-economic difficulties for Greece"
*Council Dir 90/531, [1990] OJ L297/1 on procurement procedures of entities in the water, energy, transport and telecommunications sectors	Extra time period for implementation of the obligations contained in the Directive	3 years 5 years	Spain Greece and Portugal	The opening up of contracts in these sectors "might have an adverse effect" on Spain's economy, and Greece and Portugal "will have to sustain even greater efforts"
**Council Dir 92/13, [1992] OJ L76/14 on co-ordination of provisions re the application of Community rules on procurement procedures of entities in the water, energy, transport and telecommunications sectors	Extra time period for implementation of the obligations contained in the Directive	2 years 4½ years	Spain Greece and Portugal	The need to take account of the additional periods given to those Member States in Directive 90/531, above

Table 2 cont.
* signifies a measure adopted under the dual legal basis of Articles 47 (ex Article 57) *and* 95 (ex Article 100A)
** signifies a measure adopted under Article 95 (ex Article 100A) without Article 47 (ex Article 57)

Directive	*Type of provision*	*Length of differentiation period*	*Member state*	*Reason given*
Council Dir 92/49, [1992] OJ L228/1 p. co-ordinating provisions on direct insurance other than life insurance, and amending the 3rd non-life insurance Directive	Derogation from provisions on calculation of premiums	2 years	Germany	Article 8c (now 20) EC whereby "account should be taken of the extent of the effort which must be made by certain economies at different stages of development" (not clear how Germany fits into this)
	Derogation from obligation to include compulsory insurance against accidents at work	5 years	Denmark	
	Special provisions for contracts covering risks exclusively in one of the Member States	3 years 5 years 5 years	Spain Greece Portugal	
Council Dir 92/96, [1992] OJ L360/1–27 on co-ordination of provisions relating to direct life insurance and amending the 3rd life assurance Directive	Extra period to implement obligations re contracts in respect of which these Member States are the Member State "of commitment"	1½ years 1½ years 4½ years	Spain Portugal Greece	Article 20 (formerly 8c) EC Treaty: "the extent of the effort which must be made by certain economies at different stages of development

Council Dir 93/22/EEC, [1993] OJ L141/27 on investment services in the securities field (harmonisation/mutual recognition of authorisation provisions	Derogation from obligation to permit investment firms from other Member States to have indirect access to their regulated markets	18 months 4½ years	Any MS which does not permit its own credit institutions to have such access Spain Greece and Portugal	The obligation in this Directive constitutes a significant reform for those MS, and its consequences for them needs to be assessed
* Council Dir 93/37, [1993] OJ L199/54 on co-ordination of procedures for the award of public works contracts	Extra period for implementation of the obligations contained in the Directive	2½ years 3½ years 3½ years	Spain Greece Portugal	None given
* Council Dir 93/38, [1993] OJ L199/84 on co-ordination of the procurement procedures of entities in the water, energy, transport and telecommunications sectors	Extra period for implementation of the obligations contained in the Directive	3 years 4 years 4 years	Spain Greece Portugal	Opening up of contracts in the relevant sectors "might have an adverse effect on" the Spanish economy and the Greek and Portugese economies "will have to sustain even greater efforts"
** Council Dir 93/7, [1993] OJ L74/74 on the return of cultural objects unlawfully removed from the territory of a Member State	Extension of the time limit for implementation	3 months	Belgium, Germanyand the Netherlands	"the nature of their legal systems and the scope of the changes to their legislation necessary to implement this Directive"

8

EMU and the Catch–22 of EU Constitution-making

FILIP TUYTSCHAEVER*

1. EMU FUNDAMENTALS

ON 3 MAY 1998, the European Council decided, in accordance with Article 121(4) (ex Article 109j(4)) of the EC Treaty, that 11 Member States fulfilled the conditions necessary for the adoption of the single currency on 1 January 1999.[1] In accordance with Article 122(4) (ex Article 109k(4)) of the EC Treaty, these Member States are referred to as "Member States without a derogation".

Greece did not fulfil the necessary conditions because it did not comply with any of the convergence criteria mentioned in the four indents of Article 121(1) (ex Article 109j(1)) of the EC Treaty: its average inflation rate and its long-term interest rate were above reference value, its government deficit was excessive, and the Greek drachma did not participate in the Exchange Rate Mechanism ("ERM") in the two years ending in February 1998. Notwithstanding this, its national legislation, including the statute of its national central bank, was compatible with the requirements on the independence of the European Central Bank ("ECB") and the national central banks, as laid down in Articles 108 (ex Article 107) and 109 (ex Article 108) of the EC Treaty and the Statute of the European System of Central Banks ("ECSB").

Sweden fulfilled the convergence criteria concerning average inflation and long-term interest rates, and its government deficit was not excessive. However, the Swedish crown had never participated in the ERM. Furthermore, the Swedish government had failed to adjust its national legislation to the obligations imposed on it by Articles 108 (ex Article 107) and 109 (ex Article 108) of the EC Treaty and the Statute of the ESCB. Accordingly, Sweden also did not fulfil the necessary conditions for the adoption of the single currency. As opposed to the Greek government, the Swedish government was pleased with

* Member of the Brussels Bar; Assistant in European Law, Free University of Brussels. I would like to thank Joanne Scott and Hervé Bribosia for their insightful and stimulating comments on an earlier draft of this chapter.

[1] Council Decision 98/317/EC of 3 May 1998 in accordance with Art. 109j(4) of the Treaty [1998] OJ L139/30.

this result. In actual fact, it had sought it on purpose, since it had indicated all along that it did not aspire to single currency membership in the first wave. However, unlike Denmark and the UK during the negotiations of the Maastricht Treaty, Sweden had not been able to obtain a facility to opt out unilaterally from Stage Three of EMU during its negotiations to accede to the EU. It is therefore difficult to see how the Council could have decided not to include Sweden in the euro-area had it fulfilled the necessary conditions. Under these circumstances, the Swedish refusal to participate could have led to a serious institutional crisis. It thus suited more or less everybody that Sweden failed (intentionally) to fulfil the necessary conditions.

In accordance with Article 122 (ex Article 109k(3)) of the EC Treaty, Greece and Sweden have been given the status of "Member States with a derogation". This entails that a number of Treaty provisions, mentioned in Article 122(3) of the EC Treaty, do not apply to them, and that their voting rights are suspended for Council decisions taken on the basis of these provisions. In such cases, a qualified majority shall be defined, in accordance with Article 122(5) of the EC Treaty, as two-thirds of the votes of the representatives of the Member States without a derogation weighted in accordance with Article 205(2) (ex Article 148(2)) EC Treaty, and unanimity of those Member States shall be required for an act requiring unanimity.

Together with Greece and Sweden, Denmark and the UK also remain outside Stage Three of EMU. By virtue of the "Protocol on Certain Provisions relating to [the UK]" and the "Protocol on Certain Provisions relating to Denmark", these Member States extracted a right to opt out of the single currency. More specifically, they were authorised to notify the Council of their intentions with regard to participation in the third stage, before the Council's assessment of the fulfilment by the Member States of the necessary conditions for the adoption of the single currency.

Following the negative outcome of a referendum on the ratification of the Treaty on European Union ("TEU"), Denmark made use of this facility at an early stage, namely at the European Council meeting in Edinburgh on 11–12 December 1992. Thereby, it activated the Protocol on certain provisions relating to Denmark at the date of entry into force of the TEU, i.e. 1 November 1993. According to the Protocol, the effect of the Danish opt-out is that all Articles and provisions of the TEU and the Statute of the ESCB referring to a derogation shall be applicable to Denmark. In other words, Denmark is put on the same footing as the Member States with a derogation.

On 30 October 1997, the UK also gave notice to the Council that it did not intend to move to Stage Three of EMU.[2] As opposed to that on Denmark, the Protocol on certain provisions relating to the UK does not simply put the UK on the same footing as a Member State with a derogation, but sets out in a detailed way the various effects of the UK's non-participation in Stage Three of EMU.

[2] See recital 21 to the preamble to Council Reg. 974/98 of 3 May 1998 on the introduction of the euro [1998] OJ L139/1.

If anything, the previous considerations show that flexibility (or, as it will be referred to hereafter, differentiation or differentiated integration) has entrenched itself into the Treaty provisions on EMU, the centrepiece of the post-TEU EC legal order. From a historical perspective, this is hardly surprising. Indeed, as opposed to many other fields of EC/EU policy, recourse to differentiation has always been accepted quite naturally with respect to the achievement of the EMU. From the outset, proposals for EMU have espoused views on European integration which partially abandoned traditional dogmas about the universality of EC law and the uniformity of its application, and which, inspired by a good dose of common sense (it is after all impossible to ignore differences in the Member States' levels of socio-economic development), have opted in favour of a more gradual approach to integration, or one which does not necessarily involve the participation of all Member States at the same time.

Examples of the link between differentiation and the road to EMU are there for the taking. Presumably, the most well-known example can be found in the 1975 *Report on European Union*, where former Belgian Prime Minister Tindemans argued that it was impossible to submit a credible programme of action in the field of EMU if it was deemed absolutely necessary that in every case all stages should be reached by all the Member States at the same time. Therefore, it ought to be allowed that:

> —within the Community framework of an overall concept of European Union . . . and accepted by the Nine,
> —and on the basis of an action programme drawn up in a field decided upon by the common institutions, whose principles are accepted by all,
> (1) those States which are able to progress have a duty to forge ahead,
> (2) those States which have reasons for not progressing which the Council, on a proposal from the Commission, acknowledges as valid do not do so,
> —but will at the same time receive from the other States any aid and assistance that can be given them to enable them to catch the others up,
> —and will take part, within the joint institutions, in assessing the results obtained in the field in question.[3]

Tindemans' concern to safeguard the objective of EMU by allowing those Member States which, according to certain convergence criteria, are economically able to forge ahead as an *avant-garde* was consolidated in the Treaty of Maastricht. However, as expressed most clearly by the Danish and UK position in Stage Three, the Treaty provisions on EMU also include differentiation that originates from a radically different viewpoint on the role of differentiation in the European integration process; namely that differentiation must not

[3] "Report on European Union", *Bull. EC*, Supp. 1/76, 20–1. Even earlier, see the Final Communiqué of the Hague Summit, held on 2 Dec. 1969 (i.e. at the end of the original transitional period), where the Heads of State and Government already agreed that "a *plan in stages* should be worked out during 1970 with a view to the creation of an economic and monetary union"; a plan that can be found in the final report to the Commission by the Werner Committee ([1970] OJ C136/1).

necessarily be grounded on socio-economic differences but may also be a consequence of political squabbles between the Member States. This view has also been present since the first important practical steps towards EMU were taken. It will, for instance, be recalled that the European Monetary System ("EMS") was based on a non-legally binding resolution of the European Council of 5 December 1978,[4] which left it to each Member State to decide whether or not to join the EMS.[5] In other words, long before the TEU gave Denmark and the UK a facility not to participate in Stage Three of EMU, the EMS already recognised that non-participation need not always be based on motives pertaining to the Member States' socio-economic performance. "As John Usher has stated, 'in a sense the EMS is an agreement between all the Member States that those who so wish will be bound by the rules and make use of institutions created under Community law'. Consequently, it can be seen as a forerunner, if not a precedent, for later forms of differentiation within the Community system, including the Social Protocol under the Maastricht Treaty, the special treatment of the United Kingdom and Denmark in respect of monetary policy, and enhanced cooperation under the Amsterdam Treaty".[6]

The present contribution is situated in this context. Its purpose is two-fold. First, it aims at using differentiation in EMU as a starting-point better to understand differentiation in EU law in general, and differentiation in the Treaty of Amsterdam in particular. To this end, Section 2 will, following some preliminary remarks on the meaning of the concept "differentiation", show that differentiation in EMU is capable of telling us many things about the politico-legal choices involved in the use of a given form of differentiation in the broader context of the EU, as well as the reasons for those choices, and the consequences thereof. Section 3 then offers brief comment on the extent to which EMU is paradigmatic for the development of the EU constitution as a whole.

2. E(M)U DIFFERENTIATION IN A NUTSHELL

A. Differentiation?

Tradition has it that we intuitively link concepts such as unity, uniformity, cohesion, integration and supranationality to what is known to be the Community method ("*la méthode communautaire*"). On closer view, it nonetheless appears that this practice relies to a large extent on an inherited,

[4] *Bull. EC*, 12/1978, pt. 1.1.11. The EMS's operating procedures were laid down in an Agreement of 13 Mar. 1979 between the Central Banks of the Member States: see *Compendium of Community Texts* (Luxembourg: OOPEC, 1980), 50.

[5] Art. 3 of the Resolution.

[6] F. Snyder, "EMU Revisited: Are We Making a Constitution? What Constitution Are We Making?" in P. Craig and G. De Búrca (eds.), *The Evolution of EU Law* (Oxford: Oxford University Press, 1999), with reference to J. Usher, *The Law of Money and Financial Services in the European Community* (Oxford: Clarendon Press, 1994), 141.

somewhat idealised, view of the European integration process and its trajectory and does not correspond to what is actually taking place. In reality, the Community method has always been multi-faceted and much more complex than it at first appears. For one, it has always incorporated various forms of differentiation.

In the legal realm, the concept of "differentiation" can be given essentially two meanings.[7] First, in a broad sense, it has been used to refer to instances where the Member States (or EU citizens) are not subjected to a uniform legal regime, even though it concerns a matter which falls within the scope of application of the Treaties. On this view, differentiation is inherent in the integration process; it accords with general principles which underpin the EC/EU and which permit the Member States to continue to exercise their concurrent competence even after EC/EU intervention, provided of course their action is in conformity with their Treaty obligations.

Viewed from this perspective, the economic policy-making part of EMU, for instance, permits more differentiation than its monetary policy-making part. Indeed, according to Article 4(1) (ex Article 3a(1)) of the EC Treaty, the activities of the Community shall include, amongst others, "the adoption of an economic policy which is based on the closer coordination of Member States' economic policies", whilst according to Article 4(2) (ex Article 3a(2)) of the EC Treaty, its activities will include "the definition and conduct of a single monetary policy and exchange-rate policy". In other words, economic policies are left mainly to the Member States, which can continue to exercise their powers within the framework of Community rules, whereas in Stage Three of EMU the conduct of monetary policy is in principle situated exclusively at the Community level, thereby excluding concurrent Member State action (apart from that which may be exercised by way of delegation from the Community). There are exceptions to this rule. Certain Member States are, indeed, not subject to the same transfer of competence with respect to monetary policy matters. It is within this context that a second, narrower, meaning of the concept of differentiation emerges.

In this narrower sense, the concept of differentiation has been used to refer to instances where EU primary or secondary law, actually or potentially, permits the Member States (or regions within the Member States) not to be subjected to the same legal regime; that is, where some Member States (or regions within Member States) are, actually or potentially, excluded from the scope of application of primary or secondary law or where the rights and obligations imposed on some Member States are, actually or potentially, different from those imposed on others.

Viewed from this perspective, the Treaty provisions on EMU contain differentiation in that they envisage the possibility of the creation of groups of

[7] For more details see F. Tuytschaever, *Differentiation in European Union Law* (Oxford: Hart Publishing, 1999), 2–3, and H. Bribosia, "De la subsidiarité à la coopération renforcée" in Y. Lejeune (ed.), *Le Traité d'Amsterdam: Espoirs et déceptions* (Brussels: Bruylant, 1998), 50–1.

Member States that are subjected to different legal regimes: the Member States without a derogation, those with a derogation, and Denmark and the UK, which were entitled to postpone their participation on the basis of considerations extraneous to the criteria applicable in the normal line-up to EMU. It is this second, narrower, conception of differentiation that has served, albeit implicitly, as a background for most discussions on the matter. The present chapter is no exception to this rule.[8]

B. A Categorisation of Differentiation, and its Context

Whilst taking issue with various categorisations that have been developed in the past,[9] I believe that the following parameters are essential as building-blocks for a legal-formal categorisation of differentiation, and as a starting-point for an analysis of the political hinterland of differentiation: differentiation in primary *v.* secondary law; actual *v.* potential differentiation; positive *v.* negative differentiation; temporary *v.* non-temporary differentiation; and general *v.* specific differentiation. Schematically, the relationship between these parameters can be represented as follows:[10]

Parameters for a Categorisation of Differentiation in EU Law

	Primary law	
	Positive differentiation	*Negative differentiation*
Actual differentiation	(temporary or non-temporary differentiation; general or specific differentiation)	(*ibid.*)
Potential differentiation	(*ibid.*)	(*ibid.*)
	Secondary law (=differentiation in accordance with the principle of non-discrimination)	

Let us now take EMU as a background to discuss briefly each of these parameters and the various ways in which they are put to work when it comes to transposing political compromises to the legal realm.

[8] In this paper, I will focus exclusively on inter-state differentiation (i.e. differentiation between the Member States), and not on intra-state differentiation (territorial differentiation, differentiation between regions of Member States). On territorial differentiation, see the chapter by Jacques Ziller elsewhere in this volume.

[9] Examples are E. Grabitz and C. Iliopoulos, "Typologie der Differenzierungen und Ausnahmen im Gemeinschaftsrecht" in E. Grabitz (ed.), *Abgestufte Integration. Eine Alternative zum herkömmlichen Integrationskonzept?*, Ergebnisse eines Forschungsprojektes des Institut für Integrationsforschung der Stiftung Europa-Kolleg Hamburg (Kehl am Rhein/Strasbourg: N.P. Engel Verlag, 1984), 31–46; A. Stubb, "A Categorization of Differentiated Integration" (1996) 34 *JCMS* 283–95.

[10] A different "optical reading" is discussed in Tuytschaever, n. 7 *supra*, 124.

(i) Differentiation in Primary v. Secondary Law

The link between differentiation and the principle of non-discrimination is fundamental to the study and the understanding of differentiation. Having regard to the Court's jurisprudence, differentiation in secondary legislation which is not based on an authorisation in primary law must respect the principle of non-discrimination. According to settled case law, discrimination consists in "treating either similar situations differently or different situations identically".[11] The Court has also referred to the fact that "[d]iscrimination in the legal sense consists of treating in identical manner situations which are different or treating in a different manner situations that are identical".[12] In other words, to the extent that the Court requires that different situations must be treated differently, secondary legislation must differentiate between the Member States (albeit that this depends on the discretion which the Community enjoys in a given field of policy). In this respect, it is of course important to know which grounds the Court accepts as lawful grounds for differentiation. Generally speaking, it appears that the Court accepts different treatment of the Member States, citizens, etc. if and when such treatment is based on economic and/or social, i.e. "objective", differences, and that it refuses to endorse differentiation where this is based on purely political, "subjective", grounds.[13] Consequently, when there is political disagreement between the Member States, the Court's stance on the principle of non-discrimination prevents the adoption of decisions which apply only as far as the willing Member States are concerned and which create no obligations for the unwilling Member States.

The Member States may of course want to circumvent this case law. To this end, they may try to take advantage of the fact that it is sometimes difficult to distinguish between objective and subjective differences. As Helen and William Wallace wrote, objective differences "may be defined in slippery terms . . . or . . . some special point [may be] dressed up as objective when it is actually a difference in national preference or policy provision or cover for a commercial advantage".[14] In their capacity as masters of the Treaty, the Member States can

[11] E.g., Case 8/82, *Kommanditurgesellschaft in der Firma Hans-Otto Wagner GmbH Agrarhandel* v. *Bundesanstalt für Landwirtschaftliche Marktordnung* [1983] ECR 371, para. 18; Case 56/86, *Coopérative Agricole d'Approvisionnement des Avirons* v. *Receveur des douanes de Saint-Denis and Directeur régional des douanes de la Réunion* [1987] ECR 1525, para. 15.

[12] E.g., Case 1253/79, *Dino Battaglia* v. *Commission* [1982] ECR 297, para. 37.

[13] This principle was worded in the mid-1980s in a seminal study on differentiation by C.-D. Ehlermann, "How Flexible is Community Law? An Unusual Approach to the Concept of " 'Two Speeds' " (1984) 82 *Michigan Law Review* 1289. See also H. Wallace and A. Ridley, *Europe: The Challenge of Diversity* The Royal Institute of International Affairs (London/Boston/Henley: Routledge & Kegan Paul Ltd., 1985), 40: "[d]ifferentiation is admissible neither legally nor economically if solely as a result of political obstruction by the defecting Member State(s)". Interestingly, the chapter by Gráinne De Búrca elsewhere in this volume shows that sometimes no objective justification is given, not even for differentiation pertaining to what usually is considered to belong to the "*noyau communautaire*".

[14] H. Wallace and W. Wallace, *Flying Together in a Larger and More Diverse European Union* (The Hague: Netherlands Scientific Council for Government Policy, Working Document W87/1995, June 1995), 50.

also go a step further and strike deals in primary law which authorise differentiation in secondary law as a consequence of political differences between the Member States and exclude the Court's powers, which do not extend to deciding on the validity of primary law.

The Treaty provisions on EMU are a good example of this interaction, not to say tension, between differentiation in primary and secondary law. The provisions are very detailed, notwithstanding the fact that in view of the principle of non-discrimination many details could have been left to secondary legislation. For instance, the convergence criteria which determine the Member States' participation in Stage Three of EMU could have been agreed at the level of secondary law. Similarly, the derogations for the Member States which do not fulfil these objective convergence criteria could have been authorised by secondary law alone.[15] Instead, EMU was inserted in primary law, as it were, as a finished product. Most likely, this is because EMU belongs to the realm of high politics and can be seen as the outcome of an intricate web of compromises, often highly technical, between varying interests of a variety of actors who were anxious to take as many precautions as possible to avoid unintended consequences at the level of secondary law. The logical thing to do then is to carve EMU in stone in the Treaty itself, thereby avoiding the risk of blockage of the decision-making process due to discussion on any given aspect of EMU, accepted during the intergovernmental conference ("IGC"), but subsequently called into question again.[16]

As opposed to the derogations for the Member States that do not fulfil the conditions for the adoption of the single currency, the right for Denmark and the UK to opt out of the single currency, irrespective of whether or not they fulfil the necessary conditions, lacks any objective justification. It is based exclusively on the political unwillingness of those Member States to participate on the same footing as the others. Accordingly, in light of the principle of non-discrimination, it had to be authorised by primary law.

It is this practice of using primary law in order to escape the Court's powers that led Deirdre Curtin to the famous catchphrase that the Maastricht negotiators "hijacked" the *acquis communautaire*.[17] More commonly, this practice is referred to as integration *à la carte*. It can be best understood against the background of the intergovernmental procedure for Treaty revision. Giving in to the political unwillingness of one or several Member States and granting them, if need be, *à la carte* status in primary law with respect to a given matter, is a

[15] See also C.-D. Ehlermann, *Increased Differentiation or Stronger Uniformity*, EUI Working Paper RSC No 95/21, 1995, 10.

[16] The fact that the Treaty provisions on EMU were carved in stone at Maastricht was confirmed during the 1996 IGC, which carefully avoided to re-open negotiations on any aspect of EMU. The Amsterdam Treaty, indeed, does not modify the Maastricht Treaty at all as far as EMU is concerned. It did not even effect purely technical changes, such as replacing "ECU" by "euro".

[17] D. Curtin, "The Constitutional Structure of the Union: A Europe of Bits and Pieces" (1993) 30 *CMLRev*. 46.

means to secure Treaty ratification. Obviously, this problem only occurs at times of constitutional change, when political conflicts concerning the scope of EU intervention and, by extension, concerning the prospective direction of the integration process or the end-stage of European integration, surface between different groups of Member States. As it keeps step with the frequency of intergovernmental conferences, the tension between primary and secondary differentiation has become more important in the 1990s. The Treaty of Amsterdam confirms this. Indeed, despite the opposition of an overwhelming majority of Member States against further special-interest exemptions before and during the 1996 IGC, a number of such exemptions were granted in as many Protocols annexed to the TEU and the TEC.[18]

(ii) Actual v. *Potential Differentiation and General v. Specific Differentiation*

A second dimension of the categorisation of the different forms of differentiation concerns the fact that differentiation in primary or secondary law does not always take effect as soon as these enter into force. In practice, it is much more frequent that primary and secondary law provide only for the coming into being of a differentiated regime in the future, and require further action by the common institutions, any given Member State(s) or both before a differentiated regime is effectively established. Hereinafter, this distinction is referred to as the distinction between actual or potential differentiation.

Actual differentiation concerns certain specifically designed Member States only, whilst potential differentiation may concern either all Member States or only some of them. In other words, actual differentiation is specific, whilst potential differentiation can be general or specific.

Practice shows that in order to respond to the fact that one or several Member States are in an objectively different situation from the others, primary and secondary law have traditionally provided for potential/general differentiation. Inversely, political differences between the Member States have been translated into actual/specific differentiation in primary law.

Since the start of Stage Three of EMU was envisaged on 1 January 1997 at the earliest, the Treaty provisions on EMU only formed the basis for future differentiation; in other words, they embodied potential differentiation. Unlike other examples of potential differentiation (but on account of the fixed time frame underpinning the phased approach to EMU), they specified when further action had to be taken. This move from potential to actual differentiation was accompanied by both general and specific differentiation: general in that there are generally applicable, objective conditions for the adoption of the single currency which any given Member State must (choose to) fulfil before it can move from

[18] More specifically, the "Protocol on the application of certain aspects of Article 7a of the [EC Treaty] to the [UK] and Ireland", the "Protocol on the position of the [UK] and Ireland", the "Protocol on Denmark" and the "Protocol integration the Schengen acquis into the framework of the [EU]".

being an "out" to becoming an "in"; specific in that two specifically designed Member States, i.e. the UK and Denmark, were granted an opt-out facility for purely political reasons. It will be recalled that the use of opt-outs was unprecedented and announced a different sort of integration *à la carte*—different in that opt-outs do not translate political differences between Member States into primary law exemptions with immediate effect, but into exemptions that can be activated unilaterally by the Member State(s) concerned at any given time in the future. Obviously, the use of opt-outs was inspired by the fact that Stage Three of EMU did not start upon the entry into force of the Treaty but was planned only at a later date. Alternatively, the UK and Denmark surely would have demanded tailor-made exemptions with immediate effects.

In an attempt to counter the infiltration of EU primary law by controversial specific differentiation, actually or potentially granting one or several Member States (in practice, nearly always the same ones) a special interest exemption,[19] the negotiators of the Amsterdam Treaty, where confronted with political differences between the Member States, actively sought to move toward potential/general differentiation (*in casu*, enhanced or closer co-operation). The advantages of such a move are obvious: potential/general differentiation is more open-ended and more anonymous; it does not involve specifying the Member State or group of Member States for whose benefit a given differentiated arrangement has emerged; it is therefore capable of avoiding commotion about the exceptional treatment of one or several Member States; and it can be applied potentially to a whole variety of different situations. Yet, there is also an important downside to it. Whilst actual/specific differentiation by way of definition deals with the specific situation of a very limited number of Member States, potential/general differentiation simply authorises differentiation for all Member States in the future. In certain fields that deal with hard core economics, e.g. EMU, such authorisation can be easily controlled by means of the definition of objective criteria that condition the future divide between the Member States. (In the previous section, it was shown that in such cases the authorisation may even be dealt with exclusively at secondary law level.) Conversely, when it is used to respond to political divisions between the Member States, potential/general differentiation enables the adoption of what used to be "constitutional" decisions at secondary law level. Put differently, if no conditions are imposed on its application, it authorises the unconditional adoption of as many opt-outs as there are Member States having objections to EU intervention in any given field, and refusing to participate as a consequence thereof.

It is against this backdrop that it can be understood that strict procedural and material conditions have been imposed on the use of this form of differentiation. For instance, traditionally the best examples of potential/general differentiation, i.e. safeguard clauses, have always been subjected to Community control

[19] In addition to the Danish and UK opt-outs, reference can also be made to the former Protocol on social policy and the Protocol on the acquisition of property in Denmark.

on the limited number of grounds provided in primary law which the Member States can invoke to escape their Treaty obligations. The presence of such conditions is even more striking in the enabling clauses for closer co-operation of the Treaty of Amsterdam. (In fact, many predict that these conditions will be the main reason for the anticipated limited usage of closer co-operation.) In stark contrast to closer co-operation, constructive abstention, which came to replace closer co-operation in the second pillar, lacks any material conditions imposed on its authorisation. Legally speaking, constructive abstention is not even authorised; it is simply declared by any given Member State. However, this does not mean that constructive abstention is without any obligations on the Member State(s) using it. On the contrary, they must not only accept that the decision commits the Union, they must also, in accordance with Article 23(1) (ex Article J.13(1)) TEU, "refrain from any action likely to conflict with or impede Union action based on that decision".

Returning to the main argument, the move from actual/specific to potential/general differentiation, sought by the negotiators of the Amsterdam Treaty in cases where they were confronted with insurmountable political differences between the Member States, has been only moderately successful. This is because the Member States that really wanted their particular demands to be taken into consideration, as they had done before at Maastricht, made sure to extract pre-determined differentiated regimes in their favour.

(iii) Positive v. *Negative Differentiation and Temporary v. Non-temporary Differentiation. The institutional consequences thereof*

In the previous section, I put safeguard clauses and the Treaty provisions on EMU in a single category on the basis that both usually stand for potential/general differentiation. It nonetheless goes without saying that they are very different from each other in many additional respects. In terms of the study of differentiation, one difference is particularly acute, in that safeguard clauses authorise the Member States, provided they fulfil certain conditions, not to participate in a common regime for a given period of time, to stay behind as it were, whereas the Treaty provisions on EMU authorise certain Member States, i.e. those fulfilling the necessary conditions for the adoption of the single currency, to move ahead as an vanguard. I will refer to this increasingly important distinction as the distinction between positive and negative differentiation, and define these parameters as follows: negative differentiation is differentiation which, actually or potentially, excludes one or several or all Member States, either temporarily or non-temporarily, from a rule which is adopted by all Member States. Conversely, positive differentiation is differentiation which occurs when primary law permits a limited number of Member States to adopt rules which, either temporarily or non-temporarily, apply only as far as they are concerned.

The Treaty provisions on EMU combined both. They incorporated trend-setting positive differentiation inasmuch as they authorised the ins to adopt rules which applied only as far as they were concerned (and envisaged the creation of a proper institutional framework to this end); and negative differentiation inasmuch as they granted the UK and Denmark an opt-out from the normal line-up to the adoption of the single currency.

The distinction between positive and negative differentiation, as suggested above, is closely linked to that between temporary and non-temporary differentiation, which has also played an increasingly important role in recent years. In the pre-TEU EC legal order, differentiation, with very few exceptions, was temporary (i.e. expressly limited in time), its rationale being to allow the Member States to pursue the same objectives at different intervals depending on their socio-economic performance.[20] In recent years, differentiation has increasingly been applied to instances of political differences between the Member States. As a result, it appeared impossible to maintain the principle that differentiation must be temporary. Accordingly, the temporary nature of differentiation, favourable in terms of the medium- and long-term uniformity of the application of EU law, was abandoned in the Treaty of Maastricht and, more recently, in the Treaty of Amsterdam, and this in spite of attempts expressly to limit differentiation in time[21] or to apply the model of EMU. Especially as regards the distinction between Member States with or without a derogation, this (EMU) model is characterised by a more creative use of the element of time, whereby explicit deadlines and fixed time-limits are replaced by a number of objectives (*in casu*, convergence criteria) that can be pursued by the Member States at a more individual pace. This mode of integration is commonly referred to as multi-speed integration. During the 1996 IGC, it soon appeared that it would not be possible to turn back time. Accordingly, the idea that differentiation must be temporary, whether it be in the sense of being expressly limited in time or in the sense of multi-speed integration, rapidly lost ground and disappeared entirely in the course of the 1996 IGC. The results of the IGC are in keeping with this: none of the differentiation the Treaty of Amsterdam adds to the EU legal order incorporates a teleology towards the achievement of previously agreed common objectives and the establishment of a common regime for all Member States.

Non-temporary differentiation, especially when it is used in combination with positive differentiation that permits a limited number of Member States to adopt rules which apply only as far they are concerned, raises a number of difficult questions concerning the relationship between participating and non-participating Member States. The Treaty provisions on EMU exemplify this very well. Together with the Protocol on social policy,[22] they represent the first that

[20] Paradigmatic in this respect is Art. 15 (ex Art. 7c) EC.

[21] See, e.g., the *Reflection Group's Report*, SN 520/95, 5 Dec. 1995, para. 15.

[22] Although it is counter-intuitive, the Protocol on social policy was an example of positive differentiation in that the 12 "High Contracting Parties" authorised 11 (later 14) Member States to have recourse "to the institutions, procedures and mechanisms of the Treaty for the purpose of taking among themselves, and applying as far as they are concerned the acts and decisions required for giving effect to the [Agreement on social policy]".

have tried to give a workable answer to these questions. They have, in so doing, broken with at least one longstanding tradition; namely that differentiation must not have repercussions on the composition of the common institutions.[23] I consider this development toward differentiation with institutional consequences as one of the most important, if not the most important, contemporary development in the use of differentiation, if only because it is linked very closely to the fundamental issue of the creation of sub-systems within the framework of the Treaty, with their own membership, rules and procedures, and their own institutional set-up, whereby the single institutional framework is increasingly, as I believe Christiaan Timmermans once referred to it, becoming a *trompe l'œil*. Obviously, the possibility of creating such sub-systems, and the likelihood of short-circuits between them, increases when a generalised system of differentiation (such as closer co-operation) is available to the Member States.[24]

Yet, even in the relatively self-contained world of EMU, the establishment of a *modus operandi* between the ins and outs[25] is not without problems. I would like to conclude this section by briefly pointing to various efforts to establish a workable balance between the proper functioning of an economic and monetary *avant-garde* and the maintenance of sufficient procedural and substantive links with the outs in order to avoid the ins and outs drifting apart for good.[26]

On the one hand, the Treaty provisions on EMU limit the influence of the outs on the activities of the ins. In addition to what was already mentioned in the introduction, namely that the voting rights of the outs are suspended for Council decisions with respect to Stage Three matters, they are also not entitled to participate in the appointment of the members of the Executive Board of the ECB, i.e. its President, Vice-President and other members,[27] who are nationals of the Member States without a derogation.[28] The Governors of the national

[23] The pre-TEU Community legal order, with one exception (to be found in Art. 109 of the 1972 Act of Accession), indeed, does not offer any example of differentiation with institutional repercussions: see Ehlermann, n. 13 *supra*, 1285.

[24] Once again, this shows the importance of the conditions imposed on closer co-operation. In this respect, attention can be drawn in particular to the impact of the condition that closer co-operation may only be used as a last resort (Art. 43(1)(c) (ex Art. K.15(1)(c)) TEU). In practice, this is likely to mean that closer co-operation (at least in the Community pillar) will, almost as a matter of fact, pertain to a single Commission proposal, i.e. an individual legal act, which cannot be adopted by virtue of the normal decision-making procedures. This in turn probably means that the likelihood that it will lead to the coming into being of genuine sub-systems, or could be used to this end, is remote.

[25] Hereafter I use this concept to refer to the Member States with a derogation, Denmark and the UK collectively. For obvious political motives, these Member States are also sometimes referred to as the "pre-ins".

[26] This paper does not deal with the consequences of differentiation on the external relations of the euro-area. See, on this matter, Tuytschaever, n. 7 *supra*, 170–83; C. Ziliolo and M. Selmayr, "The External Relations of the Euro Area: Legal Aspects" (1999) 36 *CMLRev*. 273–349.

[27] Art. 123(1) (ex Art. 109l(1)) EC. See Decision taken by common accord of the Governments of the Member States adopting the single currency at the level of Heads of State or Government of 26 May 1998 appointing the President, the Vice-President and the other members of the Executive Board of the European Central Bank [1998] OJ L154/33.

[28] Art. 11.2 of the Protocol on the Statute of the ESCB and the ECB, as read in conjunction with Art. 43.3 of the same Protocol. For the UK, see Art. 8 of the Protocol on certain provisions relating to the UK.

central banks of the outs are also not part of the Governing Council of the ECB.[29] On the other hand, the Treaty assures a connection between the ins and the outs by means of the creation of the General Council, which will remain the third decision-making body of the ECB as long as there are outs. The General Council comprises the President and the Vice-President of the ECB and the Governors of all national central banks.[30] Its tasks are not really important; they are mainly advisory and are meant to contribute to the outs' preparation for participation in Stage Three of EMU.[31] The General Council's true significance is symbolic, in that it is a forum where the ins and the outs meet on a regular basis.

Partly because of the dynamics of economic and monetary integration (and the relationship between the two) and partly because the Treaty provisions on EMU do not govern all aspects of Stage Three of EMU in the same detail (they are parsimonious especially in so far as the substantive, as opposed to the procedural, relationship between the ins and outs is concerned), practical arrangements for the orderly functioning of the euro area meanwhile have evolved outside the Treaty. These practical arrangements, like the Treaty provisions on EMU, bear out the dilemma of positive differentiation, namely how to put to work the principle of non-intervention of the outs in the legislative activities of the ins, whilst simultaneously creating enough centripetal forces to pull the outs towards participation in those very same activities.

The strengthening of the relation between the ins and the outs beyond the Treaty provisions was addressed by the European Council held in Dublin in December 1996 when it was decided that it was appropriate to replace the existing ERM by a new exchange-rate mechanism ("ERM 2").[32] The creation of the ERM 2 was confirmed by a resolution adopted by the European Council held in Amsterdam in June 1997 "on the establishment of an exchange-rate mechanism in the third stage of economic and monetary union".[33] According to the resolution, the ERM 2 "will help to ensure that Member States outside the euro-area participating in the mechanism orient their policies to stability, foster convergence and thereby help them in their efforts to adopt the euro". In addition, it may assist, if necessary, the Member States outside the euro area participating in it when their currencies come under pressure.[34] Since the ERM 2 has been established in the same way as the original EMS—i.e. by way of a resolution of the European Council implemented on the basis of an agreement between the ECB and the national central banks laying down the operating procedures of the

[29] Art. 8 of the Protocol, Art. 10.1. For the UK, see Art. 8 of the Protocol on certain provisions relating to the UK.

[30] Art. 45 of the Protocol on the Statute of the ESCB and the ECB.

[31] See *ibid.*, Art. 47, and the Rules of Procedure of the General Council [1999] OJ L75/36.

[32] *Bull. EU*, 12/1996, I.3 and I.33.

[33] Resolution 97/C236/03 of the European Council on the establishment of an exchange-rate mechanism in the third stage of economic and monetary union [1997] OJ C236/5, pt. 1.3.

[34] *Ibid.* Note that it belongs to the tasks of the General Council to monitor the functioning of the ERM 2.

exchange-rate mechanism[35]—the participation of the outs, like participation of the Member States in the original ERM, is voluntary. However, "Member States with a derogation can be expected to join the mechanism".[36] Meanwhile, the Greek drachma and the Danish krone have joined the ERM 2 with effect from 4 January 1999.

Secondly, the "Stability and Growth Pact" (which combines two regulations—on the strengthening of the surveillance of budgetary positions and the surveillance and co-ordination of economic policies[37] and on speeding up and clarifying the implementation of the excessive debt procedure[38]—with a resolution of the European Council of Amsterdam of June 1997[39]) is primarily aimed at assuring that the ins continue to comply with the convergence criteria, in particular with keeping their government deficit within the 3 per cent of the GDP reference value. At the same time, however, the Stability and Growth Pact pulls the activities of the outs closer to those of the ins to the extent that they are required to submit yearly updated convergence programmes. These programmes are the counterpart of the stability programmes which the ins must submit. Their objective is to permit the Council to examine whether the medium-term budget objective which the convergence programmes must contain provides for a safety margin to ensure the avoidance of an excessive deficit, whether the economic assumptions on which the programme is based are realistic and whether the measures being taken and/or proposed are sufficient to achieve the targeted adjustment path towards the medium-term objective and to achieve sustained convergence.[40] In other words, their objective also is to strengthen the relationship between the ins and the outs, notably by providing for an instrument on the basis of which the Council can examine whether the budgetary and economic policy guidelines of the outs are directed towards fulfilling the conditions for joining the euro area and can, if need be, address recommendations to the Member State concerned to take the necessary adjustment measures[41] or to take prompt corrective measures and make its recommendation public.[42]

Lastly, the ongoing search for a balance between the ins and the outs is presumably best illustrated by the controversy surrounding the workings of the

[35] Agreement of 1 Sept. 1998 between the European Central Bank and the national central banks of the Member States outside the euro area laying down the operating procedures for an exchange rate mechanism in stage three of EMU [1998] OJ C345/6.

[36] *Ibid.*, pt. 1.6. For a critique of the fact that the ERM 2 has not been established on the basis of binding Community legal acts and hence does not sufficiently reflect the ECB's exclusive competence concerning the matter, see J.-V. Louis, "A Legal and Institutional Approach for Building a Monetary Union" (1998) 35 *CMLRev.*, 70–2, and Ziliolo and Selmayr, n. 26 *supra*, 309–13.

[37] Council Reg. 1466/97/EC of 7 July 1997 [1997] OJ L209/1.

[38] Council Reg. 1467/97/EC of 7 July 1997 [1997] OJ L209/6.

[39] Resolution 97/C236/01 of the European Council on the Stability and Growth Pact [1997] OJ L236/1.

[40] Art. 9(1) of Council Reg. 1466/97/EC, n. 38 *supra*.

[41] *Ibid.*, Art. 10(2).

[42] *Ibid.*, Art. 10(3).

"Euro Council" (or "Euro X", now "Euro 11"). The idea of creating an informal body to co-ordinate the economic policies of the ins was originally mooted by France as a kind of political counterweight (a "European Economic Government") to the powers of the strictly independent ECB. After France convinced Germany to drop its initial reticence, the French and German finance ministers were able to announce agreement on the setting up of such an informal body at the end of the Franco-German Economic and Financial Summit on 14 October 1997. The Euro Council would provide a forum for swapping economic information and statistics, and it would act to survey economic situations and prepare for joint international encounters, such as the G–8. Notes would be compared on the budget front, and the group's members would also debate employment policies, structural reforms and could be called upon to address the scope for market adjustments, tax reforms and wage trends. According to Theo Waigel, former German finance minister, one of the main tasks during Euro Council meetings would be to apply Article 99 (ex Article 103) of the EC Treaty, in respect of which he spoke about examining economic policy fundamentals, a thorough implementation of the early warning system provided for in the Stability and Growth Pact as well as recommendations for practical action if need be.[43]

The project to set up a Euro Council composed exclusively of the ins immediately raised a storm of protest from the outs. Fearing they would find themselves sidelined from a body that (although it would be informal) could end up wielding considerable influence, particularly in the sense that it could be used as a way of establishing consensus among the ins that would then be presented to the rest of the EU as a *fait accompli* and would leave the Ecofin Council an empty shell, they demanded a seat on the Euro Council. Arguing that the problem did not come from the Euro Council but from the outs' non-participation in the euro and that the outs were not supposed to have a voice in a group that was intended to manage a currency that was not their own, the ins refused to give the outs a seat as a right. The French finance minister, Dominique Strauss-Kahn, for instance, compared it to the fact that "married couples don't want anybody else in their bedroom".[44]

For the time being, the skirmish concerning the Euro Council and the involvement of the outs in its activities has been settled by the European Council held in Luxembourg in December 1997. In spite of heavy UK pressure,[45] the outs failed to secure full membership of the Euro Council. In a resolution, it was agreed that "the ministers of the States participating in the euro area may meet informally among themselves to discuss issues connected with their shared specific responsibilities for the single currency. The Commission, and the European

[43] *European Report*, No 2260, 18 Oct. 1997.

[44] *European Report*, No 2273, 3 Dec. 1997, II.3.

[45] See, e.g., "Britain rejects EMU club proposal", *Financial Times*, 10 Dec. 1997, 1; "Europe's single currency. An insiders' club", *The Economist*, 6 Dec. 1997, 34.

Central Bank, when appropriate, will be invited to take part in the meetings."[46] It is only where "matters of common interest are concerned, [that] they will be discussed by ministers of all Member States".[47] Nevertheless, "[d]ecisions will in all cases be taken by the Ecofin Council in accordance with the procedures determined by the Treaty".[48]

In practice, Euro 11 now meets for about two hours before most Ecofin gatherings. From time to time, the main source of contention in the Euro Council compromise, namely the fact that it lacks a definition of the issues that will be considered of common interest between the ins and the outs, surfaces, namely whenever it is proposed to expand Euro 11's agenda and suggested that such expansion must not necessarily lead to an increased involvement of the outs. In the recent past, for instance, alarm bells rang when the Finnish Presidency, in keeping with earlier French proposals, argued in favour of an expansion of Euro 11's agenda to include general employment policy questions, tax policy, surveillance of individual Member States' economic performance and how to foster euro-area high-technology industries.[49]

Bearing in mind that the Treaty does not govern all aspects of EMU in the same detail, one may wonder whether it would not be possible to apply the provisions on closer co-operation to Stage Three of EMU in order to permit the ins to elaborate the substantive dimension of the euro area in a more formal way than is presently the case. In this respect, it is, to say the least, odd that during the 1996 IGC EMU, although it occupies a central place in the post-TEU EC legal order, has never been put (neither by a Member State[50] nor by the Commission[51]) on a negative list of matters where closer co-operation was to be excluded as a matter of course. One may wonder whether this is purely coincidental, or whether it resulted from some sort of tacit understanding, or whether some knew and others forgot and the former did not for whatever reason inform the latter.

Be that as it may, the actual results of the 1996 IGC are less encouraging inasmuch as the application of closer co-operation to Stage Three of EMU is concerned. Whilst it certainly cannot be excluded as a matter of course, several conditions imposed on closer co-operation in the Community pillar drastically limit its potential application to Stage Three of EMU. In this respect, reference can be made to various conditions. First, the fact that closer co-operation may not affect the competences, rights, obligations and interests of those Member States which do not participate therein (Article 43(1)(f) TEU) could of course be

[46] Resolution 98/C35/01 of the European Council of 13 Dec. 1997 on economic policy co-ordination in Stage 3 of EMU and on Treaty Arts. 109 and 109b of the EC Treaty [1998] OJ C35/1, pt. 6.

[47] *Ibid.*

[48] *Ibid.*

[49] *European Voice*, 3–9 June 1999, 1.

[50] See for the Italian negative list, CONF 3914/96, 24 Sept. 1996, and for that of the Dutch Presidency, CONF 3813/97, 11 Feb. 1997 and CONF 3835/97, 4 Mar. 1997.

[51] CONF 3805/97, 23 Jan. 1997.

used by the outs as a powerful argument to prevent the authorisation of closer co-operation. Secondly, even if the outs do not object, which seems unlikely ever to occur, account must be taken of the conditions laid down in Article 11(1)(a) and (d) of the EC Treaty, according to which closer co-operation may not concern areas which fall within the exclusive competence of the Community and must remain within the limits of the powers conferred upon the Community by the Treaty. Whilst the former condition directs closer co-operation in EMU away from its monetary dimension towards its economic dimension, the latter condition, which was added only during the last weeks of the negotiations[52] and reflects the fears of certain Member States that closer co-operation may be used to circumvent the recourse to the procedure for revision of the Treaties, requires the presence of a legal basis in the Treaty and prevents closer co-operation in fields where the Community does not have competence. I believe that it is this condition that is likely to obstruct efforts formally to develop EMU's economic dimension on the basis of closer co-operation and, in so doing, to create a more formal European Economic Government.

Take, for instance, the aforementioned Stability and Growth Pact, originally proposed by former German finance minister Waigel in November 1995 as the "Stability Pact for Europe", which provided for the automatic imposition of sanctions on the ins that would breach the deficit ceiling of 3 per cent, whereas under Article 104(11) (ex Article 104c(11)) of the EC Treaty, it is clearly for the Council to decide on the imposition of fines. Because of this, the German Federal Ministry of Finance anticipated that the Stability Pact would take the form of an international treaty[53]—i.e. the Stability Pact for Europe as a kind of "Economic Schengen". Irrespective of whether or not the ins would have been able legally to conclude such an international agreement, it is the best possible indication that the Stability Pact for Europe went beyond the Community's competence and could not be based entirely on the Treaty itself. Because of this, the automatic imposition of sanctions ultimately was replaced by a quasi-automatic imposition pursuant to a solemn political undertaking laid down in the aforementioned resolution of the European Council held in Amsterdam in June 1997.[54] After the entry into force of the Treaty of Amsterdam, a different result (in terms of automatic imposition of sanctions) cannot be achieved by way of applying closer co-operation to the fields covered by the Stability and Growth Pact. The condition that closer co-operation must remain within the limits of the powers conferred upon the Community prevents this.

What remain for closer co-operation then are the possibilities offered by provisions that open the way for a simplified Treaty revision procedure. In the case

[52] F. Dehousse, "Les résultats de la Conférence intergouvernementale", *Courrier hebdomadaire*, No 1565–1566, 1997, 45.

[53] For more details on this matter, see H.J. Hahn, "The Stability Pact for European Monetary Union: Compliance with Deficit Limit as a Constant Legal Duty" (1998) 35 *CMLRev*. 80–3, and Snyder, EMU Revisited, *l.c.*

[54] N. 35 *supra*.

of the economic dimension of EMU, reference can be made to Articles 99(5) (ex Article 103(5)) and 104(14) (ex Article 104c(14)) of the EC Treaty,[55] which could be used to underpin some of the activities of the Euro Council, although the outs may want to avoid this by all means.[56] In addition to this, closer co-operation (as suggested by the Dutch Presidency in the run-up to the Amsterdam Summit[57]) could be used to elaborate the accompanying measures of an economic and monetary union, e.g., indirect taxation, environment, and employment conditions, which have their own legal bases in the Treaty.

3. EMU AND THE EU'S CONSTITUTION

EMU is not only a useful guide through the maze of differentiation in the EU's legal order. It is also, more broadly, as Francis Snyder rightly suggests, a metaphor for European Union and EU constitution-making.[58] Put differently, even though EMU "provides a lens that resembles a kaleidoscope more than a telescope" and even though its metaphorical meaning is "partial, incomplete and inconsistent",[59] it may help us to discern some of the guiding principles underlying the constitutionalisation of European union.

Originally a marginal Community activity (cf. the original EMS), EMU currently plays a central role in the post-TEU EC legal order, even to the extent that it has been said to be Europe's sole remaining political project.[60] This development has not been possible without importing differentiation into the EC's legal order, both to take account of the objective differences between the Member States and to accommodate their political differences with regard to the adoption of a single currency. Now that it is at the centre of the post-TEU EC legal order, it is possible to witness efforts to develop Stage Three of EMU

[55] Note that these provisions have been used to establish the two regs. that form part of the Stability and Growth Pact, nn. 39 and 40 *supra*.

[56] See on this, European Parliament, Committee on Institutional Affairs, *Report on the implementation of the Amsterdam Treaty: implications of closer co-operation*, A4–0257/98, 1 July 1998 (*rapporteur*: Friedhelm Frischenschlager): "[a]re they designed to develop the economic aspects of EMU (in the wider sense, i.e. including social and fiscal matters?) Nothing could be less certain given that any Member State—provided that it cites its reasons of national policy—is at liberty to prevent a vote being taken by a qualified majority on introducing closer co-operation. On top of this, closer cooperation must not affect the competences, rights, obligations and interests' of non-participating Member States and must not distort competition between the Member States." See also the minority opinion by the vice-chairman of the Committee on Institutional Affairs Georges Berthu: "it is surprising to see the Amsterdam Treaty define forms of cooperation in abstracto, with a wealth of detail, whilst carefully sidestepping the sphere of closer co-operation which would have been most useful in the immediate future—that of the single currency. For the time being the 'euro 11 Council' still has unofficial status, despite the alleged importance of its role": *ibid.*, 14.

[57] CONF 3813/97, 11 Feb. 1997.

[58] F. Snyder, "EMU—Metaphor for European Union? Institutions, Rules and Types of Regulation" in R. Dehousse (ed.), *Europe After Maastricht. An Ever Closer Union?* (Munich: Law Books in Europe, 1994), 63–99.

[59] *Ibid.*, 99.

[60] F. Dehousse, n. 52 *supra*, 52.

further, sometimes by means of marginal instruments, such as non-legally binding resolutions of the European Council. As suggested above, it is likely that this will lead in turn to efforts to apply new forms of differentiation to Stage Three of EMU, in particular to its economic dimension, in order to pull these activities from the periphery towards the centre. Whilst mainly concerning the ins, these developments will surely also affect the present and future involvement of the outs in Stage Three. In the long run, I believe that the *avant-garde* created in Stage Three of EMU, and consolidated in the way described above, will be able to exercise sufficient traction effects, and produce sufficient centripetal force, so that the distinction between the ins and the outs will disappear and all Member States with a derogation, present and future, and those with an opt-out, will adopt the single currency.[61]

In the broader context of the EU, developments which are similar to those that have occurred and continue to occur in the field of EMU can be identified. That is, more and more matters that were previously dealt with on the basis of intergovernmental co-operation between some or all Member States outside the Treaty framework have been brought under the Treaty's umbrella. Whilst this has led to a continuing growth of the EC/EU's scope of intervention, it has not always been possible immediately to incorporate matters under the Treaty's umbrella on the basis of the Community method, as perceived traditionally in terms of the universality of EC/EU law and the uniformity of its application (that is, apart from differentiation flowing from the application of the principle of non-discrimination). In recent years especially, two major alternatives have been put to work. For matters that most Member States consider very sensitive (*in casu,* common foreign and security policy and justice and home affairs), the Treaty of Maastricht created a new pattern of extra-Community "intergovernmental" co-operation under the Treaty's umbrella (the "second" and "third pillars") within which the national veto was retained and the involvement of the European Parliament, the Commission and the Court carefully circumscribed or even downright excluded. In addition to this, use has been made of differentiation, which has resulted either in intergovernmental co-operation under the Treaty's framework between only some Member States or in differentiated integration under the Community pillar. It goes without saying that the greater the scope of EU intervention, the greater the likelihood that the use of differentiation will flow from political differences between the Member States, as it is increasingly likely that the extension will concern matters that go to the heart of national sovereignty.

Compared to the TEU post-Maastricht, the TEU post-Amsterdam seems to indicate that intergovernmental co-operation under the Treaty's umbrella is only a transitional stage and that, in a second stage, a two-fold, interrelated,

[61] On the fact that the current outs are already preparing themselves to participate, see P. Beaumont and N. Walker, "The Euro and European Legal Order" in P. Beaumont and N. Walker (eds.), *Legal Framework of the Single European Currency* (Oxford: Hart Publishing, 1999), 169–94, *passim.*

development is likely to take place: one consisting of a movement toward integration under the Community pillar (the process of "communitarisation"[62]) and one consisting of a development towards increased membership of differentiated integration. Because the Member States disagree on the extent of the EC/EU's powers or because certain aspects are, implicitly or explicitly, excluded, it is sometimes possible to discern a complementary stage. This may imply the coming of a full circle, when some Member States, once again, resort to intergovernmental co-operation outside the Treaty or when some or all of them make a move toward informal co-operation at the fringes of the EC/EU. In such cases, the EC/EU, time after time, has been able to spread its tentacles to make these activities gravitate toward the centre, if need be by means of differentiation. In light of this, it should not surprise us that attempts will be made to apply closer co-operation to recent initiatives at the EC's periphery, e.g. to fill out the economic dimension of Stage Three of EMU. This would be entirely in keeping with the fact that many actors involved in the 1996 IGC considered closer co-operation as a means of keeping certain initiatives that would otherwise take place outside the Treaty framework under the Treaty umbrella. For instance, the December 1996 "General Outline for a Draft Revision of the Treaties" of the Irish Presidency stated that "(s)everal Member States have emphasized the importance of any enhanced cooperation developing inside rather than outside the Union",[63] and the January 1997 Commission's "Policy Paper on Flexibility/Enhanced Co-operation" that "if no solution is found within the Treaty, the danger then is that flexibility may be applied outside that context".[64] More recently, in a resolution on the implications of closer co-operation adopted on 16 July 1999, the European Parliament also considered "that the creation of an institutional framework for developing closer co-operation is preferable to such cooperation taking place outside the Treaty system".[65] Obviously, the extent to which differentiation is able to prevent intergovernmental co-operation or to incorporate existing intergovernmental initiatives in the Treaty framework depends on the requirements imposed on its use in the Treaty framework, and their restrictive or extensive interpretation. Accordingly, "(w)hile the Treaty provisions set out a plethora of conditions designed to remove the risk of fragmenting the single institutional framework and the existing body of Union law, a quite different risk is emerging, namely

[62] Communitarisation also pertains to certain sub-movements, e.g. constitutional development due to the use of so-called "passerelles" that make it possible to communitarise certain matters without need to amend the Treaty, see ex Art. K.9 TEU and presently Art. K.14 TEU; and, for matters already falling within the ambit of intervention of the EC, the move from unanimity to qualified majority voting, which in turn can give rise to actual or potential differentiation. An example of the latter, for instance, is ex Art. 100a(4) EC Treaty, the price to be paid for the fact that the Single European Act allowed measures which had as their object the establishment and functioning of the internal market to be adopted by qualified majority.

[63] CONF 2500/96, 5 Dec. 1996.

[64] CONF 3805/97, 23 Jan. 1997, 2.

[65] European Parliament, Resolution on the implementation of the Amsterdam Treaty: implications of closer cooperation [1998] OJ C292/143.

that because the provisions are too restrictive, they will not be applied and consequently the desire of some Member States to advance the process of integration will take the form of closer cooperation outside the Community framework".[66]

Until recently, the idea that differentiation under the Treaty's framework is an alternative for intergovernmental co-operation outside the Treaty and vice versa was regarded as a no-win situation; a Catch–22. On the one hand, intergovernmental co-operation outside the Treaty framework has been heavily criticised because of its lack of transparency, its democratic deficit and the absence of an independent judicial review mechanism. Therefore, integration under the Treaty has been widely favoured. On the other hand, integration within the Treaty framework by means of new patterns of extra-Community co-operation and, above all, by means of differentiation, has likewise been rejected, mainly because it has been perceived as posing a serious threat to the uniqueness and strength of the Community legal order. At present, most consider this view to be outdated. Differentiation under the Treaty's umbrella is, indeed, increasingly accepted as a potentially meaningful instrument to prevent groups of Member States starting work together on an intergovernmental basis outside the Treaty when hampered in their efforts for further integration under the Treaty, or to incorporate existing intergovernmental initiatives between a limited number of Member States into the Treaty framework.

The reasons for this development, this move beyond a perceived Catch-22, are various. To some extent, they concern the fact that different kinds of differentiation are used nowadays. In this respect, I believe that positive differentiation, in spite of its inherent booby traps, has been most instrumental in shifting the weight of argument from the unwilling to the willing Member States and, more generally, in connoting positive ("*avant-garde*", "strengthened solidarities", "closer co-operation") instead of negative (derogations, exemptions and "opt-outs') feelings to the phenomenon of differentiation. To some extent, they also concern the fact that differentiation, even if it is based on political disagreement between the Member States, has frequently turned out to be, so to speak, a single frame out of a motion-picture film. Indeed, experience has shown that differentiation, whatever form it takes, frequently is not an end-stage, but a stepping stone towards further communitarisation for all Member States. In other words, when they are confronted with one another for a sufficiently long time, the practice of integration nearly always seems to win from the ideology of differentiation.

In this respect, reference can be made to a number of developments which have taken place over time and which, to a greater or lesser extent, have gone through the different phases mentioned above: for instance, to the development

[66] European Parliament, Committee on Institutional Affairs, *Report on the implementation of the Amsterdam Treaty: implications of closer cooperation*, A4–0257/98, 26 June 1998 (*rapporteur*: Friedhelm Frischenschlager), 12.

from the intergovernmental 1989 Social Charter to the Protocol on social policy and the Agreement attached to it, to the abolition of the Protocol and the Agreement and the UK's fully-fledged participation in the social dimension of integration under the EC Treaty. Or the development from the intergovernmental activities of the TREVI Group to the provisions of the third pillar regarding co-operation in the fields of justice and home affairs, to the partial communitarisation of these provisions by way of the new Title IV of the EC Treaty on "visas, asylum, immigration and other policies related to the free movement of persons"; or to the integration, albeit more hesitantly, of the Schengen *acquis* into the framework of the EU, i.e. the amended third pillar and the EC Treaty[67]; and, finally, to the even more hesitant, yet long blossoming, relationship between the EU and the WEU.[68]

In summary, rather against the grain of received ideas, I believe it is possible to conclude, at least for the time being, with an optimistic note on the increased use of differentiation in the EU's legal order. Particularly when it is seen against the background of one of the main guiding principles of EU constitution-making, i.e. the permanent interaction that takes place between intergovernmental co-operation outside the Treaty and integration under the Treaty,[69] differentiation emerges as an important instrument to permit constitutional change and development. That is, in practice, differentiation frequently turns out to be the first decisive step towards communitarisation of a given matter for all Member States. To the present day differentiation has been favourable to integration, not the opposite

[67] See Council Decision 1999/436/EC of 20 May 1999 determining, in conformity with the relevant provisions of the [EC Treaty] and the [TEU], the legal basis for each of the provisions or decisions which constitute the Schengen acquis [1999] OJ L176/17. Note that the UK, which extracted an exemption from the incorporation of the Schengen *acquis* (see Art. 4, first sentence, of the Protocol integrating the Schengen *acquis* into the framework of the EU), has already asked to take part in certain provisions of the Schengen *acquis*. On 20 July 1999, the Commission adopted a favourable opinion on the request, see IP/99/550, 20 July 1999.

[68] See recently Council Decision 1999/404/CFSP of 10 May 1999 concerning the arrangements for enhanced co-operation between the EU and the WEU [1999] OJ L153/1.

[69] For more on this interaction, see the chapter by Bruno de Witte elsewhere in this volume.

9

Flexibility and Social Policy

CATHERINE BARNARD*

1. THE MANY MEANINGS OF FLEXIBILITY

IN MANY WAYS, social policy represents a microcosm of the flexibility debate in the European Union. For constitutional lawyers the UK opt-out from the "Social Chapter" provides a textbook study of the "strong" form of flexible governance where one Member State, with the consent of the others keen to integrate more deeply, is not obliged to follow a particular Community policy-for political or economic reasons.[1] While the advantages of such flexibility are clear—the UK's opt-out from the Social Chapter (and EMU) enabled it to sign the Maastricht Treaty and allowed the other Member States to maintain the momentum of integration—subsequent events have brought into sharp focus the drawbacks of such flexible governance.

While the strong form of flexibility has attracted most attention, other "softer" forms of flexibility permitting more minor types of differentiation have long been tested in the social field, before the term itself became vogue. In particular, different legislative vehicles have been used to accommodate the diversity in the Member States' approaches to regulating employment relations, and those legislative measures themselves provide scope for "internal" flexibility. More recently, different methods of governance of the employment relationship have been employed. No longer is legislation the sole channel for enacting social norms—European collective agreements, negotiated by the social partners, can replace substantive legislation. Indeed, the function of social partners has extended beyond the role of legislators and they have become important new actors in the governance of the Community.

On the other hand, to labour lawyers the term "flexibility" has different, and often much less favourable, connotations than it has to constitutional lawyers, for it suggests the undermining of hard-won legal standards of protection. In the 1980s, faced with the pressure of rising unemployment, the need to adapt to new technologies and the competitive models of the "flexible" labour markets of the

* I am very grateful to Gráinne de Búrca for her most helpful comments.

[1] This is the sense of flexibility understood in Art. 11 (ex Art. 5a) EC.

USA and Japan,[2] political attention shifted towards the need to make domestic markets more flexible in order to cure unemployment. According to some neo-liberals, the existing European social model based on a system of social protection and collective employee representation had obstructed the operation of labour markets, limiting the necessary adjustments to changing demand, hindering innovation and restricting job creation.[3] They argued that employment would only be created through the *deregulation* of employment legislation and dismantling the institutional barriers to wage flexibility.

Thus, to labour lawyers, as Deakin and Read point out,[4] the "elusive" term flexibility can mean both changing patterns of demand and supply for labour as well as changing (and usually removing) protective regulation. On the demand side, innovative methods piloted by the highly productive "flexible firm" provide the model. This model focuses on employers' strategies concerning the form in which labour is contracted, enabling employers to vary labour inputs according to fluctuations in demand. This flexibility can take a variety of forms: *numerical* flexibility allows the firm to modulate the numbers employed; *working time* flexibility permits the firm to raise or lower hours through overtime or through variations to normal hours; *financial* flexibility links remuneration directly to output; and *functional* flexibility refers to the multi-skilling of workers permitting them to move between tasks and adapt their working practices to new technical or organisational requirements.[5]

On the supply side, by contrast, flexibility manifests itself in terms of the growth of non-standard employment—such as part-time work and temporary employment. Such "atypical" employment may be demanded by certain sections of the workforce who were previously unable to gain access to employment, due to their inability or unwillingness, often for family reasons, to commit themselves to full-time, permanent, standard employment. Policies supporting supply-side flexibility enable individuals to move between different forms of work while retaining the value in their "human capital" and preserving their career path. To date, sex discrimination legislation has helped to achieve some of these objectives.[6]

[1] B. Hepple, "Aspects of Flexibility in Labour Law" (1987) 1 *Zeitschrift für auslandisches und internationales Arbeits- und Socialrecht* 280; B. Hepple, *European Social Dialogue—Alibi or Opportunity*, IER, 1993 and T. Treu, "Labour Flexibility in Europe" (1992) 131 *International Labour Review* 497.

[3] J. Addison and W. Siebert, "The Social Charter of the European Community: Evolution and Controversies" (1991) 44 *Industrial and Labor Relations Review* 597.

[4] S. Deakin and H. Reed, "Between Social Policy and EMU: The New Employment Title of the EC Treaty" in J. Shaw (ed.), *Social Law and Policy in an Evolving European Union* (Oxford: Hart, 2000). What follows in this section draws heavily on this excellent work.

[5] See Deakin and Reed, n. 4 *supra*.

[6] See C. Barnard, "Gender Equality in the EU: A Balance Sheet" in P. Alston (ed.), *The EU and Human Rights* (Oxford: OUP, 1999), although cf T. Hervey and J. Shaw, "Women, Work and Care: Women's Dual Role and Double Burden in EC Sex Equality Law" (1998) 8 *Journal of European Social Policy Law* 43.

The other manifestation of flexibility for labour lawyers concerns regulation. In some Member States (most notably the UK under the Conservative government), a "flexible" labour market is one without regulation, where the market is able to operate unimpeded by rigidities created by centralised collective bargaining, high unionisation rates, the "tax wedge" of employment taxes and social security contributions, job protection legislation and earnings related unemployment benefits.[7] For this reason, flexibility became synonymous with deregulation and was viewed by many labour lawyers with suspicion. Even where flexibility offered some benefits for those previously excluded from the workforce ("supply-side flexibility") the reality has been that these workers are poorly paid and gain little chance of career advancement.[8]

In the EU the approach towards flexibility is more sophisticated. The Treaty of Amsterdam itself does not contain a deregulatory agenda. Not only does the Treaty incorporate the Social Policy Agreement into a new Social Chapter in the EC Treaty but Article 2 talks of "a high level of employment *and* social protection" (emphasis added) and "equality between men and women", as well as "sustainable and non-inflationary growth, a high degree of competitiveness and convergence of economic performance". As various Community documents make clear, in particular the Green Paper entitled *Partnership for the New Organisation of Work*,[9] the new emphasis is on flexibility at the level of the firm *combined with* security for workers. This document is imbued with notions of rights and responsibilities: the worker who takes on the responsibility to be flexible will be rewarded with greater security[10]: this is the stakeholder society. This represents an attempt to find a "Third Way" between the "Anglo-Saxon" model of deregulation, low unemployment and fewer welfare benefits, and the European model of job protection, high unemployment and generous welfare provision.

At the heart of the "Third Way" debate is the idea that decision-making should be deeply rooted in notions of partnership and decentralisation, as the *Partnership* Green Paper recognises. It says that the social partners have a key role in achieving this balance between flexibility and security, at the macro level in terms of negotiating collective agreements, and at the micro level in terms of ensuring the development of new forms of industrial relations built on a basis of co-operation and common interest "since efficient production requires enhanced levels of both trust and commitment in firms".[11] It is here that the constitution and the labour law debates about flexibility begin to converge. It is also here that we begin to see the links between flexibility and subsidiarity, the two

[7] H. Siebert, "Labour Rigidities: At the Root of Unemployment in Europe" (1997) 17 *Journal of Economic Perspectives* 43, cited in Deakin and Reed, n. 4 *supra*.

[8] L. Dickens, *Whose Flexibility? Discriminaiton and Equality Issues in Atypical Work* (London: IER, 1992).

[9] COM(97)127.

[10] G. Kenner, "The EU Employment Title and the "Third Way': Making Soft Law Work?" (1999) 15 *IJCLLIR* 33, 45–6.

[11] COM(97)127.

"conservatory" principles of Community law,[12] and the tensions that arise at their confluence. I shall consider these issues in the third part of my chapter. First, I shall examine the concept of flexibility in social policy from the perspective of a constitutional lawyer.

2. GOVERNANCE AND SOCIAL POLICY

A. Variable Geometry: Strong Flexibility

The earliest example of strong flexibility in the social sphere was the adoption of the non-binding Community Social Charter 1989 which the UK did not sign, and the Social Chapter (the Social Policy Protocol (SPP) and the Social Policy Agreement (SPA)) from which the UK secured an opt-out. Ehlermann describes these as examples of "variable geometry": different positions being taken by the states in terms of substance and not just time. He says "the common arrangement is disapproved of by the outsiders, either in principle or in details. They are allowed to benefit from an exceptional arrangement allowing them to leave the common provision unapplied and there is no time limit on the exceptional arrangement".[13] Putting it another way, the hard core proceeds more rapidly towards greater integration and refuses to be held back by those "soft" states standing on the periphery.[14] This desire for greater integration was expressed in the SPP which provided that the (then) 12 agreed that the 11 Member States "wish to continue along the path laid down in the 1989 Social Charter" and that they have adopted the SPA "to this end". This Agreement was annexed to the Protocol.[15] Both the Agreement and the Protocol were without prejudice to the provisions of the Treaty, particularly those relating to social policy which constitute an integral part of the "*acquis communautaire*". There was much debate about the legality of the opt-out. [16] The prevailing view[17] was that since the

[12] A. Dashwood, "States in the European Union" (1998) 23 *ELRev*. 201.

[13] C.D. Ehlermann, "Differentiation, Flexibility, Closer Cooperation: The New Provisions of the Amsterdam Treaty" (1998) 4 *ELJ* 246, 247.

[14] J. Shaw, "The Treaty of Amsterdam: Challenges of Flexibility and Legitimacy" (1998) 4 *ELJ* 63, 66.

[15] However, as B. Fitzpatrick, "Community Social Law After Maastricht" (1992) 21 *ILJ* 199, 200, points out, while it is clear that the agreement is annexed to the Protocol, which in turn is annexed to the TEU, the agreement is expressed to be an annex to the Treaty of Rome—para. 3.

[16] M. Weiss, "The Significance of Maastricht for European Social Policy" (1992) 8 *IJCLLIR* 3; C. Barnard, "A Social Policy for Europe: Politicians 1 Lawyers 0" (1992) 8 *IJCLLIR* 15; E. Vogel-Polsky, *Evaluation of the Social Provisions of the Treaty on European Union*, Report prepared for the Committee on Social Affairs, Employment and the Working Environment of the European Parliament, DOC EN\CM\202155, cited in P. Watson, "Social Policy after Maastricht" (1993) 31 *CMLRev*. 481, 491. See also the submissions made in *R.* v. *Secretary of State for Foreign and Commonwealth Affairs, ex parte Lord Rees Mogg* [1993] 3 CMLR 101. For critiques of these views, see P. Watson, above, 491–4 and E. Whiteford, "Social Policy after Maastricht" (1993) 18 *ELRev*. 202, 203–4.

[17] Watson, n.16 *supra*, 488, EIRR, *Maastricht and Social Policy—Part Two*, European Industrial Relations Review 239, p. 19, Whiteford, n. 16 *supra*.

Protocol was an agreement by the 12 Member States that only 11 were to be bound by the new social provision,[18] then according to Article 239 EC (now Article 311), protocols annexed to the Treaty form an integral part of the Treaty. The Protocol on Social Policy was therefore part of the Treaty of Rome and thus part of Community law.[19]

Consequently, once the Maastricht Treaty came into force, European Community social policy was subject to two free-standing but complementary legal frames of reference—the EC Treaty and the Social Chapter. This presented a difficult choice for the Commission: to use the Social Chapter and bind the 11 or to use the EC Treaty to bind the 12 but with only a slim chance of the measures being adopted. It suggested a compromise solution. It said that it would decide on a case-by-case basis whether to use the Agreement on Social Policy.[20] However, in the case of health and safety proposals (an area which received a degree of support from the UK) the Commission said that it would give priority to instruments which enabled a decision to be taken by all 12 Member States.[21] In the White Paper on Social Policy[22] the Commission noted the "strong desire of all Member States to proceed as twelve wherever possible" and hoped that "Union social policy action will in future once again be founded on a single legal framework".[23] It added that a single legal framework is "vital if the integrity of the law and the principle of equal opportunities for all in the Union are to be upheld".[24] Nevertheless, it concluded that "the desire to act as 12 cannot be used as an excuse for standing still".[25]

The mechanics of using the SPA were complex.[26] The SPP authorised the signatories to use the institutions of the Community.[27] Therefore, the Commission still proposed legislation aimed at implementing the Agreement; the European Parliament and ECOSOC were consulted and the measure was adopted by the Council. If a unanimous vote was required, the Protocol said that all 11 Member States should agree; if qualified majority voting was required, 44 votes out of a possible 66 were needed.[28] The UK did not take part in the "deliberations and

[18] N. Burrows and J. Mair, *European Social Law* (Chichester: Wiley, 1996) 6.

[19] Similarly, since the Protocol provides that the agreement on social policy is annexed to the Protocol, which in turn is annexed to the Treaty, the Agreement also forms part of Community law.

[20] Commission Communication concerning the application of the Agreement on social policy, COM(93)600, 14, para. 8.

[21] *Ibid.*

[22] COM(94)333, 27 July 1994.

[23] COM(94)333, 13. See also COM(93)600, the Commission's Communication concerning the application of the Agreement on Social Policy.

[24] *Ibid.*

[25] *Ibid.*

[26] See G. Brinkman. "Law Making under the Social Chapter of Maastricht" in P. Craig and C. Harlow (eds.), *Law Making in the EU* (The Hague: Kluwer, 1998); B. Bercusson, "Maastricht—a Fundamental Change in European Labour Law" (1992) 23 *IRJ* 177 and "The Dynamic of European Labour Law after Maastricht" (1994) 23 *ILJ* 1.

[27] Art. 1 SPP.

[28] Art. 2(2) SPP. This became 54 votes out of 76 after the accession of Austria, Finland, and Sweden.

the adoption by the Council of Commission proposals made on the basis of this protocol and the above-mentioned agreement".[29] The Protocol did not, however, prevent British Commission officials from drafting proposals, British MEPs from participating in Parliamentary debates and voting, British members of ECOSOC from expressing their views, nor the British judge from participating in any case where the Court was required to give judgment—all acting as part of the supranational institution for which they worked rather than as official representatives of the UK. The Protocol also did not prevent the British CBI from participating in UNICE, the European employers' organisation, and the British TUC in the European TUC when negotiating collective agreements under the SPA.[30] Conversely, any financial consequences, other than administrative costs entailed by the institutions, did not apply to the United Kingdom.[31]

The arrival of the new Labour government in May 1997, with its commitment to sign up to the Social Chapter, presented its own difficulties: for obvious reasons, the Social Chapter made no express provision for an opt-in.[32] How was this to be achieved? At Amsterdam a new section was included in the Treaty entitled "The Union and the Citizen". This contained an amended chapter on "Social Provisions", incorporating into a single chapter (and revising) both Articles 117–121 of the EC Treaty and the Maastricht SPA (now Articles 136–145), and was agreed by all 15 Member States. This bound the UK for the future.

As for the past, various proposals were put forward as to how the UK could "sign up" to the four pieces of legislation adopted under the SPA: the European Works Council (EWC) Directive 94/95,[33] the Directive on Parental Leave,[34] the Directive on the Burden of Proof,[35] and the Directive on Part-time Workers.[36] It was first suggested that the UK could implement the Directives into national law without waiting for the Article N TEU (now Article 48 TEU) amendment process to be completed. This presented substantial difficulties at domestic level.[37] As a result, the Community readopted the Directives under Article 100

[29] Art. 2(1) SPP. For a similar approach, see also the Protocols concerning Title IV (ex Title IIIa) Part Three EC. Compare Art. 44 (ex Art. K16) which provides that "all members of the Council shall be able to take part in the deliberations, only those representing participating Member States shall take part in the adoption of decisions".

[30] See text attached to n. 15 *supra*.

[31] Art. 2(3) SPP.

[32] See G. Gaja, "How Flexible is Flexibility under the Treaty of Amsterdam" (1998) 35 *CMLRev.* 855, 859.

[33] [1994] OJ L254/64.

[34] Council Dir. 96/34/EC of 3 June 1996 on the framework agreement on parental leave concluded by UNICE, CEEP and the ETUC [1996] OJ L145/4.

[35] Council Dir. 97/80/EC [1998] OJ L14/6.

[36] Council Dir. 97/81/EC [1998] OJ L14/9.

[37] If the UK's opt-out is seen as a derogation from the provisions of the EC Treaty, then the procedure laid down by s. 2(2) of the European Communities Act 1972 would not apply. This means that primary legislation would need to be adopted. Further, national legislation in other countries, particularly in respect of the EWC Dir., would also need to be amended to take account of the UK's inclusion. Finally, even if the UK did adopt legislation via this route, there might have been a problem concerning the jurisdiction of the ECJ.

(now Article 94), requiring a unanimous vote in Council.[38] This required further national legislation in other Member States as well as in the UK, particularly in respect of the EWC Directive, to take account of the UK's inclusion.

Three lessons can be drawn from the five years of the UK opt-out from the Social Chapter.[39] First, the mechanics and practicalities for opting back in remain complex and have ramifications for all Member States and not just the state which has exercised the opt-out. Secondly, only four pieces of legislation were adopted during this period. It seems that despite the avowed intention of the 11 in the SPP "to continue along the path laid down in the 1989 Social Charter" they did so with little enthusiasm in the absence of the UK. Thirdly, in a globalised market, measures—in particular transnational measures—adopted by a few cannot be confined to national frontiers, and will inevitably have an effect on the many. This can be seen most clearly in respect of the EWC Directive[40] requiring the establishment of an EWC in the case of multi-national companies employing more than 1,000 workers with at least 150 workers in each of two Member States. British multi-nationals with plants on the Continent were obliged to set up EWCs or their equivalent, even though the UK government had had no input in negotiating the legislation. Many companies extended the EWCs to their UK employees (for example United Biscuits, BP, ICI, Courtaulds, GKN and Natwest). Foreign-owned companies such as Panasonic and TNT also set up consultative bodies in response to the Directive and included their British operations.[41] Thus, the UK could not fully insulate itself from the effects of the Directive.

So far I have examined the most dramatic form of flexibility, variable geometry, envisaging the highest level of variability and therefore the greatest fragmentation. However, since its inception the Community has been forced to address the question of flexibility, albeit at a lower level of variability and without the label attached, to accommodate the 15 Member States, each with its own complex body of social legislation and diverse system of industrial relations.[42] On the one hand, the so-called Romano-Germanic states (for example, France, Germany and Italy) have a system characterised by comprehensive legislation governing various areas of working conditions and employee representation. In these countries the state tends to play a central role in industrial relations. On the other hand, in the Nordic countries the state assumes a relatively limited role

[38] Council Dir. 97/75/EC [1998] OJ L10/24 (consolidating legislation [1998] OJ L10/11) on parental leave; Council Dir. 98/52/EC [1998] OJ L205/66 on burden of proof; Council Dir. 98/23/EC [1998] OJ L131/10 (Consolidating legislation [1998] OJ L131/13) on part-time work; Council Dir. 97/74/EC [1998] OJ L10/22 (consolidating legislation [1998] OJ L10/22)

[39] See C. Barnard, "The United Kingdom, the 'Social Chapter' and the Amsterdam Treaty" (1997) 26 *ILJ* 275–82.

[40] See generally Lord Wedderburn, "Consultation and Collective Bargaining in Europe: Success or Ideology?" (1997) 26 *ILJ* 1.

[41] See S. Hargreaves, "Social Europe after Maastricht: Is the United Kingdom Really Opted-out" (1997) 19 *JSWFL* 1.

[42] For full details, see A. Ferner and R. Hyman, *Changing Industrial Relatuins in Europe* (Oxford: Blackwell, 1998).

in industrial relations. The cornerstone of this system is a series of labour market collective agreements, including a permanent basic agreement which is seldom challenged or amended. The Anglo-Irish system differs again. Traditionally, it is also characterised by the limited role played by the state in industrial relations, a system described as voluntarism. When compared to the Romano-Germanic system neither the individual nor the collective relationship is subject to extensive legal regulation, despite a trend towards legislative intervention over the last two decades. Reconciling, or at least accommodating, these different traditions at European level has long proved difficult and controversial.[43] This has made uniform governance an impossibility, prompting the development of innovative, "softer" flexible solutions.

B. "Softer" Forms of Flexibility

(i) Flexibility in the Choice of Legislative Instruments

Regulations, seen by many as the epitome of uniformity, have never been used to set EC employment standards. The principal regulatory vehicle has been Directives which, by their very nature, allow for a degree of flexibility or differentiation in the way in which EC norms manifest themselves in the 15 Member States. This flexibility is increased by the use of Directives setting minimum standards which Member States are free to improve upon,[44] and those which are only framework in nature.[45] The importance of these types of Directives was recognised in the Council Resolution on certain aspects for a European Union Social Policy.[46] It said Community legislative acts must[47]:

—take account of the situation in all Member States when each individual measure is adopted and neither overstretch any one Member State nor force it to dismantle social rights;
—avoid going into undue detail but concentrate on basic, binding principles and leave the development and transposition to the Member States individually and, where this is in accordance with national traditions, to the two sides of industry;

[43] See C. Barnard, "EC 'Social' Policy" in P. Craig and G. de Búrca (eds.), *The Evolution of EU Law* (Oxford: OUP, 1999).

[44] Art. 118a EC (now Art. 137(2)) provides that the Council shall adopt, by means of Dirs., minimum requirements for encouraging improvements, especially in the working environment as regards the health and safety of workers. Thus, the Dirs., adopted on this legal basis set minimum standards: e.g. Dir. 89/391/EEC on the introduction of measures to encourage improvements in the safety and health of workers at work [1989] OJ L183/9, and the daughter dirs.; and Dir. 93/104/EC on working time [1993] OJ L307/18.

[45] See nn. 89–91, *infra*.

[46] Council Resolution of 6 Dec. 1994 on certain aspects for a European Union Social Policy: a contribution to economic and social convergence in the Union [1994] OJ C368/6.

[47] Para. 17.

—be flexible enough and confine themselves to provisions which can be incorporated into the various national systems;
—include clauses which allow the two sides of industry room for manœuvre on collective agreements;
—contain review clauses so that they can be corrected in the light of practical experience.

Stressing the diversity of the national systems, the Resolution states that it considers "unification of national systems in general by means of rigorous approximation of laws an unsuitable direction to follow as it would also reduce the chances of the disadvantaged regions in the competition for location".[48]

This approach has now been confirmed by the Protocol on the application of the principles of subsidiarity and proportionality included in the Amsterdam Treaty. Articles 6 envisages that:

> The form of Community action shall be as simple as possible, consistent with satisfactory achievement of the objective of the measure and the need for effective enforcement. The Community shall legislate only to the extent necessary. Other things being equal, directives should be preferred to regulations and framework directives to detailed measures. Directives as provided for in Article 189 [now Article 249] of the Treaty, while binding upon each Member State to which they are addressed as to the result to be achieved, shall leave to the national authorities the choice of form and methods.

This Protocol highlights the convergence between the concepts of the softer form of flexibility which leaves space for differences in policy between the Member States, and subsidiarity which allows more room for action and choice at national or local level.

Another consequence of the desire for flexibility in social policy was the increasing use of soft-law measures. Most of the EC legislation adopted under the 1974 and 1989 Action Programmes was legally binding, hard law. The Medium Term Action Programme,[49] 1995–7 and its successor, 1998–2000,[50] by contrast, were characterised by their heavy reliance on soft-law measures,[51] which are persuasive rather than coercive in character.[52] This shift had already been flagged by the conclusions of the Edinburgh Council on the implementation of Article 3b (now Article 5) on the principle of subsidiarity[53] which said

[48] Para. 18.

[49] COM(95)134 final.

[50] COM(98)259.

[51] See also F. Snyder, "Soft Law and Institutional Practice in the European Community", EUI Working Paper, Law No. 93/5, Klabbers, "Informal Instruments before the European Court of Justice" (1994) 31 *CMLRev.* 997 and J. Kenner, "EC Labour Law: The Softly, Softly Approach" (1995) 11 *IJCLLIR* 307.

[52] See, e.g., the integration of equal opportunities into the Structural Funds (94/C231/01 [1994] OJ C231/1), balanced participation by men and women in decision-making (95/C168/3 [1995] OJ C168/3) and Council Recommendation 96/694/EC [1996] OJ L319/11, and equal participation by women in an employment intensive growth strategy in the EU (94/C368/02 [1994] OJ C368/2).

[53] *EC Bull.* 12/1992, 25–6, Council Conclusions II, Guidelines, 3rd para., point 3.

that "[n]on-binding measures such as recommendations should be preferred where appropriate. Consideration should also be given where appropriate to the use of voluntary codes of conduct."[54] The Commission endorsed this view, suggesting that recourse to the most binding instruments should only be as a last resort.[55]

Soft-law measures have also formed the principal legislative vehicle under the new Employment Title which the European Council decided to put into effect before the Treaty of Amsterdam came into force. This was agreed at an extraordinary meeting of the European Council in Luxembourg on 20–21 November 1997 (the so-called Jobs Summit). Under the "Luxembourg process" the first guidelines outlining policy areas for 1998 were agreed by the Member States and adopted by the Council of Ministers.[56] The Member States were then obliged to incorporate these guidelines into National Action Plans (NAPs). As Kenner points out,[57] the various instruments issued under the Employment Strategy are no more than methods of Community guidance or rules which create an expectation that the conduct of Member States will be in conformity with them, but without any accompanying legal obligation. Presidency conclusions, Commission Communications, annual reports, and even the employment guidelines themselves, all come into the category of soft law. This, he notes, has certain advantages. The flexibility of soft laws allows the Community institutions to stimulate European integration by building on and around existing Treaty objectives without directly creating legal obligations. They are a kind of informal law-making by exhortation.

(ii) Flexibility within the Legislative Instruments—"Internal Flexibility"

Increasingly, flexibility manifests itself within the Directive. Three diverse examples serve to illustrate this. First, from the earliest days of EC social policy Directives have aimed at only partial harmonisation. Directive 77/187/EEC on transfers of undertakings[58] and Council Directive 75/129/EEC on collective redundancies[59] provide a good example. Both require consultation with "those representatives provided for by the laws or practices of the Member States". In the UK worker representation has traditionally been channelled through independent and recognised trade unions (the so-called single channel approach) so when implementing Directives 77/187 (EEC and 75/129/EEC the UK required that consultation be with recognised trade unions.[60] While this may have been

[54] See generally S. Sciarra, "Social Values and the Multiple Sources of European Social Law" (1995) 1 *ELJ* 60, especially 78–9.

[55] SEC(92)1990 final.

[56] Council Resolution of 15 Dec. 1997 on the 1998 Employment Guidelines [1998] OJ C30/1.

[57] Kenner, n. 51 *supra*, 57–8.

[58] [1977] OJ L187/61/26 as amended by Council Dir. 98/50/EC [1998] OJ L210/88.

[59] [1975] OJ L48/29, as amended by Council Dir. 92/56/EEC [1992] OJ L245/3, and consolidated by Council Dir. 98/59/EC [1998] OJ L225/16.

[60] S. 188 of the Trade Union and Labour Relations (Consolidation) Act TULR(C)A 1992 provided: "[a]n employer proposing to dismiss as redundant an employee of a description in respect of which an independent trade union is recognised by him shall consult representatives of the union

less problematic in the late 1970s when union recognition was high, both levels of recognition which was entirely optional for employers,[61] and trade union membership have declined substantially since then. As a result, in *Commission* v. *UK*[62] the Commission argued that the UK had failed to fulfil its obligations under Articles 2 and 3 of Directive 75/129/EEC on collective redundancies by not providing a mechanism for the designation of workers' representatives in an undertaking where the employer refused to recognise such representatives.[63]

The Court of Justice agreed with the Commission and rejected the UK's arguments that since the measure was a partial harmonisation directive the UK system need not be changed. The Court said that in both the Directives on Collective Redundancies and Transfers of Undertakings[64] "the Community legislature intended both to ensure comparable protection for workers' rights in the different Member States and to harmonise the costs which such protective rules entail for Community undertakings". As a result, the (Conservative) UK government passed legislation[65] requiring an employer to consult with either employee representatives elected by the affected employees, *or* if the employees were of a description in respect of which an independent trade union was recognised by the employer, representatives of the trade union.[66] Originally, employers could choose which group to consult; now the consultation must take place with a recognised trade union where one exists.[67] These new rules marked the first substantial inroad into the single channel.[68] They also reflected the dual-channel approach of the Continent, where worker representation is conducted through both trade unions and elected worker representatives. Thus, paradoxically, rulings of the Court of Justice have served to create uniformity rather than diversity. This suggests that, in fact, in the name of securing effective protection of Community law and harmonisation of costs, there is not much room for flexibility.

The second example of internal flexibility can be found in the so-called Article 13 voluntary agreements permitted by Council Directive 94/95/EC on European Works Councils.[69] Article 13 provides that where an agreement was already in existence by 22 September 1996[70] which covered the entire workforce, the

about the dismissal in accordance with this section". Reg. 10 of the Transfer of Undertakings (Protection of Employment) (TUPE) Regs. 1981 contained a similar provision.

[61] See now s. 1 of the Employment Relations Act 1999.

[62] Case C–383/92 [1994] ECR I–2479.

[63] The Commission made a similar allegation in Case C–382/93, *Commission* v. *UK* [1994] ECR I–2435 in respect of Dir. 77/187/EEC on transfers of undertakings. See generally P. Davies, "A Challenge to Single Channel" (1994) 23 *ILJ* 272.

[64] Dirs. 75/129/EEC [1975] OJ L48/29 and 77/187/EEC [1977] OJ L61/27, respectively.

[65] The Collective Redundancies and Transfer of Undertakings (Protection of Employment) (Amendment) Regs. 1995, SI 1995/2587.

[66] *Ibid*. Reg. 3(1), reg. 9(4).

[67] The Collective Redundancies and Transfer of Undertakings (Protection of Employment) (Amendment) Regs. 1999, SI 1999/1925.

[68] See generally Davies, n. 63 *supra*.

[69] [1994] OJ L254/64 as amended by Council Dir. 97/74/EEC [1998] OJ L10/22. A similar procedure is envisaged in Art. 3 of the proposed Dir. on informing and consulting workers, COM(98)612.

obligations contained in the Directive did not apply. 386 such agreements were signed by the September 1996 deadline,[71] including 58 signed by British companies. This highlights the spillover effect of the Social Chapter from which the UK government had secured an opt-out[72] and the development of "privatised" flexibility, that is differentiation not for particular Member States but for particular companies.

The third example of internal flexibility can be found in the provisions allowing the most affected Member States more time to implement certain more controversial Directives. This is an example of "multi-speed" Europe.[73] Ehlermann says that there can be no objection in principle to this sort of exceptional, time-limited arrangement if it can be based on objective circumstances that justify the distinction. The Young Workers' Directive 94/33/EC[74] and the Working Time Directive 93/104/EC[75] provide examples of this form of flexibility. According to Article 17(1)(b) of the Young Workers Directive, the UK "may refrain from implementing" certain provisions on working time and night work for a period of four years. The Commission is to report on the effects of this provision and the Council "shall decide whether this period should be extended".

The Working Time Directive 93/104/EC also made provision for two exceptions, one time limited and one merely to be reconsidered. Both were negotiated by the British (Conservative) government, although the UK was not expressly named, and the British (Labour) government has taken advantage of both in enacting the implementation legislation.[76] The first "exception" concerns the possibility of an individual opt-out from Article 6 on the maximum 48-hour working week. Article 18(1)(b)(i) provides that Member States need not apply Article 6 provided certain, detailed conditions are satisfied. This provision must be re-examined before 2003 (Article 18(1)(b)(i)). Anecdotal evidence suggests that this exception is being used extensively by employers.[77] The second "exception" provided for delayed implementation of the four weeks' paid annual leave contained in Article 7. According to Article 18(1)(b)(ii), Member States had the possibility of "making use" of a transitional period of not more than three years from 23 November 1996. This derogation was provided on condition that, during the transitional period, every worker received three weeks' paid annual leave which could not be replaced by an allowance in lieu, except where the employ-

[70] The date by which the Dir. should have been implemented ;15 Dec. 1999 for the UK or earlier if the date of transposition in the UK was before then—Art. 3(1) of Dir. 97/74/EC [1998] OJ L10/22.

[71] See P. Marginson, M. Gilman, O. Jacobi, and H. Krieger, *Negotiating European Works Councils: An Analysis of Agreements under Article 13*, European Foundation of Living and Working Conditions, EF9839.

[72] See text attached to n. 15 *supra*.

[73] According to Ehlermann, n. 13 *supra*, 247 "multi-speed" Europe involves time-limited exceptions: "one or several Member States are allowed, either in the Treaty or in Regulations, Directives, Decisions, not to apply a norm valid in principle for all Member States *temporarily*".

[74] [1994] OJ L216/12.

[75] [1993] OJ L307/18.

[76] SI 1998/1833, as amended by SI 1999/372.

[77] C. Barnard, "The Working Time Regulations 1998" (1999) 28 *ILJ* 61.

ment relationship was terminated. Although the UK took advantage of this possibility,[78] the UK's own belated implementation of the Directive—it came into force in Great Britain only on 1 October 1998—meant that the delay was less useful for employers than first appeared, and the implementing legislation was extremely complex.

(iii) Flexibility and the Choice of Actors

In order to facilitate the adoption of the Directives on Young Workers and Working Time, the EU was perhaps wise to allow for the possibility of delayed implementation for the UK. In the UK the legacy of collective *laissez-faire* meant that the state has traditionally abstained from regulating key aspects of the employment relationship, notably pay and working time, leaving these to be negotiated collectively. The two Directives on Working Time represented a cultural clash between the Romano-Germanic countries, with their history of centralised regulation of issues such as working time, and the abstentionist Anglo-Saxon tradition. The Working Time Directive does, however, envisage a substantial role for the social partners. The Directive provided that not only could the "social partners" implement the Directive,[79] but "collective agreements or agreements between the two sides of industry" could be used both in setting certain standards, such as the duration and terms on which a rest break could be taken,[80] and in derogating from those standards.[81] Yet, once again the desire for flexibility and diversity has led, for the UK at least, to greater complexity. For the reasons outlined above,[82] in the UK the identification of the "two sides of industry" has been problematic. The result has been an awkward compromise and the introduction of further unfamiliar terms. The British Working Time Regulations[83] permit three types of agreement: first, collective agreements as defined in section 178 TULR(C)A 1992 with independent, recognised trade unions; secondly, "workforce agreements" which are designed to provide a mechanism for employers to agree working time arrangements with workers who do not have any terms and conditions set by collective agreement[84]; and thirdly, relevant agreements which are defined as any provision of a collective agreement,[85] a workforce agreement, or any other agreement in writing which is legally enforceable as between the worker and the employer. The last limb in the definition of a relevant agreement removes any collective component from the negotiation. Once again, the quest for flexibility has led to

[78] Reg. 12(1) but Reg. 12(10) provides that on and after 23 Nov. 1999 the entitlement will rise to 4 weeks.

[79] See n. 75 *supra*. See also Arts. 137(2) and (3) EC (ex Arts. 2(2) and 2(3) SPA).

[80] Art. 4.

[81] Art. 17. This is most unusual: collective agreements usually improve upon it statutory protection.

[82] See the text attached to nn. 60–8.

[83] SI 1998/1833.

[84] Sched. 1, para. 2.

[85] This collective agreement must form *part of a contract* between him and his employer.

further regulation and there is little evidence, in the UK at least, that this procedural route is being used by employers.

Thus, the Working Time Directive provides a further example of internal flexibility being achieved by introducing a new set of actors. It creates a space in which the social partners can negotiate for better standards and—contrary to the Continental legal tradition[86]—for worse. This is an example of "controlled flexibility"[87] or "reflexive labour law". Using Rogowski and Wilthagen's terminology, the Directive influences centres of reflexion within other social subsystems—the social partners. In becoming reflexive the form of legal regulation changes from substantive to procedural law.[88]

The possibility introduced by the Maastricht Social Chapter for the European Social Partners, UNICE, CEEP and ETUC, to negotiate European level collective agreements, provides a further example of this phenomenon. Once negotiated, these agreements can be extended to cover all workers by means of a directive[89] in a legislative process akin to the "negotiated laws" which operate in certain Member States. The agreement is annexed to the directive and, out of respect for the autonomy of the social partners, cannot be amended by the Council in the process of adopting the measure. These agreements take reflexivity one stage further: it is the (interprofessional) European-level social partners who are negotiating a framework collective agreement which in turn provides space for the national (interprofessional or sectoral) or subnational (enterprise, or plant) level social partners to act. The framework Directive on Parental Leave provides a good example of this. It envisages two main rights: men and women workers are entitled to parental leave for at least three months on the birth or adoption of a child and workers are entitled to time off on the grounds of *force majeure* for urgent family reasons.[90] The agreement then provides, *inter alia*, that Member States and/or management and labour may specify "the conditions of access and modalities of application of this clause".[91] This is so-called "negotiated flexibility" or, using Ferner and Hyman's terminology, "centrally co-ordinated decentralisation"[92] which has operated in a number of Member States in the 1990s. The flexibility seems to lie in the nature of the regulatory process as well as in the nature of the resulting legislation which allows room for the national and subnational social partners to act. Whether this legislation is more flexible than legislation that would have been adopted by the

[86] Lord Wedderburn, "Collective Bargaining at European Level: The Inderogability Problem" (1992) 21 *ILJ* 245.

[87] See also Art. 4a(2) of the amendments to the Transfer of Undertakings Dir. 98/50, noted by Davies, n. 63 *supra*, 369.

[88] R. Rogowski and T. Wilthagen in "Introduction" R. Rogowski and T. Wilthagen (eds.), *Reflexive Labour Law* (The Hague: Kluwer, 1994), 7.

[89] The English version of the SPA provided for a "decision". This has been interpreted to mean any legally binding instrument, including a dir. See Arts. 138(4)–139.

[90] Clause 3(1).

[91] Other key matters left to the Member States and/or management and labour can be found in Arts. 2(3)(a)–(f), and 2(7).

[92] Ferner and Hyman, n. 42, *supra* xvi.

traditional legislators is far from clear. Arguably collectively negotiated legislation benefits from greater legitimacy than traditional legislation given that it is being negotiated by representatives of groups that are directly affected by it. It therefore represents a form of industrial, if not parliamentary, democracy. On the one hand, this process demonstrates a form of subsidiarity — not just in the vertical sense envisaged by Article 5 (ex Article 3b(2)) (Member State or Community level) but in the horizontal or multi-layered sense that different tasks can be assigned to different actors.[93] On the other hand, the EU's emphasis on centralised bargaining sits uncomfortably with the trend towards decentralised, plant level bargaining found in various Member States.

The role for this more flexible formof regulation was recognised in the Commission's Green Paper on *Partnership for a New Organisation of Work*[94] which considered how to develop the "flexibility firms need".[95] One solution offered was a certain softening of excessively rigid rules to accommodate developments such as "downsizing, outsourcing, subcontracting, teleworking, networking and joint ventures . . . for which traditional labour law provisions do not appear to have adequate answers".[96] This implies "the likely development of labour law and industrial relations from rigid and compulsory systems of statutory regulations to more open and flexible legal frameworks".[97] This raises "fundamental questions concerning the balance of regulatory powers between public authorities (legislation) and the social partners (collective bargaining) and between the social partners and individual employees (individual employment contracts) which may well mean greater scope for derogations from legislative standards through not just collective agreements but also individual contracts of employment.[98]

This suggests that DGV's position is not one of flexibility through deregulation but an argument for the *proceduralisation* of labour standards, as Rogowski and Wilthagen identified. This involves an acceptance that the role of legislation should be predominantly facilitative, rather than prescriptive, in nature. A similar shift can be observed within the labour law systems of most of the mainland Member States over the past decade, where provisions for derogating from statutory standards, particularly in the areas of working time and the use of flexible forms of employment, have become widespread. However, while this approach allows for diversity in the national systems and experimentation, it is not without its difficulties; these include the potential dilution of individual employment rights (in particular the right to equality of treatment) and the generation of inequalities between different categories of workers and between different workplaces and sectors. Moreover, if too much emphasis is

[93] See also E. Philippart and G. Edwards, "The Provision on Closer Cooperation in the Treaty of Amsterdam: The Politics of Flexibilitty in the European Union" (1999) 37 *JCMS* 87.
[94] COM(97)127.
[95] COM(97)127, Executive Summary.
[96] *Ibid.*, para. 42.
[97] *Ibid.*, para. 44.
[98] *Ibid.*, para. 43.

placed on the individual, as is the case of the Article 18(1)(b)(i) derogations from the Working Time Directive,[99] there may be little to distinguish internal flexibility through proceduralisation from flexibility through outright deregulation.[100]

The new importance of the social partners, particularly at European level, raises questions about their legitimacy or, in the language of Continental labour lawyers, their "representativity". Although the SPA did not define "management and labour" the Commission carried out a study of the social partners across the EU, and subsequently issued a communication[101] setting out the criteria according to which the social partners would be determined for the purposes of the SPA consultation. This took a two-fold approach: "informal" consultation which would be as wide and inclusive as possible, and the "formal" negotiation stage for the purposes of Article 4 SPA (now Article 139 EC) for which only the "established" social partners of UNICE, CEEP and the ETUC were included.[102] UEAPME, the organisation for small and medium sized enterprises, challenged its exclusion from the negotiations on parental leave before the Court of First Instance,[103] arguing that, as it was represented in the "informal" consultation, its exclusion from the formal negotiation stage was unlawful. The CFI did not agree. It said that the consultation stage was separate from the negotiation stage, and that there was no general right of those consulted in the informal stage to take part in the negotiations under Articles 3(4) and 4 SPA (now Articles 138(4) and 139). Further, it said that the Commission and Council were obliged, in carrying out their roles under Articles 3(4) and 4 SPA, to act in conformity with the principles governing their action in the field of social policy. In particular, the Commission was obliged by Article 3(1) SPA (now Article 138(1)) to promote consultation of management and labour and facilitate dialogue by ensuring balanced support for the parties. This obligation was interpreted by the CFI as imposing a duty on the Commission to examine the representativity of the signatories to agreements proposed for implementation at the Community level under Articles 3(4) and 4 SPA (now Articles 138 and 139). The CFI noted that this was particularly important in the case of this procedure, from which the European Parliament was excluded. On the facts it found that the particular constituency which UEAPME claimed to represent—small and medium-sized undertakings—was adequately represented by UNICE, one of the parties to the agreement.[104] The key feature of this judgment is that CFI does appear to condone the "contractual" nature of the law-making proce-

[99] See text attached to n. 75 *supra*.

[100] See Barnard and Deakin, n. 114 *infra*.

[101] COM(93)600 final.

[102] This approach was confirmed in subsequent Commission Communications. See COM(96)448 final; COM(98)322 final.

[103] Case T–135/96 *UEAPME* v. *Council* [1998] ECR II-2335. See L. Betten, "The Democratic Deficit of Participatory Democracy in Community Social Policy" (1998) 23 *ELRev*. 20.

[104] See E. Szyszczak, "The New Parameters of European Labour Law", in D. O'Keeffe and P. Twomey (eds.), *Legal Issues of the Amsterdam Treaty* (Oxford: Hart, 1999). The appeal of Case C–316/98 UEAPME to the Court of Justice was removed from the register, 2 Feb. 1999.

dure involving the social partners, which may promote "privatisation" of European social law.[105]

The success of the social partners in using their new powers to negotiate European-level collective agreements has been mixed. The first attempt to negotiate an agreement (on European Works Councils) ended in failure and the Commission had to step in to push the proposal through the usual legislative route.[106] However, they did succeed in negotiating three agreements: on parental leave,[107] part-time work[108] and fixed-term contracts.[109] The directives on atypical work, in particular, stand at the confluence between the constitutional lawyer's and the labour lawyer's understanding of flexibility. Negotiated by the European social partners as framework agreements, setting minimum standards extended to all workers by a directive, providing space for the national or subnational actors to flesh out the substantive terms as well as to implement the provisions, these collective agreements are also intended to serve employment objectives. In the words of Clause 1 of the Framework Agreement on Part-time Work:

> The purpose of the framework agreement is
> (a) to provide for the removal of discrimination against part-time workers and to improve the quality of part-time work;
> (b) to facilitate the development of part-time work on a voluntary basis and to contribute to the flexible organisation of working time in a manner which takes into account the needs of employers and workers.[110]

Here lies elements of both demand and supply side flexibility, considered in the first section, as a way of addressing the problems of unemployment in the EU. These issues will now be considered.

3. FLEXIBILITY AND EMPLOYMENT

In 1996 the unemployment rate stood at around 5 per cent in the USA compared to the average unemployment rate of virtually 11 per cent in the 15 EU Member States.[111] Growing concerns about the EU's persistently high level of long-term unemployed led to the inclusion of a new Employment Title in the Amsterdam Treaty and its early implementation at the Luxembourg jobs summit in November 1997 where a series of guidelines for Member States' employment

[105] See N. Bernard, "Privatisation of European Social Law: Reflections around the UEAPME Case" in J. Shaw (ed.), *Social Law and Policy in an Evolving European Union* (Oxford: Hart, 2000).

[106] European Works Council (EWC) Dir. 94/95 [1994] OJ L254/64.

[107] The Dir. on Parental Leave (Council Dir. 96/34/EC of 3 June 1996 on the framework agreement on parental leave concluded by UNICE, CEEP and the ETUC, [1996] OJ L145/4).

[108] Council Dir. 97/81/EC [1998] OJ L14/9.

[109] Council Dir. 99/70/EC [1999] OJ L175/43.

[110] Cl. 1.

[111] *OECD Employment Outlook*, OECD, 1997 Table A and *Employment in Europe* (Luxembourg: OPEC, 1997), 117.

policies were drawn up. Do these guidelines awaken the labour lawyers' fears of job creation through a low wage, low skill, unprotected workforce?

The guidelines have centred on four main "pillars".[112] The first of the pillars is *employability*, which focuses on the prevention of long-term and youth unemployment by the means of vocational education and training and active labour market policies including the placement of young workers in work experience schemes and subsidies to employers offering training. Secondly, the *entrepreneurship* pillar attempts to make the process of business start-ups more straightforward, and incorporates steps to revise regulations affecting small businesses. The deregulatory aspects of the Employment Strategy can be most clearly seen in these first two pillars.

The *adaptability* pillar has provided the main focus for demand side flexibility, in particular "functional flexibility" and working time flexibility. According to the 1998 Employment Guidelines the social partners are invited to negotiate, at the appropriate levels, agreements "to modernise the organisation of work, including flexible working arrangements, with the aim of making undertakings productive and competitive and achieving the required balance between flexibility and security". Finally, the *equal opportunities* pillar has been concerned with raising awareness of issues relating to gender equality in terms of equal access to work, family friendly policies and the needs of people with disabilities. This focuses on the supply side notion of flexibility. It also suggests that flexibility does not necessarily equate with deregulation because under this pillar certain social rights are envisaged. On the other hand the tension between deregulation and equal opportunities can be seen in the Part-time Work Directive.[113] On the one hand Member States and the social partners are required to observe the principle of equal treatment between full- and part-time employees and, facilitating the demand-side objective of the Directive, employers are required to provide information to workers on the possibility of transferring between full and part-time work. On the other hand, a deregulatory agenda can be detected in the requirement that Member States must identify and review potential obstacles to part-time work and, where possible, eliminate them.

This brief survey indicates that, even under the Employment Guidelines, flexibility does not equate with deregulation. Instead, it is combined with security for workers, as the 1998 Guidelines indicate. This can be seen most clearly in the Partnership Green Paper which identifies the challenge for social policy as being:

> how to develop or adapt policies which support, rather than hinder, fundamental organisational renewal and how to strike a productive balance between the interests of business and the interests of workers, thereby facilitating the modernisation of

[112] Council Resolution of 15 Dec. 19997 on the 1998 Employment Guidelines [1998] OJ C30/1. See C. Barnard and S. Deakin, "A Year of Living Dangerously? EC Social Rights, Employment Policy, and EMU (1999) 30 *IRJ* 355.

[113] Council Dir. 97/81/EC [1998] OJ L14/9.

> working life. An essential objective is to achieve such a balance between *flexibility and security* [emphasis added].[114]

The answer lies in an "improved organisation of work" which, although unable "of itself to solve the unemployment problem", may nevertheless "make a valuable contribution, firstly, to the competitiveness of European firms, and secondly, to the improvement of the quality of working life and the employability of the workforce".[115] In the Commission's eyes the Social Partners at all levels have a key role in reconciling the objectives of both flexibility and security and thus modernising working life. In particular they need to focus on training, working time, facilitating the diversification of working relations, as well as new forms of work, ensuring the optimum conditions for the introduction of new technology and promoting equal opportunities.[116] Thus, the Green Paper adds that flexibility within organisations will be encouraged by reinforcing mechanisms for employee participation at the level of the plant or enterprise; "the role of workers in decision making and the need to review and strengthen the existing arrangements for workers' involvement in their companies will . . . become essential issues".[117] Consequently, the Commission's proposed directive on information and consultation of employees at national level has assumed a greater importance.[118]

These documents reveal elements of "third way" thinking, based on partnership[119] and decentralisation. Constitutional soft flexibility (internal flexibility and flexibility in choice of actors) is being used to achieve labour market flexibility, in particular functional flexibility at the micro level. The role of the social partners is not, however, confined to this level. The social partners also have a role at the macro level where the social dialogue is seen as playing an important part in the formulation of wage determination policies which are compatible with employment growth. This was highlighted at the Cologne summit where the European Council noted that:

> For a consistent policy mix to be implemented successfully, it is helpful to have a fruitful macroeconomic dialogue between Social Partners, fiscal and employment policymakers and monetary policymakers within existing institutions. In the course of this dialogue, the starting position and future prospects could be discussed on the basis of statistical data and analyses, and ideas could be exchanged as to how, while retaining their respective responsibilities and preserving their independence, those involved consider that a policy mix can be achieved that is conducive to growth and employ-

[114] COM(97)127 final, para. 11.

[115] *Ibid.*, para. 4.

[116] COM(98)592, 4.

[117] COM(97)127, para. 44.

[118] In Mar. 1998, the private sector employers' confederation, UNICE, refused to enter into negotiations with ETUC and CEEP; (1998) 29, *European Industrial Relations Review*, 1. However, the Commission has now proposed its own draft proposals: COM(98)612.

[119] For a discussion of partnership in the context of the structural funds see J. Scott, "Law, Legitimacy and EC Governance: Prospects for 'Partnership' " (1998) 36 *JCMS* 175.

ment under conditions of price stability.[120]

The economic guidelines also envisage a neo-corporatist role for the Social Partners in tripartite, national-level dialogue over the employment consequences of EMU. The 1999 guidelines provide that "[f]or wage developments to contribute to an employment-friendly mix, the Social Partners should continue to pursue a responsible course and conclude wage agreements in Member States in line with the general principles set out in previous Broad Economic Policy Guidelines",[121] in particular that real wage levels should be pegged below increases in productivity so as to provide incentives for investment. As Deakin and Reed point out, these documents indicate a role in suppressing wage growth which sits unhappily with the traditional role of trade unions.[122] In this context it is harder to detect either constitutional or employment flexibility, other than in terms of the actors used. It does, however, highlight the importance of third way ideas of partnership, albeit at a centralised rather than decentralised level. Nevertheless, the importance of social dialogue as a mechanism for promoting the appropriate conditions for growth should not be underestimated; indeed it is reflected in experiences at Member State level. Some Member States, such as Italy, Spain and France, have a long tradition of tripartite bargaining between government and the Social Partners over labour costs, flexibilisation and wage growth.

4. CONCLUSIONS

Traditionally, fragmentation or flexibility has been the characteristic of EC social policy in order to maintain the momentum of further integration. However, since the early 1990s there has been a shift in emphasis: flexibility both in the labour law and constitutional sense has been used less to achieve integration than as a central tool in the management of the economy to foster growth. The role of the social partners, at both the European level and the micro level, is to assist in the "modernisation" of working arrangements at enterprise level, providing the basis for functional flexibility and hence for competitiveness at enterprise level. Governance of the firm is organised at two opposite extremes—the EU and the enterprise level. This is an extreme form of subsidiarity, one possibly not contemplated by those pressing for its inclusion in the

[120] See also Recommendation 97/249, para. 2(iii) which calls on the Commission to promote social dialogue at Community level "notably on macroeconomic policy issues"; the Commission communication of 20 May 1998 on *Adapting and Promoting the Social Dialogue at Community Level* also notes that "the incorporation of a new Employment Title in the Amsterdam Treaty and the application of these arrangements has changed the nature of the tripartite dialogue": COM(98)322, at 10.

[121] See also Council Resolution 97/C 236/02 on growth and employment which said that the Social Partners should "fully face their responsibilities within their respective sphere of activity": para. 13.

[122] See n. 4 *supra*.

Maastricht Treaty, and an extreme form of flexibility. Both terms—subsidiarity and flexibility—share two striking features. First, the simplicity of the words disguises a multitude of meanings which can appeal to a variety of audiences: their central appeal lies in their malleability—or, dare I say, flexibility. Secondly both terms are paradoxes: the desire to achieve flexibility can lead to both uniformity and rigidity; the desire to achieve subsidiarity can lead to centralisation. The social sphere demonstrates these tensions very clearly.

10

Flexibility and European Law: A Labour Lawyer's View

MIGUEL C. RODRIGUEZ-PIÑERO ROYO

1. PRELIMINARY REMARKS[1]

THE PRESENCE of some contributions by labour lawyers in a book about Flexibility in European law can be easily justified from the perspective of European legal theory itself. For a labour lawyer, at least for a labour lawyer used to operating in a continental legal culture such as the Spanish, such a presence is on the contrary rather surprising. This surprise comes from the fact that all labour lawyers consider flexibility as a topic of their own, a question which affects only labour law, on the one hand; and a concept that has been elaborated and analysed exclusively by labour lawyers, on the other. Only those who have also devoted themselves to the study of European law are aware of the fact that it is a big topic for academics in EU law, having produced an enormous amount of literature and debate over the last few years. The very notion of flexibility, although having been analysed already in the 1970s,[2] started being a major one particularly after the Maastricht summit, when academics and politicians began to use it as a conceptual framework for explaining some of its outcomes[3]; later on, it continued to be an instrument for explaining some particular provisions of the Amsterdam Treaty.[4]

[1] This contribution has its origin in my intervention as a discussant in the seminar on "The Constitution of the EU; From Uniformity to Diversity", which took place at the European University Institute in Apr. 1999. I was in charge of acting as a discussant for two of the lectures, the one by Prof. Weatherill on "Closer Cultural Co-operation", and the one by Prof. Barnard on "From Uniformity to Flexibility: Aspects of Social Policy". In these pages, however, I will deal exclusively with questions related to labour law, the field in which I usually work.

[2] According to J. Shaw, "Flexibility and legitimacy in the Domain of the Treaty Establishing the European Community", in M. den Boer, A. Guggenbühl and S. Vanhoonacker, *Coping with Flexibility and Legitimacy after Amsterdam* (Maastricht: European Institute of Public Administration, 1998), 87.

[3] See J. Shaw, "The Treaty of Amsterdam: Challenges of Flexibility and Legitimacy" (1998) 4 *ELJ* 63; also A. Stubb, *The Amsterdam Treaty and Flexible Integration: A Preliminary Assesment*, Draft Paper presented at the conference of the International Political Science Association at Seoul, Aug. 1997.

[4] L. Metcalfe, "Flexible Integration in and after the Amsterdam Treaty" in den Boer, Guggenbühl and Vanhoonacker, n. 2 *supra*, 11.

A relatively new concept, then; nothing to do with the experience labour law has had with flexibility, as it has been dealing extensively with it for at least 30 years so far. There are consequently in labour law some experiences which could be shared with European law scholars. This will be, then, the objective of these pages, to try to identify some key aspects of our experience in coping with flexibility in labour law, and apply them to the concept of flexibility which is being used in European law: because, as we will soon see, each sector of legal studies is working with a concept of flexibility which is rather different from the others. There will be a "Flexibility", with a capital letter, which will refer to the concept of flexibility which this book is all about; and a flexibility, with a small letter, which will be used when talking about the labour lawyers' understanding of this concept. These pages will address the lessons a legal scholar can learn from "flexibility", in order fully to understand the real implications of "Flexibility". Therefore the question of "Flexibility in European labour law" will not be addressed in this chapter[5]; some remarks about European labour law will anyway, be, unavoidable.

Perhaps this objective might appear somehow presumptuous, as it means in a way "teaching" European lawyers from the experience of labour law. And this is indeed a branch of law traditionally looked upon by legal scholars as a relatively new one, with little dogmatic construction and a lot of ideological content. In this particular case, however, some teaching can be justified, if only because European law is even newer than labour law as a branch of the legal order, and, of course, because flexibility has been a central concept of labour law debates for some 30 years. But there is another factor which explains this utility of labour law, its own identity as a branch of the legal order, which makes it particularly interesting from a legal theory point of view.

This is a relatively original idea, which deserves some further explanation: although labour law is a relatively new and unimportant branch of the legal order, dealing with a very limited aspect of social life and with little interaction with other branches of law, it receives a lot of attention from legal theorists and experts in other branches of law. There are some intrinsic elements in it which are very interesting to academics: to give a clear example, the coexistence of state and private regulations of labour relations, through statutory law and collective bargaining, a coexistence which you cannot find in other branches of the legal order, and which explains why labour law has been used as a ground for explaining some of the most recent theories about law and the legal order.[6] Other aspects of labour legislation, such as the treatment of social conflict or the balance between economic and social goals, are also absent in other, more traditional branches of law. From this point of view labour law is an "anomalous"

[5] There is another chapter of this book, that by C. Barnard, which is devoted precisely to this analysis.

[6] See A. Lo Faro, "Teorie autopietice e diritto sindacale" (1993) 1 *Lavoro e Diritto*, 163.

sector of the legal order, as the late Professor D'Antona used to say[7]; and therefore it can be used, in the very well-known words of Professor Giugni, as an excellent observatory from which future trends in legal studies can be foreseen. This application of our experience with the concept of flexibility to European legal studies is but another expression of this methodological utility.[8]

2. LABOUR LAW AND FLEXIBILITY: THE LESSONS FROM AN ODD COUPLE

A. Some Elements of a Definition of Flexibility

Labour law has always had some travelling companions in its century-long history. In the last decades this has clearly been the idea of flexibility. The central debate in labour law everywhere has been about flexibility and its role in the governance of labour relations. This debate has been a major force for change in the regulation of labour markets in most industrial relations systems around the world, and none of them, even the traditionally most "flexible" ones, has escaped from its effects. The main idea in this debate is extremely clear, and thus seductive to most actors in the labour market: labour laws were designed and put into force at the moment at which the situation of the labour market allowed them to grant workers a high level of protection; these protective laws, however, produced a level of rigidity in the management of the labour force which was also high. Afterwards the situation changed dramatically, as a consequence of a number of factors: increased international competition, technological change, changes in the market for goods and services due to new consumers' attitudes. In this new scenario, traditional labour law has become old-fashioned, inadequate for governing a labour market in transformation; these new circumstances produce a fast rhythm of change, and thus firms and workers have to adapt themselves continuously and immediately to face it. This adaptation is impossible with traditional labour law, because its regulations are too rigid. What you need is flexibility, the possibility of reacting and adapting yourself to changes; a flexible labour law, then, is one whose rules and regulations allow firms to respond to these changes in the market. In other words, changing markets force firms to be flexible if they want to be competitive; and this is possible only if labour law itself is flexible too.

[7] M. D'Antona, an Italian professor of Labour Law, was killed by the *Brigate Rosse* in Rome shortly after the seminar took place which was the origin of this book; the quotation comes from his work "L'anomalia post-positivista del diritto del lavoro e la questione del metodo" (1990) 1–2 *Rivista Critica di Diritto Privato*, 207.

[8] Some authors defend the leading role of labour law in the development of European law: see P. Rodiere, "Sur les effets directifs du Droit social communautaire" (1991) 4 *Revue Trimestrielle de droit européen* 318; M. Rodriguez-Piñero Sr., "La contribución de la jurisprudencia social del T.J.C.E. a la construcción del orden jurídico comunitario", in *Scritti in onore di Giuseppe Federico Mancini* (Milan: Giuffré, 1998), i, 471.

This idea is hardly a new one. The same arguments have been on the table since the very beginning of state intervention in the labour market; the trade-off between workers' protection and economic performance, fundamental then, is still the economic basis of the whole of the flexibility debate. But at the time as this debate was starting in Europe there was another factor which made a difference: the economic crisis, beginning in the early 1970s, which had an immediate effect on employment levels. With the threat of rising unemployment throughout western countries, flexibility found the element it lacked to complete the equation which made it unbeatable: markets are dynamic, but labour law is rigid; this makes it difficult for firms to adapt, and thus they lose competitiveness; not being competitive enough, they cannot survive, and therefore they are expelled from the market[9]; and this, of course, produces unemployment. Then, labour law's rigidities are the cause of unemployment; in order to fight it you need flexibility in labour law.[10]

The reasoning is simplistic but effective, especially at a moment when unemployment became the main concern of all governments and social actors.[11] The demand for flexibility was not justified on an ideological or political basis, but it was instead grounded on sound economic, and therefore technical, reasons, far from any attempt to modify the balance of powers in the industrial relations systems. Flexibility was not an end in itself, but rather a mean of reaching the real objective, full employment and competitiveness. And, finally, flexibility did not mean a permanent change in the conception of labour law; on the contrary, it was only a temporary response to a critical situation in the labour market, and things would return to normal as soon as it was over. At that time, in fact, flexible labour laws were considered a mere reaction to temporary circumstances, an "emergency labour law" ("*diritto del lavoro dell'emergenza*" was what Italian labour lawyers used to call it); its impact on labour relations or its technical soundness was therefore not very important, as these new rules were not here to stay.

For labour lawyers flexibility was not, as it still is not, a well-defined concept; on the contrary, it is a broad idea which implies a number of different legislative techniques, its common objective being the only element which gave some unity to all of them. Under this umbrella almost any reform of pre-existing labour law could be explained. One could talk, then, about "internal" and "external" flexibility, about "wage flexibility" or "numerical flexibility". You could use the term to denote a reform of redundancy law, a reduction of the cost of dismissals, a reduction in the protection of the social security system, or an exclusion of

[9] See A. Toffler, *La empresa flexible* (Barcelona: Editorial Planeta, 1986).

[10] For a general analysis of this reasoning, see the various studies collected in the book by A. Jeammaud and A. Lyon-Caen (eds.), *Droit du Travail, democratie et crise économique* (PUF Montpellier: 1986). There is a Spanish translation, published in Madrid in 1990 by the Spanish Ministry of Labour and Social Security: *Derecho del Trabajo, democracia y crisis.*

[11] One must not forget that Europe was at that moment just entering a golden period for employment and economic growth.

some groups of workers from a given piece of legislation.[12] Labour lawyers had to make an enormous effort to clarify this question, trying to define the boundaries of this elusive concept and to distinguish it from others such as deregulation or individualisation, the effects of which on the labour market were perceived at the same time.[13] In this aspect our flexibility looks like European law's Flexibility, the difficulties of which for a definition have been pointed out by almost all authors.[14]

B. Flexibility in Labour Law at the Turn of the Century

Almost 30 years later, the scenario we are facing has little to do with the promises offered in the early 1970s. Flexibility has not performed in labour law as we expected, showing a strength and a dynamic thrust that could not be foreseen.[15] Perhaps this is the most relevant conclusion a labour lawyer can reach from the flexibility experience, from the perspective of the turn of the century: how this notion has evolved in unexpected directions; and how its effects have also been very different from what one could have expected 30 years ago. For, and this is the central point of these pages, the same could very well happen with the idea of Flexibility which is being used in the analysis of European law.

The first unexpected aspect of flexibility is that it came to stay. Although the circumstances have changed dramatically the flexibility discourse maintained its presence in the evolution of national labour laws for years. It was not an urgent and temporary response to a momentary, critical situation of the labour market, as it pretended to be: once national labour laws accepted it, they applied it all the time.

At a given moment flexibility subtly evolved; from being an external element of labour law, no more than a general objective to the accomplishment of which its rules had to adapt; it became an intrinsic principle governing the whole system. It was no longer enough to grant a given level of flexibility through the reform of labour laws; the objective then was to build up a "flexible labour law", a normative system which was flexible in all the stages of the legislative process, from law-making to implementation and interpretation. This meant, among other changes, an increasing regulatory power for collective bargaining, a general tendency towards diversification of workers' and firms' status under the law, and a renewed role for the contract of employment in the definition of terms and conditions of employment. Somehow flexibility managed to get inside

[12] For an overview of the European experience with flexibility, see T. Treu, "Labour Flexibility in Europe" (1992) 131 *International Labour Review*, 497.

[13] There is a very serious attempt to distinguish all these concepts in S. Del Rey Guanter, "Desregulación, juridificación y flexibilidad" (1989) II *Relaciones Laborales*, 753.

[14] Shaw, n. 3 *supra*, 87.

[15] A classical comparative work about flexibility in European labour law can be found in R. Boyer (ed.), *La flexibilité du travail en Europe* (Parı́s: Fédération Européenne de Recherches Economiques, 1986).

the genetic code of labour law, invading it and, in a way, contaminating it as well. In this framework labour law's traditional objectives were almost forgotten, as soon as flexibility requirements left little space for them.

By doing this, the rule of flexibility changed its scope of application. Originally the advocates of flexibility focused on same aspects of the regulation of the contract of employment and of collective bargaining; now flexibility is a test against which every single aspect of labour market regulation is analysed. It is, in a way, a general tool for governing labour relations in every national system, as it can be applied everywhere. Almost a philosophy for those operating in the labour market, a life-style for each and every aspect of it. When it reached this level, flexibility was out of control, as it could be used anywhere, at any time; as a consequence of this the processes of change in labour law became extremely fast, so fast that even their original proponents had to accept that they had gone too far sometimes.

Flexibility altered dramatically the balance of powers in the industrial relations system.[16] Although its defenders considered flexibility as a purely neutral objective, as a technical adaptation to new market forces, in practice it meant the acceptance of a given interpretation of the labour market, probably the most conservative one, with its priorities and means. Those promoting a more protective, state-controlled model of labour market regulation found themselves swimming against the mainstream. What was originally technical soon showed its ideological content.[17] This is why it was an "interesting" debate, but also an "interested" one, self-seeking and biased.[18] Probably this explains why flexibility in labour law, accepted as it is everywhere, nonetheless lacks a kind of legitimacy other principles of labour law enjoy. It is still considered a "managerial instrument", a partisan notion the effects of which are unevenly distributed among the many actors in the industrial relations system.

One must point out the enormous power of the notion of flexibility. As we have seen, it has settled itself in the very nucleus of labour law, as if it were one of its natural components; and it has spread its effects to all its sectors. And all this without losing its pretended technical and non-ideological nature. But not only this: probably what is most relevant about the notion of flexibility is its power as an argument in the labour law debates.[19] It has acted as a factor providing legitimacy to almost any reform of existing labour laws and, at the same time, denying any to its opponents. The word itself is fortunate, as it sounds modern, dynamic, full of positive connotations. Flexibility's opposite is rigidity, at least in purely grammatical terms, and this is not a value which is easy to

[16] A complete analysis of this question can be found in A. Martin Artiles, *Flexibilidad y Relaciones Laborales* (Madrid: Consejo Económico y Social, 1995).

[17] According to the words of G. Lyon-Caen, "La bataille truquée de la flexibilité" [1985] *Droit Social*, 801.

[18] These are the words, whose translation probably does not work that well, used by Prof. Rodriguez-Piñero Sr, in an article which had a big impact on Spanish labour law academia; see "Flexibilidad: ¿un debate interesante o un debate interesado?" (1987), *Relaciones Laborales*, 14.

[19] M. Regini (ed.), *La sfida della flessibilità* (Milan: Franco Agneli, 1988).

defend these days. Non-flexibility was related to unemployment, lack of competitiveness, the old-fashioned defence of unions' privileges. Those advocating a defence of traditional labour law's values found themselves with no argument strong enough to oppose it.

This does not mean, of course, that flexibility had no positive impact on labour law. It proved to be a highly efficient instrument with which to fight the crisis, having some positive effect on employment levels. It undoubtedly increased the efficiency of western firms. And it altered the terms of traditional labour law debates, introducing into it questions like economic efficiency, adaptability and costs; a change that, in the 1970s when it all started, was probably very necessary. No one can deny that the flexibility debate has been the major force for change in labour law in recent decades.

At the en of the day, perhaps the best way to explain in a few words labour law's experience with flexibility would be by saying that its introduction into all national labour laws meant an implicit social agreement that was never honoured: the trade-off all actors in the labour market accepted was one through which workers and unions exchanged a reduction in statutory protection for productivity and employment. This agreement never worked, and the sacrifice some sectors of the labour market had to make did not turn into full and high quality employment. Flexibility turned out to be a principle difficult to manage, the effects of which could not be foreseen and controlled.

This explains how the very notion of flexibility, strong as it is, seems to be somehow exhausted nowadays. There are even some voices saying that flexibility is over, and that labour law is facing new challenges at the turn of the century.[20] And this opinion could be true, as the general disappointment with the idea of flexibility is forcing its advocates to search for new justifications for further attacks on what is left of traditional labour law. Globalisation seems to have taken its place as the central question for debate in the labour law arena.[21] The focus now is no longer on the demand of flexibility to face changes in the market, but in the need to reduce costs and improve productivity to resist increased international competition[22]; the debate, at the end of the day, is always the same, the very same contradiction between social and economic priorities in the regulation of the labour market.[23]

[20] See J. Pollert (ed.), *Farewell to flexibility*? (Oxford: Blackwell, 1991).

[21] For a general view of these debates see J.M. Gonzalez Limon and M.C. Rodriguez-Piñero Royo, "Integración económica y derechos sociales: aproximación al marco actual" in F. Mariño and C. Fernandez Liesa (eds.), *Política social internacional y europea* (Madrid: Ministerio de Trabajo y Asuntos Sociales, 1996). See also X. Blanc-Jouvan, "L'internationalisation des rapports de travail" in Autorii Varii, *Les transformations du Droit du Travail* (París: 1989); L. Compa and S. Diamond (eds.), *Human Rights, Labor Rights and International Trade* (Philadelphia, Penn.: University of Pennsylvania Press, 1994), *passim*; and W. Sengenberger and D. Campbell (eds.), *International Labour Standards and Economic Interdependance* (Geneva: International Institute for Labour Studies, 1994).

[22] N. Valticos and G. von Potobsky, *International Labour Law* (2nd edn., Deventer: Kluwer, 1995), 17; G. Lyon-Caen and A. Lyon-Caen, *Droit Social International et Européen* (8th edn., París: Dalloz, 1993), 1.

[23] In the words of J.C. Javillier, "Pragmatism and Innovation in International Labour Law" (1994) 4 *International Labour Review* 254.

3. FLEXIBILITY IN EUROPEAN LABOUR LAW

So far for flexibility with a small "f", the notion of flexibility traditionally known in labour law. Now let us turn to Flexibility, with a capital "F", the meaning of the word which has been used in European law in recent years. Because even though labour law has over the years developed its own concept of flexibility, European labour law shares with the rest of the European legal order the application of the general techniques of Flexibility which this book is about. The debates on what is or is not European labour law is far from being over.[24] For the purposes of this chapter I will consider as "European labour law" all the law-making production of European institutions and social actors in the areas which have traditionally been considered as labour law at a national level; that is, the regulation of terms and conditions of employment, of collective labour relations and of social protection.

In this section I will try to identify the different instruments which European labour law has developed to reach a certain level of Flexibility (section 3A), as well as give some information about the reasons which have forced European institutions to do so (section 3B). The concept of Flexibility I will be working with will be the general one, as it has been developed and defined by European law theorists. It is a general notion which implies a wide range of different notions, having in common the same model of flexible integration.[25] Legislative categories such as "variable geometry", "multi-speed integration", "opting-out", or "*à-la-carte* integration" will consequently be dealt with in these pages.[26] All these are legislative techniques used by European institutions in the adoption or in the implementation of pieces of European legislation; and they have been used in the development of a European labour law as well.[27]

A. Flexibility in European Labour Law: A Long-lasting Relationship

European labour law has been a privileged object of study for those defending the notion of Flexibility as an instrument for explaining some recent developments in the European legislative process. Even though labour lawyers themselves have not dealt directly with this question hitherto,[28] in general studies

[24] As an example of these debates, see B. Bercusson, *European Labour Law* (London: Butterworths, 1996; and C. Barnard, "EC Social Policy" in P. Graig and G. de Búrca, *The Evolution of EU Law* (Oxford: Oxford University Press, 1999).

[25] M. den Boer, A. Guggenbühl and S. Vanhoonacker, "Introduction", in den Boer, Guggenbühl and Vanhoonacker, n. 2 *supra*, 87.

[26] A. Stubb, "A Categorization of Differentiated Integration" (1996) 43 *Journal of Common Market Studies* 283.

[27] A general evaluation of the development of EU labour law from this perspective can be found in C. Barnard and S. Deakin, "European Community Social Law and Policy: Evolution or Regression?" [1997] *Industrial Relations Journal European Annual Review* 131.

[28] The only work on flexibility on European labour law I am aware of is the chapter in this book by Catherine Barnard.

about this question examples from European labour law are used all the time, some of them having become real paradigms of Flexible law. The most relevant aspect of European labour law to this purpose has probably been the Social Protocol of the Maastricht Treaty, which has been generally considered a clear case of "*à-la-carte* integration", announcing some of the techniques which would eventually be widely used throughout the Amsterdam Treaty. But this is not the only aspect of European labour law which can be analysed under this perspective. As we will see, European labour law is, generally speaking, a rather Flexible sector of the European legal order, as the legislative techniques Flexibility is about are widely used in it.

The very idea of a European labour law implies some level of Flexibility by itself.[29] Its main objective is to govern the impact of European economic integration on the labour market, mainly by avoiding disruptions of competition in the common market as a consequence of the differences in national labour laws.[30] European labour law is, then, a new expression of integration through law, whose main instrument, the directive, is by definition a Flexible source of law.[31]

European labour law is flexible, to begin with, *in its own production*. The number of different legal instruments through which it is, or has been at a given moment, developed is high, much higher than is common in other sectors of the European legal order,[32] first, because it uses extensively the more Flexible of all the common legal instruments of European law, such as directives and the different kinds of soft-law measures.[33] Beside the common Article 249 EC instruments, you find others specific to the labour law area which are used exclusively in this particular field of European law: European collective agreements; directives implementing European collective agreements; agreements implementing European directives; directives binding just some Member States (under the Maastricht Treaty's Social Protocol). We even have a norm so Flexible that its own legal nature is still unclear: the 1989 Community Social Charter of Workers' Fundamental Rights, which was not signed by all Member States, and the effects of which on the Member States' legal orders was doubtful.

[29] For a general study of this question see F. Duran Lopez, "La armonización de los ordenamientos laborales de los Estados miembros de la CEE. Problemas, alternativas y soluciones" [1990] *Revista de Instituciones Europeas* no. 1, 1990, 70.

[30] A complete analysis of this concept appears in C. Erickson and L. Kuruvilla, "Labor Costs and the Social Dumping Debate in the European Union" [1994] *Industrial and Labor Relations Review* 28; see also N. Adnett, "Social Dumping and European Economic Integration" (1995) 5 *Journal of European Social Policy* 1.

[31] See generally Barnard, n. 24 *supra*, 479.

[32] S. Sciarra, "Social Values and the Multiple Sources of European Social Law" [1995] *European Law Journal* 60.

[33] For some examples of the use of soft law in the labour law area of European legal order see F. Beveridge and S. Nott, "A Hard Look at Soft Law", in P. Craig and C. Harlow, *Lawmaking in the European Union* (London: Institute of Advanced legal Studies, 1995), 285. See also J. Kenner, "EC Labour Law: The Softly, Softly Approach" (1995) 11 *The International Journal of Comparative Labour Law and Industrial Relations*, 307.

European labour law is Flexible *in its contents* as well. In most of its pieces of legislation you find general principles which Member States are to define in their own national legal orders; different alternatives for Member States or even for employers for putting their normative obligations into practice; a variety of systems for protecting the same workers' rights. Some examples may illustrate this point: European directives on non-discrimination on the grounds of sex, which set some general principles and objectives which Member States are to attain, leaving them wide areas for deciding which instruments and normative techniques will be used in every case; the EC directive on employer's insolvency (Directive 80/987/EEC of 20 October 1980, OJ 28 October 1980) which establishes the obligation for Member States to maintain a "guarantee institution", whilst every one of them is free to define according to a few rules set out in the Directive itself. Generally speaking European labour law tends to be Flexible in its content because there is a general opinion according to which its purpose is just to set minimum standards of protection; being a "minimal" labour law its regulations should leave space for Member States to improve on their contents.

European labour law, finally, is Flexible *in its implementation*, in its translation into Member States' national legal orders. Here again we find a wide range of possibilities. Probably the most extreme is the opting-out technique, widely used in the 1990s, which allowed the United Kingdom to remain outside the scope of application of the directives passed under the Maastricht Treaty's Social Protocol.[34] But this maximum-level Flexibility is not common. Much more widespread, and therefore of more interest for this chapter, is the "more favourable provisions" clause, which appears in all labour law directives. According to this proviso, whose historical origin can be found in international labour law, the directive's regulations are but a minimum standard that Member States are free to improve[35]: "this Directive shall not affect Member States' right to apply or introduce laws, regulations or administrative provisions more favourable to the protection of the safety and health of workers or to facilitate or permit the application of collective agreements or agreements concluded between the two sides of industry which are more favourable to the protection of the safety and health of workers", as Directive 93/104/EC says.[36] Through this technique its implementation turns into a completely different process, a process in which European law acts as a legitimacy test for national labour laws. Now this minimal character of European directives is defended by the EC Treaty itself: according to its Article 137(5), "the provisions of this Article shall not prevent any Member State from maintaining or introducing more stringent protective measures compatible with this Treaty". From the perspective we are

[34] C. Barnard, "The United Kingdom, the Social Chapter and the Amsterdam Treaty" (1997) 9 *Industrial Law Journal* 275.

[35] Although it is a central element in the dynamic of European labour law the studies of this clause are scarce. One of them is M. Alonso Olea, "Directivas comunitarias y normas nacionales (el carácter mínimo de las directivas sobre seguridad e higiene en el trabajo y la posible mayor protección de la norma nacional)" [1991] *Revista de Instituciones Europeas* 9.

[36] In its Art. 15.

using in this chapter, all labour law directives allow a Flexible implementation of their provisions.

These are not the only Flexibility techniques you can find in the field of European labour law. Very common in it too is the use of exemptions to and derogations from its regulatory contents, allowing Member States, and sometimes employers themselves, not to apply them to a limited group of workers. This technique is so common that in almost every single labour law directive you find an Article on "Definitions" that deals mainly with its scope of application and of non-application; sometimes you also find specific Articles on "Derogations". The use of the implementation period as an instrument for granting some Flexibility to Member States in this phase of the legislative process is also rather common; therefore it is relatively frequent to find different time requirements for Member States with regards to their implementation duties, either for certain of them or for specific provisions from the directive.

These techniques are common in all areas of European law, labour law not being particularly original in this regard. But in addition to these there are others which can be considered typical as regards European labour law, for instance, the role of collective bargaining in the implementation of European directives.[37] Now there is almost a need for all labour law directives to permit the implementation of their provisions through collective agreements, even after the Court of Justice has expressed its reservations regarding this technique.[38] The EC Treaty itself recognises this as one of the possible alternatives for putting into practice labour law directives: according to Article 137(4), "a Member State may entrust management and labour, at their joint request, with the implementation of directives"; not all directives, but only those adopted pursuant Article 137(2) and (3), but this recognition is strong enough to make of this a "normal" alternative to the use of a state's regulative powers.

In this context collective bargaining is seen as a source of national labour law, operating in close co-operation with state-produced legislation; the choice of one source or the other is accepted as long as the directive's regulatory objective is fulfilled. In either case the directive is implemented. In some cases, though, the role of collective bargaining goes further: in Directive 94/95/EC on European Works Councils (Directive 93/104/EC, of 23 Oct. 1993, OJ 13 Dec. 1993) the Directive itself does not apply to those enterprises which already had pre-existing voluntary information and consultation agreements at the time the Directive came into force. These particular collective agreements act not as an implementation instrument, but as an alternative to the application of the directive itself.

The use of Flexibility techniques in European labour law is so extensive as to justify the analysis of EU law from this perspective. There is another fact,

[37] A general study of this role in C. Adinolfi, "The Implementation of Social Policy Directives through Collective Agreements" (1988) 25 *CMLRev*.

[38] A. Pilati, "Problemi della contrattazione collettiva europea" (1992) 3 *Rivista Italiana di Diritto del Lavoro* 5.

though, that draws our attention even more, and that is that the level of Flexibility has increased in recent years. Any directive adopted in the 1990s has accumulated more favourable provisions clauses, some derogations, transitory periods and implementation through collective bargaining, all these elements being by now part of its normal content. In the last few years this process has gone even further, and the EU has produced in the labour law area some prominent examples of Flexible law. It is beyond controversy that both Directive 93/104/EC on Working Time and Directive 94/95/EC on European Works Councils are clear cases of extensive use of Flexible instruments (94/95/E of 22–IX–1994, OJ 30–IX–1994) combined to produce an enormously high level of Flexibility, without any precedent in European labour law. Even those two pieces of legislation were eclipsed, though, when Directive 98/50/EC on the Transfer of Undertakings was enacted.[39] In this new Directive, a central one in the development of European labour law, Flexibility is no longer confined to its implementation or to the moment of its application, it is indeed in its very regulatory content, allowing Member States an enormous number of options in regulating the transfer of undertakings in their own national labour legislation.

The "normalisation" of social policy at the Amsterdam Treaty, with the inclusion of the Social Protocol in the place where it belonged, the text of the Treaty itself, must not mislead us.[40] It is true that the disappearance of the "double channel" for adopting labour law directives has meant a reduction of the level of Flexibility in this particular area of European law; thus one of the most prominent examples of Flexibility in European law, which has been used very often as a finished sample of these techniques, has been ruled out. This reduction in the level of flexibility, nonetheless, occurs in the context of a general process which is going in the opposite direction.

Flexibility, then, is a factor the importance of which is growing in the design of European labour law. Moreover, it seems as if European labour law is having a "role-model" effect in the spreading of Flexibility throughout other sectors of the European legal order, particularly with the "opting-out" technique developed for the Social Protocol adopted at the Maastricht summit, and used elsewhere after the Amsterdam reforms.[41] European labour law has been used once again as an experimentation field for the development of European law.

[39] For an analysis of this directive see M.C. Rodriguez-Piñero Royo, "Transmisión de empresas y Derecho Europeo" in A. Ojeda Aviles, J. Gorelli Hernandez and M.J. Rodriguez Ramos, *La transmisión de empresas en Europa* (Bari: Cacucci Editore, 1999), 1.

[40] Barnard, n. 34 *supra*, 275.

[41] Shaw, n. 3 *supra*, p.100; see also M.C. Rodriguez-Piñero Royo, "Aspectos sociales del Tratado de Amsterdam" in J. Aragon Medina (ed.), *EURO y Empleo* (Madrid: Servicio de Publicaciones del Consejo Económico y Social, 1998), 55.

B. Flexibility in European Labour Law: Elements of an Explanation

It is clear, then, that European labour law is a Flexible branch of the European legal order, a very Flexible one indeed. This fact could lead us to draw some conclusions from its experience that could be used to explain some future developments in other areas of European law. This could be misleading, in my opinion, because there is a previous question which should be answered before coming to any conclusion from this experience: why is there such Flexibility in European labour law? If the answer is that it is a consequence of its features as a supranational, European law, then probably what has happened in it could be helpful for other areas of EU law. If, on the contrary, it responds to its being a regulation of the labour market, to its being a kind of labour law, then the utility of its experience with Flexibility is not so clear.

The question about the justification of these levels of Flexibility is, then, crucial. In my view, there is no clear answer to this question. But what it is out of discussion, in my opinion, is that there are some particular features of labour law that explain why there is such a high level of Flexibility in its regulation. This does not mean, of course, that these features are exclusive to labour law, and that this makes of European labour law a singular branch of EU law with its own principles and dynamics. Evidently there are some problems that European labour law shares with other areas of EU law, and therefore Flexibility mechanisms would be helpful in all of them; if not, the export of European labour law techniques we have just seen would have been impossible. Nonetheless, I think that the main explanation of this Flexible character of European labour law lies in its being a branch of labour law, rather than in being "European".

It is true that many of the Flexibility techniques used by European labour law were designed to face a very specific political problem that appeared in the 1980s, the British veto to the development of an European Social Policy.[42] Institutions such as the opting-out, the long transitional periods or the exemptions for groups or workers were used to this purpose. This British opposition to a certain European policy was not a common thing at that time; now it seem that it is an attitude which many Member States are adopting with regard to different sectors of EU intervention, which makes of European labour law a good example of how to develop a given policy without the unanimous support of all Member States; harmonisation "*à la carte*", "variable geometry" and the like would have been the terminology we labour lawyers could have used in analysing the situation of European labour law from the early 1980s on. Flexibility has been both a technical and a political response to some Member

[42] This critical period of European labour law has been well studied. Among many others, see P. Sandler, "Players and Processes: The Evolution of Employment Law in the EEC" (1985), *Comparative Labour Law Journal*, 3; B. Hepple, "The Crisis in EEC Labour Law" (1987) 16 *The Industrial Law Journal* 77; and C. Ortiz Lallana, "Mercado Unico y Europa Social. Límites y dificultades para una aproximación legislativa" (1992) 5 *Revista de Trabajo y Seguridad Social*, 65.

States' resistance to any advance in the construction of an European social model.[43] And it has proved to be the only way through which EU institutions have been able to keep the European Social model alive.[44]

In many other cases, on the contrary, the need for Flexibility techniques is a consequence of some distinctive features of labour law and of the different industrial relations systems.[45] To begin with, the presence of unions and employers' associations in the legislative process, a peculiarity which is exclusive to labour law, produces a very strong demand for Flexibility in any national labour law. This demand is even stronger when we talk about building a labour law for the European integration process. Flexibility is demanded in the production of European labour law because there are some collective actors, at both a national and a European level, who demand to participate in the law-making process, just as they do at the national level. Pluralism in labour relations is a common feature for all Member States, being a part of the so-called "European Social Model". A European integration process without their participation would not have been acceptable.[46]

But the need for Flexibility is even stronger at the moment of implementation of EU labour law. In traditional areas of law law-making is the exclusive competence of the state; therefore, the implementation of European law does not produce any particular problem, as it remains a legal relationship between EU and Member States' institutions. In labour law things are completely different: law-making is a combination of public and private players and processes, and therefore the implementation of EU law must take into account the role of collective law-making. Traditional implementation mechanisms are far too rigid to be useful by themselves in this area, and they are consequently adapted; this is the function of techniques such as the "more favourable provisions" clause and the implementation through collective agreements.

Other aspects of national labour law impose on EU institutions the need for a high level of flexibility. The main one is the strong diversity that exists between them, as inside the EU you can find national systems belonging to traditions as different as the Continental, the Scandinavian or the Anglo-Saxon. Labour laws are strongly national,[47] they are the result of historical and cultural developments belonging to each national state, and so it is extremely difficult to design a common regulation in a directive that would be acceptable for all Member States, and that would be operative in all of them. Harmonisation of labour

[43] See A. Lo Faro, "EC Social Policy: The Dark Side of European Integration" [1992] *Comparative Labour Law Journal* 3.

[44] D.C. Dowling Jr., "From the Social Charter to the Social Action Program 1995–97: European Union Employment Law Comes Alive" (1996) 29 *Cornell International Law Journal* 43.

[45] I have studied this question in detail elsewhere; see M. Rodriguez-Piñero Royo, "El proceso legislativo europeo y el Derecho Social Comunitario" (1999) 12 *Revista del Ministerio de Trabajo y Asuntos Sociales* 13.

[46] A general analysis of this question appears in L. Betten, "The Democratic Deficit of Participatory Democracy in Community Social Policy" [1998] *European Law Review* 20.

[47] Lyon-Caen and A. Lyon-Caen, n. 22 *supra*, 133.

laws has turned into a very difficult matter; or, in other words, labour law is a very bad subject for harmonisation.[48] There are even some authors calling our attention to the crisis of the traditional harmonisation techniques in this area of the EU legal system.[49] Flexibility in European labour law is a response to these difficulties.

Here we find what we could call a "harmonisation paradox": the more different national labour laws are, the more you need the intervention of the EU in order to ensure a certain level of harmonisation; but, at the same time, the more different national labour laws are, the less likely you are to get this EU intervention. Even when harmonisation is possible, new and less rigid legal instruments are needed to put it into practice: exemptions, alternative regulations and the like.

All this makes me wonder whether we are creating a new problem for the legitimacy of European labour law: if it is designed as a response to the impact of European economic integration on the labour market, its main objective is to harmonise national labour laws; this would be its justification, what makes it acceptable under the subsidiarity test, because this effect cannot be achieved through national labour law exclusively. But if the EU is increasing the level of Flexibility in European labour law, then this harmonisation objective will not be possible. Will European labour law be legitimate then under the subsidiarity test, as an intervention which can be justified only on the grounds of harmonisation, but that does not produce any?

As a conclusion, I would say that European labour law is Flexible mainly because is a branch of labour law. Member States have also developed national labour laws which using this terminology would be called Flexible. When building a labour law adequate to act as a basis for supporting European social policy the need for Flexibility grows exponentially. Therefore, the opportunity of using the case of European labour law as evidence to support the existence of a general tendency of Flexibilisation in EU law is not so clear.

4. A CONCLUSION: FLEXIBILITY, GOOD, BAD OR NONE OF THE ABOVE?

In this chapter I have presented a concept of flexibility which has been central in all the debates about labour law in the last three decades. This concept has turned out to be extremely powerful, becoming a nuclear element of labour law itself, after having been presented as a temporary solution to a critical moment in Western countries' labour markets.

Any opinion about flexibility coming from a labour lawyer must be accepted with some reservations, as all of us share some prejudices against this notion.

[48] See P. Watson, "Harmonization of Social Security and Labor Law" 1984 4 *Comparative Labor Law* 1.

[49] According to A. Lo Faro, *Funzioni e finzioni della contrattazione collettiva europea*, Ph.D. Thesis (Florence: European University Institute, 1997), 72.

From this point of view flexibility and labour lawyers have always been, as some said in the early 1990s, an "odd couple".[50] But one cannot forget that to some degree labour law forced itself to suffer a transformation in order to accept most of the demands for flexibility, thus becoming a flexible labour law. Labour law academics themselves opened their minds to this concept, and there is even a "flexible labour law generation", formed by those who started studying labour law in the 1980s, when the flexibility debate was hot everywhere. Generally speaking labour law accepted its promises of change, and the strong defence of the traditional model of labour law was soon over. By doing this, however, we have also seen its effects; we know how it works. Therefore we have all the legitimacy to talk about it, to point out its power and to warn about its natural tendency to increase it.

Labour law's flexibility and European law's Flexibility have some common elements, although they must be considered as completely different notions, each having its own dynamic and mechanisms. The elements they share, however, justify the utility of our experience as labour lawyers in order to evaluate the introduction of Flexible elements into modern EU law. And although we might be biased and prejudiced against the notion of flexibility, nevertheless we should warn against it: it is a very powerful notion, the long-term effects of which are difficult to foresee. Once you accept it as a natural element of any legal system, it becomes difficult to control, because it gets its own thrust. It tends to become an end in itself, rather than an instrument; and therefore any intervention which is labelled "flexible" is automatically legitimated. Its limits are so vague and ill-defined that almost anything can be considered an instrument of flexibility.

This could be the most significant implication from the labour law experience with this notion: beware of Flexibility. The impact of flexibility on labour law has been tremendous, deep and far-reaching. Mostly because its a formal, rather than a material concept, a label you put on legal institutions according to certain vague objectives no one can be opposed to. Much of this might happen with EU law's Flexibility, because it is a formal notion as well. Under this common denomination many different techniques are grouped together as pursuing one common aim. We must not forget, however, that Flexibility is just an instrument, that what matter are the political objectives all actors have in every area of the European integration process.

There is a tendency to support Flexibility as an intrinsic element of the European integration process.[51] This is easy to understand: it sells rather well as a notion which can justify almost anything; any expression of Flexible law is

[50] The expression is from a Spanish professor of labour law, and from the "flexible labour law generation": P. Perez de los Cobos, "La flexibilidad y la doctrina: la extraña pareja" [1991] I *Relaciones Laborales* 79.

[51] According to E. Philippart and G. Edwards, "The Provisions on Closer Co-operation in the Treaty of Amsterdam: The Politics of Flexibility in the European Union" (1999) 37 *Journal of Common Market Studies* 87.

consequently positively evaluated. But any labour lawyer can remember how our best-known case of Flexible law, the Social Protocol of the Amsterdam Treaty, was strongly criticised[52] because it was an exit rather than a solution[53]; and its development was a continuous source of conflicts, forcing Member States to get rid of it at the Amsterdam summit. Under the Flexibility perspective, this Protocol was a remarkable example of modern, progressive, Flexible European law; an example deserving to be followed.

A final thought: it seems to me that in many cases the notion of Flexibility does not appear in the debate until the moment when the rules have already been set. In other words, that it is not an objective set in advance, but it appears when the outcomes are analysed and justified. The question would be, then, whether Flexibility is a real directive element in the European integration process, or is just a concept which is being used to justify its outcomes instead. Whether we are really looking for Flexibility in the construction of Europe, or we are just using it to rationalise our defeats in the realisation of this project[54]. Indro Montanelli, the famous Italian writer, said once that only wars that are lost produce heroes. If this is true, maybe it is also true that only political defeats produce slogans and labels; like Flexibility.

[52] P. Lange, "Il Protocollo Sociale di Maastricht: perché l'hanno fatto? [1993] *Stato e Mercato* 9.

[53] According to M. Rodriguez-Piñero Sr., "De Maastricht a Amsterdam: derechos sociales y empleo" (1998) 4 *Relaciones Laborales* 1.

[54] See H. Wallace, "Flexibility: A Tool of Integration or a Restraint on Disintegration" in K. Neunreither and A. Wiener (eds.), *Amsterdam and Beyond: Institutional Dynamics and Prospects for Democracy* (Oxford: Oxford University Press, 1999).

11

Finding Space for Closer Co-operation in the Field of Culture

STEPHEN WEATHERILL

1. INTRODUCTION

IT HAS BECOME axiomatic that the provisions on "closer co-operation" introduced by the Treaty of Amsterdam are very restrictive and that, at least if applied rigorously and literally, they will rarely be available to Member States proposing to develop forms of co-operation to which all their partners in the Union choose not to sign up. This chapter tests that assumption in one area that has been mooted as a candidate for breeding closer co-operation, that of culture. The conclusion is that the orthodox reading is well-founded and that closer co-operation is difficult to envisage, at least according to a formal reading of the Treaty provisions. This view is largely based on the obstruction to permissible closer co-operation caused by the Treaty's insistence that such arrangements shall neither affect other Community policies nor distort conditions of competition between Member States. It is shown that such rigid compartmentalisation is largely incompatible with the well-established pattern of development "by spillover" in the EC system. In so far as proposed closer co-operation cannot be sealed off from the tendency of the EC system to spread its sphere of influence, then it is not permitted. The chapter proceeds to doubt whether the Treaty provisions should be read so restrictively and demonstrates techniques for adopting a more flexible approach to their interpretation. It is argued, at a more general level, that flexibility—of which Treaty-based closer co-operation is but one manifestation—is of critical importance in the further design of the European integration project. However, for all its appealing resonances as a method for breaking institutional and constitutional deadlock, and despite its inevitable rise in a geographically and functionally expanding Union, flexibility carries the risk of deepening still further the gulf between elite plans and popular understanding. The emergence of blocs comprising different groupings of states in different spheres of activity under the authority of the Treaty provisions governing closer co-operation will make the patterns of European integration ever more complex. The European Union suffers from an alarming and growing transparency deficit.

2. THE EXPANSION OF THE EC'S COMPETENCE

Since the entry into force of the Single European Act in 1987, one of the more prominent trends in the evolution of the EC legal order has been the expansion of the scope of the EC's formal competence combined with adjustments to the constitutional impact of the exercise of that competence. Classic notions of Community exclusivity acquired at the expense of national competence through the pre-emptive effect of secondary legislation doubtless retain a role in the construction and maintenance of an integrated market, but in many areas Community exclusivity in fields occupied by the Community is not the norm. Space is left for local choices. Manifestations of these trends include what was Article 100a(4), becoming since the entry into force of the Amsterdam Treaty on 1 May 1999 the rather more sophisticated mechanism found in Article 95(4)–(9), and, broader, the technique of minimum harmonisation. This seam is also studded by opt-outs and derogations in individual measures or even in the Treaty itself, as illustrated by the arrangements for social policy manufactured to accommodate British intransigence at Maastricht and finally laid to rest by the Amsterdam Treaty. Of course, this is by no means an exhaustive list of the types of shift which exemplify the Community's incompetence to regulate many sectors to the exclusion of any national-level contribution. Moreover, in detail, the nature and purpose of these techniques differ. But viewed in combination they convey the broad impression that in the wake of the geographical and functional expansion which the Community has lately undergone, involving in turn the shaping of a Union, the constitutional relationship between Community intervention and residual national competence must be modified. It can no longer be as clean-cut as was promised by classic notions of Community field occupation, within which the Community's action pre-empts scope for rule-making by the states. Uniformity yields.

Subsidiarity too may be taken to lie on this trajectory. It indicates anxiety among the Member States about the expansion of Community competence and it represents a (tentative, imprecise) method for states to tap on the brake. Much of the tension felt by the Member States since the entry into force of the Single European Act may be seen to emerge as contortions designed to reshape elements of the influence over Community decision-making previously secured by the unanimity requirement in Council, but surrendered in such overt fashion to the rules of Qualified Majority Voting in Council. There is an obvious ambiguity which attaches to the general readiness of the Member States to secure acceleration of the decision-making process, thereby to remove blockages rooted in minority objections, while at the same time individual Member States seek methods to insulate their own particular anxieties and eccentricities from majority rule. Dynamism is splendid—for others. For observers of the Court, this phenomenon connects to the "legal base" cases such as that concerning the "Working Time" Directive, *United Kingdom* v. *Council*,[1] in which minority dis-

[1] Case C–84/94, [1996] ECR 5755, challenging Dir. 93/104, [1995] OJ L307, 18.

sentient states seek to throw their lifebelts over a legal base which requires unanimity once their political objections expressed in Council have drowned in the sea of Qualified Majority Voting. Thus far the Court has exhibited little readiness to lend succour to such attempts to secure minority protection from subjection to EC rules agreed by the majority.[2] Conversion of political disagreement into questions of legal validity of this type is the inevitable consequence of the Treaty's incremental growth, which has thrown up often irrational anomalies between cognate areas of regulatory activity which depend for legislative amplification on different voting rules in Council (and, in addition, different levels of Parliamentary involvement[3]). The Court, insistent that choice of legal basis is not to be left to the whims of the political institutions, has taken on a thankless task in attempting to resolve politically sensitive conundrums bequeathed to it by the erratic process of Treaty revision. These regrettable discrepancies have been reduced, though by no means eliminated, by the Amsterdam Treaty.[4] Incentives to convert political argument into legal challenge to choice of legal base are diminished post-Amsterdam.[5]

Uniformity may have less deep roots in the EC system than has traditionally been assumed, or at least publicised,[6] but today its very value is the subject of constructive debate. This chapter is based on the premise that "closer co-operation" under the Amsterdam Treaty is properly situated in this broader context. Closer co-operation under the Amsterdam Treaty is a specific manifestation of the quest for flexibility in the EU's shaping which has animated much of the political debate in the period leading up to agreement at Amsterdam. It is a further step down the road towards enhanced Community-level policy-making which nevertheless does not inevitably implicate common action on a uniform basis taken by all the Member States. The widening of action in these circumstances will, for some (minority) Member States, result in no surrender of competence at all, let alone (for example) merely the loss of a right to depress standards surrendered in a regime of minimum harmonisation. Integration is accelerated, but some states do not even board the new car added to the train. Elements of diversity prevail. This is inevitable (and, in my submission,

[2] See also, e.g., Case C–233/94, *Germany* v. *Parliament and Council* [1997] ECR I–2405. Such challenges frequently also feature reliance on alleged violation of principles such as proportionality and (thus far less clearly) subsidiarity. On the Court's positioning generally see G. De Burca, "The principle of subsidiarity and the Court of Justice as an Institutional Actor" (1998) 36 JCMS 217.

[3] A tension which has also provoked litigation; contrast the outcome of Case C–300/89, *Commission* v. *Council* [1991] ECR I–2867 with that in Case C–155/91, *Commission* v. *Council* [1993] ECR I–939.

[4] E.g. in relation to the two cases mentioned in the previous note, co-decision is now the rule for both legal bases, excepting only cases of unanimity in Council plus mere consultation of the Parliament provided for by Art. 175(2) (ex Art. 130s(2)). Moreover, a discrepancy arises because Art. 176 (ex Art. 130t) establishes a principle of minimum harmonisation while Art. 95 (ex Art. 100a) is less permissive of Member State variation.

[5] Challenge by outvoted minorities aggrieved by perceived violation of general principles of Community law remains a live possibility, n. 2 *supra*.

[6] For an early confession, see C.-D. Ehlermann, "The Internal Market Following the Single European Act" (1987) 24 *CMLRev*. 361. See also de Búrca in this volume.

desirable) as the Community expands far beyond an integration-only or even an integration-first agenda. The underlying challenge remains how to break the deadweight of unanimity through acceptance of diminished uniformity, but without thereby toppling the system into irreversible fragmentation. This is not a new challenge. It can be seen to underlie eruptions of uncommonality such as "Maastricht social policy" and the structure of Economic and Monetary Union. But the Amsterdam Treaty carries the debate on to a new plane. It attempts to provide a framework rooted in the Treaty for determining what types of "flexibility" are permitted and what are not. This is to be planned, not *ad hoc*, disunity. Articles 43 and 44 TEU, supplemented in the first pillar by Article 11 EC and in the third by Article 40 TEU, empower a majority of Member States to develop closer co-operation amongst themselves without specifying the subject areas in which this is allowed, nor even those in which it is not. The criteria are not sector-specific.[7]

Culture offers a potentially good example of some of these trends. The orthodox, though in at least some sectors outmoded, connection between Community action and the seizure of exclusivity in the field is explicitly set aside in the provision on Culture added to the EC Treaty at Maastricht. Community competence is carefully confined by the Treaty. Article 152 (ex Article 128) EC refers to contributions by the Community to "the flowering of the cultures of the Member States, while respecting their national and regional diversity"; and to Community action "aimed at encouraging cooperation between Member States" and "supporting and supplementing" state action. Moreover, action which is taken under the co-decision legislative procedure is limited to the adoption of "incentive measures", with harmonisation of laws explicitly excluded. Culture offers a good illustration of the truth that the Community cannot feasibly simply replace its Member States as the regulator in all or many fields. However could such a shift anyway be imagined in the field of culture? The Community supplements action taken elsewhere.

3. THE CRITERIA FOR "CLOSER CO-OPERATION"

The label "closer co-operation" is imbued with an appealingly positive resonance of progress. Like the broader phenomenon of "flexibility", of which closer co-operation is a Treaty-defined sub-set,[8] it is an idea which seems to defy scepticism. How could its virtue be denied? Indeed, in its suggestion of managed and non-exclusionary[9] deepening of collaborative endeavour by most, but not all,[10] Member States, closer co-operation seems to hold out the promise of

[7] Although Art. 11(1)(c) EC forbids closer co-operation that concerns citizenship of the Union.

[8] See A. Stubb, "A Categorization of Differentiated Integration" (1996) 34 *JCMS* 283.

[9] On subsequent entry by initial non-participants, see TEU, Art. 43(1)(g); EC, Art. 11(3); and TEU, Art. 40(3).

[10] The rule requiring a majority is found in Art. 43(1)(d) TEU.

openly planned and explicitly justified variation sector by sector, while refusing the allure of rigid, all-or-nothing two-speed models or, worse still, *à la carte* models. Different *blocs* of closer co-operation will engage different combinations of states, depending on the subject matter in issue. The groupings will not be static. But it is in the more detailed appreciation of the criteria which must be satisfied before the Treaty sanctions closer co-operation that a rather different impression emerges. The criteria are forbiddingly difficult to satisfy. They are, indeed, unremittingly negative, focusing on what must *not* follow from closer co-operation. This provides a warning that, for all its appeal, closer co-operation also carries with it the threat that it may inflict damage on the integrity of the legal order. In the European Union flexibility is at best an ambiguous virtue.

The criteria built into the provisions on closer co-operation in the Amsterdam Treaty will rarely be satisfied. Accordingly closer co-operation under the new provisions is not likely to be common.[11] Cultural closer co-operation provides a useful testing-ground for this assumption. For reasons amplified in section 4 below, I find the assumption well-founded. There is a "hemming-in" effect, whereby the spread of Community activity over decades makes it hard to envisage what is really now left to some but not all Member States to pursue by way of the provisions governing closer co-operation invented at Amsterdam.

A brief glance at the relevant criteria provides ample support for this verdict. Article 43 TEU operates as form of "master provision", in the sense that closer co-operation falling within the sphere of either the first or third pillar must comply with its pre-conditions in addition to those stipulated within the pillars themselves (by Article 11 EC and Article 40 TEU respectively). Article 43 forbids co-operation which affects the *acquis communautaire*. It also excludes co-operation which affects the competences, rights, obligations and interests of non-participants. These are already very high hurdles. Awareness of the extraordinary expansion of Community activity over the last four decades, propelled recently by periodic Treaty revision but also over a longer period by legislative activity based on a generous reading of available Treaty powers, in particular

[11] Commentators naturally choose different points of emphasis, but all share the view that the availability of closer co-operation is heavily restricted by the Treaty; see, *inter alia*, V. Constantinesco, "Les clauses de coopération renforcée" (1997) 33 *RTDE* 751; J. Shaw, "The Treaty of Amsterdam: Challenges of Flexibility and Legitimacy" (1998) 4 *ELJ* 63; G. Gaja, "How Flexible is Flexibility under the Amsterdam Treaty?" (1998) 35 *CMLRev*. 855; L. Favret, "Le Traité d'Amsterdam: une révision à minima de la Charte constitutionnelle de l'Union européenne" (1997) 33 *CDE* 555; C.-D. Ehlermann, "Engere Zusammenarbeit nach dem Amsterdamer Vertrag: Ein neues Verfassungsprinzip?" (1997) 32 *EuR* 362; C.-D. Ehlermann, "Differentiation, Flexibility, Closer Co-operation: The New Provisions of the Amsterdam Treaty" (1998) 4 *ELJ* 246; G. Edwards and E. Philippart, "Flexibility and the Treaty of Amsterdam" CELS, Occasional Paper 3, (Cambridge: 1997); S. Langrish, "The Treaty of Amsterdam: Selected Highlights" (1998) 23 *ELRev*. 3; N. Walker, "Sovereignty and Differentiated Integration in the European Union" (1998) 4 *ELJ* 355; J. Usher, "Flexibility and Enhanced Cooperation" in T. Heukels, N. Blokker and M. Brus, *The European Union after Amsterdam* (Deventer: Kluwer, 1998), ch. 14, 253–71; N. Kotzias, "Die Regierungskonferenz und die flexible Forderung der Integration" in F. Breuss and S. Griller, *Flexible Integration in Europa: Einheit oder Europe à la carte?* (Berlin: Springer Verlag, 1998), 1–40.

Articles 94, 95 and 308 (ex Articles 100, 100a and 235) EC, allied to the dynamic contribution of the European Court, breeds an instinctive feeling that one would be perplexed to discover many, even any, areas that fall within the sphere of Community competence yet within the confines of which co-operation could be envisaged that would be untainted by an effect on the *acquis communautaire* or on the interests of non-participants.

Article 11 (ex Article 5a) EC, applying only to closer co-operation within the first pillar, the EC, reinforces the impression that the new provisions will be triggered only rarely. It excludes co-operation which affects Community policies, actions or programmes; or which restricts trade between Member States or distorts the conditions of competition between Member States. Yet what does not fall foul of at least one of these pre-conditions? For purposes of illustration, it is worth playing the textual game. It is not difficult to list a large number of Community directives in the fields of social, environmental and consumer policy which are adopted on the stated basis that diversity between national regimes in the fields in question causes inequality in the conditions of competition within the Community. Consequently, harmonisation of laws in the areas in question is treated as justified under Articles 100 or 100a of the Treaty (Articles 94 and 95 post-Amsterdam). If one transplants the notion that conditions of competition are affected by disparity between national laws to the arena of closer co-operation, one would suppose that a system within which some, but not all, Member States develop new rules while others do not participate inevitably breeds competitive distortion. Any such plans for closer co-operation would therefore fall foul of Article 11 EC. So the historical record of harmonisation of diverse national laws prompted by competitive distortion undermines the potential for closer co-operation, which must not create competitive distortion.[12] This seems to impose severe restrictions on the possibilities for some but not all Member States to intensify their joint endeavour by relying on the Amsterdam Treaty's innovation. Of course the political context of harmonisation differs significantly from that of closer co-operation. The batch of harmonisation directives concerning social, environmental and consumer policy was in the main adopted on the basis of Article 100 or 100a, both of which emphasise the impact of national laws on the market. The reason for this choice does not lie in any developed analysis of the structure of markets and their relationship with legal intervention. Rather, it reflected the limitations of available legal bases elsewhere in the Treaty pending Treaty revision which has amplified the Community's competence in the relevant fields, combined with a past readiness in the Council to use the harmonisation programme as a cover for policy-making in politically fashionable areas in which unanimous support existed. Formal questions of legal validity associated with the meaning of distortion of

[12] For more detail, see S. Weatherill, " 'If I'd Wanted You to Understand I would have Explained it Better': What is the Purpose of the Provisions on Closer Co-operation Introduced by the Treaty of Amsterdam?" in D. O'Keeffe and P. Twomey, *Legal Issues of the Amsterdam Treaty* (Oxford: Hart Publishing, 1999).

competition were not of practical relevance. Such a political context will not necessarily today condition the interpretation of Article 11(a)(1)(e) EC. This background dictates that analogies between stated rationales for harmonisation and the criteria laid down in the new Article 11 EC may mislead, but embedded deep within legal reasoning is the manipulation of context, and historical representations of the breadth of the notion of distortion of competition may come to be relied on to provide constitutional ammunition for opponents of a particular form of proposed closer co-operation.

As a general observation, the criteria which must be satisfied before closer co-operation may proceed betray a strong anxiety to protect both the acquired strengths of the Community and Union system and the position of the non-participant states. This is not betrayed by the substantive criteria alone. The arrangements invented for managing the authorisation of use of the new provisions are similarly restrictive and, in particular, place a blocking power of sorts in the hands of the Member States which do not plan to participate in the proposed closer co-operation. Article 11(2) EC permits a member of the Council to declare that, "for important and stated reasons of national policy", it intends to oppose the granting of an authorisation by qualified majority. This may lead to a default setting of referral by qualified majority vote to the Council, meeting in the composition of the Heads of State or Government, for decision by unanimity. Article 40 TEU provides for a similar possibility, with the ultimate power to decide by unanimity resting in the hands of the European Council. To this extent, a veto is available, although reasons must be supplied for the state's opposition. It is furthermore specifically provided in Article 43 TEU, the master provision, that closer co-operation shall be "open to all Member States and allows them to become parties to the co-operation at any time, provided that they comply with the basic decision and with the decisions taken within that framework". Procedures are elaborated (in slightly different ways) in the relevant provisions in the first and third pillars.[13] This opportunity to join later, once the closer co-operation has taken shape and its merits may be assessed, may induce sceptical non-participants not to exercise their veto at the outset. However, the overall impression of these provisions is that they are heavily laden with restrictive conditions and that occasions on which they may be used will be relatively few.

4. "HEMMING IN": THE EXAMPLE OF CULTURE

The less Community legislation (or the less activity generally, including soft law) in an area, the better the prospects for discovering permissible triggering of the provisions on closer co-operation under the first pillar. The less active the Community has been in a particular policy field, the less there is to be "affected"

[13] N. 9 *supra*.

by closer co-operators. One would anticipate closer co-operation to be most obviously viable in areas which fall within Community competence (as they must, according to Article 11(1)(d) EC), but which are not "hemmed in" by a substantial body of Community activity. Culture may seem a candidate area for closer co-operation, because it is not an area in which the Community has been energetic. This impression is instructively misleading. In fact there is plenty of "hemming in" by contiguous policy areas, for culture does not exist in a legal vacuum.[14] Examples may be drawn from several areas.

A. Intellectual Property

Closer co-operation in culture would have to avoid trespassing on the *acquis communautaire* as it affects intellectual property rights, which would rule out potentially appealing methods for inducing cultural growth, such as an offer of relatively more generous periods of copyright protection. The abundant case law dealing with the impact of Articles 28–30 (ex Articles 30–36) on national intellectual property law provides evidence of the tangle that has drawn together the law of market integration and the interests that underpin national choices about the conferral of exclusive rights on innovators; and it is by no means the case that the Court feels able to draw a bright line between integration and cultural protection, nor that it automatically subordinates the latter to the imperatives of the former.[15] Article 28 (ex Article 30) does not inevitably depress levels of protection and remuneration of right-holders to the lowest common denominator in the Community. The Court is prepared to accept the force of regulatory motivations which compete with a focus on integration.[16] So, for example, in *Warner Brothers* v. *Christiansen*[17] the Court refused to allow Danish concern to defend a rental market in video cassettes existing separately from that for sale to be undermined by the more liberal system preferred in the United Kingdom. Warner Brothers held rights in the United Kingdom and in Denmark. Cross-border trade in videos released by the company in the United Kingdom market, where no distinct rental right existed, could lawfully be suppressed by it in the Danish rental market in conformity with Articles 28–30. In

[14] For surveys of EC activity, see M. Niedobitek, *The Cultural Dimension in EC Law* (Deventer: Kluwer, 1997); J.A. McMahon, *Education and Culture in EC Law* (London: Athlone Press, 1995); B. De Witte and H. Post, "Educational and Cultural Rights" in A. Cassese, A. Clapham and J. Weiler, *Human Rights and the EC: The Substantive Law* (Baden-Baden: Nomos Verlagsgesellshaft, 1991).

[15] See generally S. Weatherill and P. Beaumont, *EU Law* (3rd edn., London: Penguin Books, 1999), ch. 26; H.-W. Micklitz and S. Weatherill, *European Economic Law* (Aldershot: Dartmouth, 1997), ch. 7.

[16] In a context broader than only intellectual property, see S. Weatherill, "Recent Case Law Concerning the Free Movement of Goods: Mapping the Frontiers of Market Deregulation" (1999) 36 *CMLRev*. 51; and, more generally, M. Poiares Maduro, *We the Court* (Oxford: Hart Publishing, 1998).

[17] Case 156/86, [1988] ECR 2605.

this way, local choices about cultural protection were respected by the Court in its shaping of the law of free movement in the EC. A similar pattern emerges from its ruling in *EMI Electrola* v. *Patricia Import*.[18] EMI sought to exclude from Germany Cliff Richard records imported from Denmark. The records had been marketed perfectly lawfully by a third party in Denmark, because although EMI had held protection in Denmark parallel to that in Germany, the protection had expired after 25 years, whereas that in Germany would endure for five further years. To disallow EMI from relying on its copyright protection in Germany in such circumstances would imply the use of the law of free movement in the hands of the parallel trader in effect to depress the period of protection to that of the least generous state in the Community. Advocate General Darmon described this as a major risk "for artistic creativity in the Community, an essential aspect of this Europe of culture which everyone desires".[19] The Court's ruling reflects this concern. It concluded that EMI's rights to rely on its copyright in Germany were not exhausted, notwithstanding the persisting obstacle this placed on product market integration. The consequence of these rulings is to protect the reward of right-holders and to confine the ability of parallel traders to exploit grey markets.

The function of intellectual property rights under national law in remunerating invention is prominent in the Court's thinking in *EMI Electrola* in its application of Articles 28–30 EC, but it may also be observed in the Court's appreciation of Community legislative initiatives in the field of intellectual property. For the Court in *Metronome Musik GmbH* v. *Music Point Hokamp GmbH*[20] any diminution in the scope of rights has "inevitable repercussions" for innovation. The Court upheld the validity of Article 1(1) of Directive 92/100, which creates an exclusive rental right, spelling out, with reference to phonogram producers, the importance of the function of an exclusive right in remunerating and therefore rewarding investment in creativity. In its judgment the Court made passing reference to cultural development, specifically (what was then) Article 128 EC.

B. Broadcasting: The Treaty Provisions

Broadcasting is another sector which demonstrates the entangling of cultural policy with trade policy.[21] The imposition of obligations on broadcasters (or publishers generally[22]) to respect and/or to reflect local culture would be forced

[18] Case 341/87, [1989] ECR 79.

[19] *Ibid.*, 91.

[20] Case C–200/96, [1998] ECR I–1953.

[21] See more fully R. Craufurd Smith, *Broadcasting Law and Fundamental Rights* (Oxford: Clarendon Press, 1997).

[22] A recent extra-EU example is provided by the dispute between Canada and the USA about Canadian rules designed to protect its magazine industry in particular and cultural diversity in general. A panel report, in part reversed by the Appellate Body, found in 1997 that Canada was in

to tread a wary line around the demands of the law of product and service market integration under Articles 28(30) and 49(59) EC, amplified by relevant secondary legislation which attempts to develop Community-level rules which reconcile the concerns of cultural policy, typically addressed at national level and apt to fragment the market, with the demands of integration. A Member State which restricts cross-border trade in, for example, the transmission of television signals or cable relay will in principle fall foul of Article 49 EC.[23] A state may be able to justify restrictions imposed on the free movement of services. Rules designed to secure cultural aims such as pluralism and freedom of expression may be permissible in the general interest, even where they restrict trade, but those rules must be applied without discrimination based on nationality (so local suppliers must be subject to the same rules) and they must be proportionate in their effect to the end in view.[24] In *Bond van Adverteerders* v. *Netherlands*[25] the Court decided that it was not permissible as a matter of "public policy" to restrict cable relay of non-Dutch programmes containing advertisements targeted at Dutch viewers in order to reserve advertising revenues for a public institution established in the Netherlands. In any event, the permissibility of state acts derogating from fundamental economic freedoms in Community law must be justified, *inter alia*, with reference to fundamental rights. In *ERT* v. *Dimotiki*[26] the Court interpreted the scope of the freedom to provide services "in the light of the general principle of freedom of expression embodied in Article 10 of the European Convention on Human Rights". State restrictions on broadcasting had to be justified with reference to principles contained in the European Convention, including freedom of expression, mediated through the general principles of Community law.[27] This provides a particularly vivid demonstration of the open-textured nature of the law of free movement, for the Court allows it to be fed not simply by influences from elsewhere in the fabric of Community policies but even from outwith the formal constitutional limits of the EC legal order.

Moreover, the viability of state monopolies under EC law is challenged by Article 86 (ex Article 90) EC, which exerts further constraints over the autonomy of Member States to organise the structure of the broadcasting sector in pursuit of cultural objectives. The Court has insisted that the first paragraph of Article 86 does not mean that state monopolies are automatically unlawful. In *Italy* v. *Sacchi*[28] it stated that "nothing in the Treaty . . . prevent[s] Member

breach (WT/DS31), but, after Canada sought to devise different techniques for achieving its goals which were unacceptable to the USA, final resolution of the dispute was delayed until 1999: "Canada and US agree magazine deal", *Financial Times*, 27 May 1999, 7.

[23] Case 52/79, *Procureur du Roi* v. *Debauve* [1980] ECR 833.

[24] E.g Case C–148/91, *Veronica* [1993] ECR I–487; Case C–353/89, *Commission* v. *Netherlands* [1991] ECR I–4069.

[25] Case 352/85, [1988] ECR 2085.

[26] Case C–260/89, [1991] ECR I–2925.

[27] Cf., in the area of free movement of goods, Case C–368/95, *Vereinigte Familiapress Zeitungsverlags und -vertriebs GmbH* v. *Heinrich Bauer Verlag* [1997] ECR I–3689.

[28] Case 155/73, [1974] ECR 409.

States, for considerations of public interests, of a non-economic nature, from withdrawing radio and television broadcasts, including broadcasts by cable, from the field of competition, by conferring on one or more institutions the exclusive right to operate in this field". But the Court's increasing readiness to find, in particular, abuses contrary to Article 82 (ex Article 86) EC committed by state monopolies has led to the perception that its approach comes close to a notion of "inevitable abuse". This arises where the exclusivity conferred leads to demand exceeding supply—that is, to a malfunctioning market.[29] This severely limits the scope for shaping state monopolies that do not violate the first paragraph of Article 86 (ex Article 90). It is possible that an infringement of Article 86(1) EC may be justified under Article 86(2), but this exception is to be narrowly interpreted. In the result, it is possible that a state broadcasting monopoly may be treated as failing to meet demand for broadcasting services, leading to a violation of Article 86(1). Such a breach may be justified under Article 86(2) in the case of a public-service broadcaster, but this would not be easy to achieve. For present purposes, the key point is the difficulty in tracing the permitted scope of cultural protection in EC trade law; and, especially, the virtual impossibility of separating out culture from trade law. The sensitivity of this balance is well illustrated by Article 16 EC, an innovation of the Amsterdam Treaty. This provides that:

> Without prejudice to Articles 73, 86 and 87, and given the place occupied by services of general economic interest in the shared values of the Union as well as their role in promoting social and territorial cohesion, the Community and the Member States, each within their respective powers and within the scope of application of this Treaty, shall take care that such services operate on the basis of principles and conditions which enable them to fulfil their missions.

"Services of general economic interest" are clearly cherished; but not to the point where they can be placed above Articles 73 (77), 86 (90) and 87 (92), the key Treaty provisions which have been shaped in such an active manner by the Court. The Amsterdam Treaty also appended to the EC Treaty a Protocol on the System of Public Broadcasting in the Member States. This provides that:

> The provisions of the Treaty establishing the European Community shall be without prejudice to the competence of Member States to provide for the funding of public service broadcasting insofar as such funding is granted to broadcasting organisations for the fulfilment of the public service remit as conferred, defined and organised by each Member State, and insofar as such funding does not affect trading conditions and competition in the Community to an extent which would be contrary to the common interest, while the realisation of the remit of that public service shall be taken into account.

[29] E.g. Case C–41/90, *Höfner and Elser* v. *Macrotron GmbH* [1991] ECR I–1979; Case C–320/91, *Paul Corbeau* [1993] ECR I–2533.

This offers a further example of the anxiety to emphasise the key role of public services, but to admit that their operation cannot be immunised from EC trade law.[30]

C. Broadcasting: The Secondary Legislation

Secondary legislation in the field confirms the indissociability of trade policy and regulatory choices. The "Television without Frontiers" Directive[31] provides in Article 2a(1) that "Member States shall ensure freedom of reception and shall not restrict retransmissions on their territory of television broadcasts from other Member States for reasons which fall within the fields coordinated by this Directive". Its aim is to integrate markets for television broadcasting, but also to re-regulate the European market (within its field of application). It offers a text-book example of the "dual function" of harmonisation, whereby the establishment of common rules at Community level serves to level the playing field on which integration may proceed, but also involves choices made at Community level about the content of the common rule which will govern the conduct of business at Community level, in replacement for market-fragmenting diverse national rules. So, for example, Articles 10–21 govern the conduct of "[t]elevision advertising, sponsorship and teleshopping". "All forms of television advertising and teleshopping for cigarettes and other tobacco products shall be prohibited"; television advertising for alcoholic beverages must comply with defined criteria. Articles 22–22b cover the "[p]rotection of minors and public order".[32] The objective of integrating the market is furthered by the almost complete absence of situations explicitly foreseen in the Directive in which broadcasting services may be suspended by the receiving state. The exceptions are found in Article 2a(2) and arise in the event of a breach of Article 22 relating to impairment of "the physical, mental or moral development of minors" and/or Article 22a forbidding broadcasts containing "any incitement to hatred on grounds of race, sex, religion or nationality", but even then the power to suspend services is available only where further substantive and procedural thresholds are crossed. The infringement of Article 22 and/or Article 22a must be manifest, serious and grave, there must have been at least two prior infringements in the preceding 12 months and the receiving state must have engaged in consultation of a

[30] See also Resolution of the Council (and the representatives of the governments of the Member States meeting within Council) concerning public service broadcasting [1999] OJ C30/3.

[31] Dir. 89/552, [1989] OJ L298, 51 amended by Dir. 97/36, [1997] OJ L202, 43. On the recent amendments in particular, see B. Drijber, "The Revised Television without Frontiers Directive: Is It Fit for the Next Century?" (1999) 36 *CMLRev*. 87; L. Woods and J. Scholes, "Broadcasting: The Creation of a European Culture or the Limits of the Internal Market" (1997) 17 *YEL* 47.

[32] Note also the (increasing) role of soft law alongside formal binding rules contained in dirs.: e.g. Council Recommendation 98/560 on the development of the competitiveness of the European audiovisual and information services industry by promoting national frameworks aimed at achieving a comparable and effective level of protection of minors and human dignity [1998] OJ L270/48.

defined type with broadcaster, Commission and transmitting state. The Directive contains a strong impetus towards freedom of transmission by limiting the power of the receiving state through heavy reliance on the principle of "home country control" over broadcasters. Misconduct by the home state should be remedied by Commission intervention or, in appropriate circumstances, action before national courts, and not by retaliatory action against the broadcaster.[33] The Commission has chosen to stress the importance of home country control "in an audiovisual environment which—thanks to the proliferation of broadcasting capacities due to digital technology—favours the growth of transnational services".[34] The Directive also includes in Articles 4–9 provisions entitled "[p]romotion of distribution and production of television programmes", including the hotly controversial targets for reservation of exposure to "European works". This strategy should be read alongside the rather more outward-looking "MEDIA II" programme, which aims to support the competitiveness of the European audiovisual sector through development of technology and training of professionals.[35]

D. Other Examples of the Involvement of EC Law and Policy in Culture

The purpose here is not to criticise the priorities which emerge from this pattern of complex policy-making, but rather to confirm the unfeasibility of the sharp divide between joint regulatory endeavour pursued by some Member States and the resulting impact on the *acquis communautaire* suggested by the innovative Amsterdam Treaty provisions on closer co-operation. The list of areas where cultural policy and trade integration must establish a *modus vivendi* rather than separate lives could be extended,[36] but brief examples must suffice to conclude this explanation. Restrictions on the movement of art treasures implicate the law of product market integration. This is an area which has been the subject of secondary legislation which attempts to develop Community-level rules which place cultural policy within a framework of market integration.[37] Financial support for cultural activity would be subject to the State Aid provisions.[38] Culture does not exist in a vacuum in any context, and certainly not within the framework of Community law. Once culture is put in its broader context, it is plain that it connects with a great deal of relevant Community activity. This

33 Case C–11/95, *Commission* v. *Belgium* [1996] ECR I–4115. But see the Court's careful distinction between action against a broadcaster and (the greater scope for) action against an advertiser drawn in Joined Cases C–34/95, C–35/95 and C–36/95, *Konsummentombudsmannen* v. *De Agostini Forlag AB and TV-Shop I Sverige AB* [1997] ECR I–3843.

34 2nd report on the application of Directive 89/552, 1997 (European Commission, Brussels).

35 Dec.95/563, [1995] OJ L321/25; Dec.95/564, [1995] OJ L321/33.

36 See references at n. 14 *supra*.

37 Reg. 752/93, [1993] OJ L77/24, implementing Reg.3911/92, [1992] OJ L395/1; Dir.93/7, [1993] OJ L74/74.

38 See, for an application of this principle in a particular sector, A. Bartosch, "The Financing of Public Broadcasting and EC State Aid Law" [1999] *ECLR* 197.

breeds an appreciation of the difficulty of imagining forms of closer co-operation which do not fall foul of the prohibition contained in Article 11(1)(b) EC against affecting Community policies, actions or programmes. A final example may be taken from the fruitless attempts to insulate football from the application of the Treaty in the Court's high-profile ruling in *URBSFA* v. *Bosman*.[39] The Court in *Bosman* was quite unprepared to treat submissions based on protection of culture (and, similarly, appeals to subsidiarity) as effective to block the subjection of sport to the rules of Community law once it was satisfied that fundamental Treaty freedoms were imperilled by the restrictive rules imposed by football's governing authorities.[40] The method for reflecting the special interests of sport was through possible justification of its rules against standards recognised by Community law,[41] not by placing sport in a compartment legally immune from the Community system.[42] It is the perception that the Community system has evolved and continues to evolve that demonstrates the ease with which mooted cultural closer co-operation will become (impermissibly) enmeshed in the *acquis communautaire*. This is more than a technical point of interpretation. It is emblematic of the dynamic interdependence of policy areas which has nurtured the spread of the Community legal order over decades.

The process of embedding cultural policy into other aspects of Community policy is no accident. The quest permeates documentation produced during the 1990s, the decade during which cultural policy has taken shape at Community level in the wake of the insertion into the EC Treaty of a Title on Culture by the Maastricht Treaty.[43] A Council Resolution of 20 January 1997 dealt with the integration of cultural aspects into Community actions.[44] It adheres to the instruction in the fourth paragraph of what was Article 128, now Article 151, that the Community shall take cultural aspects into account in its action under other provisions of the Treaty and reflects on experience gained in this regard thus far. The Resolution asserts that "culture forms an integral part of Community action and contributes to the objectives of the Community through

[39] Case C–415/93, [1995] ECR I–4921.

[40] There is a close similarity with submissions designed to shelter education policy from the rule against nationality discrimination which were advanced without success in Case 235/87, *Matteucci* v. *Communauté française of Belgium* [1988] ECR 5589.

[41] See S. Weatherill, "European Football Law" in Academy of European Law (ed.), *Collected Courses of the Academy of European Law* (Deventer: Kluwer, 1999), vii, Book I, 339–82.

[42] Exceptionally, rules of "purely sporting interest" may be treated as non-economic and therefore untouched by Community law even if discriminatory on grounds of nationality; cf. Case 36/74, *Walrave and Koch* v. *UCI* [1974] ECR 1405. This concession seems to extend to the composition of national representative teams, but it is instructive that in *Bosman* the Court was resolute in refusing to accept its relevance to nationality-based rules affecting the composition of club teams. In 1999 the Commission, responding to the Declaration on Sport attached to the Treaty of Amsterdam, has been engaged in shaping the framework within which it proposes to apply EC law to the sports sector. See S. Weatherill, "The Helsinki Report on Sport" (forthcoming).

[43] A search of EUR-lex's directory of Community legislation in force, 16.40 Culture, conducted on 30 July 1999, revealed 23 separate pieces of secondary legislation, of which only one pre-dated 1990. The vast majority is non-binding.

[44] [1997] OJ C36/4.

enhancement of citizenship and personal and human development". It is also stated that "the Community must have careful regard to the impact of other policies on culture", making explicit reference to the single market, including issues connected with free movement, the Community's internal policies, audiovisual and telecommunications policies, and external relations. These concerns are to be tracked in future, initially by the Commission.

E. A Glance at International Economic Law

The interconnections revealed between culture and trade policy constitute only a relatively minor illustration of a wider phenomenon in EC law and, increasingly visibly, in international economic law too. Precisely the same sort of complex mix between trade liberalisation and competing interests in regulatory protection increasingly confronts NAFTA, MERCOSUL and the evolving World Trade Organisation in a broad sweep of areas from environmental protection to consumer protection, human rights to labour standards. On some accounts "trade law proper" should exclude acknowledgement of such issues; on others, such concerns should be inserted directly into the adjudication process where a trade barrier is created by local regulatory choices in order to permit evaluation of competing interests; a different perspective again holds that matters provoking regulatory attention should be the subject of separate transnational agreed regimes (which demands that attention be paid to the interlinkage of trade-related regimes and differently motivated initiatives governing, for example, labour standards). Different governments may hold different preferences in different sectors at different times. The implications of the choices are further finessed by the need to take a stance on the initial rule governing the impulse towards trade integration; are states required to apply only a standard of non-discrimination in their regulatory regimes or, more intrusive, must they justify even rules which apply in a non-discriminatory manner where those rules impede access to their markets by out-of-state traders? In contemplating these issues the EC model offers intriguing, though constitutionally and institutionally distinguishable, analogies for the newer transnational regimes of trade liberalisation. This is a growth area for academic research and its significance in practice is potentially considerable. Of direct relevance to the present paper, the lesson is that the separation of the impact of regulatory initiatives (albeit by most but not all EU Member States) from existing patterns of policy integration pursued by the EC, which is envisaged by the Treaty provisions on closer co-operation, is extremely difficult to sustain. This has direct implications for builders of closer co-operation, instructed by the Treaty to tip-toe around any effect on Community policies. It is a dance that demands remarkable agility.

F. Non-discrimination

Even if space for closer co-operation in matters such as culture or, similarly, education could be imagined in conformity with the Treaty provisions, the necessary element of general access to the benefits created for the enjoyment of all Union citizens, which secures compliance with Article 11(1)(c)'s insistence on absence of discrimination, diminishes the attraction of such arrangements. Why would a group of states choose to incur costs if the benefits accruing cannot be limited to their own nationals? It is a charter for free-riders. There may be circumstances in which the likelihood of free-riding is in practice small, perhaps for reasons of geography or language, but in general the rule of non-discrimination acts as a further deterrent to use of the new arrangements on closer co-operation.[45]

G. The Limited Scope of Community Competence in Culture

A distinct element in appreciating the confined space for imagining forms of closer co-operation in the field of culture arises in relation to the Community's limited powers under the Title on Culture in the EC Treaty. The Community's competence in the field of cultural activity is carefully confined to a supportive role. Article 152 (ex Article 128) EC refers to contributions by the Community to "the flowering of the cultures of the Member States, while respecting their national and regional diversity"; and to Community action "aimed at encouraging co-operation between Member States" and "supporting and supplementing" state action. The adoption of "incentive measures" is envisaged; harmonisation of laws is explicitly excluded. This in turn limits the scope of "closer co-operation" in the cultural field, for Article 11 (ex Article 5a) limits co-operation to the powers conferred on the Community by the Treaty. No more may done by closer co-operators than may be done by the Community as a whole. The only additional point to be made in this context is that the extent to which the Community may use Articles 94, 95 and 308 (ex Articles 100, 100a or 235) in the field of culture—which raises questions of choice of legal base—also impacts on the scope of permissible closer co-operation. This impinges on the still broader question of the current constitutional role of Article 308 (ex Article 235). It may be questioned whether the steady elaboration of specific competences at times of periodic Treaty revision has reinstated a practical edge to the notion of "attributed competences" at the expense of Article 308's role. For law-making affecting culture in particular, whether pursued by way of closer co-operation or as a more orthodox form of Community law binding all the Member States, this would take the form of suspicion that, if envisaged action

[45] There is an echo here of the fact pattern of Case 235/87, n. 40 *supra*, although the Court treated that case as involving discrimination against workers resident in the state concerned.

is not capable of fit within Article 152, it should not be capable of being pursued via Article 308 either. This would suggest the apparently paradoxical conclusion that the conferral of formal competence on the EC in fields such as culture has limited the permissible scope of EC intervention in the field. But curtailment of the reach of Article 308 may indeed be the consequence of the elaborations performed at times of Treaty revision, and may demonstrate the shift in identification of the limits of Community's competence away from political choices made (by unanimity) in Council to a more transparent, sector-specific defined system. This is part of the trend mentioned in section 2 above, whereby the rise in opportunities for the adoption of binding EC legislation without unanimous support among the Member States has stimulated closer attention to methods for fixing the limits of EC competence or, at least, for insulating states from the full effects of rules to which they have not given their consent in Council.

5. IS THERE A FUTURE FOR "CLOSER CO-OPERATION"?

A rigid textual analysis of the relevant Treaty provisions appears to lead to the conclusion that little can be done in the name of "closer co-operation". Fundamentally, the reason for this finding lies in the severe difficulty in separating out areas in which closer co-operation may flourish without spilling over into forbidden areas in which the Community is already active. I have argued elsewhere that in order to make the provisions operational, they should be applied in a softened manner.[46] For example, although it is not permitted of closer co-operation under Article 11 EC that it should "affect" Community policies, this should be taken to involve only a prohibition against any *adverse* effect. This would free space for closer co-operation even where the "hemming in" effect of existing Community activity looms large. Similarly, the insistence against closer co-operation which would restrict trade between Member States should be read subject to a possibility of justification—a "rule of reason" which serves as a general principle of interpretation that softens the impact of Community rules across the whole sweep of Community activity, most prominently Articles 28, 49 and 81, weakening the plain words of a prohibition found in the Treaty. So, for example, closer co-operation which might result in non-discriminatory technical rules concerning, for example, environmental protection or cultural promotion which would impede cross-border trade would not be automatically ruled out. Just as a single state would be permitted to impede trade where able to demonstrate that the regulatory objective in question serves an interest recognised as higher than that of trade integration within the framework of the *Cassis de Dijon* case law,[47] so too such permission should also be extended to a group of states acting under the provisions on closer co-operation.

[46] Weatherill, n. 12 *supra*.
[47] Case 120/78, [1979] ECR 649; see Weatherill and Beaumont, n. 15 *supra*, ch. 17.

So cultural or environmental protection ought to be a permissible focus of closer co-operation even where goods or services originating outwith the territory of the participating Member States suffer obstructions to their market access, provided the closer co-operators demonstrate the strength of the interest pursued by their strategy and, naturally, compliance with the ubiquitous proportionality principle. This infuses life into the provisions on closer co-operation and also connects their application to the general development of the Community system towards recognition of multi-functional regulatory activity on several levels, extending beyond the earlier predominant focus on opening borders to trade.

The possibility of reading the text governing closer co-operation in a softer way than may initially appear apt is supported by normative perspectives that this indeed should be done. Flexibility in general, and closer co-operation in particular, are intimately associated with the prospects for imminent enlargement of the Union into Central and Eastern Europe.[48] The Commission has been careful to insist that potential new members are expected to assume the full obligations of membership, albeit with the assistance of the familiar device of transitional periods within which adaptation to the *acquis communautaire* will be secured according to a timetable of priorities. Of course, such absorption of Community rules is also under way in the applicant states. Nonetheless, although there is no hint that the enlargement of the Community is to occur at the expense of existing "uniformity"[49] in the application of Community law, it is also clear that the influx of new members will make progress in decision-making in common all the more difficult to achieve. It is in this context that closer co-operation could play a role in reconciling pursuit of both deepening and widening. There would be more states and more policy-making—but, inevitably, without all the Member States climbing aboard, at least initially. This pattern seems vital to avoid the process of enlargement being seen to stifle innovation and it affords a strong reason for striving to make operational the closer co-operation system fashioned at Amsterdam.

A further, and perhaps stronger, reason for searching for methods to maximise the opportunities for drawing on the provisions on closer co-operation lies in the damage that would be done were Member States to abandon the new patterns as unworkable and instead to devise quite different, *ad hoc* systems to accommodate their thirst for flexibility within the scope of Union competence. The Amsterdam Treaty does not exclude such novelties, for Article 43(1) TEU is drafted to provide that the provisions on closer co-operation are no more than permissive. But this is perilous. The arrangements for opening borders to the movement of people established by some but not all Member States under the Schengen agreement provide a powerful illustration of the alarming features of intransparency and dearth of effective supervision which attach to systems which accept the need for transnational decision-making but which assume the

[48] For an Austrian collection of relevant essays with a geographically understandable emphasis on enlargement, see Breuss and Griller, n. 11 *supra*.

[49] If this is an accurate depiction of the current situation! See section 2 above.

viability of national-level political and judicial scrutiny of those decisions.[50] Although it is constitutionally comforting that such devices adopted by some but not all Member States are formally required to comply with EC norms in so far as they touch fields within which the EC is competent,[51] the preference to evade the EU system significantly reduces the effectiveness of supervision. It is therefore submitted that concern to minimise recourse to such murky, extra-EU models represents a meritorious objective. Would-be closer co-operators should not be frustrated in their ambition to employ the Amsterdam innovation. This can be secured only by a flexible reading of the criteria that must be complied with by closer co-operators. It is therefore submitted that the gateway criteria for Treaty-based closer co-operation should be applied in a flexible manner in order to encourage their use. It might be noted in conclusion that the institutional context is relevant. The establishment of a control mechanism heavily dependent on consensus among the Member States, embracing an effective veto even by a non-participant over planned closer co-operation, is likely to minimise the likelihood of direct challenge before the European Court to planned closer co-operation. But the future elaboration of a political reading of the nature of the criteria governing closer co-operation cannot obscure the formal possibility of supervision by the Court. This is clear from Article 46 TEU.

The enduring impression is that closer co-operation is associated with an ambiguous, and potentially unstable, dynamic. In this respect it offers a revealing window on the broader debate about flexibility. The Treaty provisions on closer co-operation seem to promise managed and non-exclusionary deepening of collaborative endeavour, tailored to conditions prevailing in specific sectors. They eschew the notion of a rigid "hard core" or a two-speed Europe, within which some states subscribe to the meat of the Union's endeavours while others float loosely around on the periphery. They envisage that the identity of the participating and the non-participating states may vary, depending on the sector in question and depending on the time in question, for states that choose not to join a *bloc* of closer co-operation may nonetheless sign up subsequently. On the other hand, although closer co-operation promises more flexibility within the Union than a pattern of concentric circles, it is not an *à la carte* free-for-all. The conditions that must be satisfied before closer co-operation may proceed are carefully set out in the Treaty, suggesting a foundation of constitutionalised orthodoxy which is protective of the Union's core mission and achievements. The pattern is a great deal more calculated and adaptable than, for example, the desperate eleventh-hour "flexibility" invented to by-pass the impasse over social policy at Maastricht. One aspect only may serve to illustrate this point; the

[50] For a particularly powerful critique see D. Curtin and H. Meijers, "The Principle of Open Government in Schengen and the European Union: Democratic Retrogression?" (1995) 32 *CMLRev.* 391. One of the achievements of the Amsterdam Treaty is to absorb Schengen into the Union Treaty system, albeit not without considerable awkwardness; see Weatherill and Beaumont, n. 15 *supra*, 647–63.

[51] Art. 10 EC. See, e.g. Case 44/84, *Hurd* v. *Jones* [1986] ECR 29.

Social Policy Protocol-plus-Agreement could not be adjusted to allow for the change in government in the United Kingdom in 1997 but rather had to be killed off by a full-blown Treaty amendment agreed at Amsterdam. Closer co-operation, by contrast, offers a system that is much more amenable to periodic adjustment according to political taste. Yet, for all these positive observations about the potential of closer co-operation, the criteria remain extraordinarily restrictive; as if the Member States were sufficiently anxious about the threat of fragmentation that they defined closer co-operation (almost) out of existence. The threshold conditions give the impression of concern to infuse the new provisions with the spirit of the EC's institutional, constitutional and substantive structure and, indeed, to anchor them into EC method, but to exercise a control based on denial that activity taken in their name shall affect the *acquis communautaire*. The extended treatment provided above of the direct and indirect shaping of cultural policy in the EC legal order demonstrates that a literal reading of the pre-conditions for closer co-operation virtually strips them of operational utility, because of the unavoidable patterns of spillover between policies which have characterised the long-term evolution of the EC system.

6. CONCLUSION

On the one hand, the message seems to be that the provisions on closer co-operation represent an attempt to supply a constitutional framework for making sense of the wider phenomenon of "flexibility", which, as an attempt to describe a system beyond uniformity, has deteriorated into little more than a vague slogan. On the other hand, perhaps the very narrowness of the Treaty provisions informs us that flexibility is to be disallowed within a constitutional legal order. However, I doubt that such a self-defeating interpretation is appropriate. For reasons articulated in section 5 above, I feel that the provisions on closer co-operation should be read generously to the would-be participants. Techniques for achieving this result are sketched in section 5. In part, this is desirable in order to bring such arrangements under the EC's institutional and constitutional umbrella, rather than leaving them in some extra-EU netherworld. But also it is encouraging to aspire to the use of closer co-operation as an element which reflects a multi-level appreciation of the dynamic potential inherent in transcending bi-polar arguments about either state action or Community action. Closer co-operation stands in between the two extremes. In this sense it operates in a more subtle and, potentially, adaptable way than the subsidiarity principle in attempting to fix the level at which action should be taken in a geographically and functionally expanding Union. It might be noted that such notions are potentially particularly appealing in relation to culture, which has shapes far more varied than "Scottish", "British", "Italian" or "European". Admittedly that perspective in turn leads to concern about intransparency; and to questions whether the construction of a *demos* at European level, not to replace but to supplement national or local *demoi*, may be fatally undermined by the construction of new *blocs* of shifting size lying somewhere between state and European Union. In that sense, flexibility is associated with questions of legitimacy, but it may damage the quest for legitimacy. However, despite that real anxiety, I would place flexibility, at least packaged in the form of closer co-operation, alongside opt-outs, minimum harmonisation and other devices designed to accommodate the tensions in the EU system caused by geographical and functional expansion. "Uniformity" is overstated both as a description of past practice and as a normative underpinning of future planning. Flexibility is inevitable, but, consistent with perceptions that integration in Europe is a process rather than a journey towards a fixed end, its precise contours are not yet, and perhaps never will be, clearly articulated.

12

Flexibility, "Proceduralization", and Environmental Governance in the EU

JOANNE SCOTT*

1. INTRODUCTION

THIS CHAPTER takes the form of a case study in flexibility, and examines shifting patterns of environmental governance in the EU. It focuses in particular upon what may be called the "flexibility in implementation" approach, and exemplifies this model by reference to the Directive on Integrated Pollution Prevention and Control (IPPC).[1] The chapter argues that while the flexibility in implementation model is characterised by an endorsement of substantive differentiation in environmental standards in the EU, it is nonetheless (relatively) prescriptive in establishing *procedures* according to which Member State implementation is to be achieved. This chapter also examines the nature of these procedural constraints, relating for example to public participation and information exchange, and does so against the backdrop of recent theoretical debates about the changing nature and premises of environmental regulation, and the associated demise of rigid "command and control" style approaches. Viewed from any one of a number of theoretical perspectives—be it "responsive regulation", systems theory or deliberative politics—the Community's (procedurally constrained) flexibility in implementation model emerges as having much to commend it. It nonetheless raises important practical, legal and normative questions. Among these is the issue of the appropriateness, from a constitutional perspective, of Community intervention in the "procedural lives" of the Member States.

It will be apparent that the concept of flexibility used here is concerned with the nature and intensity of Member State discretion in the implementation of Community law, specifically directives. It is not concerned with "closer co-operation" in the Amsterdam sense, or even with "opt-ins", "opt-outs", derogations or exceptions. It seeks rather to illustrate that such are the regulatory

* I would like to thank Kenneth Armstrong, Graínne de Búrca, Marise Cremona, Carole Lyons, Donald McGillivray, Wade Mansell, and the other Florence workshop participants for their comments and suggestions. The usual disclaimers apply.

[1] Council Dir. 96/61/EC [1996] OJ L257/26.

techniques increasingly deployed by the Community in the environmental sphere, that there is considerable scope for "differentiation" in Member State implementation responses. Flexibility thus refers to the substantive choices which Member States make in implementing directives. However, alongside the issue of substantive flexibility, this chapter is also concerned with the nature and intensity of Community law constraints on the manner in which implementation decisions are arrived at. It is thus also concerned with the issue of procedural flexibility; flexibility in terms of the choice of procedures instituted by Member States for the implementation of Community law.

The chapter begins with a brief account of the IPPC Directive, focussing in particular upon the concept of Best Available Techniques which underpins it. This first section seeks, very briefly, to illustrate the nature and scope of Member State substantive discretion in the implementation of the Directive. The second part of the chapter examines the flexibility in implementation model against the backdrop of three recent important contributions to the environmental governance debate. It will be seen that the values which underpin these theoretical contributions also resonate in the context of the IPPC. The third part of the chapter examines the procedurally constrained flexibility in implementation model from the perspective of the Community law principles of subsidiarity and proportionality. Contrasting instrumental and dignitarian approaches to "proceduralisation", this considers the rationale for, and legitimacy of, Community-level constraints on Member States implementation arrangements and procedures.

2. THE IPPC DIRECTIVE: SUBSTANTIVE FLEXIBILITY IN IMPLEMENTATION

The IPPC Directive seeks to control pollution arising from the industrial activities listed in Annex 1 of the Directive, laying down measures designed to prevent or, where this is not practicable, to reduce emissions to air, water and land.[2] It establishes a number of broadly defined general principles to be taken into account pursuant to the industrial licensing system mandated by the Directive.[3] Operating permits granted to the relevant industrial installations are to include emission limit values (or equivalent parameters or technical measures) for pollutants—in particular those listed in Annex III—likely to be emitted from the installation concerned in significant quantities.[4] These emission limits (performance standards[5]) or their equivalent are to be based upon the principle of Best

[2] Council Dir. 96/61/EC [1996] OJ L257/26 Art. 1.

[3] N. 1 *supra*, Arts. 3 and 4.

[4] N. 1 *supra*, Art. 9(3).

[5] I am drawing here on A. Ogus, *Regulation: Legal Form and Economic Theory* (Oxford: OUP, 1994) who distinguishes between different kinds of "command and control" instruments for environmental protection; from the most prescriptive (specification standards) which mandate the type of technology to be used, to the least prescriptive (target standards) which regulate ambient environmental quality e.g. the concentration of a given pollutant in the environment. "Performance"

Available Techniques (BAT), without prescribing the use of any technique or specific technology, but taking into account (*inter alia*) the technical characteristics of the installation concerned, its geographic location and local environmental conditions.[6] This concept of BAT represents the core of Member State obligations under the IPPC Directive. It provides a framework within which they are to exercise their regulatory discretion, and constitutes the principal, though by no means the exclusive, source of substantive flexibility in the implementation of the directive.

The concept of BAT is profoundly open-ended and is characterised by ambiguity and uncertainty. It is predicated upon recourse to a wide range of economic, technical and technological considerations, as well as upon cost-benefit and (practical) feasibility concerns.[7] Not only are such considerations themselves barely defined, but the status and role of the various factors, and the relationship between them, is far from clear. Thus, for example, while "costs and advantages" are to be taken "into consideration" in assessing the "availability" of the relevant industrial techniques,[8] the Directive does not seek to constrain Member States in their measurement and/or assessment of the relevant costs and benefits, or establish a threshold according to which "excessive" is to be defined in the cost/benefit stakes. Similarly, and equally nebulously, Annex IV lays down a range of factors to be taken "into account generally or in specific cases" in defining BAT, "bearing in mind the likely costs and benefits of a measure and the principles of precaution and prevention". Methodologically open-ended, and normatively weak, the concept of BAT tactfully blends a range of regulatory approaches and priorities, generating a hybrid form apparently acceptable to all by virtue of its exaggerated flexibility.

The substantive flexibility which inheres in the concept of BAT, and hence the indeterminacy of the performance standards to be derived therefrom, highlights the salience of the implementation phase in the environmental governance equation in the EU, and the importance of the siting of political authority for

standards (emission standards) lie in between these two in that they place a cap on the quantity of pollution which may be emitted but do not prescribe the use of any specific technology to achieve this result. Such standards may focus on a particular plant, or may establish, e.g., a country-wide emissions limit. BAT, as discussed here represents a technology (specification) standards. However, it takes the form of a so-called "benefits-based" technology standard, in that it injects cost-benefit considerations into the choice of appropriate technology. Thus, although specification standards are normally viewed as the most prescriptive form of command and control instrument, in the case of benefits-based specification standards their prescriptiveness is reduced, and these tend to be the form of command and control regulation preferred by efficiency-oriented economists. For a fuller discussion of this subject see J. Scott, *EC Environmental Law* (Harlow, Longman, 1998) ch. 2.

[6] N. 1 *supra*, Art. 9(4).

[7] N. 1 *supra*, Art. 2(11) and Annex IV. The IPPC Dir. thus represents a mélange of two approaches generally conceived (in the United States especially) as alternatives. Feasibility is defined in the light of a range of considerations, including cost-benefit concerns. For an interesting discussion of these two approaches, and for a suggestion of how they might be usefully combined (though in a manner which is different from the IPPC approach) see D.A. Farber, *Eco-Pragmatism* (Chicago, Ill.: Chicago University Press, 1999).

[8] N. 1 *supra*, Art. 2(11).

implementation. Implementation clearly involves the exercise of substantial discretion and, in the case of BAT, a choice between competing and contested environmental methodologies and assessment techniques. Hence one of the most crucial questions arising is who is to put flesh on the bare BAT bones. This is an issue addressed more closely in the next section. Suffice it for now to note that the IPPC Directive represents a departure from a committee- (comitology-) based approach to implementation, in favour of Member State flexibility. It equally eschews the independent agency model, notwithstanding a role for the European IPPC Bureau, in favour of broad Member State autonomy in implementation. It exemplifies Community law at its least substantively prescriptive, and the potentially open-ended nature of Community level "harmonization". As an "alternative" model of environmental governance in the EU, it cries out for normative engagement, throwing up a variety of conceptual challenges, and yielding uncertain results.[9]

3. NEW APPROACHES TO ENVIRONMENTAL GOVERNANCE AND THE IPPC DIRECTIVE

Recent years have seen the emergence of a multitude of proposals for achieving more effective forms of environmental governance. Rooted in a variety of theoretical traditions, and exhibiting important differences, as well as striking similarities, these purport to identify strategies for improved environmental decision-making under conditions of dramatic and endemic scientific and social uncertainty.

Among the most interesting of recent contributions, due not least to its ready accessibility, is that of Daniel Farber.[10] In seeking to articulate what he describes as BART (best available regulatory techniques) Farber focuses not only upon the criteria to be applied by the relevant regulatory authorities but also, crucially for our purposes, upon the manner in which decision-making is structured, both institutionally and procedurally. As far as the former is concerned he supports the application of a "hybrid" feasibility and cost benefit test. Thus, briefly, environmental risks should be reduced to the extent feasible subject to considerations of gross (economic) disproportionality. As for the latter (decision-making structures), Farber emphasises a number of considerations and values. Most

[9] For a cross-section of competing perspectives and evaluations of comitology, useful by way of background in assessing this "alternative" approach, see C. Joerges, and E. Vos (eds.), *European Committees: Social Regulation, Law and Politics* (Oxford: Hart Publishing, 1999), and especially the divergent contributions by C. Joerges (at 311–38) and J.H.H. Weiler (at 339–50). For an illustration of the discretion enjoyed by Member States, see the DETR's statement that consideration is being given to the interrelationship between the climate change levy agreements and IPPC, and in particular to whether such agreements could constitute compliance with Art. 3(d) which requires that installations be operated in such a way that energy is used efficiently. Thus, such sites would be exempt except in relation to basic energy management measures. I am grateful to Keith Brogan for this point.

[10] N. 7 *supra*.

important perhaps is his commitment to flexible environmental regulation, in the sense of regulation which is responsive and dynamic rather than static, and which is capable of learning and adapting on the basis of new information and experience. In a book which is based throughout on practical examples, and upon an impressive analysis of the scientific and economic premises of environmental protection decisions, his conclusion that "one of the main lessons we should learn from the last three decades is the centrality of learning to the enterprise of environmental protection" deserves to be taken seriously.[11]

Farber seeks to identify a number of features associated with responsive and dynamic environmental regulation, albeit that he does so only schematically. He focuses in particular upon the value of (supervised) decentralisation of environmental decision-making within a federal state, in view of the tendency of federal regulation to be "insensitive to differences in technological and economic constraints and to variations in environmental problems",[12] as well as insufficiently "nimble" in its capacity to respond and adapt. His preference for decentralisation speaks also to his conception of federal states as laboratories engaging in regulatory experimentation, and hence as constitutive of, as well as responsive to, new environmental knowledge. In this respect Farber stresses the importance of mutual learning and information exchange between different levels and spheres of government. More generally, Farber's preoccupation with the need to generate new information and to accumulate experience leads him to lay stress upon mechanisms self-consciously designed to foster such learning, such as programme monitoring, reporting and evaluation, and database design and development. As Kenneth Armstrong observed in his comments on this chapter: "this is an interesting new take on 'regulatory competition'—pluralism as a means of improving knowledge, rather than as a more Darwinian competition of the fittest".

Farber is not oblivious to the dangers associated with decentralisation, and hence proposes that this take shape against a backdrop of "clear, enforceable [Federal] performance standards . . . to ensure that delegation does not turn into deregulation".[13] Also important in this respect is his (little explored and briefly stated) emphasis upon participation ("heavy" involvement) by environmental groups and community representatives in order to "keep the 'deals' honest and to ensure enforcement".[14] Tied to this no doubt is his concern with procedural regulation, information disclosure, public hearings etc., as a means of preventing abuse of environmental authority, be it by a federal agency or local government body.

Farber is by no means alone in the values to which he subscribes. Indeed there are those who would claim that these values already find concrete expression in

[11] *Ibid.*, 179.

[12] *Ibid.*, 181.

[13] *Ibid.*, 183. Elsewhere Farber talks of Federal environmental "goals" (and elsewhere again a "congressionally mandated environmental baseline") thus suggesting a preference for quality as opposed to performance standards at federal level.

[14] *Ibid.*

recent environmental practice in the United States, and beyond. Particularly interesting in this respect is the recent work of Fung, Karkkainen and Sabel.[15] Representing an effective blend of the empirical and the normative, this seeks to lead us in the direction of a new "information-based model of environmental regulation". They begin with the following observation:

> The United States is in the midst of a pervasive and fundamental reorientation of environmental regulation, as improbable as it is un-remarked. The practical core of this alternative regime is an exchange in which units—such as firms or institutions corresponding to ecosystems, as well as their respective subunits—are granted discretion to achieve environmental performance targets in return for detailed reports on and proposals to improve current practices. This combination of local experimentation and central pooling of experience produces an informative disequilibrium that forces continuous improvements in both regulatory rules and environmental performance while heightening the accountability of the actors to each other and the larger public. In this rolling-rule regime, the regulator uses reports on proposals and outcomes to periodically reformulate minimum allowable performance standards, desirable targets, and migration paths from the former to the latter. In pursuing these targets as they see best, local actors provide the information necessary to progressively revise the goals, and receive back information on the performance of others that guides further experimentation.[16]

Like Daniel Farber, the authors of this piece place emphasis upon the value of (conditional) decentralisation (subject to certain guidelines); institutional learning through information exchange and continuous experimentation at both local and national level; the flexibility and revisibility of standards set, both at the centre and within constituent localities; and accountability through access to information, transparent "benchmarking", and ("deep") citizen participation. Unlike Farber's work, however, this new approach is accompanied by a particular brand of theoretical baggage; a brand to which Charles Sabel at least has been long committed.[17] What is being proposed is the emergence of a "directly deliberative form of participatory democracy" with the stress about the deliberative, in the sense of the "directly deliberative polyarchy" outlined in Sabel's earlier work.[18] The success of this new information based regime, or so the authors claim, lies in the practical deliberation which it encourages between "initially antagonistic parties"; a "problem solving process [involving] disciplined consideration of alternatives" and leading "protagonists to the discovery

[15] A. Fung, B. Karkkainen and C. Sabel, *After Backyard Environmentalism: Towards a New Model of Information-Based Environmental Regulation*. This can be found on Charles Sabel's homepage at: http://www.law.columbia.edu/~cfs11/index.html.

[16] A. Fung, B. Karkkainen and C. Sabel, *After Backyard Environmentalism: Towards a New Model of Information-Based Environmental Regulation*, 1.

[17] See generally his papers on his website (n. 15 *supra*).

[18] See "Directly-Deliberative Polyarchy" (with Josuha Cohen). Here the authors observe that "[i]deally, then, directly-deliberative polyarchy combines the advantages of local learning and self-government with the advantages (and discipline) of wider social learning and heightened political accountability that result when the outcomes of many concurrent experiments are pooled to permit public scrutiny of the effectiveness of strategies and leaders": at 1.

of unanticipated solutions provisionally acceptable to all".[19] The notion of deliberation is predicated upon a commitment to dialogic reason. Participants engage with alternative perspectives on the basis of competing arguments, and with a willingness to revise preferences in the result of justifications proffered. A deliberative polity is one which is debate-based as opposed to (pluralistically) bargain-based, and in which reason, as well as expert and popular participation, enhances the legitimacy and the effectiveness of regulatory outcomes.

It might appear as though the "new approaches to environmental governance" debate is an exclusively (North) American phenomenon, albeit that Sabel's work in particular draws upon European traditions in political theory (especially Habermas). In so far as there is a European equivalent, transcending the stale "command and control" v. "economic instruments" dichotomy, this has been largely inspired by insights from systems theory. Most notable in this respect, in the environmental sphere, is the contribution of Karl-Heinz Ladeur (also a contributor to this volume), and his conception of "co-operative learning in transnational networks".[20] Ladeur, like Farber and Sabel *et al.*, focuses upon the institutional dimension of environmental decision-making, positing the need for heterarchically organised public/private co-operative networks dedicated to problem solving under conditions of complexity and uncertainty. Laying emphasis upon the "methodological and procedural aspects of decision-making",[21] he, like his US counterparts, favours procedurally structured flexibility, with a view to opening up new and innovative avenues for regulation, and for facilitating reflexivity through monitoring, assessment and co-operation, including mutual observation, between networks. Flexibility in implementation should, according to Ladeur, be accompanied by "a general interpretative topos into the legal systems [of the Member States] imposing consideration of possible harms inflicted on other Member States".[22] Here, as elsewhere, he advocates a revised and expanded role for the European Environment Agency; a central authority able to facilitate and mediate co-operation and mutual learning.

The above summaries cannot do justice to the richness of the literature under discussion; especially to the theoretical underpinnings upon which it rests. Nonetheless, they serve to reveal the centrality of certain values in the quest for more effective environmental governance. Five values, in particular, may be identified as central and (more or less) common to the three contributions under discussion; *flexibility* facilitating differentiated responses to environmental problems; *decentralisation* of responsibility for environmental problem solving within a framework of multi-level governance; public/private partnerships implying intense *participation* for non-governmental actors, including industrial and environmental associations and citizen groups; *reflexivity* pointing to

[19] N. 15 *supra*, 8.

[20] "Towards a Legal Concept of the Network in European Standard-Setting" in Joerges and Vos, n. 9 *supra*, 169.

[21] *Ibid.*, at 165.

[22] *Ibid.*, at 168.

the importance of continuous learning and adjustment of solutions, at all levels, in the light of new information and experience; and *deliberation* between different groups and levels and spheres of government, implying a more consensual approach to decision-making, albeit against a backdrop of the contestability of the relevant knowledge base.

These five values, taken together, offer a new perspective on environmental governance according to which initiatives within the EU may be approached and assessed. They stand in contrast to the values more commonly brought to bear upon analyses of EU law, which centre upon its unique (relative to other transnational systems of law) capacity to compel obedience, in view of its constitutional commitment to supremacy and effective enforcement. It is in the light of these values that this chapter will now turn once again to the IPPC Directive.

A. Flexibility

The substantive flexibility which inheres in the IPPC Directive was adumbrated above by reference to the fluidity of the concept of BAT. Nonetheless the framework constituted by BAT is not the only substantive constraint attaching to Member States in their exercise of implementation choices. As advocated to varying degrees by the commentators discussed above, IPPC conceives a continuing role for substantive standards introduced at EU level. In this sense the IPPC Directive, like the new approaches described above, is parasitic upon old ideas, and more specifically upon traditional command and control regulatory instruments. Target standards in particular have an important role to play, Article 10 providing quite simply that:

> Where an environmental quality standard requires stricter conditions than those achievable by the use of best available techniques, additional measures will in particular be required in the permit, without prejudice to other measures which might be taken to comply with environmental quality standards.[23]

As will be seen below, this preference for target standards does not imply that the IPPC Directive fails to address one of the most important shortcomings associated with these; namely the free rider problem arising as a result of the exportation of polluting emissions.

Less straightforward, though important, is the role of Community-level performance (emission) standards in the context of the IPPC Directive. Article 18(1) reminds us that the Community's conversion to flexibility, against a backdrop of bottom-line quality standards, is equivocal. This provides for the adoption of Community-level emission limit values (performance standards), within the

[23] N. 1 *supra*. It is less certain to what extent these target standards represent the baseline in the sense that Member States are entitled to depart from BAT where this is not necessary to achieve compliance with these standards. This is envisaged in the accompanying memorandum, but not explicitly sanctioned by the Dir., although the ability (under Art. 9) to take local environmental conditions into consideration in applying BAT could be construed in this way.

parameters of the Directive, where the need for Community action has been identified. According to the explanatory memorandum, there "may" be no need for such action where broadly comparable limits are set across the Community, and where the effect on competitiveness (of such differences as do emerge) is minimal. "Where, however, standards are very different, so affecting competitiveness, future proposals under the framework of this Directive are much more likely in order to ensure the effective functioning of the internal market".[24] The Community thus retains an ongoing capacity to introduce performance standards, and any decision to do so will be contingent upon Member State behaviour in implementing the Directive, and upon the information which the Member States provide. This not only is indicative of the continuing legacy of the "harmonization of conditions of competition" rationale which underpinned Community environmental initiatives for so long, but may also be represented as a form or variant of "escalation" as conceived by the "responsive regulation" school. According to this, regulation should pursue the least burdensome approach (starting in all probability with self-regulation) but be underpinned by a willingness to escalate regulatory intervention according to a "pyramid of interventionism" in the event that the privilege of self-regulation is exploited leading to "socially suboptimal compliance with regulatory goals".[25] The problem here lies not in the principle, but in the nature of the definition of suboptimal, having regard to the quest for competitive equilibrium in the internal market. Notwithstanding criticism, notably from a law and economics perspective, the Community retains an attachment to a conception of "fair" competition predicated upon a degree of regulatory harmonisation.[26] It should be further noted in this respect that, even in the absence of new Community emissions standards, the IPPC Directive will operate against the backdrop of existing target and performance[27] standards laid down in the directives listed in Annex II, and in other Community legislation. Thus, in the end, the new flexible approach represented by the IPPC Directive will exist alongside, rather than instead of, other forms of regulatory intervention.[28]

B. Decentralisation

In so far as the IPPC Directive rests upon Member State flexibility in implementation, it implies a decentralisation of responsibility for environmental decision-making. The nature of the decentralisation which it promotes will depend in

24 COM(95)88 final, 12.

25 I. Ayers and J. Braithwaite, *Responsive Regulation: Transcending the Deregulation Debate* (Oxford: OUP, 1992), 38.

26 For a representative critique of "federal" emission standards (and for that matter quality standards) from a law and economics perspective see R. Revesz "Federalism and Environmental Regulation" [1999] *Yearbook of European Environmental Law* (Oxford: OUP, forthcoming).

27 See n. 5 *supra*.

28 Subject, however, to the transitional provisions in Art. 20 and the timetable laid down for the repeal of certain directives.

part upon the level of government at which BAT is to be articulated, be it national, regional or local. This issue will have important implications for the degree of differentiation of standards which will be tolerated in the implementation of the Directive, and hence the decentralisation theme is closely tied to that of flexibility discussed above. The extent to which Member States enjoy flexibility in identifying the governmental authority with responsibility for defining BAT will be crucially important in clarifying the limits to flexibility and differentiation within the framework of the IPPC Directive.

Responsibility for determining the outcome of permit applications, and for attaching conditions to permits granted, lies with the "competent authority or authorities" designated by the relevant Member State. It is these authorities which are to be responsible for carrying out the obligations arising from this Directive.[29] Member States enjoy considerable autonomy in establishing or identifying such authorities, and attempts to restrict that autonomy have conspicuously failed.[30] It is thus conceivable, and in practice inevitable, that such authorities will be situated at a variety of different levels of government, in the different Member States. In some cases regional and local bodies will be endowed with responsibility in this respect. Thus, and this is the crucial question in clarifying the nature of the decentralisation achieved by the Directive, if it is assumed that it is for these authorities to bring their own conception of BAT to bear, then it is equally fair to assume that within any one Member State, a variety of conceptions of BAT will emerge for any given industrial sector. This would then imply the emergence of different standards for different undertakings within a given Member State, and consequently differentiation within as well as between states.

The Directive is not very helpful in this respect. It provides, in defining the notion of "available" techniques, that technical and economic viability (taking into consideration *inter alia* the costs and advantages) are to be assessed according to the average rather than the individual operator in the relevant industrial sector.[31] But it does not identify the parameters of the pool according to which the average is to be assessed. If we assume a coincidence between the scale of the pool and the jurisdiction of the competent authority, then the scale of the pool will vary according to the level of government at which the authority is situated, and different averages in terms of cost/benefit balancing and overall economic

[29] N. 1 *supra*, Art. 2(8).

[30] See, e.g., Cases 372–374/85 *Ministère Public* v. *Oscar Traen & Others* [1987] ECR 2141, esp. para. 17, and generally J. Jans, *EC Environmental Law* (London, Kluwer, 1995) 119–41. See, however, e.g., Art. 18 EMAS (Council Regulation 1836/93 [1993] OJ L168/1), where the Member State is charged with ensuring that the composition of the competent bodies is such as to guarantee their independence and neutrality. Note that the European Court's judgments have started to reflect the flexibility in implementation paradigm. In Case C–293/97 (*Standley* v. *Metson*) [1999] ECR I–2605 the Court observed that the Nitrates Directive may be applied by Member States in different ways, this not being incompatible with the nature of it, given that it does not seek to harmonise national laws but to protect the environment.

[31] N. 1 *supra*, Art. 2(11) referring to techniques developed on a scale which allows implementation in the relevant industrial sector.

viability will result in different conceptions of BAT and, consequently, in the imposition of different emissions standards in different localities within a single Member State. To put it differently, if the identity of the competent authority is crucial in defining the reference point according to which the "average" is to be determined in the context of assessing the availability of techniques, then Member State flexibility in the application of the BAT will be enhanced by virtue of Member State flexibility in conferring legal and constitutional identity upon that authority. According to this scenario, differential standards may reflect not only objective geographic and environmental differences between localities (such as may certainly be taken into account in applying rather than defining BAT[32]) as well as differences in the scale of the relevant undertakings, but also the relative economic strengths or weaknesses of particular plants making up only part of the relevant industrial sector within that Member State, or the particular cost/benefit constellation which characterises a region or a locality, rather than the Member State as a whole.

In assessing the accuracy in law of the above scenario implying a coincidence between level of implementing authority and BAT, it is important to note the existence of a number of factors which militate against it. First, Article 11 of the Directive provides that the competent authority follow, or be informed of, developments in BAT, thus connoting a passive and reactive, rather than proactive and creative, role for them. Secondly, and again by no means conclusively, the explanatory memorandum accompanying the revised IPPC proposal hints at a conception of BAT operating at national, rather than sub-national, level. Thus, for example, it provides that "it is proposed that in the first instance it will be for each *Member State* to require emission limit values based on BAT for the industrial sectors coming under the provisions of the Directive"—thus linking industrial sector and the national level—and that "[t]he initial standards set at *Member State* level should . . . be elaborated with a common [BAT derived] framework".[33] This might be taken to imply that the "average" according to which BAT is to be ascertained is a national one, and that (national) BAT-derived emissions standards may be adjusted in the light of the factors laid down in Article 9 (including location and environmental conditions) but not in view of economic viability or cost/benefit concerns operating at plant, local or regional level. While considerations of responsiveness, experimentation and regulatory adaptability might tend to militate against a unitary Member State conception of BAT, as indeed would the Community's regional cohesion objective, such a conclusion would mitigate the criticism most commonly levelled against benefits-based performance standards such as BAT; namely the danger that more efficient firms will be required to pay a high regulatory price for their earlier economic successes. Though the issue of the level at which BAT is to be conceived remains uncertain in law, and normatively contested, it serves to

[32] N. 1 *supra*, Art. 10(4).
[33] N. 24 *supra*, 4 and 5 (emphasis added).

remind us that the scope and implications of flexibility will depend upon the nature of those factors accepted as legitimately grounding difference, and hence upon a close reading of the Directive at hand. It is by no means beyond doubt that considerations justifying differentiation between Member States will, or ought to, also serve to rationalise differentiation within states.

C. Participation

If the theoretical contributions outlined above were vague as to how, and by virtue of what mechanisms, intensive public participation in environmental decision-making is to be achieved, the IPPC Directive is no less so. It is apparent that this Directive subjects Member State flexibility in implementation to a number of important procedural constraints. In this sense the model which emerges takes the form of procedurally constrained flexibility in implementation. One of the most important procedural constraints concerns public participation in the licensing process. The Directive lays down mandatory requirements in this respect, whilst defining them only in the broadest of terms. Thus, without prejudice to the exceptions laid down in the Access to Environmental Information Directive,[34] applications for permits are to be made available to the public for an appropriate period of time, in order to enable it to comment upon them before a licensing decision is reached. Any decision adopted, as well as subsequent updates, shall be made available to the public, as will an inventory of principal emissions and the sources responsible for these on a three-yearly basis.[35] This obligation to consult will, in the circumstances laid down in Article 17(1), also connote an obligation to consult the public of other Member States on the same basis.[36] Public participation is to be further facilitated through a variety of transparency constraints. Thus, for example, applications for permits are to include a non-technical summary,[37] and the Commission is to publish the results of exchanges of information between Member States and the industries concerned.[38]

D. Reflexivity

The Directive's interest in promoting reflexivity in environmental decision-making is apparent from a number of provisions of the Directive. First and foremost is the obligation incumbent upon operators of industrial installations to include a wide range of information in their permit application, thus seeking to

[34] Council Dir. 90/313 [1990] OJ L158/56.
[35] N. 1 *supra*, Art. 15.
[36] N. 1 *supra*, Art. 17(2).
[37] N. 1 *supra*, Art. 6(1).
[38] N. 1 *supra*, Art. 16(2).

expand the knowledge base according to which governmental decisions are adopted.[39] Also important in this respect is the plethora of information-exchange mechanisms established,[40] the emphasis upon monitoring and the dissemination of the results thereof,[41] and the necessity of periodically revisiting permitting decisions adopted, even in the absence of substantial changes to the plants concerned.[42] Significant too are the transboundary co-operation requirements laid down,[43] and the obligation to include in the permit "provisions on the minimization of long-distance or transboundary pollution".[44] Article 16(3) in particular is self-conscious in its commitment to reflexivity. This imposes an obligation on the Commission to publish reports on the implementation of the Directive, and on its effectiveness compared with other Community environmental instruments. In this sense the mechanisms are in place to facilitate the kind of mutual and continuous learning envisaged in the experimental approaches discussed above. The IPPC model appears to be conceived as a trial, whose future will depend upon the results of the prescribed effectiveness analyses.

E. Deliberation

The value of deliberation may be thought to underpin many of the procedural devices outlined above, and especially those relating to public consultation and transboundary co-operation. Discussion here will, however, focus upon one dimension of the deliberation phenomenon, namely the role and functioning of the European IPPC Bureau (EIPPCB) based in Seville, the technical arm of the International Exchange Forum. The EIPPCB collects information and drafts BAT reference documents for the Commission to publish as a means of disseminating information to the permitting authorities, industry and other interested parties.[45] These BAT reference documents (known as BREFs) are non-mandatory documents to be used by national authorities in defining BAT. They are drawn up within the framework of Technical Working Groups (TWGs), the composition of each of which is listed on the EIPPCB website.[46] What is striking about these TWGs, and what distinguishes them most starkly from their comitology implementation counterparts, is the breadth of the membership which they ought, in principle, to encompass according to official literature of the Bureau. Alongside representatives of the Member States and the Commission, it is stated that delegates from industry and civil society in the form of

[39] N. 1 *supra*, Art. 6.

[40] N. 1 *supra*, Art. 11, 16(1) and 16(2) and, in the context of transboundary co-operation, Art. 17(1).

[41] N. 1 *supra*, Arts. 14 and 15(2) and (3).

[42] N. 1 *supra*, Arts. 12 and 13.

[43] N. 1 *supra*, Art. 17.

[44] N. 1 *supra*, Art. 9(4).

[45] See the EIPPCB website at: http://eippcb.jrc.es/.

[46] *Ibid.*

environmental associations are to sit. Decisions are, where possible, adopted by consensus. Multi-level and multi-actor in nature, these groups, in principle, transcend the technocratic elitism of Commission implementation committees, and operate on a basis which is supposed to be more transparent. The concept of deliberation is one which is hard to define, and yet harder to verify empirically. Moreover, in terms of their composition the TWGs may be as easily conceived in terms of pluralist bargaining as in terms of deliberative reason. Nonetheless, the diversity of the voices which they are intended to encompass is such as to render them a better candidate for deliberative democracy than their comitology cousins on whose behalf such ambitious claims have recently been made.[47]

4. PROCEDURAL CONSTRAINTS ON MEMBER STATE IMPLEMENTATION: RATIONALE AND LEGITIMACY

Thus far this chapter has explored the theme of Member State flexibility in the implementation of EC environmental law. It has exemplified the issues arising by way of a case study approach, focussing upon the important IPPC Directive. The previous section examined the nature and (uncertain) scope of Member State flexibility, as well as the values upon which this approach might be thought to rest. On the basis of this analysis it was observed that the IPPC Directive gives rise to a model of environmental governance which is characterised by "procedurally constrained flexibility in implementation". A number of procedural constraints were identified including public participation, transboundary consultation, information exchange, and the obligation periodically to revisit decisions adopted. The importance of this procedural dimension was highlighted by reference to recent theoretical contributions to the environmental governance debate. According to these, flexibility and decentralisation in environmental governance need not be synonymous with deregulation and declining environmental quality. Such values need not represent a failure of (supranational) governance but may, when coupled with appropriate procedural innovations, be indicative of a new (improved) approach, capable of transcending the shortcomings associated with more traditional command-and-control techniques.

The observations in the previous section were not intended as an apology for this new approach. As noted there, the benefits which it will yield remain uncertain, and many questions remain, relating not least to the functioning of the EIPPCB and role of the reference documents which emerge. The point, quite simply, was to observe that flexibility, when combined with a range of additional (procedural) values, may be conceived as a regulatory virtue rather than as a threat.

[47] See Joerges and Vos, n. 9 *supra*. I am tentative in putting forth these claims, in part because of the absence of empirical evidence to support or undermine even such tentative claims. In addition, looking at the membership lists on the website, it is immediately striking that industry representatives in practice dominate to a very great degree indeed.

But, it should be emphasised again, that it is the accompanying "proceduralisation" of Community environmental law—the very fact of Community intervention in the "procedural lives" of the Member States—which is conceived as capable of imbuing flexibility with its creative potential, as a means of stimulating better environmental governance.

It is upon this procedural dimension that this section will focus. It will address the constitutional context and constraints within which this takes shape in the EU, having regard in particular to the Community law principles of subsidiarity and proportionality. This discussion is underpinned by one certainty. Process-based accounts of law are currently very much in vogue, reflecting the radical value pluralism which characterises modern (transnational) society, as well as their (sometimes) capacity to legitimate existing (non-majoritarian) institutional structures and practices. Nonetheless, their wide appeal notwithstanding, such accounts cannot be regarded as somehow politically neutral or value free. The way in which citizen participation in public life is organised will reflect deeply rooted conceptions of the relationship between the individual, community and state. A commitment to the deliberative ideal implies a belief in rational argumentation which will result in the silencing of certain voices; the "mad", the "fanatic", or the merely inarticulate. The idea of process without substance may be convenient, but for all that it remains an illusion.[48] It is with this in mind that the task of assessing the basis and appropriateness of Community procedural regulation should be approached.

Turning now to the rationale for Community procedural intervention, three (sometimes overlapping) justifications will be proposed, and some of the issues which they raise explored. Broadly these may be described as follows.

A. Substitution Approach

The most obvious justification for Community regulation of Member State implementation procedures takes the form of a substitution-style argument. Put simply, this is predicated upon the claim that regulation of implementation procedures operates to obviate, or at least attenuate, the need for substantive intervention. Thus, procedural constraints should be viewed as a price to be paid for (more) substantive flexibility.

B. Effectiveness Analysis

Closely related to the substitution approach, and best viewed as a continuation of the same argument, is an effectiveness analysis. This again may be simply

[48] For a critical legal studies critique of the modern obsession with reason see P. Schlag, *The Enchantment of Reason* (Durham, North Carolina, London: Duke UP, 1998)). See also N. Duxbury, *Patterns of American Jurisprudence* (Oxford: OUP, 1995), ch. 4, for an overview of the nature and persistence or "process" in US legal and constitutional theory.

stated. Community-level procedural intervention serves to facilitate substantive flexibility by securing the effectiveness of environmental outcomes by different means. Thus, substantive flexibility, when operating within a framework of procedural constraints, need not imply a diminution of the Community's capacity to contribute to its stated (environmental) Treaty objectives. According to this perspective, procedures are conceived instrumentally, as a means of promoting the emergence of better outcomes.

C. "Dignitarian" Defence

The dignitarian defence rests upon the "intrinsic" rather than the "instrumental" value of procedures.[49] It seeks to disassociate procedures and outcomes, and lays emphasis upon the procedural journey rather than the destination to which it leads. There is, of course, not consensus as to the nature of the intrinsic values said to reside in "fair" or "appropriate" procedures. As Richardson notes:

> The emphasis on the role of process as the protector of independent values is common to the dignitary approach to process which has been influential in the United States. The precise details of the approach vary. For some commentators the requirement that an individual be treated fairly is grounded in a notion of justice derived from social contract theory, for others it springs from natural rights, from fundamental liberal values, or from Kant's injunction condemning the treatment of individuals merely as means. Whatever the precise foundation of the approach, however, the claim is made that the need to provide procedural fairness, particularly in the form of participation, springs from the obligation to respect a person's dignity and autonomy as a human being.[50]

Thus, the dignitarian defence, like the effectiveness analysis, remains usefully open-ended and susceptible to adjustment in the light of philosophical predilection and ideological standpoint.

From the point of view of the EU, it is not hard to see that a combined substitution/effectiveness approach may serve it well. Any one of the procedural constraints imposed by the IPPC Directive would in principle be susceptible to justification in these terms. Indeed in some cases vague allusions of this sort are to be found in the memoranda accompanying the proposals.[51] This thesis may be illustrated by way of an example. As observed above, the concept of BAT operates principally against a backdrop of Community-level target (ambient

[49] This language is drawn from L. Tribe, *American Constitutional Law* (2nd edn., New York: The Foundation Press, 1988) 663–77. Tribe is one of the most outspoken and effective advocates of the intrinsic value of procedural due process protection in the US constitution. For a general UK-based discussion of the instrumental v. intrinsic debate see G. Richardson, "The Legal Regulation of Process" in G. Richardson and H. Genn (eds.), *Administrative Law and Government Action* (Oxford: OUP, 1994), 105, and, for a comparative study, D. Galligan, *Due Process and Fair Procedures* (Oxford: OUP, 1997).

[50] Richardson, n. 49 *supra*, 113–14 (footnotes omitted).

[51] E.g., n. 24 *supra*, 12.

environmental quality) standards. It may be argued that recourse to this style of command and control instrument (as opposed to a more prescriptive form of command and control intervention) is made possible by virtue of the accompanying provisions on transboundary co-operation between Member States. One of the principal shortcomings of target standards is their limited capacity to address the issue of transboundary pollution externalities. To the extent that a state exports polluting substances beyond its territory, these emissions will not prejudice ambient (e.g. air) environmental quality in that state. This is a shortcoming which is mitigated within a framework of bilateral negotiations, thus ensuring the resonance of non-national interests in the domestic political order.

To take another example, the myriad IPPC provisions on information exchange, transparency and consultation may be justified in terms of their capacity to expand the knowledge base according to which decisions are adopted. Public participation may be defended in the name of contextual or local knowledge, and transparency requirements in the name of effective enforcement. And so this list could go on.

Application of the substitution/effectiveness defence raises, in its own terms, two specific questions in a Community setting. First, there arises the issue, endemic to the subsidiarity debate,[52] of the Community's obligation properly to motivate (reason) its actions. It is only when the Community pins its justification colours to the mast that the credibility and proportionality of its intervention may be assessed. This obligation to give reasons must apply regardless of the (procedural or substantive) nature of the obligations imposed on the Member States.

Secondly, there arises an important, and strangely neglected, issue. Even if the logic of substitution/effectiveness is accepted, it cannot be uncritically assumed that a (any) procedural price for (more) substantive autonomy is one which Member States will, or ought, to be willing to pay. On the contrary, from a subsidiarity/proportionality viewpoint, the loss of procedural autonomy implied ought to be assessed relative to the associated gains in substantive flexibility, with a view to determining whether the procedural route does indeed represent the least intrusive or prescriptive alternative. This, of course, is not a task which will yield right answers and precise outcomes. It is a question of judgement rather than of measurement, and one which is further complicated by the injection of effectiveness considerations into the assessment equation. To the extent that procedural mechanisms may, as many now claim, induce better environmental outcomes, how is "better" to relate to "more" or "less" prescriptive in terms of the intensity of intervention. How much "better" will compensate for (how much) "more" Community intervention? In addition, as is clear from the remedies case law of the Court,[53] and from experiences in the sphere of

[52] See generally G. de Burca, "The Principle of Subsidiarity and the Court of Justice as an Institutional Actor" (1998) 36 *JCMS* 217.

[53] Think, to take a parochial example, of the impact of the *Factortame* litigation on the system of public law remedies against the crown in the UK.

structural funding and the application of the "partnership" principle,[54] Community procedural intervention however apparently restricted in its scope, tends to spillover into the "domestic" sphere. It is apparent that procedural regulation may involve quite intense regulation, albeit in the form of systems of supervision and surveillance through notification, exchange and audit etc. The costs associated with such regulation may not be clear, and the ability of Member States to assess these costs will depend in part upon how accustomed and equipped they are to perform regulatory impact assessments.

If the instrumentalism of substitution/effectiveness raises questions, it also carries risks. It is predicated upon empirical claims as to outcomes which are by no means unassailable, and which have been subjected, for example, to a powerful public choice critique.[55] According to the instrumentalist perspective, procedures are only as good as the outcomes which they produce, and have no value independently of those outcomes. Thus, citizen participation, for example, may be sacrificed where it does not contribute to public welfare, conceived according to the public choice model in terms of the sum of individual preferences. Access to judicial review may be restricted where the costs associated with this (especially in terms of delay) are higher than the benefits which accrue. Outcome is all, and what the Community currently gives in terms of procedural rights and obligations, it may equally calmly eschew in the name of effective outcomes. To take one recent example, the Community's current proposal for a directive on strategic environmental impact assessment[56] specifically precludes access to the courts to seek review of planning and development decisions adopted. From an instrumental perspective this may not be condemned as wrong, other than in terms of the threat which it poses to the quality of outcomes. Welcome back the benign dictator. All, it seems, has been forgiven. Consider also in this respect the manner in which the European Parliament has been excluded from direct participation in "comitology" proceedings, the justification being framed in terms of the efficiency of the decision-making process.

Yet even if one accepts that procedures, especially perhaps those relating to citizen participation, have an intrinsic value in contributing to good rather than merely effective governance, the proper role of the Community in shaping implementation procedures within the Member States is still not clear. It is far from easy to conceive of how the Community might justify its interventions in this respect. An agency model, such as applies in the context of Community law general principles in their application *vis-à-vis* the Member States, is less than persuasive in the context of the IPPC where the procedural precepts in question do not bind the Community itself. Equally, the agency model was developed by

[54] See, for country case studies in this respect, L. Hooghe (ed.), *Cohesion Policy and European Integration* (Oxford: OUP, 1996).

[55] For an overview and reference to the relevant literature, see F. Bignami, "The Administrative State in a Constitutional System of Checks and Balances: Lessons for EC Comitology from American Rulemaking", Harvard Jean Monnet Working Paper 4/99, (http://www.law.harvard.edu/Programs/JeanMonnet/papers/index.html), 43–7.

[56] For the Commission's amended proposal see COM(99)73 final.

commentators (in relation to general principles), where the line separating Community and Member State authority was essentially functionally drawn, having regard in particular to the limited institutional resources of the Community, in for example collecting duties and levies within the framework of the common commercial or agricultural policies. In the context of the IPPC Directive, division of authority is motivated less by functional considerations than by constitutional principles and constraints. It is not that the Community enjoys authority which it chooses to cede to the Member States, but rather that the Community, within a framework of shared competence and shared responsibility, must justify its exercise of authority and must do so in a manner which is consistent with the principles of subsidiarity and proportionality. The implementing authority which rests in the hands of the Member States should thus not be conceived as a conditional gift bestowed by the Community. It "belongs" to the Member States which act, not as agents or servants, but as masters in their own homes. In this sense any analogy between the United States and the applicability of the Administrative Procedures Act (APA) *vis-à-vis* federal states may also be misleading. The "notice and comment" procedures established therein are binding upon the states where they seek, and receive, federal authorisation to administer certain programmes, or make certain rules, instead of a centralised federal agency, such as the Environmental Protection Agency. In such a scenario the state is acting "in lieu" of the Agency and is thus bound by the same procedural constraints.[57]

More generally analogies with the United States are problematic, though in certain respects revealing. It is, of course, the case that federal states are subject, under the Fourteenth Amendment to the US Constitution, to procedural due process requirements in the administrative sphere. The procedural protection derived therefrom is thus constitutionally guaranteed, rather than conferred by statute. The scope of the protection provided is constrained in a number of important respects.[58] Crucial for our purposes is the fact that it yields only in respect of individualised administrative acts, not where citizens are affected "*en masse*", and not in relation to administrative rule-making or policy formation.[59] The point here is not so much that in the United States participation rights would not be guaranteed under the due process clause in the case of an industrial licensing application—unless this were to imply a specific loss of the kind envisaged (life, liberty or property) for a given individual—but rather to note the importance of the level of decision-making in determining the nature and scope of the procedural protection to accrue. While it is generally accepted that the kind of procedural protection available under the due process clause (generally implying an adjudicative process of some sort) becomes "more important

[57] N. 55 *supra*, 27.

[58] See generally Tribe, n. 49 *supra*, 663–768.

[59] *Bi-Metallic Invest. Co.* v. *State Board of Equalization*, 239 US 441 (1915) and *O'Bannon* v. *Town Court Nursing Center* 447 US 773 (1980) and Tribe, n. 49 *supra*, 766–8.

the closer the government's focus approaches the singling out of individuals",[60] it has equally been argued that its restricted scope of application rests upon "overly formalistic distinctions between government rule-making and rule-applying".[61] Thus, Tribe has argued against the all or nothing jurisprudence of procedural due process, in favour of a more nuanced response which would imply different shades and varieties of participation rights according to context. A "continuum" between adjudicative process and representation of interests "would establish a range of procedural mechanisms". These, he argues:

> would not have to be written in constitutional stone. Instead, the decisions might frame a constitutional common law, leaving legislatures with the power to design other methods of protecting the individual's participatory interests. Thus, such a jurisprudence could effect a "remand to the legislature", prodding it to discover and develop new systems of "due process" more compatible with the needs of the administrative state.[62]

There seems to me to be much in this discussion which is enlightening for the EU generally, and for the IPPC case study under discussion more particularly. It serves first to highlight important limits to the procedural protection endowed by the Directive. Public consultation is to form part of the licensing procedure. There is nothing in the Directive which obliges Member States to create a space for public participation in the adoption of the framework within which such licensing decisions are adopted, for example in defining BAT or in establishing the methodologies for so doing. The nature of the discretion exercised by competent authorities in granting, or refusing to grant, permits, and in attaching conditions thereto, will vary widely according to the nature of this framework. Powers exercised by a competent authority in one state may be vested in a national, regional or local legislature in another or, alternatively, in a (more or less) independent agency or quasi-government authority. Consequently, the scope of application of the procedural prescriptions in place will vary according to Member State practice. This may be hard to defend in "intrinsic" terms, but it is harder still to justify according to the logic of instrumentalism.

Secondly, and crucially, discussion of "due process" serves to locate the issue of procedural protection in a constitutional setting. Due process protection is part of the constitutional identity of the United States, and disputes about its rationale, availability and scope are conducted in precisely these terms. And herein lies an important lesson for the European Union. It is hard—perhaps impossible—to justify the pursuit of non-instrumental procedural values in Community legislation on a piecemeal, barely articulated (now you see them, now you don't) basis. For such process values to bind the Member States they must, like the values of liberty, democracy and respect for fundamental human rights,[63] form part of the

[60] *O'Bannon* v. *Town Court Nursing Center* 447 US 773 (1980) and Tribe, 766 (footnotes omitted).

[61] *Ibid.*, 1683.

[62] *Ibid.*, 767.

constitutional settlement of the EU, as reflected in its founding treaties and/or in the case law of the European Court. To the extent that process equals politics, albeit politics disguised by the more familiar language of effectiveness, it is incumbent upon the Community both to acknowledge and justify its role; in so far as process is conceived in terms of good rather than minimally effective governance, it is hard to see how it can do without recourse to the language of constitutionalism and constitutional protection.

A final issue highlighted by the US example relates to the flexibility which inheres in procedural due process, and in APA notice and comment requirements. The standards applied constitute minimum standards only, and even then there is no single set of uniform rules steadfastly applicable to all situations. Adequate protection may be achieved by a range of diverse procedural mechanisms, and it has fallen largely to the courts to determine the "bottom line" in terms of the procedures to be followed. If "information" and "interest participation" are two of the "principal characteristics of American rulemaking", the third is "extensive judicial review".[64]

Similarly, in the context of the IPPC Directive, procedural aspects are defined in only the most general of terms. Thus, for example, the public shall have "an appropriate period of time" to comment upon permit applications, and decision reached by the competent authority shall be made available to the public (with or without reasons, it would appear). Transboundary information exchange is to "serve as a basis for any consultations necessary in the framework of the bilateral relations between the two Member States on a reciprocal and equivalent basis".[65] Transparency guarantees operate subject to the broadly defined exceptions laid down in the Access to Environmental Information Directive.[66]

A creative "remand to the legislature" *à la* Laurence Tribe, or a meaningless sop to the latest fashion accessories; transparency, participation and deliberation? It is a truism to assert that this will depend, in part, upon the role of the courts and upon their willingness to scrutinise, evaluate and, where necessary, condemn the procedural mechanisms put in place within the Member States. If, as at present in the EU, the instrumental/dignitarian divide remains unspoken and unexplored, and the role of each and the relationship between them equivocal, it will fall to the courts (as in both the UK and the US) to articulate their own conception of the value of process, and of the interests which it is intended to serve and protect; constitution building by whatever name.

[63] It should of course be noted the EU, and its Member States when acting within the scope of Community law, are already "constitutionally" bound by certain process values in so far as these derive protection under the European Convention on Human Rights, and particularly Art. 6 thereof. See generally Galligan, n. 49 *supra*, 214–21 and M. Hunt, *Using Human Rights Law in the English Courts* (Oxford: Hart Publishing, 1998).

[64] N. 55 *supra*, 41.

[65] For evidence that the ECJ appears to regard failure properly to implement such obligations relating to transboundary consultation see Case C–365/93, *Commission* v. *Greece* [1995] ECR I–499 and Case C–186/91, *Commission* v. *Belgium* [1993] ECR I–851.

[66] N. 34 *supra*.

5. CONCLUSION

The conclusion may be brief. In the environmental sphere "flexibility", in terms of differentiated standards, has not come alone. It has, in keeping with the spirit of the age, been accompanied by a "proceduralisation" of Community environmental law. Condemned by some as deregulation by another name, the constitutional, as opposed to environmental, propriety of this model has been barely considered. If, in many respects, the "procedurally constrained Member State flexibility in implementation" model examined here is normatively attractive, it opens up a new debate about Community intervention in the procedural lives of the Member States which represents a new stage in the constitutional development of the European Union. Lurking behind the most obscure issues of policy lie profound issues of regulatory and constitutional politics. The longest journey begins with a single step.

13

Flexibility and "Co-operative Law": The Co-ordination of European Member States' Laws—The Example of Environmental Law

KARL-HEINZ LADEUR

1. TRANSNATIONAL LEGAL RELATIONSHIPS IN THE EC

FLEXIBILITY IN the European Community is a paradigm which is discussed primarily with reference to the distribution of competences between the supranational, the intergovernmental and the state levels. New forms of a kind of transnational fragmented intergovernmentalism are being discussed on the basis of the Amsterdam Treaty, which tries to integrate into Community law forms of co-operation between Member States which draw upon traditional international law approaches. However, even here the focus is still on state-related forms of law which should be a part of the integration process. However, to my mind, the processual and a-centric character of European law is due not merely to the provisional nature of the project which has not yet reached its final institutional destination. The specific open character of European integration has to be taken as an autonomous form of its own, creating many new relational, heterarchical, transnational legal relationships that call into question the close link between state and law, and above all the hierarchical structure of a system of rules.

Here what we have in mind is not even supranational legal unification in the EC,[1] the pattern of which also fits the image of a legal order imprinted by the state. The EC is however particularly interesting because of the manner in

[1] For harmonisation of law see M. Rohe, "Binnenmarkt oder Interessenverband? Zum Verhältnis von Binnenmarktziel und Subsidiaritätsprinzip nach dem Maastricht-Vertrag" (1997) 61 *RabelsZ* 1; O. Remien, "Rechtsvereinheitlichung ohne Einheitsgesetze? Zum Symposium 'Alternativen zur legislatorischen Rechtsvereinheitlichung' " (1952) 56 *RabelsZ* 300; M. Boodman, "The Myth of Harmonization of Laws" (1991) 39 *American J. Comparative Law* 699; C. Joerges, "The Europeanization of Private Law as a Rationalization Process and as a Contest of Disciplines—An Analysis of the Directive on Unfair Terms in Consumer Contracts" [1995] *European Review of Private Law* 178.

which, despite quasi-statal legal unification, there can be a number of new types of legal phenomenon that cannot be fitted into the notion of the construction of a European legal order within a European Federal State. This can be seen, first, in the fact that specifically European law has to make use of general, national administrative law,[2] itself centred in the individual Member States around the public interest seen in state terms. According to ECJ case law, however, as we know, this narrowly bipolar perception of the relationship between public and private interests is not compatible with the procedurally conceived integration requirement of the EC.[3] In practical terms this means that the interest of the EC, or of other Member States, must always also be taken into account within national law, and in the event of a conflict either the national law should not be applied, even where its meaning is clear, or new legal forms must even be created by the judge so as to attain the "*effet utile*" of the specific European law. Thus, Britain had to extend, to actions against the crown, the institution of provisional judicial relief in order to guarantee the effective enforcement of European Community law. This is a consequence of an entirely new, legally creative, conception of transnational co-operation between states, and between states and the EC, such as does not fit a classical hierarchical conception of graduated rules in a multi-level system such as a federal state.[4]

The EC is, moreover, in other respects too, developing ever more numerous forms that may be termed transnational rather than supranational, in which the impermeability of state sovereignty is transcended not just by introducing a new level to the hierarchy, but through the mutual interlacing of several legal systems (of the Member States). One might mention here the mutual recognition of product licensing[5] or—even more interesting for our discussion—the development of a hybrid organisational structure, for instance on the model of the European Environment Agency, which has a relatively independent position *vis-à-vis* the Commission. Not only do Member State administrations co-operate in its management, but above all an organizational infrastructure is built up enabling individual national environment agencies to take on overall responsibility in the European Community for discharging common responsibilities.[6]

[2] For the relationship between national general administrative law and EC law see R. Scholz, "Zum Verhältnis von europäischem Gemeinschaftsrecht und nationalem Verwaltungsverfahrensrecht" [1998] *Die öffentliche Verwaltung* 261; F. Schoch, "Die Europäisierung des allgemeinen Verwaltungsrechts" [1995] *Juristenzeitung* 109; K.H. Ladeur, "Transnationale Tendenzen in der Europäisierung des Verwaltungsrechts" [1995] *Europarecht* 227.

[3] See Case 94/87, *Commission* v. *Germany* (*Alcan I*) [1989] ECR 175; [1998] Die öffentliche Verwaltung 287 (*Alcan II*).

[4] See K.H. Ladeur, "Richterrecht und Dogmatik—Eine verfehlte Konfrontation? Eine Untersuchung am Beispiel der Rechtsprechung des Europäischen Gerichtshofs" (1996) 79 *Kritische Vierteljahresschrift für Gesetzgebung und Rechtswissenschaft* 77; see also [1990] ECR I–3437 (*BUG-Alutechnik*).

[5] See generally E. Schmidt-Assmann, "Verwaltungskooperation und Verwaltungskooperationsrecht in der Europäischen Gemeinschaft" [1996] *Europarecht* 270, at 291.

[6] See W. Kahl, "Europäisches und nationales Verwaltungsorganisationsrecht. Von der Konfrontation zur Kooperation" (1996) 29 *Die Verwaltung* 341; K.H. Ladeur, "Die europäische Umweltagentur und die Perspektiven eines europäischen Netzwerks der Umweltverwaltungen"

Admittedly this is concerned principally with informational action, and therefore not sovereign action in the strict sense, but it may nonetheless be seen as a further variant of transnational administrative co-operative law of a kind which is incompatible with either the traditional conception of sovereignty or traditional models of limitations of national sovereignty in international law.

Yet another different manifestation of this new type of legal form which is hard to fit into traditional conceptual frameworks can be seen in the example of international standardisation[7] (in its differing forms, say inside the EC or also beyond its frontiers). These standardisation processes are part of a globalisation process to the extent that they aim at producing and conventionalising stocks of "common knowledge", of great importance for, for instance, establishing quality expectations, but also in enabling network effects (e.g. the "unbundling" of the components of complex composite products and services like computers, telephone services etc.).[8]

2. TOWARDS A NETWORK-LIKE STRUCTURE OF THE EUROPEAN COMMUNITY

Taking into account the importance of non-traditional legal relationships could lead to a new conception of a "network-like" relationship between national, trans- and supra-national forms of legal integration in the EU.[9] Leaving aside the problem of the distribution of law-making competences between the EU and the Member-States, but considering instead the importance of the doctrinal "infrastructure", the "systematicity" of the reproduction of practical patterns of networking of relationships in private law-based societies, then the idea of focussing upon a transnational component of mutual co-ordination, or even irritation and reciprocal self-adaptation, including the optional approach of a harmonised civil code (dependent on practical experimentation), might appear quite plausible as a "third way" between the preservation of a national legal order and a relatively homogenous supranational order. This approach might lead beyond the idea of preserving "national identity". It would not challenge legal integration, but rather try to develop co-operative, horizontal forms of relationships between the infrastructures of law and would try to keep national

[1997] *Natur und Recht* 8; A. Kreher (ed.), *The EC Agencies between Community Institutions and Constituents: Autonomy, Control and Accountability* (Florence, EUI, 1998).

[7] See generally C. Joerges, K.H. Ladeur and E. Vos (eds.), *The Integration of Scientific Expertise into Standard-Setting* (Baden-Baden: Nomos, 1997).

[8] See B. Kahin and J. Abbate (eds.), *Standards Policy and Information Infrastructure* (Cambridge, Mass.: MIT Press, 1995).

[9] See K.H.Ladeur, "Towards a New Theory of Supranationality—The Viability of the Network-Concept" [1997] *European Law Journal* 33; for the use of the network concept in the analysis of the contemporary decline of the dtate see J.M. Guéhenno, *The End of the Nation State* (Ann Arbor, Mich.: Michigan UP, 1995); for the evolution of law in "open" states see U.Di Fabio, *Das Recht offener Staaten* (Tübingen: Mohr, 1998); for a critique of the EU as a super-state see J.J. Rosa, *L'erreur européenne* (Paris: Grasset, 1998).

law sensitive to trans-national influences, preserving the knowledge base which, hitherto, has been accumulated in the national legal order and doctrine.[10]

This approach could also explain, and lead to an acceptance of, the self-organised character of the new European law by the European Court, on the basis of practical necessities relating to the implementation of Community law, and the lack of openness of Member States' law denying it the necessary "*effet utile*".[11] This is an effect which goes beyond a reactive concept of the implementation and enforcement of European law in the traditional sense, because it refers to the proactive role of the "infrastructure" of Member State law which is used for the process of putting European law into practice. The problem comes to the fore when, for example, citizens invoke the protection of legitimate expectations granted by the general administrative law of a Member State against the revocation of a subsidy which is taken to be incompatible with European law.

In such an example, the ECJ refers to the co-operation principle in Article 10 (ex Article 5) EC as providing an adequate basis for a Member State obligation to give European law as much efficiency as possible. This is a new practice of a kind of "bottom up" effect of integration of Member State and supranational law. Member States are not only obliged to "apply" EC law but also to open their legal structures to different forms of consideration of effect and influences exercised on other Member States and the European Community as such. And at the same time, the exclusive focus of the public interest as a frame of reference for the interpretation of administrative law is set aside (e.g. the private and public interest in decisions on the conservation of illegal administrative acts have to be balanced).

3. THE PRACTICE OF THE EUROPEAN COURT OF JUSTICE WITH REFERENCE TO THE "PRINCIPLE OF CO-OPERATION"

One of the relevant cases in which the "fit" between specific European law and the general administrative law of Member States has been examined concerns a decision of the (only) German Minister of Viticulture (of *Land* Rheinland-Pfalz)—which is, of course, heavily dominated by the organisations of wine growers. On the basis of this decision, local wine growers had been granted an additional quantity of wine to be marketed, in spite of a European decision to limit the total quantity to be put on the market according to a fixed quota. This decision to exceed the fixed quota was of course illegal because it ran counter to a European norm. But when the European Commission asked the Minister to revoke his decision, the latter invoked the protection of the legitimate expecta-

[10] For administrative law see F. Schoch, "Die Europäisierung des allgemeinen Verwaltungsrechts" [1995] *Juristenzeitung* 109; K.H. Ladeur, "Transnationale Tendenzen in der Europäisierung des Verwaltungsrechts" [1995] *Europarecht* 227; for private law see Joerges, n. 1 *supra*.

[11] See Schoch and Ladeur, n. 2 *supra*.

tions of the addressees who had, in their economic strategy, relied upon the administrative act granting them dispensation from the quota.

In this case, finally, the European Court of Justice[12]—I think with good reason—referred to the "principle of co-operation" enshrined in the EC Treaty (new Article 10) in order to formulate a legal constraint on Member States to be respected in the process of the administrative implementation of European law. This was, in my view, a productive idea, though one has to admit that the protection of legitimate interests is also inherent in European law.[13] But this is a construction which takes into account the specific open architecture of the European Community. On the one hand, this case—as do many other similar cases—shows how deeply national legal concepts are transformed by the process of Europeanisation—far beyond the specific European law. The whole infrastructure of Member States' law is changed when it comes to the concrete administrative application of a norm, because general administrative instruments and concepts have to be adapted to the triangular constellation in this case. It is not only the relationship between the Member State and the European Community which is at stake, but also the interests of the other Member States which are touched by the decision as such, and by the refusal to annul it. On the other hand, this case shows the importance of national infrastructure to this process, because apparently all kinds of procedural and substantive elements of decision-making have to be taken from national administrative law. Thus, at this point there arise not only the problems of interpreting whether Member States enjoy discretion according to a specific European law, but also the degree of Member State autonomy in administrative law, and the nature of the general constraints implied by Article 10 (ex Article 5) EC and the case law of the Court.[14] Crucially, divergent standards of general administrative law concerning judicial control, discretion, annulment etc. can lead to different versions of uniform European law.[15]

[12] See Case C–289/91, *Klaus Kuhn* v. *Landwirtschaftskammer Rheinland Pfalz* [1993] ECR I–4439; also Case 44/79 *Hauer* v. *Rheinland Pfalz* [1979] ECR 3727.

[13] See Case C–375/96, *Zaninotto* v. *Ispettorato Centrale Repressione Frodi* [1998] ECR I–6629.

[14] See, from a German point of view, J. Zöttl, *Integrierter Umweltschutz in der neuesten Rechtsentwicklung* (Baden-Baden: Nomos, 1998), 192; R. Steinberg and K. Koepfer, "IVU-Richtlinie und immissionsschutzrechtliche Genehmigung" [1997] *Deutsches Verwaltungsblatt* 973; for discretion in European environmental law see Case C–361/88, *Commission* v. *Germany* [1991] ECR I–2567; Case C–355/90, *Commission* v. *Spain* [1993] ECR I–4221.

[15] See C.D. Classen, "Das nationale Verwaltungsverfahrensrecht im Kraftfeld des europäischen Gemeinschaftsrechts" [1998] *Die Verwaltung* 307; C.D. Classen, "Strukturunterschiede zwischen deutschem und europäischem Verwaltungsrecht" [1995] *Neue Juristische Wochenschrift* 2457; C.D. Classen, *Die Europäisierung der Verwaltungsgerichtsbarkeit* (Tübingen: Mohr, 1996); Th. v. Danwitz, *Verwaltungsrechtliches System und Europäische Integration* (Tübingen: Mohr, 1996); M. Brenner, *Der Gestaltungsauftrag der Verwaltung in der Europäischen Union* (Tübingen: Mohr, 1996); J. Schwarze, *Europäisches Verwaltungsrecht* (Baden-Baden: Nomos, 1988), ii; J. Schwarze, "Der Beitrag des Europäischen Gerichtshofs zur Europäisierung des Verwaltungsrechts" [1997] *Europarecht* 419; J. Schwarze, "The Convergence of Administrative Laws of the EU Member States" [1998] *European Public Law* 191; from a UK perspective see C. Harlow, "European Administrative Law and the Global Challenge", EUI Working Paper RSC 98/23, who focuses on the different relations between administration and courts in Europe; for the US see the famous *Chevron*

But this latter possibility should not lead to an expansion of the Europeanisation of the basic structure of Member States' law: the "principle of co-operation" works perfectly well in the sense of a differentiated form of "structural coupling" between specific European law and national general administrative law. (One has to admit that this evolution at the hands of the ECJ has met with severe criticism by some German law professors denouncing it as an intrusion by the European institutions in competences for general administrative law which are attributed to Member States.[16]) But if one takes a closer look at the interrelationship between European and Member State law, one cannot deny that there are some constraints imposed on national systems of administrative law which are simply inherent in the process of integration. In the wine case, it is plausible that divergent implementation processes could not be accepted because this could undermine the integrated European policy.[17] But different cases will imply different circumstances and a varying degree of Member State autonomy in implementation and enforcement. This may be exemplified by reference to a number of examples in the next section.

4. THE EUROPEAN ENVIRONMENTAL IMPACT DIRECTIVE AND MEMBER STATES' ADMINISTRATIVE LAW

A. The Heterogeneity of General Administrative Legal Systems and the Introduction of the EIA into Member States' Law

The aforementioned co-ordination problem comes to the fore in the implementation of the European Directive on Environmental Impact Assessment (EIA)[18]: beyond the process of the implementation of the Directive in the legal order of Member States, the problem of co-ordinating its application with general administrative law has to be tackled. For instance, the question has to be raised

case in which the Supreme Court accepted administrative discretion also with reference to the interpretation of law if there was no clear guidance given by Congress (467 US 837 (1984)); K.W. Starr, "Judicial Review in the Post-*Chevron* Era" (1998) 6 *Yale Journal on Regulation* 269; see generally also K.F. Kreuzer, D. Scheuing and U. Sieber (eds.), *Die Europäisierung der mitgliedstaatlichen Rechtsordnungen* (Baden Baden: Nomos, 1997).

[16] See R. Scholz, who is a former minister of the CDU, "Zum Verhältnis von Europäischem Gemeinschaftsrecht und nationalem Verwaltungsverfahrensrecht" [1998] *Die öffentliche Verwaltung* 261; F. Ossenbühl, "Der verfassungsrechtliche Rahmen offener Gesetzgebung und konkretisierender Rechtsetzung" [1999] *Deutsches Verwaltungsblatt* 1, at 7, even calls the *effet-utile* jurisprudence a "virus" which invades German public law; for the counter-position see R. Winkler, "Das 'Alcan'-Urteil des EuGH—eine Katastrophe für den Rechtsstaat?" [1999] *Die öffentliche Verwaltung* 148.

[17] See R. Streinz, "Vertrauensschutz und Gemeinschaftsinteresse beim Vollzug des Europäischen Gemeinschaftsrechts" [1990] *Die Verwaltung* 153.

[18] Council Dir. 85/337 [1985] OJ L91/30, as amended by Council Dir. 97/11 [1997] OJ L73/5. For the UK see B. Hough, "Relevance and Reasons in Planning Matters" [1998] *Journal of Planning and Environmental Law* 625; J. Alder, "Environmental Impact Assessment—Inadequacies of English Law" [1993] *Journal of Environmental Law* 203.

to what extent procedural infringements, such as the absence of an EIA at all, or neglect of relevant factual elements, to name but a few possible mistakes, necessarily will lead to an annulment of a licence or of a planning decision required to be based on an EIA.

In this respect, the legal position in different Member States is rather heterogeneous. There are different conceptions of judicial control of fact-finding in particular, and of administrative discretion more generally. Methods of control are different also as regards judicial review of technically complex matters, such as, for instance, the control of the administrative forecast of certain needs to be met by some new project to improve public infrastructure.[19] The different approaches to standing to sue can also lead to different levels of implementation of European law.[20] In Germany, standing is based upon subjective rights, the definition of which is quite difficult in multipolar legal relationships: it depends on the conception of the particular law which is evaluated according to limited or broad protective approaches. Only in the first case can the attribution of a subjective right be assumed. On the other hand, the ECJ tends to establish a rather generous conception of the subjective interest protected by a European directive. In many cases, such as in the area of consumer protection, the Court has regarded the general protection of health and other personal interests as sufficient for the assumption of individual concerns which may give access to judicial protection in the Member States.[21] These questions can, of course, be relevant in planning or other administrative decision-making procedures in which an environmental impact assessment has to be carried out; and in this respect different approaches to administrative control can lead to far more practical divergence in the implementation process than in the enforcement of the Directive as such. One cannot assume that this question can be reduced to a quantitative problem of more or less effective practical implementation. It is rather the problem of different legal systems which has to be taken into account. The problem is all the more important because the ECJ shows a tendency to set up a coherent level of protection in the European Community as a whole.[22]

[19] For German court practice see Bundesverwaltungsgericht (BVervGE) Rep. 34, 301; 45,309; K.H. Ladeur, "Die rechtliche Kontrolle planerischer Prognosen" [1985] *Natur und Recht* 81; see also, for nuclear law, Bundesverwaltungsgericht (BVervGE) Rep. 101, 347; 106, 115.

[20] See C.D. Classen, "Der Einzelne als Instrument zur Durchsetzung des Gemeinschaftsrechts?" [1997] *Verwaltungsarchiv* 645).

[21] See F. Schoch, "Individualrechtsschutz im deutschen Umweltrecht unter dem Einfluß des Gemeinschaftsrechts" [1999] *Neue Zeitschrift für Verwaltungsrecht* 457, at 463; G. Winter, "Individualrechtsschutz im deutschen Verwaltungsrecht unter dem Einfluß des Gemeinschaftsrechts" [1999] *Neue Zeitschrift für Verwaltungsrecht* 467. In an EC context see C. Hilson, "Community Rights in Environmental Law: Rhetoric or Reality" in J. Holder, *The Implementation of EC Environmental Law in the UK* (Chichester: Wiley, 1997).

[22] See Schoch, n. 21 *supra*, at 461.

B. The Example of Germany

In Germany, for instance, the abovementioned restrictive legal regime for access to courts, based on the idea of individual concern, may have considerable effect on the implementation of the EIA Directive because an individual subjective right has to be invoked.[23] In planning processes, the protection of property or individual health confers standing as far as a statute explicitly or implicitly intends to protect certain well-defined groups (e.g. neighbours).[24] Obviously, the infringement of requirements enshrined in the EIA Directive can also lead to individual harm, but in many cases they will not. The EIA procedure is not as such regarded as intending to protect individual interests.[25] Procedural requirements in general are relevant for standing only if they are closely linked to substantive interests which are themselves attributed as subjective rights.[26] In many cases there will be no possibility of judicial control at all, even if the infringement of the requirements of the Directive is evident. Recently some remarks of the Federal Administrative Court referred to the possibility that the procedure for public participation in EIA cases might have a subjective element.[27] However, as far as fact-finding is concerned, German administrative law is, at a first level, much stricter than that of most other countries in court control. It does not, in general, allow for discretion as far as the process of collecting information is concerned.[28] This approach is, on the other hand, mitigated by the fact that procedural infringements can justify the annulment of an administrative act only if there is a reasonable probability of a causal realtionship between this type of illegality and the substantive outcome of the decision as such.[29] This approach lends itself to the criticism which claims that this hypothetical construction forces the judge to adopt—in a sort of "*Gedankenexperiment*"—the role of an administrator. There are, of course, also different levels of probability which can be invoked. At a second level, there has recently been a tendency in legislation further to restrict the possibility of mistakes being made in the fact

[23] See Bundesverwaltungsgericht Rep. 67, 74, 77; 72, 15, 25; 74, 109, 110; J. Schwarze, "Grundlinien und neuere Entwicklungen des Verwaltungsrechtsschutzes in Frankreich und Deutschland" [1996] *Neue Zeitschrift für Verwaltungsrecht* 22; J. Schwarze, "Die gerichtliche Kontrolle der Verwaltung in England" [1996] *Die öffentliche Verwaltung* 771 (review of De Smith, Woolf and Jowell, *Judicial Review of Aministrative Action* (London: Sweet & Maxwell, 1995)).

[24] See Bundesverwaltungsgericht Rep. 42, 66; 67, 78; 74, 109, [1983] Deutsches Verwaltungsblatt 899; but broad protection is only given in taking-cases, not for indirect degradation of property or health, Bundesverwaltungsgericht Rep. 72, 15, 25.

[25] See Bundesverwaltungsgericht Rep.100, 238, 243.

[26] See Bundesverwaltungsgericht [1999] Neue Zeitschrift für Verwaltungsrecht 635.

[27] See Bundesverwaltungsgericht Rep.100, 238, 243.

[28] See W. Hoppe and S. Grotefels, *Öffentliches Baurecht* (Munich: Beck, 1995), §7 No.44; on the other hand, the court may have discretion concerning methods of proof, Bundesverwaltungsgericht [1999] Neue Zeitschrift für Verwaltungsrecht 635.

[29] See §46 Verwaltungsverfahrensgesetz; Bundesverwaltungsgericht [1995] Umwelt- und Planungsrecht 445, [1996] Neue Zeitschrift für Verwaltungsrecht 1012, [1999] Neue Zeitschrift für Verwaltungsrecht 550, [1998] Natur und Recht 305.

finding process in planning decisions. In the past these would quite often have been prone to annulment, because in highly complex cases allowing for the weighing of arguments and criteria, causality of procedural infringements could easily be invoked. This new legislation is part of a tendency towards deregulation which also reduces judicial protection.[30] These examples may suffice to show that one cannot even compare the standards of administrative law in Europe according to a quantitative scale. Some countries, such as France and Britain, are much more open in giving court access than is Germany. With reference to fact-finding, German administrative law is in some respects stricter than French or English law, though this is more and more difficult to demonstrate because an act whose illegality is confirmed by the judge will often in fact not be annulled. In some respects, one might even assume that procedural requirements are not taken very seriously by German administrative law because in France, for instance, serious procedural infringements in administrative procedure can lead to annulment without reference to causality.[31] This point is interesting for our discussion because it concerns the requirement of public participation in environmental procedures, in particular, in the environmental impact assessment procedure. In Germany, the illegality of such a procedure would be revealed in the court decision, but more often than not the judge would not come to the conclusion that the procedural mistake had exerted influence on the substantive outcome. In this respect, procedural requirements are given more weight in France because the procedure has a value of its own, and is not merely regarded as a potential protective measure for individual substantive interests. That is to say, the German conception of procedure is closely linked to the protection of substantive interests, and the latter can be invoked in court only if they are attributed as rights. On the other hand, not only is fact-finding subjected to strict control, but also the interpretation of the legal terms used in a statute are interpreted with binding force by the judge, whereas in most other countries this question depends rather upon whether the legislator has shown clear intentions in the legislative process which will, in this case, restrict the interpretative power of the judge. Broader concepts are understood as giving the administration a measure of discretion which can be controlled by the judge only to a very limited extent.[32] At this point, the different approaches of Member States concerning procedure and judicial control, or the role of the administration, come to the fore.

[30] See E. Gawel, "Beschleunigung im Umweltzulassungsrecht" [1999] *Die öffentliche Verwaltung* 281; H.J. Koch, "Beschleunigung, Deregulierung, Privatisierung, Modernisierung des Umweltrechts oder symbolische Standortpolitik" [1997] *Zeitschrift für angewandte Umweltforschung* 210 at 217; B. Stuer, "Die Beschleunigungsnovellen 1996" [1997] *Deutsches Verwaltungsblatt* 326.

[31] [1983] Conseil d'Etat Rep. 57. For a discussion in a UK context see G. Richardson, "The Legal Regulation of Process" in G. Richardson and H. Genn, *Administrative Law and Government Action* (Oxford: OUP, 1994).

[32] For the USA, see the interpretation of the famous *Chevron* case in M.W. Spicer and L.D. Terry, "Administrative Interpretation of Statutes: A Constitutional View on the 'New World Order' of Public Administration" [1996] *Public Administration Review* 38.

C. The Example of the IPPC Directive

The same problems can be demonstrated with reference to the Integrated Pollution Prevention Control (IPPC) Directive which will confront German administrative law with a lot of new problems.[33] This is not so relevant in terms of the introduction of the specific measures to be taken, particularly as Member States enjoy a high degree of flexibility in this respect. But in German administrative law, a licensing decision for a chemical plant, for instance—to be granted where there is no environmental harm—does not allow for administrative discretion at the first stage in which "harm" (to the environment or individuals) has to be evaluated according to emission standards. Only at the second level, concerning "precaution" does the administration have at its disposal a certain leeway of discretion ("*Standardisierungsermächtigung*")[34] but this can be used only in imposing general emisssion (ambient) standards (in general, not in individual evaluations on a case-by-case basis). On the basis of the IPPC Directive, the decision will have to be taken on a case-by-case basis, whereas the role of general guidelines integrating different forms of pollution remains unclear.[35]

The IPPC Directive creates some problems in this respect because it integrates the examination of environmental concerns for different environmental media (air, water etc.) which, to date, are more or less analysed separately on the basis of differentiated limit values for each medium. On the one hand, the IPPC model represents progress towards more complex solutions while, on the other, the integration of the examination procedure and the linking of standards to technology in general ("best available technology") imposes some constraints on such a system in so far as leeway is given for compensation for trespassing ambient standards in one medium by a quantity of emissions which remains below acceptable levels in another medium (e.g. air versus water).

D. Different Paradigms of Administrative Law in Europe

French and English legal systems are probably more open to flexible strategies of decision-making than German law is. French law is, in particular, much more generous in according discretion to administrators concerning both fact-finding and decision-making as such in complex technical cases. This is why the introduction of the EIA occurred much earlier in France—long before the EIA

[33] Council Dir. 96/61 [1996] OJ L257/26. See U.Di Fabio, "Integrierter und betrieblicher Umweltschutz" in H.W.Rengeling (ed.), *Wege zur Materialisierung des Europäischen Umweltschutzes* (Cologne: Heymann, 1996); for problems related with integrated standards of pollution see H.J. Koch, "Die IPPC-Richtlinie: Umsturz im deutschen Anlagengenehmigungsrecht?" [1997] *Umwelt- und Technikrecht* 31, at 50.

[34] See R. Wahl, "Risikobewertung der Exekutive und richterliche Kontrolldichte—Auswirkungen auf das Verwaltungs- und das gerichtliche Verfahren" [1991] *Neue Zeitschrift für Verwaltungsrecht* 409, and J. Scott in this volume.

[35] See Zöttl, n.14 *supra*, at 226.

Directive came into force. Consequently the integration of the EIA Directive into French administrative law[36] was much easier than it turned out to be in German administrative law which is more orientated towards judicial control, and has some difficulty in accepting discretion in fact-finding and the weighing of heterogeneous elements in licensing procedures (as opposed to planning decisions). However, the EIA Directive demands more flexibility with respect to environmental effects to be assessed in a more integrated way, instead of a procedure which separates different types of effects (water, air, soil etc.). English environmental law is more open to discretion in fact finding as well.[37] In many European countries the administration is also given a certain discretion in the interpretation of legal concepts as long as parliament cannot be supposed to have followed a clear regulatory strategy. In France, courts will, in normal cases, limit their control to "*erreurs manifestes d'appréciation*". Both French and English legal systems are more centred upon a procedural approach. A broader conception of discretion is, on the other hand, linked to a stricter control of procedure, whereas in Germany stricter substantive control is regarded as a legitimation for a lower level of control with respect to procedure. In France this approach to the relationship between the administration and the judiciary is connected to a hierarchical conception of the administrative state which should allow for the internal control of lower levels of administration by the centre; procedure is regarded as a limit which compensates for broad discretionary powers, and judicial control follows to a large extent the administrative rationality. This tendency is epitomised in particular by the fact that the judge can also annul a decision if the investment of public money is not justified according to the method of the *bilan-coûts-avantages*.[38] Procedural control in France is rather strict as compared to that in Germany: incomplete publication of documents, lack of a comment by an administrative body envisaged by a statute, or omission of a public announcement in EIA procedures can lead to the revocation of a decision without an evaluation of whether these mistakes might have influenced the outcome of the decision.

In Britain and the USA, the legal situation is similar, but this is due to a more political, pragmatic conception of discretion and an administrative procedure which is more open towards co-operation with business[39]—of course this element can also be found in France and Germany but it is not emphasised by the

[36] See M. Prieur, *Droit de l'environnement* (2nd edn., Paris: Dalloz, 1996), No.97.

[37] For the UK see S. De Smith, M. Woolf and J. Jowell, *Judicial Review of Administrative Action* (London: Sweet & Maxwell, 1995), 284; for France see G. Knaub, "Le contrôle par le juge administratif de l'appréciation des faits" in J. Burmeister (ed.), *Die verfassungsrechtliche Stellung der Verwaltung in Frankreich und in der Bundesrepublik Deutschland* (Cologne: Heymann, 1991), 129.

[38] See Conseil d'Etat, 28 Mar. 1997, *Association contre le projet de l'autoroute transchablaisienne* (No.170 856: excessive costs of the construction of a highway); see generally J.M. Woehrling (President of the Administrative Court of Strasbourg), "Rechtsschutz im Umweltrecht in Frankreich" [1999] *Neue Zeitschrift für Verwaltungsrecht* 502.

[39] For Britain see R. Burnett-Hall, *Environmental Law* (London: Sweet & Maxwell, 1995), 1–26; N. Haigh and F. Irwin (eds.), *Integrated Pollution Control in Europe and North America* (Washington, DC: WWF, 1990).

structure of administrative law. The search for a systematic approach to new forms of conventions allowing for co-ordination of public and private decision-making in England finds its repercussion in the Environment Act of 1995 which gives a systematic methodological preference to cost-benefit-analysis[40] as a basis for environmental decision-making which might be more compatible with entrepreneurial thinking. In France, a similar phenomenon can be observed in planning law which uses the "*bilan-coûts-avantages*" as a method of control of technical decisions[41]—a concept, which is again more adapted to an internal administrative standard of rationality. In Germany, a functional equivalent might be seen in the "proportionality principle" which is more related to a judicial approach to the control of complex administrative decision-making and which is often looked at wryly in the UK, because a judicial approach to evaluating the relation between resources to invest and goals to be met might be regarded as incompatible with the function of the judiciary because this is, of course, not the "application" of a rule in a traditional sense.

5. THE PROBLEM OF LEGAL "TRANSPLANTS" IN EUROPE

Many of the environmental reforms of the EC are not really European, in the sense that they have their own systematic framework to which Member States have to adapt. They are rather linked to a conception of reciprocal stimulation of change by transplanting new forms of environmental regulation from one country to the others. This is inevitable because Europe is composed of different legal systems, but there is no European legal system, as such. This is a reasonable approach which allows for learning and experimentation with different legal elements and methods. However, one has to bear in mind that specific rules and types of regulation generated in one country are always linked to a basic framework of general administrative law and that a body of doctrine and experience cannot just be transposed to other Member States. P. Legrand[42] has, on the one hand, observed this interrelationship in a very sensible analysis. On the other hand, he has drawn far-reaching consequences from his reflections on the identity of different legal systems and their integrative potential which keeps specific and general administrative (or private law) together. He tends to deny that anything of the kind of European law—in a meaningful sense beyond the level of superficial co-ordination of specific legal measures—is possible. One should not go so far because there is a third position between his and a superficial one which tends just to ignore or downplay the difficulties in integrating

[40] See D. Helm, "Reforming Environmental Regulation in the U.K." (1993) 4 *Oxford Review of Economic Policy* 1.

[41] See Conseil d'Etat Rep. 1971, 409 (*Ville Nouvelle Est*).

[42] See P. Legrand, "European Legal Systems are not Converging" [1996] *The International and Comparative Law Quarterly* 52; P. Legrand, "Sens et non-sens d'une codification réformatrice du droit européen" [1997] *Revue Française d'administration Publique* 227.

different types of legal systems incorporating a lot of experience, and in hammering out the inevitable structural and systemic interrelationships between different levels of law, doctrine, practical understanding, institutional support, societal expectations etc. At this point one could refer to a more flexible understanding of this "systematicity"[43] of the law which would not just deny the possibility of legal "transplants" from one system to another, but take seriously the inevitable problems of finding an adequate "fit" between specific and general components of the law. G. Teubner[44] has regarded these transplants as "legal irritants": this means new "foreign" elements can ,in fact, be transposed into a legal system but one has to allow for the emergence of an autonomous form of reaction which might alter the new component in its own way and find its own "fit" based on new, unexpected forms of linkage between the old and new components. This could be a productive idea which conceptualises forms of learning stimulated by the introduction of legal "transplants" but, at the same time, accepts that a certain transformation of European legal elements takes place in this type of implementation in a general legal system. Such an approach would imply an acceptance of a new form of flexibility which is related not to the implementation of EC directives in Member States' law as such, but to co-operation between specific European law and the general administrative law of Member States. Legal "transplants" might be conceived of as imposing constraints on the national legal systems which should stimulate a learning and adaptation process which needs a new form of a kind of "meta-dogmatics" but which should not just lead to a uniformity of administrative law.

In German law, this could lead to a kind of self-observation of the viability of the hitherto established doctrine for complex procedures of decision-making and, as a consequence, to a differentiation of the legal concepts on which the system of decision-making in environmental law is based. A kind of evolution of the established doctrine should be hoped for, but not a blind adaptation to a fictitious European requirement of effective implementation of specific legal norms without bearing in mind the inevitably creative character of the co-ordination of specific and general administrative law. (The IPPC Directive is in fact a British "transplant", whereas the EIA Directive stems from French and English law—originally , of course, from the USA.[45]) One could, for instance, think about searching for a common understanding of basic procedural requirements for an environmental impact assessment (with reference to public participation, for example) instead of trying to attain a homogeneous standard of implementation through general administrative law as such. Each Member State could try to find its own way of co-ordinating general and specific law, and

[43] See M. Van Hoecke and M. Warrington, "Legal Cultures, Legal Paradigms, and Legal Doctrine: Towards a Model for Comparative Law" [1998] *The International and Comparative Law Quarterly* 495.

[44] G. Teubner, "Legal Irritants: Good Faith in British Law or How Unifying Law Ends Up in New Divergences" [1998] 61 *Modern Law Review* 11.

[45] See S.T. French, "Judicial Review of Administrative Records in NEPA Litigation" (1993) 81 *California Law Review* 929.

the experience of each country should be used reciprocally in a process of self-observation and self-revision of legal systems. One should—to repeat—not be worried by vague feelings about "national identities" which might be at risk but take a more law-related and pragmatic approach which takes into account the "path-dependency" of legal systems[46] which use their specific systematicity for the accumulation of knowledge and for generating new options. New methods for mutual learning from "competition between rules" and institutions should be designed in the search of patterned interrelationships between legal decision-making and practical fields (e.g. pollution control). The latter should be sorted out and tested in view of functional equivalents in different legal systems. The recent development of comparative law draws attention to the "context in which a norm operates in order to evaluate the operation of the normative arrangements effectively". On the other hand, "conventional comparative law methods tend to produce little generalizable knowledge about the process of legal systems, focusing instead on the artifacts they produce".[47]

This idea might lead towards a practical way of systematic comparison and mutual observation among legal systems in the sense of introducing learning capacity into the law. Courts should take the Europeanisation of law more seriously in referring to different court practices in other Member States with respect to common problems.[48] In the age of the computerisation of legal information, this should not be an unmanageable task. Of course they should get support from methods of comparative law, which fortunately has shown a productive evolution recently. Comparative law research tends towards a more problem- and decision-oriented approach. In many complex cases, the common search for solutions to common problems beyond the formal Europeanisation of standard models is already in place. This may be observed with reference to product or environmental liability where American court practice has also been regarded and used as a "test-bed" for new options to be integrated into private law in cases of diffuse causality, or shared or collective attribution of responsibility. This type of reciprocal stimulation of learning should be based on Member States' legal systems and conceptions of general law, and allow for autonomous evolution of self-adaptation to new challenges. Otherwise the process of Europeanisation might even create more unintended heterogeneity as a side-effect, as compared to the limited and manageable degree of fluctuation openly accepted by a "co-operative" approach to transnational "irritation", as opposed to supranational uniformity. A common though not uniform European doctrine based on the mutual observation of the interrelationships between legal systems within Europe should be set up. The hostility of the German system

[46] See U. Mattei, "An Opportunity Not to be Missed: The Future of Comparative Law in the United States" (1998) 46 *The American Journal of Comparative Law* 709.

[47] See D.J. Gerber, "System Dynamics: Toward a Language of Comparative Law?" (1998) 46 *The American Journal of Comparative Law* 719.

[48] See E.A. Kramer, *Juristische Methodenlehre* (Basel/Munich: Stämpfli, Beck, 1998), 181; C. von Bar, "Vereinheitlichung und Angleichung von Deliktsrecht in der Europäischen Union" [1994] *Zeitschrift für vergleichende Rechtswissenschaft* 221.

towards discretion in fact-finding might lead to new forms of a more specific and limited type of administrative evaluation of complex licensing procedures which might also be of interest for other countries. Equally, Germany would adopt a more open perspective on discretion in fact-finding as such. This could, on the other hand, also lead to a new co-ordination of substantive and procedural law, and in compensation for more discretion in fact-finding, a greater emphasis on procedure should be conceded. This may also lead to a new combination of substantive and procedural law, especially by way of different forms of linkages between environmental quality standards which are based on immission standards, and technology-based ambient standards of pollution oriented on guidelines which are to be set up by European institutions. Taken all in all, there should not only be different normative standards of implementation but also different types of general legal systems supporting the implementation process.

6. WHAT IS TRANSNATIONAL ABOUT THIS TYPE OF EUROPEANISATION OF LAW?

According to the conception sketched above, the focus in the analysis of the process of legal integration in Europe should be more (or at least also) on the reciprocal interrelationships between different legal systems of the Member States which are used in order to attain the famous "*effet utile*" in the process of implementation of European law in the stricter sense. This should not be regarded as a kind of inertia to be abolished by more homogeneity, imposed by an extended level of harmonisation in which the general administrative (or private) law would be included. This might give more strength and vitality to Europeanisation because different types of legal systems might be used and observed in a process of competition between rules which might allow for experimentation with different forms of law and for mutual learning processes among Member States.

For the formation of European law, what this means is that the transnational component of co-operation, and of comparison of national legal systems and institutions, must be emphasised more strongly in relation to the supranational-hierarchical unification of law. "European" law has no infrastructure of its own consisting of doctrines, traditions or learning processes, which have hitherto come about primarily in the Member States.[49] This does not rule out supranational intervention, but this linkage of European and national law is to be regarded more as a process of irritation which can bring about different results in the different legal systems of the Member States,[50] but which must not be

[49] See C. Harlow, "Changing the Mindset: The Place of Theory in English Administrative Law" (1994) 14 *Oxford J. Legal Studies* 419.

[50] See B. Markesinis (ed.), *The Gradual Convergence: Foreign Ideas, Foreign Influences and English Law on the Eve of the 21st Century* (Oxford: OUP, 1994); P. Müller-Graff (ed.), *Gemeinsames Privatrecht in der Europäischen Gemeinschaft* (Baden-Baden: Nomos, 1993); for environmental law see M. Faure, "Harmonisation of Environmental Law and Market Integration: Harmonising for the Wrong Reasons?" [1998] *European Environmental Law Rev.* 169.

allowed to lead to a levelling out of all differences among national legal systems.[51] The point here is not to stress national "identities", but instead to take differing practical knowledge accumulated in the national legal systems, which ought not to be devalued, into account. It is also a decentralised search for new regulatory forms likewise not optimally to be controlled by some central body. The trend in any case under way towards global convergence of law must be underpinned by systematic practical legal comparison in courts and in legal science. But the classical model of the unitary legal system relating to a separable territory is being replaced by a transition to legal pluralism that is experimenting with a multiplicity of legal forms. In Europe, the need would be to develop, not illusory and unattainable legal harmonization according to traditional patterns,[52] but rather a system of "metadogmatics" to define the acceptable fluctuation in the formation of law, within the transnational convergence of law. This should lead to a more proactive type of transnational "co-operation of legal systems" in view of the common problem of the use of "imported" knowledge. Especially where competitive disadvantages arise for agents from different countries, this band of fluctuation in legal possibilities should correspondingly be drawn more narrowly.

In legal terms, this approach might start from the assumption that the dichotomy of private and public interests on which the protection of legitimate expectations, in particular, is based undergoes a fundamental transformation in the European integration process. Its dynamic demands an inclusion of third-party interests, such as the involvement of other Member States and their citizens who have to gain access to the European market. The consequences derived from this idea, a limited protection of private interests in cases of multilateral effects of a state measure, should be acceptable for business because they might end up in the same position. A problem of mutual compensation of cost and benefit is at stake here. State-based protection must be broadened to include the effects of the integration process in the gaze of national administrative law. This would be the reverse side of the state-based and limited traditional market economy. One could try to use "private" and "public" interests as a framework for Member State law, and as starting points for a better thought out "triangular" conception of a co-operative law which would include the new "integration" interests in the interpretation process. This might be plausible, especially in cases of regulated markets, such as that for agricultural products. (The wine case would be a good example of this.) This more specific way of building bridges between European and the general administrative law of Member States, focused as it is upon the concrete requirements of integration and not upon the abstract institutional interests of the implementation of European law as such, might be more suited to the process-like character of European integra-

[51] See the sceptical remarks of B. Markesinis, "Why a Code is not the Best Way to Advance the Cause of European Legal Unity" [1997] *European Review of Private Law* 519.

[52] See Boodman, n.1 *supra*; see also N. MacCormick, "Democracy, Subsidiarity, and Citizenship in the European Commonwealth" [1997] *Law and Philosophy* 331.

tion. In the same vein, one could explain and limit state liability for delayed implementation of European law.[53] The reasons given for expanding liability beyond the limits of Member State law should, in this case, refer not to the interest in forcing Member States to adapt but rather to the asymmetric consequences generated by divergent levels of integration. Firms would, for example, be confronted with new competitors in their own market but not get access to other markets themselves in the case of a Member State unlawfully delaying the implementation of a European directive. This would again be a specific "irritation" of Member State law related to the broadening of the concepts of "private" and "public" interests to be weighed in cases which are related to the integration process. In German law, for example, this would work because state liability is, in these cases, based on the understanding of a certain relationship between interests. And a specific variation of this conception would not question the whole construction with all the effects of incalculability to be taken into account. Established argumentation is a little too short-sighted in focusing upon the use of individual interest for the institutional interest of harmonisation as such.[54]

Otherwise, however, Member States themselves should be responsible for implementing European law, so that some differences in practical implementation in the legal systems of individual countries should be tolerated.[55] This does not exclude the fact that even supranational intervention fostering closer integration might be acceptable in some cases, but highlights simply that this need not, and should not, be the rule. There ought to be different levels of "intrusion" of European law into the general administrative law of Member States. The Amsterdam Treaty Protocol on the application of the principles of subsidiarity and proportionality may be seen as a declaration in favour of more flexibility of this kind. The focus of this chapter was on the idea that this need not generate just more heterogeneity, but that it might also contribute to a shift from supranational to more transnational co-operative processes of legal integration based upon a more profound understanding of the richness of European law.

[53] See R. Streinz, *Europarecht* (3rd edn., Karlsruhe: C.F. Müller, 1996), No.410.

[54] See Cases C–6 & 9/90 *Francovich & Bonifaci* v. *Italy* [1991] ECR I–5357; and Cases C–46 & 48/93 *Brasserie du Pêcheur* v. *Germany* and *R.* v. *Secretary of State for Transport, ex parte Factortame* [1996] ECR I–1029.

[55] For public law see v. Danwitz, n. 15 *supra*; for private law see Rohe, n. 1 *supra*.

14

From Uniformity to Flexibility. The Management of Diversity and its Impact on the EU System of Governance

ERIC PHILIPPART and MONIKA SIE DHIAN HO*

1. INTRODUCTION

THE 1990S HAVE witnessed a remarkable shift in the way the European Union (EU) fulfils its basic functions, causing uncertainty about its future trajectory. This chapter focuses on the recent changes in the management of diversity within the EU—in particular how diverse interests and ideologies of Member States are aggregated and accommodated in order to allow policy development at European level—and studies the constitutional effects of these innovations.

Against the background of more and more openly, not to say assertively, debated socio-economic and political diversity among Member States and the resulting threat of blockages of policy initiatives, the Treaty of Maastricht had already breached the fundamental rule of diversity management in the traditional European Community (EC) system, that is, the preservation of the principle of common rights and obligations for all Member States. If the new forms of differentiation introduced by the Maastricht Treaty violated what Weiler has called the "all-or-nothing effect" of EU membership[1] (that is, precluding selective application of Community obligations by Member States), they were nevertheless seen by the large majority of European actors as exceptional

* We wish to thank the participants of the April 1999 conference organised by the EUI for their most useful suggestions, as well as G. de Búrca and J. Scott for their editorial guidance. The support and ideal research environment provided by the Netherlands Scientific Council for Government Policy (Den Haag) are also to be acknowledged.

[1] Joseph Weiler recognised however in the same breath that "whereas Member States retain the ultimate political option of withdrawing from the Community and thereby disengaging from their obligation of membership . . . as long as they opt for membership they are *largely unable* to practice selective application of Community obligations" (emphasis added); J.H. Weiler, "The Community System: The Dual Character of Supranationalism" (1987) 1 *Yearbook of European Law* 267 at 297.

expedients. With an entire title dedicated to general enabling clauses for "closer co-operation" between those Member States which are willing and able to further co-operation among themselves, the Treaty of Amsterdam (ToA) has turned the exception into a constitutional principle.

Future enlargements will bring a quantitative and qualitative increase in diversity in the Union and, with it, the need for policy adaptations. A comparison of the problem-solving capacity of instruments of diversity management is thus of renewed relevance (managerial evaluation). Our evaluation encompasses instruments designed to overcome problems of integration by suppressing, diminishing, trading off, accommodating and circumventing diversity. Presented as a solution to the post-enlargement possible challenges, closer co-operation is, symbolically speaking at least, the biggest innovation since Maasstricht in terms of EC/EU methodology and constitution. In that respect, it is a natural point of reference for this comparative evaluation.

Apart from managerial utility, the enshrinement of the closer co-operation clauses in the ToA has possible far-reaching constitutional effects on the Union, calling for systemic evaluation. In our evaluation of these systemic consequences, we will focus on the effects of closer co-operation on EU governance in terms of (1) the scope, depth and output of EU policies; (2) methods of integration; and (3) institutional architecture and legitimacy. The evaluation of the effects of flexibility on these dimensions depends on the "vision" one has of the Union. For our purposes we have used the visions encompassed in four stylised models of EU governance—the Westphalian, the Intergovernmentalist, the Regulatory and the Multi-level Governance models—which each have their specific standards and prescriptions for the three dimensions mentioned above. The objective here is to assess the potential effects, if any, of closer co-operation on these dimensions. We will then, on the basis of the standards provided by the four models of EU governance, evaluate the meaning of these shifts for the future evolution of the EU system as a whole.

Section two provides the "ingredients" for the managerial and systemic evaluation. In so far as the managerial evaluation consists of a review of the "problem-solving capacity" of various policy instruments, we need to define beforehand the problems diversity can cause to EU integration (sub-section 2.1) and give an overview of the instruments developed by the Union to overcome blockages of integration (sub-section 2.2). As regards the points of reference needed for the evaluation of the systemic effects of closer co-operation, they are provided by the last sub-section with the presentation of four ideal-types of European governance (sub-section 2.3). Sections three and four deal respectively with the managerial and systemic evaluation, followed by some concluding remarks.

2. INGREDIENTS FOR THE EVALUATION

A. Diversity and Problems of Integration: A Typology

Since our criterion of—managerial—evaluation is the respective problem-solving capacity of several policy instruments, only those forms of diversity among Member States which cause problems in terms of European integration are of concern here. Integration, i.e. the development of intense and diversified economic, social or political patterns of interaction among previously autonomous units,[2] is not necessarily hindered by diversity among those units. Some interactions are eased by similarities, others require (complementary) differences. Integration is therefore not synonymous with uniformisation or even harmonisation. The specifics of the situation and policy area will determine whether diversity is an asset, an unassailable fact, a costly impediment or an obstacle. Proponents of integration should then aim at nurturing, accommodating, decreasing/transforming, circumventing or suppressing it accordingly.

The sources of potentially "paralysing" or "harmful" diversity are manifold.[3] Differences in the level of socio-economic development and the geo-economic situation can lead to conflicts between economic (sub)national interests and long-lasting deadlocks. Divergent political views, dictated for instance by the respective geo-political location or the size of the Member States may result in EU stalemate, in particular with respect to Common Foreign and Security Policy (CFSP) initiatives. Differences of institutional structures or administrative, legal and policy cultures among Member States can furthermore induce substantial differences in adjustment costs of harmonisation, resulting in strong bureaucratic opposition in particular. Diverging appreciation of what is a "fair" distribution of costs and benefits of membership can also cause ominous paralysis when manifesting itself by recurrent budgetary impasses. Last but not least, ideological divergence on the role of the state *vis-à-vis* the market, the division of

[2] W. Wallace, "The Dynamics of European Integration" in W. Wallace (ed.), *The Dynamics of European Integration* (London, Pinter Publishers for the RIIA, 1991) at 9.

[3] In the Treaties and in the doctrine, a sharp distinction has usually been made between objective (socio-economic) and subjective (political-ideological) diversity, the kinds of problems they pose and the way to solve them. The delineation between the two is however not absolute. In which category should one put geopolitical reasons or institutional/administrative differences which may underpin Member States' difficulty in endorsing a decision? "Differentiation" (i.e. difference in the treatment of Member States) has officially been based on the idea that, all Member States having accepted the *acquis* of the Union, derogations can only be based on "objective" differences. The temporariness of derogations for the purposes of adaptation is reinforced by the acceptance that any more permanent exemptions had to be justified by factors beyond Member States' control. What is "beyond" the control of a government has however often been defined in terms of "affordable" costs of adjustment, while what is "objectively" impossible has proved to be variable in time and space (cf. self-imposed adjustments to match the Economic and Monetary Union—EMU—convergence criteria). Furthermore, the definition of objective obstacles has been regularly tempered with spectacularly: for instance, the state of the public opinion has in a way been unofficially regarded as objectively preventing governments from complying with their legal obligations (cf. the case of Sweden's non-participation in the third phase of the EMU).

labour between various levels of governance or the *modus operandi* of the Union (supranational v. intergovernmental-oriented Member States) can be yet another source of "non-negotiable conflicts".[4]

Acknowledging a certain pro-interventionist bias in what we define as "problematic",[5] we distinguish between five main categories of problems which these various forms of diversity among Member States might cause to integration:

- *Problems with the development of the acquis "in house"*, i.e. developed through EU "normal" procedures. In so far as unanimity among Member States is in many cases required for further (positive) integration, diversity whatever its origins, once it reaches a certain level of sensitivity, is potentially problematic for the adoption of new policy initiatives.
- *Problems with the development of the acquis "by import"*, i.e. first developed outside the Union to be integrated at a later stage in the Treaties (cf. European Political Co-operation or Schengen co-operation). As far as unanimity presides over the main "importing" procedure, i.e. the revision of the Treaties negotiated by an Intergovernmental Conference, any significant divergence among Member States can become problematic for that mode of development of integration.
- *Problems with the adoption of the existing acquis by candidate Member States*. Differences in socio-economic development or judicial-administrative capacity can lead to problems with the adoption of the *acquis*, i.e. how existing Community legislation is incorporated and translated into the law of the Member State.
- *Problems with the application and enforcement of the existing acquis·* Both objective and subjective diversity among Member States can result in non-compliance, either because of sheer incapacity or deliberate engineering. In so far as the effectiveness of the European system relies on the implementation and enforcement of EU law by the Member States, diversity could provoke a progressive unravelling of European integration.
- *Problems with the reform of the acquis*. Historical precedents show that socio-economic and ideological diversity, but also sharp asymmetry in the price paid for membership, can block any reform of the *acquis* or restrict the options for such reform. The increased diversity of an enlarged Community

[4] See F. Scharpf, *Governing in Europe. Effective and Democratic?* (Oxford: Oxford University Press, 1999) 80 at 83.

[5] "Interventionists" argue that, in the context of diminishing capacity of the national systems confronted with globalised competition and EU negative integration (i.e. European rules prohibiting public interventions at (sub)national level), there is a need for further positive integration at the level of the Union. EU instruments able to provide public goods (redistributing resources), deal with externalities and introduce market-correcting measures (regulating markets) have to be developed. For "neo-liberals" on the contrary, the EU is only meant to establish a European-wide market, safeguard economic freedom and create a level playing field under supranational surveillance but insulated from political interference. See F. Scharpf, n. 4 *supra*, at 71; L. Hooghe and G. Marks, *The Making of a Polity: The Struggle over European Integration* (Florence: European University Institute, Robert Schuman Centre, RSCNo.97/31, EUI Working Papers, 1997) at 17.

often means that some policies become ineffective or too costly. Confronted with diverse demands for renegotiation of the *acquis* and the rigidities of decision-making processes, European decision-makers rarely manage to reform fundamental inadequacies, ending up with the adoption of policy instruments overlying existing ones.[6] Diversity is problematic because it generates more complex, less coherent and more diluted *acquis*, when it does not lead to its dismantling.

The problems of integration mentioned are interconnected. When the management of one type of problem is inadequate, one should expect to see other types of problem rising in magnitude. For instance, too much emphasis on uniformity in the development of the *acquis* is very likely to lead to growing non-compliance and/or non-enforcement. The types of problems listed above are all but one touching at decision-making. Problems of implementation and enforcement of the *acquis* (together with instruments aimed at controlling diversity—see below) belong to another *problématique* and will not be included in our managerial evaluation.[7]

B. The Toolbox for the Management of "Problematic" Diversity

In order to prevent and overcome such problems affecting integration, EU players have progressively developed a rich palette of formal and informal instruments which manage diversity by suppressing, diminishing, controlling, trading off, accommodating or circumventing it. For the sake of clarify, instruments which are often used in combination (for instance qualified majority voting and side-payments) are described separately hereunder. Since the book is focusing on flexibility, the following presentation puts special emphasis on instruments accommodating diversity.

(i) Suppressing Diversity

In many policy areas, even if the search for consensus is still pursued at great length, unanimity is no longer required. Obstacles to the development of integration can then be overcome by deciding to resort to qualified majority voting (QMV) and adopt uniformising decisions at the expense of problematic diversity. Where unanimity is still required, another way for a majority of Member States to obtain the suppression of diversity is to threaten to resort to extra-EU

[6] C. Preston, *Enlargement and Integration in the European Union* (London: Routledge—UACES, 1997) at 20.

[7] On the application and enforcement *problématique* see D. Curtin and K. Mortelmans, "Application and Enforcement of Community Law by the Member States: Actors in Search of a Third Generation Script" in D. Curtin and T. Heukels (eds.), *Institutional Dynamics of European Integration. Essays in Honour of Henry G. Schermers* (Dordrecht/Boston, Mass./London: Martinus Nijhoff Publishers, 1994).

co-operation. If co-operation among Member States taking place outside the EU framework (like the 1985 Schengen initiative) is obviously not part of the "EU" toolbox of diversity management, its evocation is an instrument in EU negotiation. It strengthens the bargaining power of some Member States over those faced with the possibility of exclusion and the potential negative policy externalities which come with it.

(ii) Diminishing (or Transforming) Diversity

Another way to manage diversity is to decrease it to an unproblematic level through instruments which contribute to a progressive convergence of all, either through "catch up" of the laggards with the best socio-economic performances (for instance, via adjustment programmes and cohesion funds), benchmarking (comparison of national practices, selection of best practices, establishment of benchmarks, peer review), or "europeanisation",[8] i.e. the development of new—transcending—European solutions (for instance, via exchange of information, staff exchange, and/or cross-training).

(iii) Controlling Diversity

In other cases, diversity's (faulty) expression rather than diversity itself is the target; EU instruments are applied only when diversity in the application of rules or implementation of policies amounts to non-compliance. The control and, if need be, sanctioning of diversity are managed mainly by the Commission and the European Court of Justice,[9] but also by independent agencies and Member States.[10]

(iv) Trading-off Diversity

Instead of having its diversity recognised (through accommodation) or agreeing to diminish it (through adjustment programmes), a Member State can decide to remove it from the equation in exchange for concessions on other issues (issue-linkage or package deals) and/or unconditional side-payments.[11] If that

[8] W. Wessels, "An Ever Closer Fusion? A Dynamic Macro-political View on Integration Processes" (1997) 35 *Journal of Common Market Studies* 267 at 299.

[9] The most notorious instrument of this category probably being the infringement procedure set in Arts. 226, 227 and 228 TEC.

[10] The obligation to present progress reports and "public shaming" are among the "soft" instruments used by the Council of Ministers and Member States to control and sanction policy slippage. These techniques are used, for instance, in the context of the EMU, for national budget management in particular.

[11] Bargaining theory suggests that if diversity among parties is less intense across different issues, with marginal gains in some issue areas more important to some than to others, blockage of policy-development in these issue areas might be overcome by issue linkage. Exchange of concessions is in that case to the advantage of both parties. See A. Moravcsik, *The Choice for Europe. Social Purpose & State Power from Messina to Maastricht* (London: UCL Press, 1998) 65 at 66 on issue linkages and side-payments.

Member State trades off its diversity against various concessions, it does not however commit itself to do anything about it. Contrary to convergence or adjustment programmes, where resources are granted on the condition that action will be taken to diminish diversity and consequently used for investment, here the side-payments can be used for any purpose.

(v) Accommodating Diversity

Accommodation of diversity implies a certain acknowledgement of diversity by way of granting a special treatment. The accommodation can be sought in a "vertical" way (through resort to subsidiarity), or in a "horizontal" way (through new forms of harmonisation and flexibility instruments). Subsidiarity has obviously not been introduced as an instrument to overcome obstacles to the development of EU *acquis*.[12] Yet it can be used as an instrument to push through a package deal by leaving the management of part of the package to other levels of government, thereby removing thorny issues from the EU agenda.

Alternatively, diversity can be accommodated horizontally at a European level either by relaxing the degree of constraint of legal regimes and policies, or by varying the participation of Member States in those regimes and policies. The first type of horizontal accommodation is usually obtained through outline legislation or framework directives. Contrary to detailed and uniformising regulations, these directives leave many aspects of the policy to the discretion of Member States. Another way to decrease the level of uniformity is to resort to the so-called "opt-up" system, laying down a "Community floor" on which individual Member States can build up a set of national measures (provided they are compatible with the Treaty). A national rule is no longer completely replaced by a single Community rule. The European intervention is then restricted to the establishment of minimal standards compulsory for all, but which do not prevent any Member States from maintaining or introducing, for instance, more stringent protective provisions in areas concerning working environment, public health, consumer protection and environment.

[12] For most governmental players, subsidiarity has been introduced as a defensive principle, intended to protect the competences of Member States (and their subnational units) against undue incursion from European actors (the European Council in Dec. 1992 was stating that "Community measures should leave as much scope for national decision as possible"). To palliate the absence of a strict delineation of competences between European and national levels, the EC Treaty imposes a double subsidiarity test on any action envisaged by the Community outside EC exclusive competences: the comparative efficiency test and the proportionality test. Indeed the principle contained in Art. 5 TEC "embraces three separate, albeit related, ideas: the Community is to take action only if the objectives of that action cannot be sufficiently achieved by the Member States; the action can therefore be better achieved by the Community because of the scale or effects of the proposed measure; if the Community is to take action then this should not go beyond what is necessary to achieve the objectives of the Treaty"; P. Craig and G. de Búrca, *EU Law—Text, Cases and Materials* (Oxford: Oxford University Press, 1998) at 127. The practical consequences of the principle are however not straightforward in the absence of a straight criterion indicating areas of EC exclusive competences.

Variation in the participation of Member States takes many forms, and this second type of horizontal accommodation requires a more detailed presentation. We have classified these forms into six categories on the basis of the following dimensions: maintaining common objectives for all Member States or not; the scope over which flexibility applies (one decision up to an entire policy area); and the choice of the framework (inside or outside the EU).

- *EC/EU policies with a differentiated application of common obligations and rights.* This form of flexibility implies that, although Member States are and remain equally committed by the Treaties, the application of the Treaties is subject to variation dictated by "objective" differences (cf. temporary derogations in the case of the accession of new Member States, specific measures taken on the basis of Article 227(2) TEC in favour of the Outermost regions—French overseas departments, the Azores—before general provisions of the TEC and common policies are applied to them).
- *EC/EU policies incorporating an element of case-by-case flexibility.* In a number of EC/EU policy areas, some or all Member States have the chance to "pick and choose" the measures which will commit them. This form of flexibility allows for permanent and, to a large extent, discretionary exemptions, that is, based more on unwillingness than inability. Member States "opting out" do not have to apply the decision of the Council, but must accept that the Union is committed by the action or position in question (cf. Article 23 TEU allowing for "constructive abstention" in the CFSP).
- *EC/EU policies established on the basis of* ad hoc *flexible arrangements (predetermined flexibility).* In this case, the exemptions granted to some Member States do not apply to individual acts or decisions (case-by-case flexibility) but to an entire policy (sub)area. Reference is often made to the "predetermined flexibility" method because the policy is established on the basis of a protocol detailing in advance all aspects of the flexibility arrangement (specific scope and procedures) for that particular area. For instance, in the case of the EMU, one part of the monetary policy is run through "normal" procedures, involving notably the (Ecofin) Council, while another part, including the monitoring of government deficits or the adjustment of the Euro exchange rate, is dealt with through "*ad hoc*" procedures and modalities, largely defined in protocols attached to the treaties. Title IV of the TEC (on visas, asylum, immigration and other policies related to free movement of persons) and Article 14 TEC (area without internal frontiers) are two other important examples in this category.
- *Intra-EU closer co-operation established on the basis of* ad hoc *flexible arrangements.* This form of flexibility authorises, sometimes informally, Member States to use the institutional framework of the EU to develop closer co-operation among themselves. Such co-operative developments take place inside the EU but are not considered as part of the common *acquis* or as EC/EU policies, even if they all build on an existing EC/EU policy or innovate

in line with EC/EU objectives. Their scope, objectives, rules and procedures are defined on an *ad hoc* or "occasional" basis (cf. co-operation for additional research programmes, within the "euro–11" group or the possibility for closer co-operation offered by the Protocol integrating the Schengen *acquis*).
- *Intra-EU closer co-operation established on the basis of the general enabling clauses set out in Title VII of the TEU.* Provided that no veto is waived at European Council level, the Council can decide by QMV to authorise a majority of Member States to make use of the institutions, procedures and mechanisms laid down by the Treaties to further co-operation among themselves in a restricted number of policy areas of the first pillar and in the entire third pillar (Article 43 TEU; Article 11 TEC and Title VI, Article 40 TEU).
- *Extra-EU closer co-operation with a direct link with the EU.* This form of flexibility refers to (intergovernmental) co-operation between EU Member States outside the EC/EU framework but which has a link with the Union. Extra-EU closer co-operation can be explicitly conceived, as the signatories of the 1985 Schengen agreement did, as a "laboratory of EU policies" whose output is intended to integrate eventually the framework of the EU. It can also be considered as "an integral part of the development of the Union", notwithstanding differences in the respective membership, as in the case of the Western European Union (WEU). The EU can go even further by establishing on that basis a structural and functional link, when it stipulates that it "will avail itself of the WEU to elaborate and implement decisions and actions of the Union which have defence implications" (Article 17 TEU).

(vi) Circumventing Diversity

Problems of integration can be solved by the development of co-operation outside the EU framework, on a formal or informal *ad hoc* basis. The failures of the CFSP, often attributed to divergence among the 15, lead large Member States—France, Germany, Italy and the UK—to form "contact groups" among themselves. In armaments production, the same Member States, which are also the main arms producers, pursue a similar multi-track approach: they co-operate in the OCCAR (Organisation of Co-operation in Armaments), to the detriment of the working group for armament policy (POLARM) established by the Council and the European Armaments Group, part of the WEU. Diversity and the institutional structure of the Union (its principles, norms, rules and procedures) are in these cases circumvented.

C. Four Visions of EU Governance

Discussions on flexibility instruments tend to focus on technical, functional and/or managerial aspects, overlooking their (side-)effects on EU governance as a whole and the strategic and ideological choices they imply for the long-term trajectory of the Union. In section four, the possible systemic effects of closer co-operation on the evolving structures of the EU will be examined, using ideal-types of EU governance: the "Westphalian", the intergovernmentalist, the "regulatory", and the "multi-level governance" model. These models do not pretend to represent "reality", but in a stylised way each of them says something about what are, will and/or should be EU policies, methods of integration, institutional architecture and legitimacy.[13] Supposing that closer co-operation has an impact on some or all of these aspects, the meaning of this impact for the future evolution of the EU system will be evaluated on the basis of the standards derived from the four models of EU governance. We present these standards here.

The "*Westphalian*" *model* portrays the EU as a political system in the making, a system which should eventually be comparable with the model characterising Western European states.[14] The analogy with the Westphalian state implies that the EU is expected to evolve in the direction of an undifferentiated institutional order across policy areas, covering all activities traditionally associated with the nation-state, including the provision of security and welfare (redistributive politics). As regards methods and procedures of integration, the Westphalian model lays considerable emphasis on comprehensive participation by all Member States, majoritarian politics (qualified majority voting) and universality of EC law. EC law should be uniform in its application,[15] even if temporary differentiation in Member States' rights and obligations can be envisaged, provided that this "flexibility" is characterised by clear centripetal dynamics. Integration should proceed through constitutionalisation, i.e. the intergovernmental agreements and treaties among the sovereign European states should evolve into a set of rules binding those states, imposing limits on the power of the new entity, guaranteeing the rule of law and endowing EU citizens with rights that are enforceable in national courts. In fact, as Weiler, Shaw and others have suggested, a majority of legal scholars have conceived this constitutionalising process as a straight line—save small deviations—towards the eventual fulfilment of governmental functions by a monocentred, and vertically

[13] Focusing mainly on new processes of governance, the literature on the multi-level governance (MLG) model offers a lot in terms of description and explanation of the current state of the EU, but relatively little in terms of prediction and prescription for the future. We have tried to develop its normative dimension in order to overcome this problem of partial incongruity between the models, using in particular recent work on legitimacy whose line of reasoning runs parallel with MLG.

[14] Philippe Schmitter has created four ideal types "to provoke a discussion" on the future of the European polity in his "Imagining the Future of the Euro-Polity" in G. Marks, F. Scharpf, P. Schmitter and W. Streeck, *Governance in the European Union* (London: Sage Publications, 1996), 121–50. The four ideal types are defined by their specific mix of territorial and functional constituencies. In his typology, the "Stato/*Federatio*" ideal type corresponds with the Westphalian model presented here, while his "*Consortio*" and "*Condominio*" ideal types have much in common with the regulatory model and the MLG model respectively described below.

[15] This is particularly true for a specific variant within the Westphalian paradigm, that is, the highly-centralised version of federalism used by A. Moravcsik and K. Nicolaïdis as their term of reference: A. Moravcsik and K. Nicolaïdis, "Federal Ideals and Constitutional Realities in the Treaty of Amsterdam" (1998) 36 *Annual Review—Journal of Common Market Studies* 16.

integrated, political system.[16] From the Westphalian perspective, the transfer of competences to the European level has to be accompanied by a much faster development of European democracy. The current structures designed to regulate European affairs are seen as lacking transparency, and the European debate and party politics as underdeveloped. Increasing the input-legitimacy of the EU by wider opening to public scrutiny and extension of the power and competences of the European Parliament (EP) is advocated as the ultimate remedy to overcome these deficits.

The *intergovernmentalist model* evaluates the EU project in terms of its potential to achieve the objectives and further the self-interest of nation-states. Pictured as a sequence of interstate bargains and interstate strategic interaction, European integration is expected here not only to preserve, but to strengthen participating nation-states, for instance by providing them with means to overcome domestic opposition to specific policies.[17] In the words of Moravcsik and Nicolaïdes, "the EU properly provides a structure to complement, co-ordinate, even in limited ways supplant the policies of nation-states, correcting for their manifest weaknesses; yet the EU has not, will not, and should not replace the nation-state".[18] From the intergovernmentalist perspective, there should be no European competence unless there is a "compelling and compatible substantive national interest" in co-operation.[19] The favoured method of integration is voluntary co-operation where diverse national interests need to be pragmatically accommodated. Veto or non-participation should therefore always be an option, as well as the revocation of previous engagements. Just as integrative methods should be seen as mere instruments serving the national interests of Member States, the institutional structure is of only instrumental value; supranational institutions are there for efficiency reasons only, reducing transaction costs and facilitating communication when compared to *ad hoc* deals.[20] Contrary to the Westphalian view, the EP has no symbolic and transcending value in itself (as the repository of democratic representation and legitimacy in the EU). Pushing the argument further it could even be said that "the very existence of the European Parliament does not sit easily with liberal intergovernmentalist theory".[21] The main explanation of the acceptance of its existence

[16] See J. Shaw, *European Legal Studies in Crisis? Towards a New Dynamic*, EUI Working Paper RSC No. 95/23, 1995, 2 and 6; J Shaw, "Introduction" in J. Shaw and G. More (eds.), *New Legal Dynamics of European Union* (Oxford: Clarendon Press, 1995) at 3; and J.H. Weiler, "The Reformation of European Constitutionalism" (1997) 35 *Journal of Common Market Studies* 110.

[17] A. Moravcsik, "Preferences and Power in the European Community: A Liberal Intergovernmentalist Approach" (1993) 31 *Journal of Common Market Studies* 509 at 510.

[18] See Moravcsik and Nicolaïdes, n. 15 *supra*, at 32; A.S. Milward, *The European Rescue of the Nation-State* (London: Routledge, 1992); and Moravcsik, n. 11 *supra*.

[19] See Moravcsik and Nicolaïdes, n. 15 *supra*, at 17.

[20] Delegation of powers does not go beyond the narrow logic of the "principal-agent model": M.A. Pollack, "The Engines of Integration? Supranational Autonomy and Influence in the European Union" in W. Sandholtz and A. Stone Sweet (eds.), *European Integration and Supranational Governance* (New York: Oxford University Press, 1998) 217 at 249.

[21] P. Craig, "The Nature of the Community: Integration, Democracy, and Legitimacy" in P. Craig and G. De Búrca (eds.), *The Evolution of EU Law* (Oxford: Oxford University Press, 1999) at 11.

would be the states recognising the practical interest of some European democratic legitimacy as a stabiliser of their European project. The resulting loss of autonomy for the states should be strictly proportional to that gain.[22]

For both the Westphalian and the intergovernmentalist models, the existing modern Western nation-state is the point of reference against which developments of the Union are judged. While the protagonists of the Westphalian model plead for a "super-state", reconstituting the national Westphalian state model at the European level, the intergovernmentalists strive for the preservation of the Westphalian state at the national level. The Westphalian state is however a "form of state" which is, in the words of Caporaso, "based on a very selective reading of the histories of a few countries (France, England, Germany)".[23] It is linked to specific social formations, specific cultural and geographical environments, as well as distinctive historical periods.[24] According to advocates of a more post-modern concept of statehood, the present "Westphalian" form of state should not be reified and projected on the evolving institutional structure of the EU as the sole and eternal expression of political authority and legal order. The recent literature on European integration has seen a number of efforts to escape from the Westphalian straitjacket, many of which cluster around the regulatory and the multi-level governance models.

The *regulatory model* considers the EU's institutions and policies as of a different nature from those of national governments. The EU is seen as a highly developed special-purpose organisation, a "*Zweckverband funktioneller Integration*" in the words of Ipsen, the primary task of which is to further objectives which are expected to be realised more efficiently at a European level than at the level of the individual Member States.[25] Protagonists of the regulatory model posit that the EU should not necessarily cover the whole gamut of policies national states usually run: if some policies are more effectively managed at another level, this level should keep that competence. Conversely, reallocation of competence should be envisaged as soon as the European level ceases to be the most efficient. Consequently, there should be a clear, albeit not irreversible, division of labour between the Member States and the European Union, where European activities will logically tend to concentrate on market integration and "risk regulation".[26] In the regulatory model, the methods have to be chosen

[22] See P. Craig, n. 21 *supra* at 12.

[23] "Form of state" refers to "conceptually possible expressions of political authority organized at the national and transnational levels": J.A. Caporaso, "The European Union and Forms of State: Westphalian, Regulatory or Post-Modern?" (1996) 34 *JCMS* 31.

[24] See the work of Robert Cox on the topic: R.W. Cox, "Gramsci, Hegemony, and International Relations: An Essay in Method", (1983) 12 *Millennium: A Journal of International Studies*; R.W. Cox, "Social Forces, States, and World Orders: Beyond International Relations Theory" in R.O. Keohane (ed.), *Neorealism and Its Critics* (New York: Columbia University Press, 1986).

[25] H.P. Ipsen, *Europäisches Gemeinschaftsrecht* (Tübingen: J.C.B. Mohr—Paul Siebeck, 1972) 196 at 200.

[26] R. Dehousse, "European Institutional Architecture after Amsterdam: Parliamentary System or Regulatory Structure?" (1998) RSC Working Paper No. 98/11, 1 at 3.

according to their contribution to the fulfilment of the functional objectives of the EU. There is no preconception in terms of variations in institutional settings and methods across issue-areas as long as they contribute to effectiveness and efficiency. The regulatory model favours delegation to supranational institutions, like the Commission or independent agencies, for those policy areas which for reasons of efficiency have to be dealt with at the European level. These institutions thanks to their special expertise are thought to be in a better position to guarantee the essential autonomy of decision and non-discriminatory application of rules.

In the regulatory model, the primary source of legitimacy also lies in the effectiveness and efficiency of the institutions ("output-legitimacy").[27] The legitimacy of the system will be increased by clear mandates and objectives for which the autonomous institutions are held accountable, and through decision-making processes sufficiently transparent to allow stakeholders to express themselves.[28] Solutions based on the principles of parliamentary democracy are seen as inappropriate for a Community which is principally concerned with economic integration and should therefore be partially shielded from the pressures of constituencies.[29]

The *multi-level governance (MLG) model* pictures the process of regional integration as a process of diffusion of state authority; upward to supranational institutions and downward to subnational regions. Moreover, political arenas are no longer seen as "nested" within the state, but more and more as "interconnected", that is to say, subnational actors now operate in both national and supranational arenas, forming dense transnational policy networks together with actors from those levels.[30] Two main approaches or variants of multi-level governance can be distinguished. Despite the existence of many different levels of government and the proliferation of transnational networks, the first variant of the model conceives the Union as a political system with a strong institutional framework, political authority and adjudicatory system (the European Court of Justice) which, as Tuytschaever rightly underlines, is binding the various multi-level networks together.[31] In this "Europe *with* the regions",[32] various regimes co-exist, each having its own division of labour among levels of government (reminding one of forms of "co-operative federalism"). The second variant of MLG—combining an extreme functionalism with a vision of subnational actors outflanking the national ones (a "Europe *of* the regions")—pictures Europe as a

[27] M. Höreth, *The Trilemma of Legitimacy—Multilevel Governance in the EU and the Problem of Democracy* (Discussion Paper, C 11, ZEI, 1998) 22–5.

[28] Dehousse, n. 26 *supra*, at 4.

[29] G. Majone, "Europe's 'Democracy Deficit': The Question of Standards" (1998) 4 *ELJ* 5.

[30] G. Marks, L. Hooghe, and K. Blank, "European Integration from the 1980s: State-Centric v. Multi-level Governance" (1996) 34 *Journal of Common Market Studies* 341 at 378.

[31] F. Tuytschaever, *Differentiation in European Union Law* (Oxford: Hart Publishing, 1999) at 253.

[32] L. Hooghe, "Building a Europe with the Regions: The Changing Role of the European Commission" in L. Hooghe (ed.), *Cohesion Policy and European Integration: Building Multi-Level Governance* (Oxford: Oxford University Press, 1996) 89 at 126.

plethora of non-hierarchical networks and regimes, in which varying and overlapping domains of functional competence interact with varying and overlapping scales of territorial aggregation.[33] With weakened or no common institutions able to tie the various regimes together, the Union is fundamentally dispersed, progressively turning itself into a "*condominio*".

When it comes to the competences of the EU, both variants agree that their extent and scope have to be determined first and foremost on the basis of subsidiarity. As already mentioned, this concept leaves considerable room for political interpretation and the two MLG variants seem to correspond indeed to very different "ideologies" of subsidiarity.[34] On one hand, reflecting the principles of German federalism[35] and fiscal federalism,[36] the more "structured" MLG variant pleads for a "master plan" for the political evolution of the Union, encompassing a clear delineation of the duties and powers of the different levels of government in Europe. Subsidiarity is, in this case, interpreted as a rule to determine which functions are most efficiently performed by which tiers of authority in the European system. On the other hand, reminiscent of Catholic social philosophy, the more "dispersed" MLG variant idealises the autonomy, sovereignty and efficiency of small social groups in a pluralist society. Subsidiarity here is the expression of the philosophical claim that democratic governance must be exerted as closely as possible to the citizen, with the result that "whatever its functions, the EU is to be a dispersed polity where most decisions will presumably be taken (and not just implemented) by other than central supranational authorities".[37] Both variants expect competences to overlap among multiple levels of governance and reject the idea that the EU will ever perform all the functions which are now covered by national states.[38] Considering that EC/EU competences encompass *de facto* most of the policy spectrum, the MLG approach has been more about listing European policies in which subnational players should be involved at decision and implementing levels, than listing policies to be excluded from EU scope. The EC Treaty already makes provision for mandatory consultation of the Committee of the Regions for part of the list, in particular education, culture, employment, social policy, regional policy and structural funds, public health, environment and transport. The most "advanced" subnational players claim that, on the basis of subsidiarity, policies

[33] P. Schmitter, n. 14 *supra*, at 138. See also J. Loughlin, "Europe of the Regions and the Federalization of Europe" (1996) 26 *Publius* 141 at 162; I. Tömmel, "Tranformation of Governance: The European Commission's Strategy for Creating a 'Europe of the Regions' " (1998) 8 *Regional and Federal Studies* 52 at 80.

[34] For a discussion of the origins and interpretations of the subsidiarity principle, see J. Peterson, "Subsidiarity: A Definition to Suit any Vision" (1994) 47 *Parliamentary Affairs* 117 at 119.

[35] F. Scharpf, "The Joint-Decision Trap: Lessons from German Federalism and European Integration" (1998) 66 *Public Administration* 258.

[36] See D. Begg, *Making Sense of Subsidiarity: How Much Centralization for Europe?* (London: Centre for Economic Policy Research, 1993).

[37] Schmitter, n.14 *supra*, at 127.

[38] Cf. G. Marks, F. Nielsen, L. Ray and J. Salk, "Competencies, Cracks and Conflicts: Regional Mobilization in the European Union" in Marks, Scharpf, Schmitter and Streeck, n.14 *supra*, at 41.

such as development co-operation, information society, citizenship of the Union, or even state aid, agriculture and energy, should also be considered as areas of shared competences.[39]

As far as the method of integration is concerned, the "structured" MLG variant remains so far laconic and vague. To some extent, its vision is one of a "variable geometry" Europe, with a core of activities in which all Member States participate, supplemented by various functional groupings in which participation is optional. The dispersed MLG variant corresponds clearly to an "*à la carte*" Europe, a polymorphic structure lacking a core, in which a variety of public and private actors will pick and choose the regimes they prefer.

As for the EU institutional structure, MLG has not yet come up with very specific prescriptions. The same goes to a lesser extent for democracy and legitimacy. Describing the multiple actors participating in European policy-making networks is one thing, building a normative theory demonstrating why this type of governance is the most legitimate is something else. The justification for the involvement of different levels of government given by the first MLG variant rests on references to output-legitimacy (a MLG system is more effective in terms of public goods delivery) and to the additional legitimacy—elected—sub-national actors bring with them into the Union. The second MLG variant, building on notions of "associative democracy" and "deliberative democracy", stresses the desirability of open-ended, flexible and informal decision structures which do not restrict participation in policy-formation and implementation to a limited number of direct stakeholders (as in the regulatory model). The justification of such a large-scale and rather indiscriminate involvement is that these loosely structured open decision networks are more responsive to society in the phase of agenda-setting, enrich the deliberation of the potential consequences of policy initiatives and generate less hierarchical policy alternatives which are better able to cope with diversity.[40] They are simply more effective in dealing with the complex problems of our times.[41]

3. EFFECTIVENESS OF DIVERSITY MANAGEMENT IN THE EU: A COMPARATIVE EVALUATION IN THE PERSPECTIVE OF ENLARGEMENT

Diversity problems linked with the next rounds of enlargement are likely to require a number of substantial policy adaptations. A comparative evaluation of instruments of diversity management is thus of particular importance. Closer

[39] Resolution of the Committee of the Regions on the outcome of the Intergovernmental Conference (IGC), CdR 305/97, Brussels, 20 Nov. 1997, point 7.

[40] B. Kohler-Koch, "La renaissance de la dimension territoriale en Europe—Entre illusion et réalité" in E. Négrier and B. Jouve, *Que gouvernent les régions d'Europe—Echanges politiques et mobilisations régionales* (Paris: L'Harmattan, 1998) 33 at 53.

[41] For a discussion of the recent normative literature on policy networks and their sources of inspiration, see Scharpf, n. 4 *supra*, 18 at 21.

co-operation, the biggest innovation in that matter and our point of reference for the comparison, is severely constricted, if not unworkable in many cases. The other instruments have shown their potential but also their limitations over the last decades. Assuming that the present toolbox might not be up to the task ahead, we have widened the comparison to a number of alternative combinations and new solutions: extension of QMV; new methods of Treaty reform; increase of resource transfers; structured flexibility extended to the second pillar[42] as well as freed from the possibility of veto by any single Member States and the most draconian enabling clauses (i.e. preserving the guarantee of openness but, for instance, forbidding only unfair competition or "significant" distortion of competition, defining ways and degrees to which closer co-operation could affect the *acquis communautaire*, etc.).

The evaluation looks successively at the effectiveness of each instrument in overcoming blockages in the development of the *acquis* in house and by import, the adoption of the *acquis* and its reform. It reviews their (dis)advantages and how closer co-operation in its present form[43] and in a more operational version compare, more specifically in the perspective of the enlargements to come. Considering the number of instruments and problems taken into account, what follows proceeds necessarily by rather large generalisations. We have nevertheless tried to highlight here and there the specificity of a number of key issue-areas, as well as the interconnectedness of the instruments. In-depth case studies are obviously needed further to refine our propositions in those respects.

A. Instruments Suppressing Diversity

In the Community pillar, decision-making by majority voting in the Council is the rule (Article 205 TEC). Unanimity still prevails in a number of important areas (budget, taxation, parts of internal market, industrial and social policy, or culture) and in the two intergovernmental pillars, even if various propositions

42 As envisaged during the 1996–7 IGC (cf. Art. J.18(1) of the Consolidated Draft Treaty Texts, May 1997) and suggested in Oct. 1999 by the Dehaene report to the President of the Commission: J.L. Dehaene, R. von Weizsäcker, and D. Simon, *The Institutional Implication of Enlargement. Report to the European Commission* (Brussels: European Commission, 18 Oct. 1999) at 8.

43 Our evaluation is based on the detailed assessment presented in E. Philippart and M. Sie Dhian Ho, "Flexibility after Amsterdam: Comparative Analysis and Prospective Impact" in J. Monar and W. Wessels (eds.), *The Treaty of Amsterdam . . .* (London: Pinter, forth.) and E. Philippart and G. Edwards, "The Provisions on Closer Cooperation in the Treaty on European Union—Politics of Multi-faceted System" (1999) 37 *Journal of Common Market Studies* 87 at 108. For additional assessments, see the very detailed work of A. Stubb, *Flexible Integration and the Amsterdam Treaty: Negotiating Differentiation in the 1996–97 IGC* (London: London School of Economics, Doctoral thesis, 1999), as well as G. Gaja, "How Flexible is Flexibility under the Amsterdam Treaty?" (1998) 35 *Common Market Law Review* 855 at 870; V. Constantinesco, "Les clauses de 'coopération renforcée'. Le protocole sur l'application des principes de subsidiarité et de proportionalité" (1997) 33 *RTD Eur.* 751 at 767; and C.-D. Ehlermann, *Differentiation, Flexibility, Closer Cooperation: The New Provisions of the Amsterdam Treaty* (Florence: European University Institute, 1998).

for the extension of QMV to those areas are regularly put forward.[44] The advantages and disadvantages of this instrument are very similar for our four categories of blockages. While unanimity should obviously not be equated with blockage,[45] resorting to qualified majority voting or extending its scope is, in the short term, the most effective way by far to override negotiation deadlocks in the development and reform of policies. A decision can be secured almost immediately, at no cost to EU finances. It applies to all Member States, avoiding the pitfall of legal fragmentation. By contrast, depending on the issue at stake, the financial and political costs for the national governments whose diversity is "outvoted" can be substantial, weighing down on the viability of policy developments obtained in that manner, especially if the distribution of the cost is perceived as unfair (cf. the scenario of orchestrated non-compliance). The repetitive use of QMV can even be experienced by the targeted Member States as "traumatic", by comparison with the slow but comforting consensus-building approach, *a fortiori* if the latter combines concessions, side-payments or acknowledgement of diversity.[46] Being repeatedly outvoted might be particularly sensitive for new members from Central and Eastern European (CEE) countries, considering the special symbolic value of a recently recaptured sovereignty. The constitution of sub-groups respecting the procedure for closer co-operation could be seen as a less "traumatic" alternative, nothing being directly imposed on the Member States choosing not to participate. All in all, QMV, because of its potential divisiveness, may not always be the most effective problem-solving technique over the long term.

As regards the import of entire (sub-)policy regimes into the EU framework, the main mechanisms are firmly based on unanimous decisions—cf. Article 48 TEU on the amendments to the Treaties and Article 308 TEC on the introduction of measures for which the Treaty has not provided the necessary powers. If QMV were to be introduced at that level,[47] its use to resolve problems of

[44] A large majority of Member States' governments agree on the necessity of QMV extension but are divided on the range of this extension. After the limited progress recorded at Amsterdam, the question is back on the agenda for the IGC 2000. Not everyone agrees, however, on the superior effectiveness of QMV in the absolute. Leading authors tend to think that QMV is not indispensable and is often introduced for reasons other than effectiveness, including in the emblematic case of the completion of the single market decided by the Single European Act (see D. Dinan, "Reflections on the IGCs" in P.H. Laurent and M. Marescеau (eds.), *The State of the European Union. Vol. 4; Deepening and Widening* (London: Lynne Rienner Publishers, 1998) at 24.

[45] Unanimity is indeed a double-edged sword. On one hand, this rule gives a huge advantage to those who favour the status quo, making reform difficult. On the other hand, "by doing so, unanimity opens the door to package deals crafted to benefit each national government", forcing the minority or even the majority to introduce undesired innovations: Hooghe and Marks, n. 5 *supra*, at 22.

[46] See, in particular, the literature on consociational systems and how the pioneering work of Lijphart has been applied to the EU by Chryssochoou: A. Lijphart, *The Politics of Accommodation: Pluralism and Democracy in the Netherlands* (Berkeley, Cal.: University of California Press, 1968); D. Chryssochoou, *Democracy in the European Union* (London and New York: Tauris Academic Studies, 1998).

[47] The most commonly discussed scheme so far is only proposing the division of the Treaties into a constitutional part for which unanimity would remain the rule and a non-constitutional part which could be reformed by a new super QMV.

integration would *a priori* have the advantages mentioned above, but could become an instrument of definitive fragmentation. As Adriano Giovanelli pointed out to us, federal systems usually recognise a right of secession, the sole remnant of the sovereignty of the federate states and the price paid for the possibility of reforming the founding act of the federation by a majority decision. Abandoning unanimity for Treaty reform should then mean the parallel introduction of the possibility of "complete withdrawal".[48] On the point of the adoption of the *acquis*, the accession procedure in fact already has much in common with QMV. Theoretically at least, negotiation is not on the contents of the *acquis*, but on how and when the applicants will apply it.[49] With the "take it or leave it" logic presiding over accession "negotiations", the current Member States—the majority—impose a set of policies and solutions to the candidates—the minority. The radical suppression of the applicant's diversity has proved to be a very effective way of overcoming problems linked with the adoption of the *acquis*, both in terms of the pace of the negotiation and the preservation of the *acquis*. It was also the source of serious backlashes when solutions were perceived as "diktats" or created "structural losers" among the newcomers.

In domains ruled by unanimity, the possibility for the majority to initiate intra-EU or extra-EU closer co-operation can put substantial pressure on dissenting Member States, thereby facilitating agreement on the development of the *acquis*. The effectiveness of this way of suppressing diversity depends on the nature of the issue under negotiation. The unwilling will give way more easily if they believe the group of the willing capable of excluding them from the benefits of the co-operation ("private goods"). The same holds for issue areas where closer co-operation is expected to cause negative externalities or induce costs for the non-participants. The effectiveness of suppressing diversity by threatening depends also on the credibility of the threat to resort to closer co-operation, credibility often increased by the participation of large Member States with adequate leadership and resources. This instrument of persuasion is, of course, not an option when it comes to reforming the *acquis*, because intra- or extra-EU co-operation for this purpose would be totally incompatible with the preservation of the EC legal order and basic obligations *vis-à-vis* the Treaties.

B. Instruments Diminishing (or Transforming) Diversity

Catch-up funds, benchmarking and "europeanising" instruments can contribute to varying degrees to the solution of all types of problems of integration. In the long term, these instruments represent probably the most effective way of solving difficulties resulting from diversity, because they operate on the roots of the problem. Cohesion by convergence is likely to produce more stable and

[48] J.V. Louis, "Quelques réflexions sur la différenciation dans l'Union européenne" in P. Manin and J.V. Louis (eds.), *Vers une Europe différenciée? Possibilité et limite* (Paris: Pedone, 1996) at 49.

[49] See Preston, n. 6 *supra*.

enduring policy outputs. The progressive weakening of cleavages should minimise indeed the probability of pendulum swings in the course of integration. For these reasons, instruments like structural funds have become central for regional policy, or benchmarking and peer review for monetary policy and compliance with internal market rules.[50] The uncertainty surrounding their performance is their main shortcoming: results can be quite divergent (cf. the record of adjustment programmes in Ireland and Greece) and/or slow to come. In the case of catch-up funds, they suppose some level of pre-existing solidarity on the basis of which net contributors consent to a significant transfer of resources and the development of substantial management structures. As for "policy transfer" methods (information exchange, best practices, benchmarking, etc.) which are much cheaper and lighter to operate, their success of course is contingent on Member States' open-mindedness about each other's practices. The extent to which those instruments are going to be effective in solving integration problems will thus depend on the urgency of achieving results, the availability of resources and the readiness of Member States to converge and europeanise.

In the context of enlargement, policy transfer is used extensively, the CEE candidate Member States being very keen to westernise quickly and thoroughly. It is likely to remain the case for some time, even if the attitude of the latter will certainly evolve to some extent after enlargement. The Union is also well aware that catch-up instruments have to be conceived on a larger scale and has embarked on an unprecedented pre-accession strategy *vis-à-vis* the CEE candidates. Intensive support is, for instance, being provided for the improvement of their judicial and administrative capacity to implement the *acquis*. Compared with the adjustments required, the current financial envelope however seems rather small. Budgetary tensions among the 15 are already high and additional transfers of resources for redistribution by the EU is very improbable at this stage. It is therefore difficult to imagine that pre-accession and post-accession programmes will do enough to secure proper adoption and implementation of the *acquis* from the moment of accession on. In such a scenario, one cannot preclude the dilution or progressive dismantling of the *acquis* confronted, among other things, with internal market problems resulting in a multiplication of safeguards and retaliation measures.

In all those respects, closer co-operation might be a quicker way to develop new and stronger regimes than what catch-up funds, soft law or policy transfer can hope to achieve. If it provides a number of institutional bridges between the "ins" and "outs", closer co-operation however offers little in terms of any more substantive commitment to solidarity. Leaving in fact the entire burden of adaptation on the shoulders of Member States who wish to join at a later stage, this expression of self-help philosophy is clearly much cheaper for the EU budget but also much more divisive.

[50] I. Begg and J. Peterson, "Editorial Statement" (1999) 37 *Journal of Common Market Studies* 9.

C. Instruments Trading-off Diversity

Issue linkages and unconditional side-payments are of relevance for problems of development, adoption and reform of the *acquis*. Package dealing obviously has its merits in so far as it is one of the longest established practices of the EC/EU and has survived the generalisation of the QMV possibility.[51] It may not be conducive to optimal decisions but guarantees a minimum of cohesiveness. Multiple linkages tend indeed to produce complex packages which are more the addition of various solutions than the expression of a coherent approach, leading in the worst cases to shaky policy design with unclear, vague or inconsistent objectives as well as inadequate or contradictory instruments. Yet the (long) search for the right balance of mutual concessions ensures that all parties have some reason for satisfaction and see the output as not entirely unfair.

If effective in lubricating agreement, the capacity of these instruments to break deadlocks is, however, not infinite. Linkage strategies depend very much on the willingness of opposing Member States to put their diversity in brackets and withdraw problematic demands from the European agenda, in exchange for concessions in other issue areas or financial compensation. This willingness is many times restricted to those instances where the adjustment costs (the domestic political costs) for the diverse Member States are moderate, excluding for instance politically sensitive sectors such as agriculture. Moreover, linkage can only overcome blockages if the other Member States are willing and able to buy off the opposing Member States with concessions elsewhere and/or unconditional side-payments. Small Member States with limited means are usually not in a position to do so, which means that there will usually be no transaction without benevolent and/or interested large and wealthy Member States. Unconditional side-payments also present the disadvantage of not addressing the source of the problem in so far as, by definition, no action is asked for in return on the part of the opposing Member States. In the long term, this exposes the EU to the necessity to buy off the same diversity time and again, straining resources and goodwill. It could institutionalise a form of free-riding, where some Member States would do little to solve their specific problems, counting on others to bail them out (cf. in the run-up to the Euro, the allegations made against Italy for its lack of monetary and budgetary discipline). Generally speaking, few governments are willing to co-operate in a system where they would have to bail out other members repeatedly. Current Member States want to make sure that the enlargement of the Union will not place them in such a situation. As for the adoption of the *acquis*, the current format of accession leaves no official room for issue linkages. The only (informal) linkage would consist of persuading the candidate to withdraw its demands against the vague promise of possible renegoti-

[51] F. Hayes-Renshaw and H. Wallace, *The Council of Ministers* (London: Macmillan, 1997) 64 at 65; J. Peterson and E. Bomberg, *Decision-making in the European Union* (London: Macmillan, 1999) at 56.

ation once it has won its "seat at the table". Put another way, the postponement of its demands is traded off against the granting of membership.

Compared with package-dealing, a revised form of closer co-operation seems more expedient and less messy. Variable geometry and its "agreement to disagree" present obviously stronger risks of "unravelling of the overarching political compromises which define the Community",[52] but the cohesive potential of trading-off instruments should not be overestimated—especially in the case of unconditional side-payments.

D. Instruments Accommodating Diversity through "Flexible" Solutions

Since instruments suppressing diversity are not available everywhere, and to the extent that means of *diminishing* and *trading off* diversity are not always sufficient to secure an agreement, a palette of accommodating methods has been developed over the years.[53] Their importance is expected to rise in the context of enlargement, in view of the substantial gap between incumbent and candidate Member States in terms of economic development or judicial and administrative capacity. On one hand, the candidates cannot afford the investments required for the adoption and implementation of the *acquis* in several sectors. On the other hand, there is no consensus in the Union on providing financial assistance comparable to that which Greece, Spain and Portugal received to help fulfilling membership's obligations. In this section, we look at the instruments accommodating diversity "horizontally" (through a new approach to harmonisation and flexible solutions) and "vertically" (through subsidiarity).

A first way of accommodating diversity boils down to what Tuytschaever calls "a lighter regulatory touch".[54] Pre-eminently suited for the development of the Community *acquis*, this new approach is based on the idea that no more harmonisation should take place than is strictly necessary for removing obstacles to economic activity. Recourse to minimum standards, mutual recognition and outline legislation has proved to be an effective method of accommodating problematic diversity, playing, for example, a key role in the completion of the single market. Negotiations are less laborious and time-consuming, being less detailed and restricted to diversity among Member States really hindering integration. Member States are free to maintain or introduce national rules better fitting local conditions, and adapt them swiftly to sectoral changes, which was not possible under previous highly detailed and encompassing legislation applied throughout the Union. In the specific context of the enlargement to come, it might be opportune to distinguish between what must be harmonised and what can be left to mutual recognition or at the discretion of the Member

[52] R. Harmsen, "A European Union of Variable Geometry: Problems and Perspectives" (1994) 45 *Northern Ireland Legal Quarterly* 129.

[53] Parts of this sub-section have been developed for Philippart and Sie Dhian Ho, n. 43 *supra*.

[54] Tuytschaever, n. 31 *supra*, at 29.

States. The danger for incumbent Member States is the way regulatory competition may develop. In the absence of a uniform legal regime, capital for example could relocate in regulatory environments where health, safety and environmental standards—that is production costs—are lower, dragging the other Member States in a race to the bottom. The new approach would, in this vision, be rather ineffective in protecting values other than trade liberalisation. Minimum harmonisation plus opt-up is in fact very much comparable to EC policies plus closer co-operation: in both cases, we have a floor on which some Member States add a number of measures committing themselves only. The main difference may be that the multiplication of individual opt-ups does not have the same integrative dimension than the efforts of a majority of Member States collectively developing more stringent standards.

A second way of accommodating diversity horizontally is through flexibility in the participation of Member States in EU regimes or policies. Various categories of instruments giving a margin of discretion to some Member States only were identified in sub-section 2.2. We evaluate their respective effectiveness hereunder.[55]

EC/EU policies with a differentiated application of common obligations and rights. Differentiation in the application of common obligations and rights is a tool which has proved to be helpful for the solution of all the integration problems we have mentioned. Transition periods and temporary derogations have been the main Community methods of accommodating diversity, allowing Member States gradually to adjust to the adoption, development or reform of the *acquis*. Among all forms of flexibility, this classical multi-speed differentiation maintains the principle of common obligations and rights, keeping legal fragmentation at its lowest. Together with the two categories which follow next, it offers the advantage of having to manage only one single *acquis* or one policy within the Union framework. To be temporarily exempted from the application of a rule might however not satisfy opposing Member States. If the rule has to be adopted by unanimity, such an accommodation will not suffice to break a stalemate leading to a cascade of vetoes. In that respect, closer co-operation is a more effective way of meeting the objection of the dissenters. An additional benefit from an integrationist viewpoint is that it restricts the later defensive panoply to a one-off veto the use of which is costly.[56] All in all, classical differentiation is most effective in the situation where all Member States are willing to co-operate, but some are unable to, even if, in the short to medium term, it is not the most efficient solution for the Member States footing the bill. In *Agenda 2000*, the Commission announced its intention of proposing transition periods limited both in scope and in duration.[57] Considering what we said

[55] Elements of this part of the sub-section have been developed for Philippart and Sie Dhian Ho, n. 43 *supra*.

[56] See n. 70 *infra*.

[57] EC, *Agenda 2000—For a Stronger and Wider Union. Vol. I. Part II. The Challenge of Enlargement* (Strasbourg: Communication of the Commission, DOC 97/6, 15 July 1997).

about adjustment costs and burden-sharing, this position could well create severe post-enlargement managerial strains. A better option might be to envisage in addition a form of multi-speed flexibility inspired by the EMU or Schengen approach. In the most demanding areas, the new Member States would not obtain derogations or be excluded, but be engaged in a scheduled process where full participation is made conditional upon meeting convergence criteria. They would go through a system of decompression stages, their diversity being largely accommodated at the beginning but having to decreased progressively.

EC/EU policies incorporating an element of case-by-case flexibility. Different types of discrete opt-outs have proved to be effective in the development of the *acquis* in-house. Constructive abstention has, for instance, eased the extension of the CFSP to peace-keeping operations. Combined with or part of predetermined flexibility packages, it has also facilitated the import of sensitive policies (in particular for social and Schengen-related issues). In that respect, constructive abstention might prepare the ground for the import of WEU *acquis*. In terms of readability, especially for third countries not necessarily aware of the EU subtleties nor keen to accept them, this formula is more predictable and less confusing than cases of a non-EC/EU policy developed in the EC/EU framework. It is also more versatile: lighter to operate because it often only requires a unilateral decision of the unwilling compared with the long procedures of closer co-operation; easier to resort to because it is more secure or less stressing for the non-participants (in most cases, their authorisation is indeed needed for each decision while it is given once for all in closer co-operation). If used sparingly, this form of flexibility is more compatible with the "indivisible" nature of some policy areas (an argument often used for external policy). It could turn out to be more effective to manage situations where the blockage rests with hesitant, i.e. unwilling but non-recalcitrant, Member States. If used repeatedly, case-by-case flexibility could amount to some sort of jurisprudential development producing a more fragmented *acquis* than what would be produced by a limited number of clearly identified groupings (that is to say, in a Union practising restricted variable geometry, what Nordic, pro-environment, . . . , groups would develop for themselves in addition to a common *acquis*). The pick-and-choose approach is indeed, in theory, the most damaging option with respect to maintaining the coherence of a general scheme. With regard to enlargement, the application of a case-by-case opt-out in the adoption of the *acquis* would clash with the rule of the full adoption of the *acquis* by new Member States, but more importantly would do that in an extremely fragmentary way. It might however prove difficult to sell a "no opt-out" approach to candidate Member States, now that opt-outs have been so generously granted to (better off) current Member States. To minimise the impression of a diktat and resulting frustrations, imaginative diplomacy will obviously be needed.

EC/EU policies established on the basis of ad hoc flexible arrangements (predetermined flexibility). This category is also primarily suited for the problem of development of the *acquis* in-house and by import. Tailor-made arrangements with *ad hoc* decision-making, burden-sharing procedures, among others, can be more complex or difficult to manage than arrangements designed according to the general rules for closer co-operation. They are indeed likely to include many expedients in order to meet all political considerations and exhaust all opportunities. As a result, this form of flexibility, together with the next one, can lead to monstrosity in terms of transparency and readability. On the other hand, it will remain a more effective policy tool if the multiple safeguards and rigid features of closer co-operation are not adapted. With predetermined flexibility, one does not have to demonstrate that the last resort has been reached, convince a majority of Member States to join in, etc. Had the EMU and the Schengen protocols been drafted according to the provisions for closer co-operation, it is likely that the policy output would have been smaller and slower to come, and most probably short of what was needed to solve the problems of the development of the *acquis*.

It might be advisable, before or soon after the accession of the first wave of candidates, to reform parts of the *acquis* by resorting to this form of predetermined flexibility. The concept of variable geometry is indeed "more appropriate for dealing with important, relatively constant differences between constellations of Member States, where the differences constitute a case for permanently distinct rules for particular groups of countries".[58] In sectors like environment, it is highly unlikely that the CEE candidate Member States will have adopted and implemented the entire *acquis* by the time of their accession. Their environmental problems are often very similar. One could therefore think of a more selective adoption of the environmental *acquis* restricted, for example, to transnational environmental protection and/or the functioning of the internal market. For the rest, different sub-regimes could be established, adapted to the realities of different groups of Member States.[59] Accommodation through predetermined flexibility would—contrary to minimum harmonisation plus individual Member States opt-outs—maintain a unified European environmental legislation. This "controlled but flexible approach towards the accession process" may be an effective regulatory strategy for the problem of the adoption of the *acquis*, but it implies transgressing the taboo of regressive flexibility.

Intra-EU closer co-operation established on the basis of ad hoc flexible arrangements. This option has in theory all the advantages and disadvantages of the previous form of flexibility with one major supplementary complication:

[58] A. Carius, I. von Homeyer and S. Bär, "The Eastern Enlargement of the European Union and Environmental Policy: Challenges, Expectations, Speed and Flexibility" in K. Holzinger and P. Knoepfel (eds.), *Environmental Policy in a European Union of Variable Geometry? The Challenge of the Next Enlargement* (Basel: Helbig & Lictenhahn, forthcoming) at 29.

[59] Carius *et al.* argue, for example, that it might make sense to release CEE candidate Member States from the obligation strictly to apply EC standards for water management. The accession countries with large areas thinly populated, in order to implement rules initially conceived for EU high-density population areas, would indeed have to make investments unjustifiable in terms of environmental benefits, Carius, *supra* n. 58.

the policy resulting from intra-EU closer co-operation is normally not part of the EC/EU *acquis* (the exception being the *acquis* resulting from the closer co-operation authorised by the protocol integrating the Schengen *acquis* into the framework of the EU). In such a configuration, one ends up with one domain managed through a number of differentiated procedures producing several policies and *acquis*. When *ad hoc* co-operation has no legislative or regulatory dimension (for instance additional R&D programmes), this managerial complication is not necessarily prohibitive. The "euro–11" formula has also proved to be effective for the type of informal and confidential co-operation required so far by monetary integration. Serious doubts are nevertheless expressed on the capacity of such arrangement to deliver if confronted, for instance, by serious asymmetrical shocks.

Intra-EU closer co-operation on the basis of the general enabling clauses set out in TEU Title VII. The provisions for closer co-operation were designed to deal with the problem of the development of the *acquis* "in-house". The result of a laborious compromise, they are said to have no or very little potential as a policy tool due to their multiple defensive and restrictive features. This corresponds in fact to a reading which implicitly uses the question of how to get around recalcitrant Member States as the main criterion for evaluation—an obvious choice in the wake of an IGC battered for months by the defiant attitude of the UK conservative government. If however one considers the use of closer co-operation in the context of "normal" disagreement, its potential is greater than it first appears. Cases where Member States do not object to other Member States co-operating more closely among themselves, are not unprecedented. While lacking interest for a policy sub-area, they are keen to manifest their positive attitude towards the Union (a sort of federal comity) and increase their political capital in a relatively easy way. A mechanism like constructive abstention is based on that very expectation and has been welcomed by many as an experiment worth making. It would therefore be unfounded to rule out that, despite its multiple vetoes and practical difficulties,[60] closer co-operation could provide a reasonably attractive solution for problems involving uninterested unwilling and not excluding willing Member States.

The problem of the development of the *acquis* by import has not been directly addressed by the new system of structured flexibility. Closer co-operation is nevertheless making a positive contribution in that respect, as it provides some principles, norms and rules recognised by all as acceptable, if not totally equitable. In other words, a regime was established which could contribute to decrease the transaction costs for future imports: the new system indeed provides a starting point for the negotiations of specific arrangements, it sets minima and maxima, it narrows down the range of options. As regards the problem of the adoption of the *acquis* by candidate Member States, the new device does

[60] On 17 May 1999, the Council's Rules of Procedure were adapted to answer some of these problems.

not help their accession by lowering the threshold in terms of the volume of the *acquis*, but it does facilitate the enlargement by contributing to reducing the anxiety of incumbent Member States about the capacity further to develop the Union once enlargement has taken place. It can also contribute indirectly to alleviating managerial concerns with the possible dilution of existing European policies. If applicants are not able to implement the *acquis* satisfactorily and if the postponement of enlargement is not an option, the only alternative solution is to segment the *acquis* and fence some of its parts to prevent their decay. It can be argued that the constitutional entrenchment of closer co-operation has, depending on the point of view, broken a taboo or opened Pandora's box, and is legitimising a number of principles which could be evoked in favour of such a regressive form of flexibility.

EU-linked extra-EU closer co-operation. By definition, this form of flexibility can only be envisaged as a solution to blockages in the development of the *acquis* in-house. When management of diversity within the EU fails, the last option is to develop those policies outside the EU framework, in the limits of Article 10 TEC stipulating that "[Member States] shall abstain from any measure which could jeopardise the attainment of the objectives" of the Treaty. Unhindered by veto participation threshold optimal groups of like-minded Member States more quickly can form and agree stronger sets of norms (cf. Benelux, Nordic Co-operation Council, etc.). But it also comes with particular managerial problems, like the development of specific structures characterised by smaller economies of scale, this against a widespread reluctance to create new international bureaucracies.[61] EU-linked extra-EU co-operation can be of great interest for the pursuit of a dialectical—some would say schizophrenic—development: for instance, thanks to the WEU formula, the EU can move closer to hard security and defence while respecting the diversity of neutral and non-aligned Member States. Because of the recognition of a link with the EU and the need to prepare for eventual fusion, co-operating Member States tend to adopt open structures and avoid offensive hegemonic behaviour. Yet it might smack of *directoire* and be a source of anxiety for the non-participating Member States, leading them to hinder the deepening of the links between the EU and extra-EU instances of closer co-operation. Unless the general clauses for closer co-operation are revised, the post-enlargement context will increase the attractiveness of more flexible flexibility, that is to say mainly extra-EU or informal intra-EU co-operation.

Subsidiarity. The last option of this palette is to accommodate diversity vertically by making use of subsidiarity and leaving parts of a policy outside the realm of the EU. Such solution by subtraction has cleared the path for many package deals developing or reforming the *acquis*. In the short term, it is partic-

[61] On the practical problems encountered by the extra-EU Schengen experience, see J. Monar, "Schengen and Flexibility in the Treaty of Amsterdam: Opportunities and Risks of Differentiated Integration in EU Justice and Home Affairs" in M. den Boer (ed.), *Schengen, Judicial Cooperation and Policy Coordination* (Maastricht: EIPA, 1997) 10 at 11 and 15.

ularly effective in areas where sub-national actors can veto the position of their country and have to be appeased by the guarantee that their *chasse gardée* will be preserved—a major concern in particular for the non-central governments of federal or strongly regionalised Member States. The resulting allocation of competences is likely to be neater than horizontal accommodation would *a priori* produce. Moreover this use of subsidiarity swiftly eases tensions over the EU budget and among Member States, but accentuates tensions within those Member States unable to deliver satisfactory solutions at national level. From the last point of view, closer co-operation could come off better. Equally non constraining, it provides in addition a possibility for "differentiated subsidiarity": some Member States stick to national solutions, whereas others choose to adopt sub-continental ones (that is, solutions jointly pursued by eight or more Member States participating in a given project).[62] In the long term, resorting to subsidiarity rather than closer co-operation would therefore, in a number of cases, be less effective, integrative and supportive option from a European point of view (if one reckons that some solidarity will necessarily develop within closer co-operation groupings). In the context of enlargement, this method might be used more extensively to justify the withdrawal or non-inclusion of costly and/or highly redistributive policies in EU schemes (cf. CAP, welfare or public health).

E. Instruments Circumventing Diversity

The records of EU-linked extra-EU co-operation and extra-EU co-operation are very similar. The latter, however, follows a much more restrictive approach *vis-à-vis* some categories of Member States (the small and/or less developed Member States usually being excluded) and supranational institutions (almost always short-circuited). Refusing EU bridges, interferences and counterweights benefiting dissenting Member States, this form of co-operation often corresponds to a naked expression of leadership. The Big Three (France, Germany, the UK) and Italy aim for instance at designing and consolidating new regimes among themselves before progressively opening up to other countries ready to act in unison with them (cf. co-operation in education or armaments production). This approach can be effective in terms of pressure put on the dissenting Member States, pace of policy development or alternative to collective intra-EU leadership, yet with all the problems of (would-be) *directoires*. Compared to closer co-operation, this instrument—by definition not preoccupied by consensus politics and completely deprived of EU legitimacy—could generate lasting

62 This idea has been discussed in the context of subsidiarity and variable geometry by Lane, then more explicitly developed by Bribosia and Tuytschaever in particular: R. Lane, "New Community Competences under the Maastricht Treaty" (1993) 30 *Common Market Law Review* 971; H. Bribosia, "De la subsidiarité à la coopération renforcée" in Y. Lejeune (ed.), *Le Traité d'Amsterdam: Espoirs et déceptions* (Brussels: Bruylant, 1998), 86 ff; Tuytschaever, n. 32 *supra*, at 242.

resentment and permanent suspicion among the excluded, preventing later integration into the EU. In the long term, this solution could also presage a proliferation of regimes parallel to the EU (duplicating or emptying existing EU/EC policies) and an accentuation in the formation of caucuses or voting syndicates. It could therefore represent one of the biggest dangers for the EU/EC integration project.

4. THE CONSTITUTIONALIZATION OF VARIABLE GEOMETRY: EVALUATING ITS IMPACT FOR THE EU SYSTEM

The repercussions of the Amsterdam provisions on closer co-operation go beyond the management of problems of integration.[63] Some problems of integration have been addressed in a specific way and with a particular institutional set-up; other remain unanswered, their blend having consequences for EU governance as a whole. Moreover, many governments tend to put a managerial spin on their systemic objectives, having learned the lessons of many inconclusive or even counter-productive debates on the finality of the Union. Managerial innovations are, for instance, used as an opportunity to step up the pace to further (federal-like) integration or break down the dynamics of the initial pre-federal mould. That being said, the actors' information is limited and their capacity to foresee future developments is impaired by the fact that the Union is moving from one unstable equilibrium to another. Some consequences may therefore simply be unintended.

Closer co-operation has a practical and a symbolic dimension. When studying the actual design of the instrument or the revised version suggested in the introduction to section 3, one needs to look at the immediate impact its application could have, but also at the wider signification of the enshrinement of its underlying principle in the Treaties. These direct and indirect systemic consequences will be evaluated from the perspective of the Westphalian, intergovernmentalist, regulatory and multi-level governance models, focusing on (4.1) the scope of EU policies, (4.2) the methods of integration and (4.3) the institutional structure and legitimacy of the EU.

A. Shrinking or Expanding the Scope of EU Policies?

Closer co-operation has been explicitly restricted to current EC/EU domains. It is intended for intensifying the level of co-operation in existing EC/EU policies, not moving into new areas. From the Westphalian perspective (which prescribes that the EU's scope should widen to cover more and more areas traditionally

[63] Large parts of the paras. dealing with the Westphalian and regulatory models were initially developed for Philippart and Sie Dhian Ho, n. 43 *supra*.

associated with the national state), it is neither progress nor a setback, in so far as it should *a priori* not lead to expansion or contraction. On closer reading however, it is not entirely neutral. On the one hand, the fact that solidarity mechanisms (i.e. helping non-participant Member States to catch up with front-runners) have no part in this scheme does not bode well for the Westphalian objective of expanding the Union's redistributive policies. On the other hand, the Amsterdam provisions could be seen as a first answer to the Westphalian ambition to curb extra-EU co-operation which negatively affects the Union scope and depth of policies.[64] The revised version of closer co-operation would, of course, represent a much more substantial progress in that respect.

The Amsterdam mechanism is, by contrast, very much in accordance with the intergovernmentalist and regulatory conceptions. While officially aiming "at furthering the objectives of the Union and at protecting and serving its interests" (Article 43 TEU), it provides in fact a way to make sure that the limits of European competence coincide more precisely with the individual interests of the Member States—a key intergovernmentalist prescription. It allows the deepening of integration where functional needs require it, which is of utmost importance for the proponents of the regulatory model. The record from the multi-level governance viewpoint is more ambivalent. Closer co-operation is *a priori* not undermining subsidiarity, the basis on which the scope and depth of EU competences must be determined according to MLG. The relative importance of the concept may even gain from it if one accepts the argument that closer co-operation amounts to "differentiated subsidiarity" (see sub-section 3.4.). Such a development is, of course, very positive for both MLG approaches. Proponents of the structured MLG variant would only deplore that closer co-operation is not contributing, to say the least, to clarifying the question of the allocation of competences. Even if its use might increase the problem-solving capacity of the system as a whole, it would necessarily add confusion to the already muddy question of who is in charge of what. The frustration for tenants of the dispersed MLG variant should be of a different nature: the Amsterdam mechanism remains centered on state actors and does not contribute to the empowerment of small groups in civil society.

B. Breaking Taboos: the End of the "Integration Through Solidarity" Method?

As far as the methods of integration are concerned, the introduction of closer co-operation means a clear departure from the Westphalian model whose

[64] For this point, we are indebted to Philippe de Schoutheete who drew our attention to the fact that closer co-operation can be seen as a consolidation of the Westphalian model as far as it gives (at least in theory) a means of avoiding occurrences similar to Schengen in the future. Amsterdam is however also seen by some as a missed opportunity or even an incentive to co-operate outside the Community framework: G. Gaja, "How Flexible is Flexibility under the Amsterdam Treaty?" (1998) 35 *Common Market Law Review* 869 at 870).

standards prescribe universal participation by Member States, uniform application of procedures and extended transparency. One could nevertheless argue that the transgression of these Westphalian prescriptions does not necessarily push the Union off a statehood course. Because of its centripetal features and integrative dynamic, closer co-operation should be conceived first and foremost as an intermediary stage, preparing the ground for further integration for all at the cost of a temporary loss of uniformity.[65] The departure from the Westphalian principle of equal rights and obligations for all Member States would only be tactical and closer co-operation amount to a new variant of the "step-by-step approach towards an ever closer union", characteristic of the Community method.[66] The challenge would then be, in the words of the Club of Florence, "to maintain the dynamism of the Community through the advances which a number of Member States are ready to make, without running the risk of a division which would later be difficult to overcome".[67]

A more significant breach of the Westphalian ethos might arise from the impact of closer co-operation on the two related issues of QMV and solidarity. During the 1996–7 IGC, closer co-operation was sometimes presented as an alternative to QMV: either less integrationist minded Member States accept the extension of QMV or they agree to let the others move forward through closer co-operation. The Amsterdam negotiators eventually decided to extend the scope of QMV and authorise closer co-operation, including in policy areas where unanimity is not the rule. The question was therefore not treated *stricto sensu* in terms of an alternative, but concessions were exchanged, the advocates of closer co-operation agreeing to dilute their demands (and with them the operativeness of the mechanism) because of pro-integrationist breakthroughs on other fronts. It is nevertheless also true that the idea of the alternative could resurface, putting closer co-operation in the way of future extension of QMV. Unwilling Member States could see its revision as a convenient solution to remove the extension of QMV from the EU agenda and break the pro-QMV coalition. Such a move could indeed lead the willing and able Member States to redirect their negotiating efforts from the unwilling onto the unable Member States, the latter having been so far more reluctant *vis-à-vis* closer co-operation than QMV. The revision of closer co-operation could be detrimental not only to the extension of QMV, but also to its exercise or practice. Once revised, closer co-operation could indeed be used in place of QMV, if the majority reckons that, for very controversial questions, outvoting the minority would be

[65] The costs of exclusion from the benefits and/or the exposure to the negative externalities of the closer co-operation should push sooner or later non participant governments to consider opting in and eventuate in a regrouping of all Member States. Among the main procedural features contributing to this centripetal process are the principle of "open door" based on objective criteria and the obligation for latecomers to accept closer co-operation's *acquis*.

[66] Y. Devuyst, "The Community Method after Amsterdam" (1999) 37 *Journal of Common Market Studies* 110.

[67] R. Dehousse (ed.) for the Club of Florence, *Europe: The Impossible Status Quo* (London: Macmillan, 1997) at 14.

too traumatic. In so far as the solidarity *problématique* is concerned, closer co-operation illustrates the emergence of a new norm: there will be no automatic solidarity mechanism between the "ins" and "outs", self-help being the rule. Yet the present system for structured flexibility is only a set of minimal rules. Solidarity schemes are not mentioned, but are not precluded either. The so-called "emergency brakes" (the right to veto the authorisation of closer co-operation "for important and stated reasons of national policy") are a powerful lever for the unables to extract catch-up measures—provided of course that the willing are resourceful, very eager to move ahead and cannot proceed through extra-EU co-operation. The suppression of the veto on the occasion of a revision of closer co-operation would remove the obligation to make concessions and let the attention paid to cohesion depend on other, wider, considerations. The EU could then depart further and further from the pro-Westphalian extension of majoritarian rule, going hand in hand with various solidarity mechanisms aimed at compensating the outvoted minority. The "integration through solidarity" method favoured by the model (that is, dealing with socio-economic diversity through multi-speed formulae, differentiation in treatment and redistributive schemes) could be progressively replaced by a combination of catch-up through self-help and temporary exclusion from various policy regimes.

Yet another serious hazard for a Westphalian type of integration is linked to the fact that no rules have set minimal procedural and institutional standards below which the import of any *acquis* would be forbidden. Precedents show that, in the process of importing, quite opposite regimes can be injected into the Community or Union framework. Before being imported into the Treaties, the European Monetary System was subjected to a radical overhaul which led to the design of the Monetary Union and the eventual introduction of elements which are among the most centralised and federal in the EU. What the European Political Co-operation underwent was mainly repackaging, leading to the creation of a separate pillar for the Common Foreign and Security Policy and its considerable dose of intergovernmentalism challenging the Community method from inside. The fact that closer co-operation does not bring any solution to the problem of the development of the *acquis* by import means that the evolution of the system remains open or vulnerable to elements developed exogenously, possibly by some Member States only, through specific procedures and not necessarily in view of their eventual integration into the Union framework.[68]

A last and highly speculative systemic consequence could be derived from the symbolic meaning of the constitutionalisation of flexibility. Closer co-operation has broken a major taboo in the domain of the development of the *acquis*, and this precedent could shake the foundations of the orthodoxy presiding over the

[68] Jörg Monar, among others, is strongly pleading for fundamental changes in the procedure for Treaty reform, arguing that the proliferation of differentiation through Treaty amendments "is approaching the threshold to irreversible fragmentation and eventual disintegration": J. Monar, *"Europe 2020" Project. The Future of European Governance* (Bruges: College of Europe, 2000) at 29.

adoption of the *acquis*. In other words, it could be an invitation to abandon or relax the principle of the integrity of the *acquis* and envisage regressive flexibility. Particularly in the context of strong political pressure in favour of a rapid enlargement to CEE or even Balkan countries which might not be able to adopt and implement parts of the *acquis*, this extrapolation of the flexibility logic could potentially form the biggest threat for Westphalian aspirations.[69]

The evaluation of the consequences of closer co-operation is, in varying degrees, more positive from the point of view of our other models of reference. Seen from an intergovernmentalist angle, closer co-operation is the ultimate expression of the right of non-participation and, by extension, of its preferred method, voluntary co-operation. Compared with the extension of QMV, the Member States can refuse to be constrained by the development of the *acquis* and keep a greater control over the process of European integration. With the "emergency brakes", closer co-operation gave in addition the symbolically important opportunity to codify in the Treaties a mechanism reminding one of the Luxembourg compromise and recognise explicitly a clear primacy of national over European "priorities".[70] The functionalist-inspired regulatory camp, having no strict methodological preconception, is satisfied with any functional improvement of the system, provided that the supranational elements are preserved in a number of policy areas. Closer co-operation, seen as a manifestation of pragmatism in terms of procedures and methods, fulfils this basic condition, even if the restrictive conditions imposed on it limit too drastically the effectiveness of the instrument. It would become a major systemic advance if its revision allowed for policy mixes better adapted to issue areas and the rebuilding of more functional "clubs". The MLG for its part would, of course, applaud the officialisation and approval of variable geometry as a method and an institutional framework (see below). Its structured variant would mainly regret that closer co-operation does not bring anything new for the subnational level of government, while its dispersed variant would be disappointed first with the inflexibility of the Amsterdam formula and the many limits placed on a "pick and choose" method.

[69] The European Commission has strongly warned against this option, for instance in the contribution to the Finish presidency tabled by Romano Prodi and the Commissioner responsible for the IGC 2000, Michel Barnier: European Commission, *Adapting the Institutions to make a success of enlargement: a Commission contribution to the preparations for the Inter-Governmental Conference on institutional issues* (Brussels: 10 Nov. 1999, IP/99/826).

[70] The triggering procedure established by Art. 40 TEU has often been abusively presented as the final codification of the Luxembourg compromise. A comparison of the texts and the practice indicates indeed that Amsterdam is a strongly edulcorated version of Luxembourg. The major differences are the obligation for the Member States evoking the possibility of a veto to justify its position, the reference to national policy instead of the much vaguer "national interest", and the exchange of a routine and anonymous veto in the Council with a more exceptional and highly publicised veto aired at the level of the European Council.

C. Minimising Risks for the Institutional Structure while Betting on Output Legitimacy?

The consequences of closer co-operation on the institutional structure of the Union are, once again, potentially more disturbing from the Westphalian viewpoint than from the three others. On one hand, closer co-operation does not create new institutions, alter significantly the inter-institutional balance of power established by the other titles of the Treaties, or change the pre-existing level of participation, political accountability and democratic control. In that respect, it is more or less neutral with regard to the evolution of the Union towards a classical parliamentary system, the strengthening of the EP and the blossoming of input legitimacy, all defended by the Westphalian model. On the other hand, it does affect negatively the transparency and openness of the EU. Access to the documentation of those co-operating more closely is likely to be problematic for non-participating Member States, and by extension for the public in general. If, following their revision, the provisions on closer co-operation are used more extensively, the complexity of the *acquis lato sensu* would increase significantly, impairing the readability and transparency of the European enterprise. More seriously perhaps, it could also dramatically distract the EU from the ideal of an undifferentiated system of governance across policy-areas. If closer co-operation is simply adding new places of interaction between some Member States for limited purposes (i.e. new *loci* of power), the institutional structure of the Union would remain compatible with the *federatio* variant of the Westphalian conceptual world.[71] If it amounts however to the formalisation of a "core Europe" (i.e. a new level of power with its special prerogatives), the new structure would simply become antinomic with the Westphalian systemic objectives. The probability of the first scenario is clearly higher and closer co-operation should be seen, from a Westphalian viewpoint, as a possible but remote risk rather than an imminent danger.

A core Europe is unlikely to emerge from the repeated use of (a revised form of) closer co-operation. First, it is not clear whether this instrument would be used to push through rather narrowly delineated projects (for instance, the creation of a European Company Statute) or more substantial policy packages (for instance, an entire code on employment, working conditions and social protection). In any case, future reinforced co-operation is expected to remain of an incremental nature and follow a sectoral logic. The fact that some Member States would participate in all instances of co-operation would therefore not necessarily put a world between them and the other Member States, or mean they share a common strategic vision on the *finalités politiques* of the Union,

[71] Federal systems, in Germany or North America for instance, have developed fora where (some) federate units co-operate among themselves or with the federal level—which the federalist jargon terms, rather confusingly for specialists of international relations, "intergovernmental co-operation".

two defining conditions of a political core. One could also point to the fact that the only group of countries likely to be part of all closer co-operation, i.e. the six founding Member States would have to work with other Member States, these partners varying with the policy area. This should undermine any attempt to act as a separate nucleus. The most serious cause of concern from a Westphalian point of view may however arise after the next waves of enlargement, if new Member States from Central and Eastern Europe happen to be more or less systematically excluded from new initiatives linked with the single currency, security and justice or defence. Confronted with a growing erosion of coherence, discipline and solidarity at EU level, most, if not all, current Member States could indeed be tempted to develop, by default, a defensive core where such erosion would be stopped or reversed.[72] In the words of Helen Wallace, "the flexibility debate might unleash the instruments and a dynamic that could give an identity and a legitimisation to the club within the club".[73]

As much as it is disputable that closer co-operation is laying the ground for core countries to establish a core Europe, it is undeniable that its introduction into the Treaties gives new status to variable geometry in the European architecture. What has been acknowledged unequivocally is a scheme where, beyond an overall acceptance of the finality of the Union (i.e. the firm commitment to the normative project defined by the founding fathers), all Member States have to participate in a number of core activities which will be supplemented by functional groupings of variable membership. This conception falls short of the ideal of an "*à la carte* Europe" shared by the intergovernmentalist and dispersed MLG models for which it is not necessary to identify core policies, but is in essence consistent with the regulatory and structured MLG logic of sub-systems designed for specific performance. Such an evolution clearly vindicates the regulatory and structured MLG approaches, their proponents applauding a more flexible architecture and the reinforcement of sectorisation, better able to deliver adequate solutions to specific policy problems.

Legitimacy and EU institutional reform have become increasingly intertwined issues in the course of the 1990s. Yet the provisions on closer co-operation have not been designed for legitimacy purposes.[74] Their use may even be detrimental in terms of input legitimacy (cf. above on the transparency issue). Nonetheless,

[72] In June 1998, at the opening of the French National Assembly debate on EU enlargement and institutional reforms, Pierre Moscovici, French Minister for European Affairs, stated very clearly that the next enlargement "raises, no doubt for the first time, the question of the limits of European construction, not only its geographical but also its 'functional' limits". Referring to enhanced co-operation as "an inevitable road towards a broader Union", he added that it does not imply any "infringement of the principle of solidarity, nor any manœuvre by the older Member States against the new ones: it is simply a virtual biological necessity in a Europe of 20 or 30": *Europe*, No. 7236, 6 June 1998.

[73] H. Wallace, "Flexibility: A Tool of Integration or a Restraint on Disintegration?" in K. Neunreither and A. Wiener (eds.), *Amsterdam and Beyond: Institutional Dynamics and Prospects for Democracy* (Oxford: Oxford University Press, 2000) 175 at 191.

[74] F. Snyder, "Comments" in M. den Boer, A. Guggenbühl and S. Vanhoonacker, *Coping with Flexibility and Legitimacy after Amsterdam*, (Maastricht: EIPA, 1998) at 114.

provided they are the key to more effective policies, they will contribute to boosting the Union's output legitimacy. If closer co-operation became an alternative to QMV, it would amount to a shift towards a system more based on output legitimacy than input legitimacy, the extension of QMV being usually combined with an increase of the powers of the EP. Should the revision of closer co-operation be exchanged in a future reform of the Treaties for the maintenance of unanimity, such a trade-off would mean a further deviation from the Westphalian legitimacy standards. Closer co-operation is also not interesting from the point of view of the dispersed MLG model. The latter pleads for more devolution and greater involvement of civil society actors (i.e. increased input legitimacy), whereas the new solution preserves a single institutional framework and is substituting one formal state-centric procedure for another. The conception of legitimacy which underpins closer co-operation is, in fact, plainly compatible only with the intergovernmentalist, the regulatory and the structured MLG model.

5. CONCLUSIONS

Enlargement will increase managerial strains within the Union by increasing the number of Member States and EU diversity. Leaving aside problems caused by sheer numbers and recognising that diversity is not intrinsically detrimental to integration, we have focused on problems diversity might cause for integration in terms of the development, adoption and reform of the *acquis*. Although governments and commentators differ in their prescriptions, it is widely accepted that the actual settings of the Union are inadequate to confront efficiently challenges ahead. This proposition was underwritten by the 1996–7 and 2000 IGCs, both mandated to increase the problem-solving capacity of the Union. Our managerial evaluation, after taking into consideration various policy instruments, is pointing at a number of logical solutions capable of increasing this capacity through procedural, institutional or substantive reforms.[75]

From an integrationist perspective, the extension of QMV is probably the most tried and tested managerial technique. The long-term effectiveness of this option would depend on the sparing use of QMV and the parallel development of far-reaching solidarity mechanisms avoiding paternalistic or patronising overtones—two conditions particularly crucial in the context of the next enlargement. Dealing with problematic diversity through a mix of QMV and catch-up funds should be a first priority, but the probability of additional resources being made available after enlargement is rather low. This approach will therefore not always be feasible. In the absence of financial means, other combinations of diminishing and/or trading-off instruments can be envisaged.

[75] These solutions are more fully developed by E. Philippart and M. Sie Dhian Ho in a forthcoming working document and in a report of the Netherlands Scientific Council for Government policy (Den Haag).

Soft law, benchmarking and policy transfer contributing to diminish diversity indeed have a genuine potential. Yet the degree of convergence they produce is uncertain and their pace usually slow. As regards instruments trading off diversity, their effectiveness has other limitations. Package dealing depends very much on the willingness of the dissenting Member States to put their diversity in brackets and the other Member States to buy it off. In times of budgetary constraints, the likelihood of large unconditional side-payments decreases, replaced by package deals with few direct financial consequences which are more difficult to construct. Irrespective of this financial dimension, they present the disadvantage of being rather messy, not addressing the source of the problem and having a limited cohesive potential. Circumventing diversity can be effective to put pressure on dissenting Member States, swiftly develop new co-operation regimes or provide leadership. Yet it comes with the practical difficulties of extra-EU co-operation, the political problems generated by *directoires* and the risk of a multiplication of parallel regimes duplicating or emptying existing EU/EC policies. It could be one of the most divisive options for EU/EC integrative ambitions.

Such a background explains the growing importance held by flexible approaches over the 1990s. Compared with the previous combinations, accommodating instruments supply less costly, traumatic, paternalistic and relatively quicker alternatives. They also involve various types of managerial problems and risks, their respective effectiveness and cost, depending on the issue at stake as well as the configuration of willing, unwilling and unable Member States. Generally speaking, and except for the differentiated application of common obligations and rights (like temporary derogations), TEU title VII closer co-operation is providing, from an integrationist perspective, a better approach to flexibility because of the following centripetal features: the capacity to put pressure on the unwilling, playing on the latter's fear of exclusion from the benefits of co-operation while "suffering" from its negative external effects; limited legal fragmentation compared to minimum harmonisation plus individual opt-outs or case-by-case flexibility; transparency resulting from the fact that normal procedures will apply (contrasting, in particular, with intra-EU closer co-operation based on *ad hoc* flexible arrangements); and minimising of risks for EU institutional structures. On the other hand, the mechanism established by Amsterdam has comparative disadvantages: extremely cumbersome procedures; disregard for the plight of the unable Member States (through the choice of self-help philosophy, implicitly expressed by an absence of direct commitment to solidarity); risk of deepening cleavages between Member States; and risk of unravelling the overarching political compromises which define the Community. No flexible solution has been supplied so far for the problem of the import, adoption or reform of the *acquis*, even if closer co-operation provides possible points of reference in those respects. Considering the balance of pros and cons listed above, the conclusion of our managerial evaluation can only be written in an "if then" form: if the extension of QMV combined with an increase in the EU budget does not materialise, it might be argued that closer co-operation should be revised to offer a better "structured flexibility", but also that further innovations will be needed in particular to solve the problem of the adoption of the *acquis*.

If revised and used extensively, in which direction could closer co-operation propel the EU? Our systemic evaluation is showing that the use of closer co-operation would move the EU system towards the regulatory and structured MLG models.[76] Falling short of the intergovernmentalist and dispersed MLG ideal of an "*à la carte* Europe", closer co-operation means the constitutionalisation and the possibility of further developing a variable geometry Europe—in which Member States are due to enter on a number of common core activities, but are allowed to create functional subsystems with variable membership. In line with the regulatory and MLG emphasis on problem-solving capacity of the Union, such a system would rely predominantly on output legitimacy. This "pragmatic" solution would also seriously threaten a number of key values at the root of the Community method and advocated by the Westphalian model, solidarity in particular. If put into practice in a self-help mode, closer co-operation might even lead to a more or less structural exclusion of the new CEE Member States from new policy initiatives. The format of closer co-operation is however partially open for negotiation and the output of that negotiation will in fact determine the actual impact of closer co-operation on the trajectory of the Union. If self-help and confidentiality are the rule, resorting repeatedly to closer co-operation might lead to the creation of a club within the club. If, on the contrary, closer co-operation is conceived in a fairly open way and accompanied by adequate bridging between the "ins" and "outs", this form of flexibility might make a substantial contribution to further expansion of the system. It would then not mean the final blow to the Westphalian model, but only to its highly centralised version, namely that of a hierarchical super-state. If applied in an integrative mode, closer co-operation would be consistent with a form of decentralised federalism, which is in fact close to the structured MLG model.

What is going to happen with flexibility? Immediately after the signature of the Amsterdam Treaty, disappointment and cynicism *vis-à-vis* the closer co-operation clauses dominated the debate with few exceptions. But, as we wrote in October 1998, the need for more structured and integrated closer co-operation was going to "be impossible to ignore".[77] The Finnish presidency saw a revival of interest for the issue, from caricatural and populist demand for a flexibility clause by William Hague playing for the Euro-sceptic wing of the

[76] In fact, the regulatory model and the structured MLG model have much in common, both emphasising functionality of methods and institutions, output legitimacy, etc. This proximity led Simon Hix to amalgamate them under the label of "new governance" in his evaluation of the merits of comparative politics: S. Hix, "The Study of the European Union II: The 'New Governance' Agenda and its Rival" (1998) 5 *Journal of European Public Policy* 38 at 65.

[77] E. Philippart, " Flexibility and Enhanced Co-operation after Amsterdam: Perspectives and Likely Scenarios", paper prepared for *Flexibility and Enhanced Cooperation in European Security Matters: Assets or Liabilities?*, Western European Union, Institute for Security Studies, Paris, 22–23 Oct. 1998.

British Conservative party, to more elaborated and balanced propositions on closer co-operation put forward by, among others, the Dehaene Report, the French Commissariat du Plan,[78] the German Stiftung Wissenschaft und Politik,[79] the Dutch government position paper for the IGC 2000 and the European Commission. The fact that the question of closer co-operation has resurfaced in the run-up to the IGC 2000 does not of course mean that significant or even incremental modifications will be part of the next package of Treaty reforms. Mobilisation is a necessary but insufficient condition for that matter, the concept and the mechanism being the object of enduring misunderstanding and reluctance. For those reckoning that, with such a tool, the Union would be better equipped to face any post-enlargement evolution, all should be done to push this reform through during the coming Intergovernmental Conference. It might indeed become much more difficult at a later stage, if unanimity remains the rule for Treaty reform and if some of the CEE countries see closer co-operation as an instrument devised to exclude them.

[78] The report is, in particular, proposing ways to development a strong "*centre de gravité*" for the Union: J.L. Quermonne, G. Andréani and M. Dehove, *L'Union européenne en quête d'institutions légitimes et efficaces* (Paris: La Documentation française pour le Commissariat du Plan, 1999).

[79] The Ebenhausen report recommends the "rehabilitation" of extra-EU co-operation rather than attempting to strengthen closer co-operation: C. Deubner, *Enhanced Cooperation of EU Member States after Amsterdam. A New Tool to be Applied or to be Avoided?* (Ebenhausen: SWP–KA 3108, 1999) at 12.

15

Relating Constitutionalism and Flexibility in the European Union

JO SHAW*

1. INTRODUCTION

THERE IS A PUZZLE underpinning this chapter. It lies in the following question: is there something inherently contradictory in considering constitutionalism in conjunction with flexibility? Can a political system or entity which claims to be "constitutional" in the sense that it conforms to the well-established and widely regarded principles of the rule of law, checks on powers and the protection of individual rights, also instantiate elements of flexibility, and, if so, what degree of flexibility? Or is such a polity inevitably sinking into the realms of the arbitrary, away from necessary elements of certainty and stability?

After an initial discussion juxtaposing the concepts of constitutionalism and flexibility (section 2), section 3 reconsiders the notion of constitutionalism in the EU, suggesting ways in which current conceptualisations and approaches are inadequate to the task of identifying and explaining the constitutional basis of the EU polity. I suggest an approach to constitutionalism which is in essence procedural, relational and dialogic. Most significantly, a definition of constitutionalism as the accommodation of difference and diversity will be deployed. In section 4 the attention shifts to the notion of flexibility. After a brief review of some key definitions and concepts of flexibility, the focus returns once more to the concepts of diversity and difference. Thus, the definition given to flexibility in this chapter has a procedural rather than a substantive character. This is because it is this procedural quality which binds together the widely differing uses of flexibility in political and legal language. Indeed, flexibility certainly appears to provide a language in which differing interests can appear to converse without actually communicating. Importing flexibility into the debate could be said to be what has kept those representing both intensified and

* Professor of European Law, University of Leeds. Thanks go to John Bell, Armin von Bogdandy, Gráinne de Búrca, Jim Tully and Antje Wiener for comments and suggestions on an earlier draft. Unfortunately, I have not been able to incorporate or respond to all the useful ideas which these commentators put forward, and, of course, responsibility for remaining errors and infelicities is mine.

diffused visions of the "integration project" round the same negotiating table. On that view, it is a "lowest common denominator"-type concept, applied by pragmatists and technocrats. But less cynically, one can also suggest that flexibility is linked to important principles of dialogic and procedural constitutionalism, including a duty to negotiate and a duty to listen to the arguments of others. It implies tolerance of partial, fragmented and interim outcomes, formulated in the knowledge that the dialogue will continue. The Union and its governance arrangements are a work in progress. It does not, however, imply an acceptance of the arbitrary or the inconsistent as the inevitable price of flexibility.

Having identified the notions of constitutionalism and flexibility, in section 5 we then revisit the flexibility v. constitutionalism puzzle in the light of the reformulations suggested. For exemplary purposes, the chapter makes use of recent debates on constitutional law and politics in Canada, in particular the Supreme Court's judgment on the *Reference on the Secession of Quebec*. In that case, the Court identified and formulated a constitutional duty on the parties involved in constitutional amendment to negotiate in good faith, a duty which would be triggered by a clearly expressed wish on the part of the people of that province to secede from the rest of Canada.[1] Although an argument around *secession* (and therefore *disintegration*) seems at first sight a poor comparator for the constitutional challenges faced by the EU and its Member States embarking upon what is conventionally described as an *integration* and *polity-formation* process, there are none the less good bases for the comparison. In the first place, there is a simple descriptive point that were Quebec to proceed with secession, it would be likely to negotiate some form of "halfway house" economic association and political links with the rest of Canada which would undoubtedly ressemble and perhaps learn from the experience of the EU.[2] Secondly, the key element of the Supreme Court's judgment is its willingness to begin thinking the unthinkable and contemplating the unpalatable—namely the secession of Quebec and the dismemberment of the Canadian body politic consequent upon the separatist demands of the *québécois*—and to consider how this possibility could be located within a process comprising constitutional civility. Similarly, EU constitutionalism is—for many of the actors implicated—the (hitherto) unthinkable. To that end, the duty to negotiate in good faith represents an interesting idea which could be imported into EU constitutionalism. Moreover, the comparison brings into focus more clearly the reasons why aspects of flexibility operating at all levels of a polity, including the constitutional, can usefully reinforce both the principles and processes which promote justice and stability in divided societies.

[1] *Reference by the Governor in Council, pursuant to s 53 of the Supreme Court Act, concerning the secession of Quebec from Canada* [1998] 2 SCR 217.

[2] P. Oliver, "Canada's Two Solitudes: Constitutional and International Law in *Reference re Secession of Quebec*" (1999) 6 *International Journal on Minority and Group Rights* 63.

In sum, through the paper the argument is developed that the Union must be, in conceptual terms at least, a *flexible polity*. Thus the presentation refutes the apocalyptic vision of flexibility as ushering in a nightmarish departure from the sense of order and the particular vision of power under limits which the legal framework has lent to the EU hitherto. However, the conclusion is based on the foundational argument that the substratum of the polity is not its legal order, but rather its discursive practices. In sum, flexibility rather precisely instantiates the open-endedness of constitutional politics within the contemporary EU.

2. JUXTAPOSING CONSTITUTIONALISM AND FLEXIBILITY

Constitutionalism and flexibility—while not exactly binary opposites—are not obviously closely linked. Indeed, the classic discussions of a constitutional polity dwell more often upon the stability and structure provided by constitutionalism as a practice of democratic politics under the rule of law, upon the provision of rights protecting individuals, and upon the imposition of limits on the exercise of power than upon the capacity of constitutions to permit flexibility or upon constitutional capacity for diversity. A common-sense understanding of law is as (one) antidote to flexibility. It creates procedures and sets standards that governmental actors must conform to. Typically these are linked to some form of remedial guarantees or rights for citizens or other stakeholders within the system. Moreover, turning to the relevance of these concepts in the context of the EU, it is apparent that since constitutionalism has hitherto frequently been invoked as a close relative of the *telos* of integration in studies of the law and politics of the EU,[3] there is what might be termed an orthodoxy of hostility to flexibility as undermining the enhancement of that constitutionalism. This orthodoxy would characterise the insertion of flexibility—both actual and potential—into the EU order by the Treaty of Amsterdam as a crude "statal grab for power".[4] The orthodox thesis is neatly expressed by Akos Toth when he argues that "as a means of ensuring the future progress of the Union, no amount of opt-out, opt-in, derogation and flexibility can provide a credible alternative" to the reforms which he advocates, namely strengthening the current constitutional elements of the Treaties in particular by altering the procedure for Treaty amendment (i.e. by making the whole system more flexible).[5] For Toth, such changes would be based on the desire precisely to preserve what are understood to be the key elements of the EU constitutional framework in the face of an increasingly hostile environment: the constitutionalised Treaty,

[3] One classic example amongst many would be G.F. Mancini, "Europe: The Case for Statehood" (1998) 4 *European Law Journal* 29.

[4] J.M. de Areilza, "Enhanced Cooperation in the Treaty of Amsterdam: Some Critical Remarks", Harvard Jean Monnet Working Paper 13/98, at 2.

[5] A. Toth, "The Legal Effects of the Protocols relating to the United Kingdom, Ireland and Denmark" in T. Heukels, N. Blokker and M. Brus (eds.), *The European Union after Amsterdam* (The Hague: Kluwer Law International, 1998).

the supremacy and direct effect of EC law and the constitutional authority of the Court of Justice. The alternative seems to risk a descent into arbitrariness, essentially at odds with the Enlightenment value of the rule of law, not to mention the moral claims of the integration project. It is to these grand ideals which the creation of a simple tension between integration (forwards) and disintegration (backwards) speaks. It is a powerful invocation of a specifically "modern" version of progress.

And yet despite the hostility of those propounding the orthodoxy of integration-through-law and the progress of constitutionalism as the inevitable, not to say cosy, partner of integration, flexibility has none the less become a pervasive element of the EU at the present time. Having always been present to some degree at a variety of levels of the EC/EU's operation,[6] one might now almost say that assymetrical approaches such as opting out/in and flexible frameworks for implementation have become guiding norms in EU governance. Flexibility in the EU context takes many different forms. At various times and in various ways, assymetrical approaches employing a multitude of differing more or less formal methods, based upon either international law or the internal law of the EU itself, have provided practical solutions acceptable to the Member States and other actors involved, in relation to challenges of governance thrown up by the evolution of the EC, and more recently the EU. This has occurred in respect of topics as diverse as economic and monetary union, social policy, the control of borders, asylum, immigration and refugees, and many aspects of external trading relations. In so doing, it has cut across divisions between "high" politics and "low" politics. The development of flexibility in relation to the formulation and articulation of policy complements the enduring use of flexibility in policy implementation in relation to many areas of the harmonisation of laws, including the internal market, consumer policy and environmental policy. The configurations of and bases for such arrangements can and do evolve over the years, as the narratives behind the rise and fall of the social policy opt-out for the United Kingdom from Maastricht to Amsterdam and the communitarisation of Schengen through the Treaty of Amsterdam both amply demonstrate. In addition, one should also cite one of the Treaty of Amsterdam's principal contributions to the flexibility matrix, which is that of making certain future instances of flexibility formally constitutionally tolerable and conceivable for the EU, in particular through the provisions of Articles 40 and 43–45 TEU and Article 11 EC.[7] All in all, as the papers in this volume amply and aptly demonstrate, it is hard to identify a field of EU law and policy-making where the flexibility debate has not resounded to a greater or lesser extent in recent years, raising a variety of different political and legal challenges to the generally acknowledged *status quo*. Simultaneously, flexibility casts doubt upon the taken-for-granted integrationist

[6] See the chapter in this volume by G. de Búrca; also C.-D. Ehlermann, "How Flexible is Community Law? An Unsual Approach to the Concept of 'Two Speeds' " (1984) 82 *Michigan Law Review* 1274.

[7] J. Shaw, "The Treaty of Amsterdam: Challenges of Flexibility and Legitimacy" (1998) 4 *ELJ* 63.

telos of "more Europe" as stating definitively the nature of the "progress" which is being sought. On the contrary, flexibility suggests that an integrationist outcome understood in those terms is not necessarily a shared goal of all Member States. It challenges the presumption that "more Europe" must be the outcome of the project of creating new supranational governance structures within the EU. It challenges us also to think about the relationships between integration and disintegration.

At the same time, constitutionalism has also become an increasingly pervasive discourse. Constitutionalism and constitutional principles as such are not explicitly articulated in the Treaties, or by the Member States in their debates around those Treaties and amendments to them. However, a value framework which can be recognised as the conventional substratum of a "liberal constitutional" edifice is now to be found in the Treaty of Amsterdam, as the Union is expressed to be founded on "the principles of liberty, democracy, respect for human rights and fundamental freedoms, and the rule of law" (Article 6 TEU). In similar terms, the practices of the institutions and the Member States—whether or not directly founded upon the Treaties—are often recognisably "constitutional" (e.g. in the use of concepts such as competence or limited powers), and the borrowing of the languages, concepts and normative frameworks of constitutionalism offers a reference point or—in constructivist terms—set of shared norms for actors. These in turn help to shape the responses of actors to external stimuli, such as a discernible global movement towards constitutionalism.[8] The impact of these shared norms is most visible in the work of the Court of Justice, with its invocation of the EC Treaty as the "constitutional charter" of the European Community in the *Les Verts* case.[9] The declaratory wording of the Treaty of Amsterdam in relation to the European Union as a whole has its strongest constitutive effect when it is viewed as cumulative upon the declaratory statements of the Court of Justice about the constitutional basis of the European Community.

Both academic scholars and commentators within the media also frequently focus upon the possibilities of constitutionalism as lending enhanced legitimacy to the struggling EU. Somewhat less frequently—certainly in the UK—these ideas are taken up by politicians as well. The general objective of such endeavours has often been to make constitutionalism more than an elite discourse and somehow to involve "ordinary" people through a constitution-building process. In terms of academic analysis, numerous variants based more or less tightly or loosely upon Habermassian discourse ethics and related ethical frameworks have been propounded, in order to suggest ways out of the impasse apparently

[8] On this see B. Ackermann, "The Rise of World Constitutionalism" (1997) 83 *Virginia Law Review* 771.

[9] Case 294/83, *Parti Ecologiste "Les Verts"* v. *European Parliament* [1986] ECR 1339; see also *Opinion 1/91: Re the Draft Agreement on a European Economic Area* [1991] ECR I–6079.

created by the absence of a pre-existing *demos* or European people.[10] Some of these arguments rely heavily upon the constructive potential of Union citizenship as an institutional framework.[11] These are useful ways of escaping what Damian Chalmers terms the "dialogue of the deaf" which occurs in relation to issues of both constitutionalism and democracy in the European Union "with those who believe in a European *demos* shouting past those who do not, and vice versa".[12]

These comments briefly chart, but do not explain, the emergence of both flexibility and constitutionalism within the EU.[13] The task of examining the forces and pressures which lie behind the demand for and supply of flexiblity and constitutionalism—along with the task of explaining in detail how these ideas and practices operate—lies beyond the scope of this chapter. Instead, it takes up the challenge of juxtaposing the two ideas, of articulating possible contradictions and of considering the nature of the existing cohabitation between constitutionalism and flexibility. One way of proceeding would be to examine the hypothesis that the Member States have enlisted the concept of flexibility as discourse and practice in order to avoid confronting and dealing with the key challenges of constructing constitutional democracy in a postnational context and of addressing the legitimacy question. Pursuing that line of enquiry would be essentially normative in its deployment of assumptions about the values of constitutional democracy. This chapter employs a rather different method by first setting out concepts of constitutionalism and flexibility understood in the context of a historically and institutionally grounded account of European Union governance and integration, in order to show that the two principles possess an important underlying intellectual consistency and coherence when applied in the postnational context which is not apparent at first blush. However, it is normative in two senses. First, it is normative in its prescription of the appropriate tools from the "constitutionalism toolkit" which should be applied to the EU and the constitutional issues which are raised in this postnational and supranational process of polity formation. Although this point is not explicitly articulated in the context of the argument which follows, which focuses first and foremost upon constitutionalism's procedural qualities, this chapter accepts as an underlying normative prescription the capacity of constitutionalism to anchor societal values within a stable framework of divided powers. Secondly, it is normative in its dissection of constitutional approaches to the question of

10 See generally on this J. Shaw, "The Interpretation of European Union Citizenship" (1998) 61 *MLR* 293 at 305–7. Examples include J. Weiler, "Does Europe Need a Constitution? Reflections upon Demos, Telos and the German Maastricht Decision" (1995) 1 *ELJ* 219 and D. Chryssochoou, "Europe's Could-Be Demos: Recasting the Debate" (1996) 1 *West European Politics* 787.

11 E.g. A. Wiener and V. della Sala, "Constitution Making and Citizenship Practice—Bridging the Democracy Gap in the EU?" (1997) 35 *JCMS* 595.

12 D. Chalmers, *European Union Law. Volume One. Law and EU Government* (Aldershot: Dartmouth, 1998), at 186; for a summary of the arguments see also B. Kohler-Koch, "A Constitution for Europe?", MZES Working Paper 8, 1999 (www.mzes.uni_mannheim.de/)

13 See e.g. A. Moravscsik and K. Nicolaïdes, "Keynote Article: Federal Ideals and Constitutional Realities in the Treaty of Amsterdam" (1998) 36 *JCMS*: *Annual Review 1997* 13.

the recognition of cultural differences within multinational and often divided polities. Because it instantiates a high degree of diversity—even if not an intense degree of conflict at present—the EU constitutes such a polity in its challenge to constitutionalism.

For constitutionalism and flexibility to be presented as complementary rather than contradictory elements of the emergent EU polity may appear to be paradoxical, but this perverse complementarity is not a unique phenomenon within the EU. It is one part of the broader paradoxical relationship between the EU and "stateness": the phenomenon of the EU as the creature of states, as apeing aspects of the behaviour of states, and yet as undermining their authority through the construction of alternative and sometimes competing spheres of authority.[14] This paradox is played out in a number of fields, where the practices of EU governance borrow from the practices of states but yet differ in crucial ways. For example, it is customary to reproach the EU for possessing a democratic deficit in so far as the ways in which laws are made at EU level do not, by any means, pass muster when measured against an ideal type of parliamentary or constitutional democracy. Yet, in practice, further development of the treasured "democratic" element of the EU in the form of the role of the European Parliament could contribute as easily to the undermining of national democratic practices as to the evolution of a European public space and a new "European democracy".[15] "European" parliamentary democracy is thus, so far, an unrealised and—to many—undesirable ideal, unhappily positioned between sometimes over-idealised visions of national democracies *within* states and the conventions of diplomatic practice *between* states which admit of little or no conception of representation and direct popular accountability. This paradoxical nature invites us to begin the process of understanding EU governance and then developing its democratisation by reconsidering well-established binary oppositions or pairs such as the state and the EU, national institutions and EU institutions, or national citizenship and Citizenship of the Union. Reflecting that paradox onto the conceptual domain, I have suggested elsewhere the utility of examining key strands of the principles of integration and "disintegration" in parallel and without automatically privileging taken-for-granted assumptions about integration in order to show how the current praxis of the EU legal and political order sustains elements of *both* principles.[16] In other words, the apparent binary opposites reveal substantial areas of overlap and constructive interaction, as with, for example, the creeping Europeanisation of national institutions, or the increase in forms of national influence over supposedly

[14] For more details see J. Shaw and A. Wiener, "The Paradox of the 'European Polity' " in M. Green Cowles and M. Smith (eds.), *The State of the European Union: Volume 5: Risks, Reforms, Resistance and Revival* (Oxford: Oxford University Press, 2000, forthcoming).

[15] On the difficulties raised by such an analysis see M. Poiares Maduro, "Europe and the Constitution: *What if this is As Good As It Gets?*", in J. Weiler and K. Wind, *Rethinking European Constitutionalism* (Cambridge, 2000, forthcoming).

[16] See J. Shaw, "European Union Legal Studies in Crisis? Towards a New Dynamic" (1996) 16 *OJLS* 231.

"European" institutions such as the EU's legislative processes. The overall objective of such an endeavour is to allow scholarship on the EU and particularly its legal order(s) to escape the constricting and suffocating preconceptions of the "integration-through-law" movement,[17] challenging taken-for-granted assumptions about why and how institutions and identities within and around the European Union are changing and transforming *beyond* or *without* a simplistic integrationist *telos*.[18]

3. IDENTIFYING CONSTITUTIONALISM IN THE EU

In the specific EU context, the root of constitutionalism, if not its modern-day flowering, is the "constitutionalisation" of the Treaties; that is, precisely the ironing out of the flexibilities and discretionary elements of the EU as international legal order, and a process of creating more rigidities, certainties and uniformities through the interactions of the Court of Justice, national courts, the political institutions and the texts of the Treaties and secondary legislation. EC law rights are conceived as universalised procedural claims, conferred upon the subjects of EC law. The uniform application and interpretation of EC law represent high constitutional values from the perspective of the Court of Justice as constitutional court. The adjective more readily used in conjunction with the EU legal order is "federal" rather than "international". The variables to which the differing national laws and constitutions of the Member States inevitably give rise are fed into the system essentially via the prism of EC law and via the Court of Justice as authoritative arbiter of conflicts and questions of interpretation and effect. That is the vision of the "constitutionalised" Treaty from the perspective of the Court of Justice, and the widespread, if not universal, acceptance of this perspective by courts at national level suggests that there are important areas of mutual reinforcement in relation to ideas about law and integration between the Court of Justice and its national interlocutors. The shared norm of integration as *telos* thus came to support the constitutional structure of the Treaties. As Kenneth Armstrong has argued, the image of the constitutionalised Treaty is one element of an instrumentalist presentation of the law in the context of the EU, implying "a broader claim concerning the possibility of social and political integration *through law*" (emphasis added).[19]

This seems to suggest a comfortable relationship between law, constitutionalism and European integration processes. This appearance of comfort is, in fact, somewhat misleading—for a number of reasons. First, the image of the

[17] This is a consistent theme in Michelle Everson's writing: e.g. M. Everson, "Beyond the *Bundesverfassungsgericht*: On the Necessary Cunning of Constitutional Reasoning" (1998) 4 *ELJ* 389.

[18] For an example of anti-teleological reasoning in relation to the EU see Z. Bańkowski and E. Christodoulidis, "The European Union as an Essentially Contested Project" (1998) 4 *ELJ* 341.

[19] K. Armstrong, "Legal Integration: Theorizing the Legal Dimension of European Integration" (1998) 36 *JCMS* 155 at 161.

constitutionalised Treaty is, to a very great extent, a unilateral projection of the Court of Justice, not a negotiated constitutional settlement between the Court of Justice and those of its interlocutors which are sceptical of the Court's *Kompetenz-Kompetenz* in relation to the scope of EC law and of the autonomy of the EU legal order. Foremost amongst these sceptical interlocutors is the German Federal Constitutional Court,[20] but the list has also included—at various times—the French Conseil d'Etat,[21] the Italian Constitutional Court[22] and the Danish Supreme Court.[23] This demonstrates the inadequacy of the somewhat monological characterisation of the EU constitution via the constitutionalisation of the Treaties. These challenges have provoked a number of responses amongst commentators and constitutional scholars in particular. One line of argument presents an alternative characterisation of the EU constitutional system as comprising *also* the national systems in a multi-level constitutionalism expressed as a *Verfassungsverbund*.[24] On that line of argument the EU constitution cannot be understood separately from the national systems, although the constitutional nature system of governance is much easier to perceive in relation to the "European Community" narrowly understood. Other characterisations have focused upon presenting the EU and its legal order as a single unit[25] and the pillar structure as effectively merged,[26] or as a "layered international organization".[27] Although there are substantial differences between these various approaches, it can be argued that what they share is a reconstruction around a much wider constitutional basis of the scholarly understanding of the nature of "integration" as shared norm and a reconsideration of the value of notions such as federalism.

Secondly, the absence of a firm empirical base of "a European constitution" functionally or ideologically equivalent to the American constitution upon which scholarship can be grounded, along with the uncertain relationship between the EU and the notion of "stateness" with which constitutionalism is historically strongly linked, together contribute to a rather slippery discourse in

[20] *Brunner* [1994] 1 CMLR 57.

[21] A consistent line was taken in case law until the case of *Nicolo* [1990] 1 CMLR 173.

[22] *Frontini* v. *Ministero delle Finanze* [1974] 2 CMLR 372.

[23] *Carlsen et al.* v. *Prime Minister Rasmussen*, judgment of the Danish Supreme Court of 6 Apr. 1998; unofficial translation available at http://www.um.dk/udenrigspolitik/europa/domeng/ (website visited: 26 July 1999). On the question of national reactions to the supremacy of EC law, see in general P. Craig and G. de Búrca, *EU Law—Text, Cases and Materials* (2nd edn., Oxford: Oxford University Press, 1998), 264–94.

[24] I. Pernice, "Multilevel Constitutionalism and the Treaty of Amsterdam: European Constitution-making Revisited?" (1999) 36 *CMLRev*. 703.

[25] A. von Bogdandy, "The European Union as a Supranational Federation. A Conceptual Attempt in the Light of the Amsterdam Treaty", draft paper, ms June 1999; *ibid*, "The Legal Case for Unity. The European Union as a Single Organisation with a Single Legal System" (1999) 36 *CMLRev*. 887.

[26] B. de Witte, "The Pillar Structure and the Nature of the European Union: Greek Temple or French Gothic Cathedral?" in Heukels *et al*. (eds.), n. 5 *supra*.

[27] D. Curtin and I. Dekker, "The EU as a 'Layered' International Organization: Institutional Unity in Disguise" in P. Craig and G. de Búrca (eds.), *The Evolution of EU Law* (Oxford: Oxford University Press, 1998).

relation to EU constitutionalism. Frequently, the analysis slips between description of observable elements of EU-level constitutional practices as empirical fact, the articulation of a normative discourse surrounding the question "does Europe need a Constitution?", and the application to the EU of various established theories of constitutionalism drawn from political theories of liberalism, communitarianism and republicanism. In particular, it is clear that debates about the political theories and political economies of constitutionalism are likely to be circular in so far as the discussion is trapped within the paradigm of the sameness/difference binary. Is the EU more or less like a state because it aspires to a form of constitutionalism? Clearly, the postnational non-state nature of the EU as an evolving political and legal object demands that prescriptions of constitutionalism at (nation) state level cannot simply be applied to the EU unchanged or barely altered. The tools of analysis are therefore badly lacking both in terms of the "thick" description of EU constitutionalism as postnational polity formation, and in terms of a normative understanding of the underlying principles of this new level of constitutional debate. As Miguel Poiares Maduro has argued, it is one thing to describe the EU constitution as "open-ended, indeterminate, discursive, sui generis, contested," but quite another to come up with proposals to deal with these issues.[28]

The argument about constitutionalism can move forward, I would suggest, only if we focus upon key procedural, dialogic and relational elements in a reworked conception of constitutionalism as the framework within which differences and similarities between social groups are uncovered, negotiated and resolved.[29] Such negotiations and resolutions are themselves not necessarily to be understood as finally determinative, but as interim solutions within a continuing conversation.[30] That procedural turn needs to pay explicit attention, however, to the postnational context. I understand postnational to be an open-textured concept used to express many of the dynamic and *sui generis* elements of the EU as an *integration* project involving the process of polity formation including constitutional processes, but understanding integration itself as a multi-textured concept. This can either comprise seeing integration as in some senses *including* disintegration, or understanding it as being in continuous interaction with (and not necessarily in opposition to) processes of disintegration.[31] Either way, the relationship is one of tension and complex interaction, not simple opposition and contradiction. In other words, postnationalism is not about

[28] Poiares Maduro, n. 15 *supra*, at 1.

[29] For further details see J. Shaw, "Postnational Constitutionalism in the European Union" (1999) 6 *Journal of European Public Policy* 579. This focus should not be taken to mean that a complete argument in relation to EU constitutionalism should ignore the normative dimension of constitution-building. Rather the limit to the argument at the present time is that before a Rawlsian "overlapping consensus" or other basis of agreement can be constructed, the terms of constitutional debate need to be made transparent.

[30] S. Chambers, "Contract or Conversation? Theoretical Lessons from the Canadian Constitutional Crisis" (1998) 26 *Politics and Society* 143.

[31] Shaw, n. 16 *supra*.

a linear movement towards a more "integrated" Europe in the conventional sense so often used by the so-called "integration-through-law" movement, but involves a reflexive critique of institutions, legal forms and identity formations beyond statist limits. Moreover, the discourse of postnationalism is essentially interrogatory. It demands, for example, that the practical and intellectual challenges to nation states posed by the twin developments of globalisation and regionalisation are reflected back upon taken-for-granted assumptions about the Westphalian system of states. It rejects simplistic views of the relationship between EC law and national law, and of evolving notions of sovereignty and sovereign authority as applied in the context of the EU. Indeed, the legal dimension of postnationalism, and especially the challenge to develop plural notions of legal systems,[32] represents a key element of reinterpreting constitutionalism beyond a "unitary" notion of the constitution, deploying an acknowledgement that the *national* constitution cannot automatically make a privileged claim for recognition.[33]

The argument about process mounted in this chapter is more than the common-sense or intuitive presupposition that political processes are important—particularly in the constitutional context where demands regarding the putative social legitimacy of ruling norms are correspondingly higher. At the level of theorising about constitutional politics, it concerns the question whether individuals and groups of individuals can negotiate their living together in a way which recognises but does not submerge differences and varying identities, and which recognises the non-fixity of constitutional settlements in the light of the infinite possibility and variability of new claims for the recognition of identities which are not envisaged at the present time. Elements of dialogue and process are frequently visible not only in discussions of EU constitutionalism, but also in the constitutional heritages of many states inside and outside the EU. The task here is to find a satisfactory theoretical grounding for the argument. To this end, the work of the Canadian political theorist James Tully proves to be particularly useful as a starting point for rethinking the EU's postnational constitutionalism since it is founded upon a linkage of constitutionalism and the negotiation of cultural recognition, as well as a normative presupposition of the acute need for "diversity awareness" amongst participants in a constitutional process.[34] It provides both a statement of the conventions which should underpin a form of

[32] On this see in particular N. MacCormick, *Questioning Sovereignty. Law, State, and Nation in the European Commonwealth* (Oxford: Oxford University Press, 1999), esp. chs. 7 and 8; MacCormick explicitly bases his reinterpretation of sovereignty upon a legal pluralism derived from an institutional theory of law which "detaches 'law' conceptually from 'state' " (*ibid.*, at p. v).

[33] Poiares Maduro, n. 15 *supra*.

[34] J. Tully, *Strange Multipicity. Constitutionalism in an Age of Diversity* (Cambridge: Cambridge University Press, 1995); *ibid.*, "Freedom and Disclosure in Multinational Societies" in A. Gagnon and J. Tully (eds.), *Justice and Stability in Multinational Societies* (Cambridge: Cambridge University Press, 2000 forthcoming); *ibid.*, "Identity Politics and Freedom: The Challenge of Reimagining Belonging in Multicultural and Multinational Societies", Conference on Reimagining Belonging, Aalborg University, Denmark, May 1999; *ibid.*, "The Agonic Freedom of Citizens" (1999) 28 *Economy and Society* 161.

reworked constitutionalism which he terms "common constitutionalism" and a method for theorising constitutional dialogue in divided societies. Tully's argument is both explicit and prescriptive about the conventions which must—perforce—underlie a constitutional process which achieves cultural recognition, which is just, and which will lead to stability within divided societies. Hence he asserts that:

> A constitution should be seen as a form of activity, an intercultural dialogue in which culturally diverse sovereign citizens of contemporary societies negotiate agreements on their forms of association over time in accordance with three conventions of mutual recognition, consent and cultural continuity.[35]

These three principles are conventions in the sense that they are:

> norms that come into being and come to be accepted as authoritative in the course of constitutional practice, including criticism and contestation of that practice. They gradually gain their authority by acts in conformity with them and by appeals to them by both sides, as warrants of justification, when they are transgressed.[36]

Tully's conventions of common constitutionalism do not at first sight appear particularly controversial. Mutual recognition is distinguished from assimilation, consent from coercion and cultural continuity from the *tabula rasa* notion which informed the unique moment of constitutional creation which occurred at Philadelphia on behalf of an essentially fictional "we, the People". The "bite" of these ideas emerges more strongly when the details of Tully's intellectual method are fed into the debate. He proposes an approach to constitution-building derived from critical concepts of understanding, definition and description drawn from the philosophy and philosophical practices of Ludwig Wittgenstein[37] specifically as an alternative worldview to that which informs so-called modern constitutionalism, which is harshly criticised by Tully as facilitating imperialistic cultural practices and substituting the assimilation, integration and transcendence of difference for its recognition and affirmation.[38] A Wittgensteinian approach supplies a way of understanding which is not a redescription of another's cultural situation in one's own language, but which reveals redescription as what it really is, namely "one heuristic description of examples among others; one interlocution among others in the dialogue of humankind". It also provides a "philosophical account of the way in which exchanges of views in intercultural dialogues nurture the attitude of 'diversity awareness' by enabling the interlocutors to regard cases differently and change their way of looking at things", and finally it links the real world and the philo-

[35] Tully, *Strange Multiplicity*, n. 34 *supra*, at 30.

[36] *Ibid.*, 116.

[37] Tully's use of Wittgensteinian thinking to develop a political philosophy for constitutionalism can be contrasted with the use of Wittgensteinian ideas about speech-acts and language in the emerging tradition of constructivist studies of the EU: see T. Christiansen, K.E. Jørgensen and A. Wiener, "The Social Construction of Europe" (1999) 6 *Journal of European Public Policy* 528 at 541.

[38] Tully, *Strange Multiplicity*, n. 34 *supra*, at 44.

sophical world by showing "how understanding occurs in the real world of overlapping, interacting and negotiated cultural diversity in which we speak, act and associate together".[39] Significantly, the account supplies a duty to hear the other side, and to listen to arguments presented in the terminology and languages of others.

In an argument which uses the baseline of Canadian constitutional debates, Simone Chambers offers general support to Tully's approach to constitutionalism as a dialogic and conversational process, rather than as a contractual one producing a fixed outcome.[40] However, she suggests that Habermassian discourse theory can provide an alternative grounding of the approach. But, as she indicates, she and Tully agree upon the fundamental principle that "constitutionalism in an age of democratic diversity is more about keeping a conversation going than getting all the parties to sign on the dotted line at one time and place".[41] Such an approach presupposes the value of flexibility in constitutional processes. The specific historical moments which generate these theorisations relate to the Canadian experience of failing to achieve a consensus across the relevant constitutional actors on what being Canadian and being subject to a Canadian constitutional settlement actually means. These problems have been acute ever since the repatriation of the Canadian constitution occurred in 1982 in circumstances which overrode the will of the province of Quebec and the majority of its people, and have persisted through the course of the negotiations of, but subsequent failure to accept, the Meech Lake and Charlottetown Accords which were intended to accommodate the situation of Quebec.[42] These constitutional problems continue against a backdrop of continuing arguments by separatists in Quebec promoting its secession from the rest of Canada, if need be by a unilateral act based upon the will of the people of Quebec. Better, in such circumstances of fundamental disagreement, Chambers suggests, to accept the new interpretation which Canada's situation seems to generate, that is, "the idea of an ongoing open conversation between diversities rather than the idea of a unitary identity for a nation-state".[43] Part of the problem, she argues, is overemphasis upon particular constitutional moments rather than the constitutional continuum. Thus a different approach will be taken if it is accepted that consti-

[39] All quotations drawn from *ibid.*, 111.

[40] Such arguments are implicitly deploying the concept of "contract" in its classical or neo-classical sense of a discrete relationship with a high degree of fixity in relation to the participants, the procedures for entering and leaving, and the contents of the contract. Interestingly, debates about contractualism in constitutional politics rarely address the challenges of understanding a contract or network of contracts as "relational", and thus as a complex and changing transaction rather than one with fixed terms, entries and exits: e.g. H. Abromeit and T. Hitzel-Cassagnes, "Constitutional Change and Contractual Revision: Principles and Procedures" (1999) 5 *ELJ* 23. On relational contract, see S. Wheeler and J. Shaw, *Contract Law* (Oxford: Oxford University Press, 1996), ch. 2.

[41] Chambers, n. 30 *supra*, at 155.

[42] For brief accounts of this situation see, e.g., Chambers, n. 30 *supra*, at 144–9, Oliver, n. 2 *supra*, and M. Walters, "Nationalism and the Pathology of Legal Systems: Considering the *Quebec Secession Reference* and its Lessons for the United Kingdom" (1999) 62 *MLR* 370 at 372–5.

[43] Chambers, n. 30 *supra*, at 165.

tutional issues are not settled once and for all, in a single constituting act. So, she argues, the referendum on the Charlottetown Accord which formulated a complex and, some would argue, unwieldy notion of what it meant to be Canadian was lost, because it became divisive rather than discursive. It became a yes/no and win/lose scenario in which the adversarial is privileged over the discursive.

Chambers continues, and concludes—in a manner that has clear resonance for a polity as diverse as the EU—that:

> it is Canada's great achievement and strength that is has built a political association without imposing unitary identity on its diverse members . . . This is the constitutional model of the future—a constitutional model that can accommodate multiculturalism and diversity.

We shall return to the relevance of the Canadian experience—specifically through the reassessment of Canadian constitutionalism by the Supreme Court in the *Quebec Secession Reference* judgment and the articulation of a constitutional duty to negotiate[44]—in section 4. However, it is clear that these proposals from Chambers, as much as the arguments mounted by Tully, are explicitly grounded upon an acknowledgement that the global rise of identity politics and consequent demands for cultural recognition represent a key challenge for constitutionalism.

The utility of these dialogic and conversational approaches to developing ideas about constitutionalism in the EU context becomes more apparent when they are allied to an illuminating reinterpretation of the Union as an "essentially contested concept" developed by Zenon Bańkowski and Emilios Christodoulidis.[45] Their approach draws upon W.B. Gallie's notion of "essential contestability", which postulates that it is possible to demonstrate that two people can disagree substantively about a certain concept and yet agree that some example could be a paradigm of that concept (e.g. democracy, and perhaps subsidiarity in the EU context),[46] but they suggest a useful gloss whereby it is the process of *contestation*, not the state of *contestability* which is crucial. This is crucially tied to an explicitly non-teleological understanding of the EU. It may be on a journey, as many people accept, but its journey has no fixed and predetermined destination, and indeed it is the journey rather than any putative destination which is placed at the centre of their analysis.[47]

Here, then, is a menu of concepts and approaches which suggests a way forward for constitutionalist thinking in the EU. It is beyond the constitutionalisation of the Treaties debate, and grounded in the indeterminate postnational

[44] See n. 1 *supra*.

[45] Z. Bańkowski and Christodoulidis, n. 18 *supra*.

[46] W.B. Gallie, "Essentially Contested Concepts" (1955–6) 56 *Proceedings of the Aristotelian Society* 167.

[47] See also M. La Torre, "Legal Pluralism as Evolutionary Achievement of Community Law" (1999) 12 *Ratio Juris* 182, 194–5, who argues for an interactionist constitution for the EU, emerging through an "open-ended" discursive process, and who deploys an argument to that end grounded in a combination of legal pluralism and a Rawlsian overlapping consensus.

territory of cultural recognition and diversity. Crucially, for the argument in this chapter, it is the first step in relating flexibility and constitutionalism in the context of the EU's ongoing process of polity formation.

4. IDENTIFYING FLEXIBILITY IN THE EU

At every level and in every dimension, the EU is a flexible polity. Its external borders are not (yet? ever?) fixed. Since the entry into force of the Single European Act in 1986, what were then the European Communities and what is now conventionally designated the European Union (taken to include the "old" Communities and the two other "pillars") have experienced profound and continuing change of a constitutional nature, affecting *inter alia* basic objectives and principles, degree of "integration" of the constituent states and law-making processes. The intensity and nature of the changes witnessed are untypical both for the liberal nation states which themselves comprise the members of the Union and for international organisations, which represent the other obvious comparator frame of reference for assessing the EU. The scholarly debate over the legal nature of the EU and possible relationships, distinctions or unities between, amongst and within what are conventionally known as the "pillars" remains unresolved.[48] However, the plural and differentiated nature of the system cannot be doubted, and the challenges for the Court of Justice and the Court of First Instance are already evident in the case law. Early examples of the these Courts grappling with border and category disputes include *UEAPME*, in which the Court of First Instance classed laws adopted under the Social Policy Agreement without the participation of the UK as "Community law[49]"; *Air Transport Visas,* in which the Court of Justice articulated a broad view of its jurisdiction to police the validity of measures, even to the extent of modestly trespassing into the domain of Co-operation in Justice and Home Affairs[50]; and the transparency and access to documents cases where the case law has developed a generally inclusive approach.[51] Moreover, elements of differentiated integration are built into the primary constitutional frame, namely the Treaties, in a variety of different forms. The legal framework for Economic and Monetary Union offers states the opportunity to "opt out" of binding primary and secondary rules agreed by all Member States in the Treaties. The post-Amsterdam arrangements in relation to Title IV of Part Three of the EC Treaty (Visas, Asylum, etc.) and the allocation of the Schengen *acquis* represent a similar type of arrangement for the UK, Ireland and (in different ways) Denmark.

[48] See the differing interpretations given by von Bogdandy, de Witte and Curtin/Dekker *supra* at nn 25–27.

[49] Case T–135/96, *UEAPME* v. *Council* [1998] ECR II–2335.

[50] Case C–170/96, *Commission* v. *Council (Air Transport Visas)* [1998] ECR I–2763.

[51] See on this Curtin and Dekker, n. 27 *supra*, at 124–6; most recently on transparency and comitology see Case T–188/97, *Rothmans International* v. *Commission*, 19 July 1999, not yet reported.

Between 1993 and 1997, the Social Policy Agreement and Protocol offered an example of the Member States unanimously allowing a proportion of the existing Member States to proceed with a more intensive form of co-operation with new legislative procedures. After the Treaty of Amsterdam, Articles 40 and 43–45 TEU, together with Article 11 EC, provide structured and conditional opportunities for similar arrangements to be set up *within* the existing Treaty framework in relation to aspects of "first" and "third" pillar policy-making, and subject to certain conditions, under the rubric of "closer co-operation".[52] The latter case is, however, one of potential, not actual, differentiation.[53] Flexible or differentiated implementation is foreseen in Article 95 EC in relation to single market decision-making, affording Member States the opportunity to raise specific major needs to justify derogations from EU measures.

The historical and contemporary prevalence of derogations in content and variable time limits for implementation in the full range of secondary EU law is well charted by Gráinne de Búrca's chapter in this collection and Filip Tuytschaever's extended study of differentiation.[54] Writers such as Alexander Stubb and Claus-Dieter Ehlermann comprehensively chart and systematise factors of variation in time, space and matter, and map these onto myriad examples drawn from EU practice and history.[55] Scholars of flexibility also frequently deploy and simultaneously seek to elucidate terms such as "multi-speed", "*à la carte*" and "variable geometry"—often in relation to these factors of variation, but not in a sufficiently consistent way to suggest that there exist uncontested definitions of these terms. Moreover, in terms of the incorporation of the practice of flexibility into the evolving EU constitutional system, while the Treaty of Amsterdam may be a key constitutional moment in the history of flexible integration in the EU, with its formal acceptance of differentiation into the core of the constitutional order and with its attempt to systematise constitutional principles of "closer co-operation",[56] none the less, as Neil Walker's analysis shows, in terms of the self-definition of the EU legal order as conventionally understood, the provisions of the Treaty of Amsterdam do not resolve the "border" problems which differentiated legal frameworks raise. In other words, they pose new and intensified challenges to the established and accepted constitutional paradigms of the EU legal order.[57] For, as Tuytschaever comments[58]:

[52] For these distinctions see J. Usher, "Economic and Monetary Union—A Model for Flexibility" (1999) 1 *Cambridge Yearbook of European Legal Studies* 39.

[53] On this key distinction see F. Tuytschaever, *Differentiation in European Union Law* (Oxford: Hart Publishing, 1999).

[54] *Ibid.*

[55] A. Stubb, "A Categorization of Differentiated Integration" (1996) 34 *JCMS* 283; C.-D. Ehlermann, "Increased Differentiation or Stronger Uniformity" in J. Winter *et al.* (eds.), *Reforming the Treaty on European Union* (The Hague: Kluwer Law International, 1996).

[56] Shaw, n. 7 *supra*; see also C.-D. Ehlermann, "Differentiation, Flexibility, Closer Co-operation: The New Provisions of the Amsterdam Treaty" (1998) 4 *ELJ* 246.

[57] N. Walker, "Sovereignty and Differentiated Integration in the European Union" (1998) 4 *ELJ* 355.

[58] N. 53 *supra*, at 247.

> Increased differentiation thus presents us with an angle from which to challenge the traditional unitarian constitutional image. Indeed, at least theoretically speaking, there must be a threshold beyond which increased differentiation transcends the mere situational or policy level, and beyond which it can *no longer be encapsulated and starts to affect the EU as a whole* [emphasis added].

This analysis could easily lead to a minimalist vision of the future Euro-polity, so far as it is based upon a normative perspective derived from, as Tuytschaever shows, the realist school of international relations with its fundamental statist orientation. This is the "flexibility equals less Europe" paradigm. Tuytschaever himself shows a marked preference for a functionalist understanding of the role of flexibility, based on concepts of spillover and rejecting the dominant paradigm of statist analysis. In normative terms, this allows a less negative position—from a constitutionalist perspective—on the effects and potentialities of flexibility. Pragmatically, this seems an understandable approach, since the history of the EU has seen functionalist positions frequently associated with a "technocratic" view of the instruments of integration. There is much to be said for suggesting that the Treaty of Amsterdam represents, above all, such a technocratic response, rather than a fundamental rethink of the integration project. As I have argued elsewhere, this has profound implications from the point of view of the legitimacy of the Union.[59]

However, this chapter presents a different perspective upon the flexibility question. A tremendous amount of scholarly effort has been expended in the attempt to capture the "essence" of flexibility, and—in recent years—to match this to the broader debate[60] regarding the Treaty-based framework, the underlying rhetoric of "variable geometry" or "Europe *à la carte*" etc., as well as the empirical reality of flexibility. Yet when flexibility is considered in relation to constitutionalism it becomes less important to discover the "truth" of either term, but rather to consider precisely that relationship and its evolution. Thus the debate changes when flexibility is understood in the context of a procedural and dialogic approach to constitutionalism. Flexibility, understood with an emphasis upon its procedural dimension rather than in terms of the outcomes which might thereby be produced, links easily to the accommodation of difference and diversity as a practice of constitutionalism. Quite different uses of the political and legal terminology, and extremely variable ideological investments in the inputs and outputs of the political bargaining processes which flexibility can promote, can be encapsulated in a sense of flexibility assisting in "keeping the conversation going", a sense which precisely builds upon the understanding of constitutionalism developed in the previous section. In other words, we should eschew a fixity of meaning in relation to flexibility, which is quite in

[59] J. Shaw, n. 7 *supra*, at 80–5.

[60] As exemplified, e.g., by F. de la Serre and H. Wallace, *Flexbility and Enhanced Cooperation in the European Union: Placebo rather than Panacea?*, "Notre Europe" Research and Policy Paper, no. 2, Sept. 1997.

keeping with the anti-teleological approach to constitutionalism suggested in section 3.

5. BACK TO THE PUZZLE OF CONSTITUTIONALISM AND FLEXIBILITY

It remains, therefore, precisely to reconsider the relationship of constititutionalism and flexibility. This chapter began with the puzzle of how constitutionalism and flexibility could be understood as linked or in an interactive relationship. This section opens out that relationship by examining it through the medium of constitutional change. Clearly, every constitution has some sort of relationship with flexibility. Most explicitly provide for some, if not all, provisions to be capable of amendment, subject to the application of certain conditions in terms of process. An "unwritten" constitution such as that of the United Kingdom is not necessarily any less or more flexible than the more common "written" variants, simply because of the absence of an explicit device for changing certain constitutional norms. Furthermore, many rights provisions which are given constitutional force have an inbuilt flexibility, for example by allowing interferences or restrictions on the part of state institutions with individual rights which do not go beyond what is permissible in a democratic society, or some similar formulation (a "margin of appreciation" doctrine, etc.). In other words, elements of both substantive and procedural flexibility are generally included in constitutions.

In formal terms, many of Canada's constitutional problems relate to that first paradigm of procedural constitutional flexibility, namely the amendment process. Some of the most vexed *legal* issues surrounding the difficult relationship between Quebec, as a province, and the rest of Canada have arisen specifically in relation to the rather rigid and certainly extremely complex amendment formulae for the Canadian constitution.[61] There is a paradox at the centre of the current Canadian constitution settlement. Although a variety of amendment formulae are written into the Constitution Act, 1982, in practice the Constitution requires unanimity amongst the provinces to bring about the types of amendments which Quebec seeks—following a long constitutional convention in Canada. However, the current version of the constitutional settlement was itself brought into being without the consent of one of the provinces, namely Quebec. This was constitutionally possible, because that settlement is the formal patriation of the Canadian constitution, the end of the formal powers of the Imperial Parliament, and its national adoption in the form of the Constitution Act, 1982. The Canadian federal government turned (one last time) to the Westminster Parliament against the will of Quebec for a repatriation and amendment process which was formally external to Canada as sovereign state. It is a settlement

[61] For an extended analysis see P. Oliver, "Canada, Quebec and Constitutional Amendment" (1999) 49 *University of Toronto Law Journal* 519.

which has proved unhappy. All attempts since then to create accord around the Canadian constitution have likewise failed, because they have not secured ratification at provincial level (the Meech Lake agreement and the Charlottetown Accord). At the same time, however, *québécois* separatist demands have increased, and there has been a referendum within the province of Quebec where the separatists failed narrowly to secure a majority in favour of secession.

Against that background, with *québécois* separatists clearly contemplating a unilateral move to secede, the Canadian federal government referred to the Supreme Court the question whether the unilateral secession of Quebec would be lawful under the Canadian constitution or under international law. In a lengthy judgment by the Court, the conclusion was reached that it would not be lawful for Quebec unilaterally to secede. Many of the detailed issues raised and discussed are directly pertinent only to Canadian constitutional law and politics.[62] However, for our purposes, the Supreme Court's extended exploration of Canadian constitutionalism in the context of ongoing conflict contains two key elements.

First, the Court elaborated a notion of constitutionalism in which a number of principles are seen as balancing each other, and incapable of operating in isolation: for these purposes, the principles of federalism, democracy, constitutionalism and the rule of law, and respect for minority rights were identified as foundational. The Court indicated that this was not a closed and complete list of constitutional principles, but it made it plain through its interpretation that it favoured an understanding of the notion and scope of constitutionalism through the medium of principles rather than rules. Secondly, although it rejected the lawfulness of a unilateral secession, the Court identified circumstances, when a clear majority of the people of Quebec had expressed a clear wish to secede, in which a duty to negotiate in good faith upon this question would be incumbent upon all actors. However, it made plain that the duty to negotiate does not give a correlative right to Quebec to secede even if there is a democratically expressed provincial will to do so. In other words, the result of the negotiation is not pre-ordained, since the other provinces may not agree to the secession because the negotiations may not be satisfactory. Equally, the rest of the Canadian provinces and the federal governmental authorities cannot remain indifferent to the democratically expressed will of one province to secede. The objective is the reconciliation of the rights and obligations of two legitimate authorities. This limitation has led James Tully to criticise some aspects of the judgment, although he regards it as ultimately of great importance "in re-orienting constitutional change around the ideal of democratic freedom of the constituent members to amend the rules of the game *en passant*".[63]

[62] For commentary see Oliver, n. 42 *supra*; special issue of the *Constitutional Forum/Forum Constitutionnel*, Vol. 10, No. 1, Fall 1998, especially A. Cairns, "The Quebec Secession Reference: The Constitutional Duty to Negotiate"; D. Haljan, "A Constitutional Duty to Negotiate Amendments: *Reference re. Secession of Quebec*" (1999) 48 *ICLQ* 447; Walters, n. 42 *supra*.

[63] Communication to the author, 21 Sept. 1999. For an extended discussion see Tully, "Freedom and Disclosure", n. 34 *supra*.

Tully's criticism is that whatever the Court's formula of "fair negotiations" in relation to the initiation of constitutional change, in practice the *québécois* people are blocked from exercising their internal right of self-determination because of the rigidity of the constitutional amendment process. The requirement (by convention) of the unanimity of the provinces represents in reality a blockage to fair negotiations. Agreement on a simplified amending formula once negotiations begin, requiring the consent of the negotiating parties, as the Supreme Court itself seems to suggest, would dissolve the blockage and make possible constitutional amendment short of secession. However, until that dissolution occurs—and the Supreme Court's judgment seems ambivalent on the question of amending formulas[64]—the Canadian constitution is for the *québécois* people (and indeed for First Nations, whose situation in relation to Treaty relations with the rest of Canada he also discusses) in reality a straitjacket.[65]

The Supreme Court's judgment has generally received a welcome—sometimes a guarded welcome—from commentators, including some based in Quebec itself.[66] Whatever the weaknesses of some of its historical and doctrinal arguments and the caveats entered by Tully, the judgment is welcomed as a starting point on a road towards a more flexible constitutionalism by "at least crystallising 'principled negotiations' into a constitutional obligation".[67] One point preoccupying commentators is the nature of that obligation, which the Court characterises as "legal" in nature, whilst as the same time indicating firmly that it will not be justiciable before the Court. What, then, might be the sanction against a constitutional actor refusing to negotiate in good faith? Interestingly, as to the tone and general approach of the judgment, it is hard to imagine that the Canadian Supreme Court has *not*, in some way, been influenced by the lively academic debate about diversity, the role of procedure and negotiation, and about the projection of the Canadian constitutional process as conversation rather than contract. Thus it seizes directly upon the challenges of constitution-making in a divided society, but one in which the preconditions of democracy must prevail and be developed. In other words, this is about constitution-making in a society where even the fiction of preceding the constitution by a statement from an implicit "we the people" is no longer acceptable (if it ever was). The best example of this will remain the historic one of the American constitution and the elite invocation of "we the people" at Philadelphia to sustain the legitimacy of the settlement. And yet, in this same society, abandoning the idea of a putative pre-political "people" does not mean abandoning the commitment to ideas of self-government, autonomy and the

[64] The impact of the judgment on constitutional amendment is discussed by D. Greschner, (1998) 10 *Constitutional Forum/Forum Constitutionnel* 19.

[65] My thanks go to Jim Tully for e-mail discussions of this question which have assisted my understanding.

[66] E.g. J. Leclair, "Impoverishment of the Law by the Law: A Critique of the Attorney General's Vision of the Rule of Law and the Federal Principle" (1998) 10 *Constitutional Forum/Forum Constitutionnel* 1.

[67] Haljan, n. 62 *supra*, at 457.

legitimacy-conferring capacity of giving consent. Here the idea of constitution as conversation rather than as contract proves extremely useful.

This brief analysis indicates some scope for mutual cross-fertilisation between the Canadian and EU experiences of constitutionalism and suggestions as to the evolving relationship between constitutionalism and the notions of flexibility expounded in this chapter. On the one hand, the willingness of the Member States to conclude flexible arrangements on an *ad hoc* basis and then subsequently to renegotiate them, or to provide mechanisms whereby Member States can opt in upon negotiation of a later agreement (e.g. in relation to Schengen and the new Title on free movement, etc.), could be said to prevent the risk of constitutional paralysis which is highlighted in relation to Canada, even though at the present time, of course, the formal constitutional amendment process in the EU (i.e. amending treaties) requires the consent of all the Member States as well as a nationally based ratification process. On the other hand, the Supreme Court's presentation of a constitutionalism based on interacting principles rather than a taut system of rules, in which the discursive practice of negotiation is given an elevated status, suggests that flexible constitutionalism should not necessarily be associated with a painful breakdown of constitutional order, but rather with a refocusing of the centre of the polity upon its discursive practices rather than its (narrowly conceived) rule-based legal order. The judgment raises, however, difficult questions about the relationship between those discursive practices and the judicial role in a constitutional system—a clear challenge to courts such as the Supreme Court and the Court of Justice. By pronouncing upon constitutionalism in this way the Supreme Court simultaneously elevates and also endangers the judicial role within a constitutional system. Moreover, none of the analysis really touches upon fundamental questions about the participants in the constitutional process, and even the identity of the ultimate constitutional authority in a polity where *demos* can have only a political and not an ethnic or even cultural meaning. The comparison articulates the nature of "voice" in constitutional processes, but tells little about the identity of the speakers.[68]

6. CONCLUSIONS

In practical terms, any conclusions drawn must be based on the acceptance that whatever the hostility of some adopting a more narrowly conceived notion of the nature of the EU legal and political order, the practice of flexiblity is unlikely to disappear from the EU in the conceivable future. Nor should it. For one thing, it helps to make the system work, through the possibility and practice of assymetrical solutions. Moreover, it also has a dialogic and—I would argue—constructive relationship with the certainty and stability provided by the rule of

[68] On this see further J. Shaw, "Process and Constitutional Discourse in the European Union", (2000) 27 *Journal of Law and Society* forthcoming.

law and constitutionalism, understood in the narrow sense of constitutional supremacy. It certainly appears that EU constitutionalism, conceived in its "classic" terms based upon the supremacy of EU law, leaves little space for the question of flexibility, unless it is accepted that allowing for flexibility means that the EU is moving "backwards" (in simplistic integrationist terms) along the continuum between (con)federal polity/legal order towards international organisation or regime. As de Areilza puts it, that would be viewing the 1996–7 Inter-Governmental Conference (IGC) as a "statal grab of power".[69] However, that would be—as this chapter has sought to show—taking too narrow a view of both constitutionalism and flexibility. It leaves the presuppositions of *national* constitutionalism untouched, although in a world of "meta-constitutionalism"[70] that seems a difficult argument to sustain. Thus the key points of the chapter have been to review exactly what is meant by these two terms and to reconsider their dialogic relationship. To that end, in addition to demonstrating the shared properties of the two concepts, the chapter has also used a comparative method which has sought to illuminate the constitutionalism of the EU by reference to the experiences of another evolving and still uncertain constitutional framework, that of Canada and Quebec. Canada and the Quebec question together suggest a different constellation of postnationalism.

In conclusion, the analysis of the relationship between constiutionalism and flexibility has been framed by a general view that constitutions are to be seen as evolving projects rather than as perfect and immutable renderings of a fixed moment which saw the exercise of political will by a popular sovereign. Viewed against the rich backdrop of the constitutional practices of many, if not most, states, that idea is a banality.[71] In the evolving European Union it remains an observation which—while not wholly innovatory—represents a useful reminder of the nature of the project.

[69] De Areilza, n. 4 *supra*.

[70] Cf. Neil Walker's contribution to this volume.

[71] My thanks go to John Bell for referring me to many examples of dialogism, multi-speedism and flexibility in national constitutional practices.

Index